Revelation

a commentary
for our time

Revelation

a commentary
for our time

PART I • Revelation 1–11

Roger Forster

Copyright © 2022 Roger Forster

Published in 2022 by PUSH Publishing

The right of Roger Forster to be identified as the author of this work has been asserted by him in accordance with the Copyright, Designs and Patents Act 1988.

Scripture is taken from:

New American Standard Bible® (NASB)
Copyright © 1960, 1962, 1963, 1968, 1971, 1972, 1973, 1975, 1977, 1995
By the Lockman Foundation. Used by permission

A catalogue record for this book is available from the British Library

ISBN-13: 978-1-912947-14-0

All rights reserved. No part of this publication may be reproduced, stored in a retrieval system, or transmitted, in any form or by any means, electronic, mechanical, photocopying, recording or otherwise, without the prior permission of the publisher.

Printed and bound in Great Britain

www.pushpublishing.co.uk

Cover design and graphics by Joseph Laycock
Watercolour paintings by Walter Hayn

Contents

Foreword   vii
Preface   ix

Approaching the text

Interpreting Revelation   2
The Four Vision structure   41
Overview of Revelation   54

Commentary

Introduction – The Communication of Christ
The Letterhead   63

Section 1 – Christ Central in the Church
The First Vision | Revelation 1:9–3:22   85
The 7 Letters   105
    Letter to Ephesus | Revelation 2:1–7   116
    Letter to Smyrna | Revelation 2:8–11   128
    Letter to Pergamum | Revelation 2:12–17   135
    Letter to Thyatira | Revelation 2:18–29   142
    Letter to Sardis | Revelation 3:1–6   151
    Letter to Philadelphia | Revelation 3:7–13   163
    Letter to Laodicea | Revelation 3:14–22   170
    The Comprehensive Church   176

Section 2 – Christ Central in Creation

The Second Vision ∣ Revelation 4:1–5:14	192
7 Seals, Trumpets, Signs & Bowls	232
The 7 Seals	243
Seals 1–4 ∣ The 4 Horsemen	245
Seal 5	263
Seal 6	274
Interlude	281
Seal 7	306
The 7 Trumpets	317
Trumpets 1–4	321
Trumpet 5	333
Trumpet 6	346
Interlude	358
Trumpet 7	416

Summary of Revelation 1—11   429

Reference Material

List of Discussion Topics	cdxxxi
Bibliography	cdxxxii
About the Author	cdxxxvii

Foreword

Academics like me trade in knowledge. However, since I saw Jesus for myself in a Cambridge College room in the summer of 1974, my thirst has been for God's wisdom and understanding. This book is suffused with it. So, to have had the privilege to comment on earlier manuscripts of Roger's reflections and to see this final version of 'Revelation – a commentary for our time', is a joy.

John's Revelation is the last Book of Christian Scripture and its summation; as Roger puts it, 'The Manifesto of Jesus for the Church'. It is a book for today – reflect upon Roger's analysis of the 7 values that Jesus expects of us as His body: love, suffering, endurance, pure teaching, holiness, genuineness, evangelism and humility; consider then how far short of that we as the Church fall. As Roger so elegantly illuminates from the text: 'This is what we are supposed to look like'. This is about us as Overcomers. We have the excitement and pressure of being in the now and the not yet of Jesus' new creation and the time to embrace it!

Yet Revelation uses highly symbolic language and *prima facie* it is obscure and its people's interpretation diverse. The imagery is profound and hidden enough to be precious as we read for example the discussion of the white stone. As Roger says: 'To be inside with the hidden-ness is to be in the intimacy of God'. This is not elitism, but an invitation in these pages to enter a new level of relationship with Jesus.

Those of you familiar with his other writings will see once again Roger's considerable, deep, but accessible theological and linguistic scholarship bringing Revelation's text alive. His profound common sense and balance demythologises, explains and interprets with symmetry and elegance *inter alia* the numerology of the book, the why and what of God's wrath and the Tribulation.

Finally, and in relation to a commentary on Revelation that probes so deeply into what it ought to mean to be a Christian – the point of writing commentaries to my mind – is not just about interpreting correctly but applying such truths to oneself in order to live correctly. When it comes to matching Roger's wisdom and teaching in these pages against the man himself: can this teaching be seen in his life? Yes, it can.

Rob George
King's College London

Preface

This is a work in two parts. Part 1 comprises an introduction to, and overview of the Book of Revelation (The Revelation of John) followed by a commentary on chapters 1 through 11. Part II is a commentary on Chapters 12 to 22 with a recap and summary.

This book is the fruit of my Christian reflection and discipleship over more than six decades on the complexity and nuances of John's Revelation. It is the end of a journey through the works of over a hundred other commentators. I have read them all with the greatest pleasure and profit. As I complete a final text though, new thoughts and insights crowd in, but one must draw a line somewhere.

Revelation has had commentators for centuries all of whom necessarily apply its relevance through the lens of their time. This is my experience too. As we come closer to the day when God puts everything right – when He aligns this age properly and finally – justifies with His final justice and puts right what He says is right, one aches and hopes that this time is now.

Nevertheless, there is a bizarre counterpoint: many people do not read Revelation because in it they see imagery and violence that they find impossible to interpret in the light of a God of Love, yet others – mostly those seeking to defend an antiChristian position – read the book precisely to imply that if this is the imagery of a God of Love they will have nothing to do with Him.

It is easy, but also right, to refer to the events of our time, though nothing has changed despite science and man's attempts at civilisation: famine, plague, war, nation pitting against nation and tyrants with free reign that the world is experiencing as I write. They are, as Mark alludes, the birth pangs as the Kingdom draws near in its fulness. I must address, therefore, as early as this preface, the wrongness of seeing God as sadistic in bringing judgment. When sin is finally destroyed by the final judgment, it is akin to the exquisite pain that carries with it the happiness of a mother seeing her child delivered safely through her suffering. For God this is the delivery of His Kingdom in all its fulness that reaches a pinnacle with the excruciating pain of Jesus' sacrifice.

In thanking people, as I surely must, it would be remiss of me not to mention first my wife Faith with her observations and our life together that have contributed in profound ways to this work's production. Her love – both of me and the text – and insights, especially in these most recent years that through a stroke has taken my ability to write for myself anymore and has caused us much frustration. Many have been my amanuenses as they have listened to my voice and transferred this to paper, but mostly admiration and thanksgiving goes to her. I am so grateful for her endurance.

Second, this book would not be here were it not for my son-in-law Dr Joe Laycock. He not only produced and edited the text, but also the figures and illustrations. They present the text attractively and colourfully to elucidate and present my thoughts in an accessible way. A key source of material for Joe's editing in this has been the scores of tapes, and their transcriptions of my preaching on this book over the years. For this I must thank the patience and commitment of Jacqui Hussein, Lydia George and Jyothi Chapman. There have also been so many well-wishers and enquirers as to when the book will appear that have kept my nose to the grindstone. Nevertheless, without Joe's perseverance and unwavering dedication, I would have given up on the project long ago. I cannot thank him enough. I would also like to thank Jenny Page and Ian Marden for their help in the important task of proofreading, and Walter Hayn for his watercolours.

Finally, I would like to thank Professor Rob George who assisted with the final proof reading and editing of the manuscript. His continual fervour to understand has set my own heart alight and his observations have quickened my understanding.

Roger Forster
Summer 2022

Approaching the Text

Before we get into the text, we need to spend a few pages looking at the background to the book of Revelation, including how other people have interpreted it, who, when, and why it was written and some of the key themes. This will give us a firm foundation to build on, and hopefully make the book a lot less daunting!

Interpreting Revelation

Schools of interpretation

We are going to start by looking at the main ways people have interpreted the book of Revelation, although there is a wide range of views within each school of thought. It is important right from the beginning to remember that the variety of interpretations exists because they have arisen from different theological positions held by those who have sought to understand the text.

There are basically four views to understanding the 22 chapters, each of which places a different emphasis on the nature of the book: the Praeterist, Historicist, Spiritual and Futurist views. As we will see, each of these four interpretations is alluded to in the text of Revelation 1. I will suggest a fifth view, a conglomeration of the other four, which seems to me to be more in keeping with Revelation itself and how it was intended to be understood. Grasping these four views will give clues as to the varied interpretations and how to guard ourselves from being too bizarre in the way we try to get hold of the truth in Revelation. Each of these approaches has its weaknesses, but having said that they all have some important validity and help us grasp a different aspect of the message of the book. So we should not set one against another to try and knock them down – truth is a little bit bigger than that. Doing this does not mean you have to agree with everything, or sit on the fence forever, but rather there is a need to appreciate one another's point of view.

It is encouraging that in the last thirty years, scholars are coming towards a common consensus of understanding over different symbols and ideas which are found in the book of Revelation. So whereas we look back into the past and see that there have been wildly divergent interpretations (and many, many commentaries written on them), we are now beginning to find unity from a scholarly point of view. While this understanding may not necessarily always result in the best application or inspiration, it does mean that as we come to the text there is something objective there, and not something that is entirely subjective. Let's start by looking at each of these four main views in turn and how they are alluded to in the text.

Schools of interpretation

1. Praeterist – applies to the first-century church only

 Written as an epistle 1:11,19

Write in a book what you see, and *send it to the seven churches*. (Revelation 1:11)

First, the Praeterist **(or** Preterist**) view emphasises that Revelation is a message for the church in the first century AD.** This view interprets most if not all of the events in Revelation as having already been fulfilled in the first century, by the destruction of the Jerusalem Temple in 70 AD, or soon after. The term praeterism comes from the Latin *praeter*, meaning 'past' or 'beyond'.

Revelation 2 says, 'To the angel of the church in Ephesus *write*' (v1) . . . *write* to Smyrna (v8) . . . *write* to Pergamum (v12), and so on. So it is quite valid to approach the book of Revelation as an epistle, written at a particular time, to a particular set of churches with a particular purpose. Therefore, first and foremost Revelation applies to the conditions and the needs of the people to whom it was written. To understand it properly, Paul's epistle to the Romans should be read in the context of the first-century church in Rome (as discussed in our commentary *Paul's Gospel*). Of course, what Paul wrote then has a lot to say to us twenty centuries later, but to interpret it and apply it to ourselves correctly, we have to understand that it has been written to the church in Rome in the first century to meet specific problems and to answer specific questions. Paul even sends greetings to his friends: to Priscilla and Aquila (16:3), Epaenetus (v5), Mary (v6) and Andronicus and Junia (v7), and so on . . . It was a real letter written to real people at a real point in time, and the same is true for Revelation.

The Praeterist view says that as the first century is the focus of the book, to really understand Revelation we have to put ourselves back there, look at what is going on, and feel ourselves in that time.

For example, everybody in the first century would have known straight away that the Harlot of Babylon sitting on the seven hills is Rome! Rome was the dominant, political power that was suppressing the Church and was famously built upon seven hills: the imagery of Revelation makes sense to a first-century mind. Indeed, the first readers of Revelation lived in the first century and would have read it as if it was written to them, and would have applied it to their world, so it must make sense in that way.

Revelation – Approaching the text

However, it is unlikely that the first readers of Revelation were 'Praeterists' in the sense that they saw its application only in relation to their situation. Indeed, the Praeterist approach was first introduced in the mid-sixteenth century by Luiz de Alcazar, a Jesuit, who was trying to defend the authority of Rome by providing an alternative to the Historicist view (see below) which was being used to attack the Pope as the anti-Christ. Other prominent Praeterists include Hugo Grotius in the sixteenth century, and more recently Moses Stuart and James Snowden.

The diagram below shows the Praeterist view interprets Revelation as being relevant to the first-century Church only.

Historical–Critical method

The main reason for the rise in the Praeterist view in the past 250 years is the historical–critical method (also known as 'Higher Criticism'), which has dominated the field of scholarly theology over that time. Historical criticism is a tool that tries to work out the exact meaning of a text in its original historical context. If Revelation is a letter written to believers in the first century, what did these words mean in the first century? Who was writing them? Why? And how was it interpreted, applied and understood by the people who received it?

This method involves taking the text from all points of view, looking at the different ways each word was used at that time in different contexts in order to build up a picture of the possible ways it would have been understood. So history, linguistics, the philosophies of the day – all these are brought to bear within this view to try and understand what the text means.

The weakness of the Praeterist view is that it usually does not go any

Schools of interpretation

further than the historical–critical method: the text is not applied and shown to be relevant to us today, and so it becomes just a historical study or intellectual exercise. This often leaves people with more questions about their faith than answers. As Christians we should use the historical–critical method to engage with the text as fully as possible, and expect it to reveal truth about Jesus in every verse of the Bible, and build our faith. Sadly, the way this method has sometimes been used to try and undermine Scripture has discouraged some from engaging with it. All Scripture points to Jesus – all the written words point to *the* Living Word. Peter wrote:

> No prophecy of Scripture is a matter of one's own interpretation, for no prophecy was ever made by an act of human will, but men moved by the Holy Spirit spoke from God. (2 Peter 1:20–21)

What the Old Testament prophets wrote was beyond what they knew (see 1 Peter 1:11–12), because while they were seeking what it was saying about the coming of the Messiah, they did not know the exact relevance of what they had written. So, while it is important to understand biblical texts in their original context, there is more to interpreting the text than simply the historical–critical method.

2. Historicist – the whole panorama of church history

 Written as a book/scroll 1:11

> *Write in a book* what you see, and send it to the seven churches. (Revelation 1:11)

The Historicist view looks upon Revelation as describing the whole panorama of church history stretched out in front of us. Revelation is not restricted to the first century AD, but, particularly starting with chapter 4, where we are caught up into heaven, through to chapter 19, where Jesus comes from heaven riding a white horse, it can be seen as a great unrolled scroll. It is just as though everything has been written beforehand and is happening according to the mind and will of God: this is how it is going to be. So Revelation can be seen as a prediction of how the Church will go through various stages. There is an allusion to this in Revelation 1:11, when it says 'write in a book' or 'scroll', which of course was the shape of books at that time. As this scroll is unrolled, we go through the chapters and move through church history. So Revelation is not only an epistle, it is also a scroll – a history book.

The Historicist view was first developed in the early twelfth century by Anselm of Havelberg, Rupert of Deutz and Joachim of Floris, and became increasingly influential over the next two centuries in the lead-up to the Reformation. In the sixteenth century Martin Luther galvanised it as the standard Reformed Protestant interpretation, and this persisted into the nineteenth century. Indeed, it was particularly attractive for Reformers as it afforded them the opportunity to attack Catholicism theologically by interpreting the anti-Christ as the Pope and Rome – the centre of the Catholic faith – as Babylon, the Harlot. However, it is noteworthy that Calvin wrote commentaries on every book of the Bible except for Revelation.

One of the weaknesses of this particular viewpoint is that if you were writing a commentary on Revelation two hundred years ago, by the time you arrived at chapter 19 you would probably interpret it as happening in your day because you wanted the Lord to return. But of course as more centuries have passed we have had to change our point of view and stretch it out a bit more. Now it is the twenty-first century, and we have to push the end along a little bit further into the future and stretch out what is in between then and now a bit more. For example, in the seventeenth century people thought the anti-Christ was the Pope. In the twentieth century people thought it was Hitler, Stalin or Pol Pot and so on. As the anti-Christ *will be* the last great evil world leader, as soon as a new one comes along we have to update our viewpoint.

So the Historicist view is not too objective a way of trying to understand what is going on – at what point in time are we relative to the events in Revelation? However, there is a certain validity in this view, because surely the word of God is not only applicable in the day when it was written, but is also applicable throughout the whole Church Age, right up to today.

Paul wrote 1 Corinthians to the church in Corinth about a very particular situation where some people were going over the top in using charismatic gifts. Paul's advice was not to crush them, but to encourage them to keep to certain guidelines. That message is not just for Corinth, but for all churches (see 1 Corinthians 14:33) – all the way through church history these things have been applicable in the right context for every generation.

So the good side of the Historicist view is that it asks, 'what is the word of God saying to me today?' rather than 'what did God say in the past?'

Schools of interpretation

The diagram below shows how the Historicist view interprets Revelation as being relevant to the whole of church history.

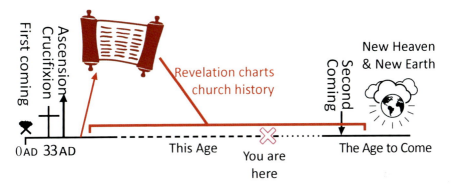

Jewish Midrash method

The Historicist view is comparable to the Jewish Midrash, which is a method of interpreting Scripture along specific guidelines. One method is to throw different verses together so that they shine on each other. Another is to dig down into the root of a particular word which reminds you of another word with the same root. The Midrash is also a way of taking a theme, pattern or motif from one passage and reapplying it into a new situation, revealing the same spiritual principles and interpretations at different points in history.

The Bible itself teaches this method. For example, the crossing the Jordan/Exile motif:

- Abraham came out of Ur and crossed the Jordan into Canaan
- Israel came out of Egypt and crossed the Jordan into Canaan
- The Exiles came out of Babylon and back into Canaan.

The same pattern is reapplied. Then in the New Testament, Jesus comes out of Egypt and into Canaan. Why? It is the same spiritual principle and interpretation being applied at these different points in history – the application is not open to misinterpretation but is governed by the motif that has already been established. Jesus also uses the Midrashic method with the Jubilee teaching, first given to Israel in Leviticus 25 when they were going through the Wilderness. At the Jubilee (7 × 7 = 49 years) slaves were set free. Later, after Israel settled in the Promised Land they didn't just have slaves, but also captives (from war) in prisons, so when Isaiah alludes to the Jubilee teaching (Isaiah 61:1–3)

Revelation – Approaching the text

he revamps it from just being about slaves to also include captives. Then, when Jesus uses the Jubilee teaching in Nazareth (Luke 4:16–19) and says, 'I have come to set the captives free', rather than just meaning slaves or prisoners, He is talking about captives to sin and to Satan. He is quoting the same Jubilee teaching, but reapplying it to bring understanding and insight.

However, recently the word 'Midrash' has been used in some circles in an ill-disciplined way to justify saying almost anything. For example, I met some Christians who maintained that you must always have Communion at noon on a Sunday, because it was the Lord's day and because Joseph dined at noon (Genesis 43:16,25)! Interpreting the Bible using Midrash is a wonderful thing, but we do need to take care not to take verses out of context.

Just like the Midrash, the Historicist view takes the basic principles from Revelation and reapplies them at different points in church history, to reveal fresh understanding in parallel contexts.

With scriptural interpretation we have already got the Historicist view written into the text of Revelation itself, which is saturated with Old Testament motifs, pictures and stories. They do not have to mean exactly what they meant in the Old Testament, but they will carry fundamental unchangeable principles with them as they are reapplied into the days of Rome. We know this took place because in the apocryphal writings and in the Dead Sea Scrolls, Jews were interpreting the minor prophets and Isaiah, but in place of the Babylonians, Medes or Persians, they applied it to the Romans. So, it is a perfectly legitimate way of interpreting, as long as it is done in a disciplined way.

3. Futurist – for the last phase of church history

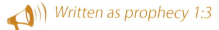 *Written as prophecy 1:3*

> Blessed is he who reads and those who hear the *words of the prophecy* and heed the things that are written in it; for the time is near. (Revelation 1:3)

As well as a letter and a scroll, in the Futurist view Revelation can be read as a prophecy. While prophecy primarily means 'to speak forth', it is rare that it does not also contain the connotation 'to speak beforehand' — *prophetes* in Greek – which takes us into the future.

Revelation is an eschatological book – a book about the last things. Nearly all biblical prophecy centres on our Lord's return, either the First or Second Coming, so if Revelation is prophecy it is going to carry us forward to the very future that we are praying and hoping won't be far off. Revelation can be seen as describing the last phase of church history – a prophecy of what will happen at the End of the Age.

One way of understanding the role of prophecy in the Bible as a whole is to regard the Bible like a five-act play that has been discovered, with one act missing: the first three acts refer to the Old Testament, the Gospels and the Acts of the Apostles, then there is a missing fourth act – the Church Age – and then comes Revelation as the fifth and final act.

In the Church Age, we have got to soak ourselves in what has happened in the past and understand it, and soak ourselves in what is going to happen in the future – that is, how God is going to wind it up. Then, under the guidance of the Holy Spirit, we ad-lib our way through the Church Age. The closer you understand God's purposes and where He is going, the better you will play your part and speed it up. If, as with some Christians, you do not bother to learn the things that have already happened in the play and have no idea where it is going to finish up, then of course you wander around and do things your own way – this just draws out the play and it goes on and on. Why don't we see the promises of His coming? Probably because a significant proportion of the Church is not fulfilling the purpose of this missing act, where we have been given the privilege of doing our own thing. So the Futurist view is important: it emphasises the prophecies that should be leading the Church on.

The Futurist view shares its roots with the Praeterist view in the sixteenth century and was also developed by a Jesuit, Francisco Ribera, in order to counter Protestant Historicist views. Both Futurist and Praeterist views aimed to stop the Pope being identified with the anti-Christ: praeterism by saying that Revelation only applied to the first century, and futurism by pushing everything from chapter 4 onwards to the End of the Age. As such, for the next 200 years Protestantism disregarded the Futurist view as Catholic self-defence theology, until it was renewed through the Brethren movement when Darby incorporated it into his Dispensationalist teaching, particularly in the Schofield Bible. It entered Protestant circles through theologians including Samuel Maitland and Isaac Williams, and has continued to gain ground through the twentieth century with scholars such as J A Seiss, Robert Mounce and George

Ladd, and especially through Hal Lindsey's book, *The Late Great Planet Earth*.

The diagram below shows how the Futurist view interprets Revelation as referring only to the End of the Age.

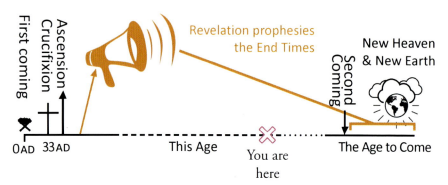

Literal Prophetic method

People who take the Futurist view tend to interpret Revelation as being literal, as this school of thought emphasises the final end event itself. It is a very popular view, especially in the USA, and is the source of many popular books and films, such at the *Left Behind* series.

Futurists are trying to work out *literally* what is going to happen on earth and in the heavens surrounding our Lord's return. However, you cannot be overly literal with the use of language in a book that is written in highly symbolic terms. For instance, in Revelation 8:7, it says that every blade of grass was burnt up, however in 9:4 the scorpions are commanded not to harm the grass when there should be no grass left!

Maintaining an absolutely literal interpretation of Revelation is difficult, although some people have tried very hard to do so. For example, in the nineteenth century renowned Bible expositors, Patrick Fairbairn and Andrew Jukes, both gave prestigious lectures where they tried to interpret everything in prophecy – particularly Revelation – in literal terms. However, as the years went on, Andrew Jukes wrote a book *Types in Genesis*, and Patrick Fairbairn wrote his classic volume *The Typology of Scripture*, both of which dealt with spiritual and parabolic interpretations of the signs and symbols in the Bible – they had completely moved away from their literal interpretations! The more you dwell in the book of Revelation you see it is dealing with signs and pictures, rather than with total literality, and you will not keep to a scientific, reductionist type of interpretation.

We need to bear in mind that nobody has seen the Second Coming yet, so nobody knows what it is going to be like, and therefore we haven't strictly got a language for it. There are bound to be things that leave us somewhat puzzled and unable to explain fully – no doubt how John would have felt while faced with the visions he saw, so he uses pictures, symbols and analogies to help explain it. In fact, Revelation 10:4 reminds us that God has deliberately withheld a complete picture of the future.

While the literal approach in the pedantic terms of linguistic analysis is not very helpful, these signs do represent something that will actually happen in the future. So the Futurist view does help show us something of what will be taking place in the End Times, even if there are some fuzzy edges where we cannot be overly dogmatic. This approach should prevent our interpretations from moving too far away from the divinely given text.

Discussion Topic: Literal interpretation of Scripture

As Christians we believe the Bible is the inspired word of God, and that what it says is true. However, there are differences of opinion in how literally we must interpret it and how we define 'truth'. Biblical Literalists insist the Bible must be interpreted as one hundred percent literally true.

A well-known example of Biblical Literalism is the Creation account in Genesis 1–2: was the whole universe created in just 6 days, ie 6 periods of 24 hours? Or are the 'days' figurative or allegorical, or a poetic device to try to begin to describe something which is indescribable? The Early Church Fathers, for example Augustine and Irenæus, as well as Christian thinkers throughout the centuries, did not interpret the 'days' of Creation as literal periods of 24 hours.

Many have held to a Biblical Literalist position because they believe it demonstrates that they take the Scriptures seriously. However, this emphasis only developed relatively recently, from the late seventeenth century onwards, in response to the historical–critical method being applied to the Bible, and alongside the rise of empiricism – the idea that scientific proof is the only way to determine truth. Together, these developments in thinking led people to try to present biblical truth in a popular scientific framework. While the critics were trying to pull the Bible apart to investigate each part separately, the literalists aimed to bind it together even more strongly.

There are problems with a literalist approach. First, the Bible uses a lot of imagery and poetry to represent and describe truth. The Old Testament is full of examples: Song of Solomon is highly poetic and metaphorical; Psalm 45 uses the glorious imagery of a royal wedding; 'the broken-hearted' will be bound up in Isaiah 61; and the prophet Nathan uses a parable to bring conviction to King David (2 Samuel 12), to list but a few. Jesus spoke in parables, using stories and metaphors to explain complex truths in a simple way (see for example the seven Kingdom parables in Matthew 13).

There is a difference between something being true and it being literal, and importantly truth does not depend upon literality. The parable of the Good Samaritan reveals truth, but that does not mean it had to have actually happened in exactly the way Jesus told it. Even if there had never been a Good Samaritan event, the parable is still true – it reveals truth about God to us. In the same way, Genesis 1–2 is true, but its truth is not dependent upon it being absolutely literal.

To counteract this problem, some Biblical Literalists qualify their literalism as applying to all passages except those clearly intended to be understood as a parable, metaphor or poem. However, in practice how it is decided which parts of Scripture are included would appear to be highly selective and subjective. A literalist approach would limit the extent to which we allow the Lord to speak to us through the Scriptures today (Hebrews 4:12).

Secondly, Biblical Literalism is not the way the Bible uses when interpreting Scripture itself – it is not a Hebrew way of thinking.

Revelation and the Old Testament

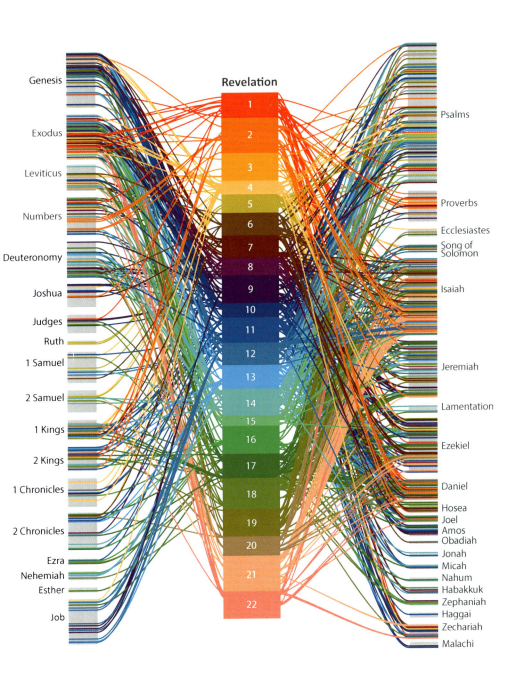

we must approach the text with that in mind. Do not worry if you are reading this and you are not yet totally familiar with the whole of the Old Testament – we will go into each reference as and when they crop up . . . so please carry on reading!

Revelation and Daniel

Revelation is steeped in Old Testament prophecy, but it is especially enriched with the book of Daniel. It is often said that to understand Revelation you must interpret it in the light of Daniel – if we do not understand Daniel, we won't fully understand Revelation. Allusions to Daniel abound in Revelation: for example, in Daniel 7 we see 'the Son of Man', 'times, time and half a time', the beast coming up out of the water, and so on. Again, if you haven't studied Daniel in depth we will be picking up the relevant bits as we go along.

Reliability of prophecy

Not only is Revelation packed full of the Old Testament, it also shares the same kind of prophetic balance – some material obviously relates to the immediate, local context, but this is linked to prophecies with a future, global perspective. This is important because it is how we gain confidence that the prophet was hearing from God – if they are correct when it comes to the immediate thing, then it gives credence and authenticity to the prophecies regarding the future. The first prophecy establishes the veracity of the one yet to come. If, however, a prophecy about the near future turned out to be wrong, then of course we would reasonably disregard what the prophet said about the End Times. For more on prophecy in the Bible, see the Discussion Topic below.

This prophetic balance is very apparent in Revelation – 'I come quickly' is written into the beginning and the end of the book and six other times in between. 'Shortly come to pass' also appears at the beginning and end of the book. This fits well with a Praeterist point of view, where the book is focused on the first century AD, and things *would* shortly came to pass, but poses problems for people who follow a strict Historicist or Futurist interpretation. Some have even said they believe that Jesus got it wrong when he gave the impression that He was coming quickly, because it has been almost 2,000 years and he *still* hasn't come again. Some have tried to argue that we should translate it as 'I come suddenly', but this isn't really satisfactory.

However, there is no real problem if we interpret using the Gestational view. In one sense, historically, some of the prophecies did come to pass quickly as the immediate and local elements were happening in the days of John, and in another sense what was happening was foretelling the future in a way that was meant to be seen as just around the corner, because we are intended to live in the tension of the soon-coming of Jesus. To carry the Gospel to the whole world is a generational job – every new generation has to be reached by its contemporaries. In the Gestational view the immediate fulfilment prophesies the future fulfilment and affirms to us the Second Coming.

It is important though to remember that there is an urgency in our Lord's return – He wants us to be praying 'Your Kingdom come' and 'Maranatha, come quickly'. The gap between the immediate and future fulfilments is not set, and depends to some degree upon us: so far it has stretched almost 2,000 years, but we will see it happen within a generation if this Gospel is preached in all the world, and then the end will come – that is the promise (compare Matthew 24:14 and 2 Peter 3:12).

Discussion Topic: The reliability of prophecy

In both the Old and New Testaments we often find prophecies for things that are just about to happen alongside prophecies that look way into the future. For instance, Jeremiah prophesied that within his lifetime Babylon would conquer Jerusalem and take the people away into exile (Jeremiah 25). But goes on to say that the time will come when God will make a new covenant with Israel – 'I will put My law within them and on their heart I will write it; and I will be their God, and they shall be My people' (Jeremiah 31:33). Jeremiah's immediate prophecies are very closely linked with his futurist prophecies, which would be fulfilled in another 500 years' time when Jesus sent the gift of the Holy Spirit.

Jesus did the same thing in Matthew 24—25, where He prophesied about the destruction of the Temple – that not one stone would stand upon another – and this prophecy was linked with prophecies about the Second Coming. Was the Temple destroyed within that generation? Yes, in AD 70! Therefore we should take seriously what Jesus says about His coming again.

As we will see, the prophecy in Revelation is also very similar: the 'Day of the Lord' is both immediate and local, but it is also future and worldwide, and the first prophecy establishes the veracity of the latter. For example, Amos prophesies judgment over Israel (local and immediate) as a 'mini' Day of the Lord, but then moves out of the immediate context and talks about the judgment of the nations in the 'maxi' Day of the Lord in the more distant future. So the first fulfilment prepares the way for understanding the universal and more distant judgment of the world – there is a connection between the first century AD and when Christ comes again. In fact, you have to develop some sort of language in which to talk about End Times events, because they have not happened before – you have to say 'It is like this . . .' In order to have a language to talk about the Second Coming, the judgment of the earth or the Kingdom of God coming to earth, you have to take the mini previews and extrapolate them into the future.

Both the Old Testament prophets and Jesus knew they were up against it when they came to prophesy because if what they prophesied did not come true and they were shown to be false prophets, they were to be executed. It would be easy just to make up prophecies about the End Times, as they would be too far away to be testable, so Old Testament prophets would say something about the immediate situation, and then prophesy about the distant end of the world. This was the test point of their prophecy.

When was Revelation written?

Given the strong theme of persecution in Revelation, the book is likely to have been written during a time of persecution of the Early Church by Rome. It is often said that there were ten major persecutions of the Church before Christianity became an official religion under Constantine. Up until Nero's reign (AD 54–68) the Roman Empire had largely been tolerant of Christianity, as it was seen as an emergent form of Judaism, which was protected under

Roman law. However, as the century progressed, and Christianity became more readily distinguishable from Judaism, and as worship of the Emperor became more fundamental, this attitude changed and believers were increasingly persecuted and martyred for not sacrificing to the Emperor.

Generally, commentators are divided between an earlier date (AD 69–70) and a later date (AD 91–96) for when Revelation was written.

Earlier date: AD 69–70

The first persecution was under Nero in AD 64–68, and from the accounts of Roman historians Tacitus and Suetonius, who had lived through Nero's reign, and later Tertullian (AD 155–230), Christians were tortured and executed in the arena:

> [Nero] falsely charged and punished with the most fearful tortures, the persons commonly called Christians, who were hated for their enormities . . . first those were arrested who confessed they were Christians; next on their information, a vast multitude were convicted, not so much on the charge of burning the city, as of 'hating the human race' . . . In their very deaths they were made the subjects of sport: for they were covered with the hides of wild beasts, and worried to death by dogs, or nailed to crosses, or set fire to, and when the day waned, burned to serve for the evening lights. (Tacitus, *Annals*)

This description is very reminiscent of the strong and violent imagery of persecution used in Revelation. The accounts of a 'vast multitude' indicate this may not have been confined to Rome, and that Christians may have been brought in from elsewhere in the Empire. With the church growing rapidly in nearby Asia Minor, persecution there seems credible.

People thought Nero was too wicked to die, so even after his death in AD 68, some could not believe he was actually dead, and a myth grew up that he would return and gather together the Parthians, ride in and overthrow the Empire of Rome: Nero would come back again – *Nero redivivus*, 'Nero re-living'. This seems to lie behind the horrific picture of the anti-Christ we see in Revelation 13, where John sees one of the beast's heads 'as if it had been slain, and his fatal wound was healed' – dying and rising again, in a parody of the resurrection. This is a literal, historical background for the prophetic idea of the seeming indestructibility of evil.

As such, Revelation being written straight after this persecution, in the period AD 69–70, seems to fit well with the historical context. This view is taken by a number of scholars including Moses Stuart, E Earl Ellis and JAT Robinson.

Later date: AD 91–96

The popular date suggested for Revelation that you will find in conservative theology is AD 91–96, when a second persecution of the Church took place towards the end of Domitian's reign. However, this wave seems to have been more of a purging of aristocrats and their close relatives. Domitian had his niece Domitilla exiled and her husband, his cousin, executed on charges of 'atheism', because they refused to worship the Roman gods. This likely meant they had become Christians, and it is fascinating that in Rome there is a plaque in the earliest-known Christian cemetery stating the land was the property of Domitilla.

The cult of Emperor worship began during the reign of Caligula, who in AD 40 ordered a statue of himself to be erected in the Jerusalem Temple, leading to a revolt amongst Jews. As such Emperor worship existed before Nero's reign, but under Domitian appears to have greatly expanded throughout the Roman Empire. In particular a temple to Domitian was built in Ephesus, including a five-metre-high statue of the Emperor, which also gives a possible historical backdrop to some of the passages in Revelation about worshipping the Beast and the Image of the Beast (for example 13:4,8,15). The first definite record of Christians being punished for refusing to worship the Emperor is from AD 113, in a letter to Trajan written by Pliny the Younger, a Roman lawyer who had served under Domitian. He wrote asking for advice on how to deal with Christians brought before him. He was unsure as to whether it was legal or not to kill them if they refused to deny their faith, and said: 'I have never been present at the examination of the Christians, and I do not know, therefore, how they are normally punished or how these cases are investigated.' It would seem unlikely he would not have had some experience of a Christian trial if there had been a widespread persecution under Domitian.

While Domitian did seemingly persecute those within his family who converted, there are no contemporary accounts of a widespread persecution of the Church at that time, either by Roman authors or from early Christian sources. The first reference to a widespread persecution of Christians under

Domitian comes in Eusebius, writing 250 years later in around AD 340, which was later expanded by Orosius. He quotes Tertullian, Irenæus and Melito, who wrote earlier, but none of whom suggest anything worse than select Christians being slandered or exiled. So it does not seem to fit as well with a theme of a large-scale persecution, but is an attractive option from the perspective of Emperor worship. However, all this is based on the academic principle that John is writing in response to things he has actually seen and experienced, and leaves little room for Revelation to be a *prophetic vision* of things that have not happened yet.

Another mainstay of the later date argument is that the Early Church Father Irenæus (AD 130–202) wrote:

> If it were necessary that [the anti-Christ's] name should be revealed in this present time, it would have been announced by him [ie John] who beheld the apocalyptic vision. For it was seen no very long time since, but almost in our day, towards the end of Domitian's reign. (*Against Heresies*)

The question is, what was it 'that was seen' near the end of Domitian's reign? The text is not clear: the words could mean 'he/she' or 'it' was seen. So it could refer to when John actually saw the vision, which would imply the later date – this is the view of most modern commentators. However, it could equally refer to the written scroll of the vision, or to 'he', John, being seen after his return from exile. Given this is foundational to the later date view, it is remarkably ambiguous.

Other arguments

There are plenty of other minor arguments for and against these two possible dates, none of which are conclusive one way or the other. These points are often academic and aimed at supporting a particular theological agenda or scholarly trend, picking sources that agree and rebutting ones that do not. As such we need to see them as opinions on things we will probably never find out. I will leave it up to you to draw your own conclusions:

- → In his epistle to the Ephesians, usually dated AD 61–62, Paul commends the church there for their 'faith in the Lord Jesus' and their 'love for all the saints' (Ephesians 1:15). If Revelation were written in AD 69–70 it does not give much time for the Church to go rapidly downhill (see Revelation 2:4). Alternatively, others date Ephesians to AD 57–59. Even so, sadly from personal experience I would suggest a church can go from being vibrant and full of the Holy Spirit to losing their first love in much less than seven or eight years.

→ In AD 60–61 there was a large earthquake in Laodicea, which devastated the city – however, Revelation 3:17 describes it as 'rich' and 'wealthy'. If the church was destroyed, was there enough time for them to rebuild and become one of the seven main churches in Asia Minor? It doesn't necessarily follow that losing their buildings would have removed their wealth. We need to be careful here, as this argument involves seeing the church as the building, whereas we know that 'church', or *ekklesia*, really refers to the people, and was the term, prior to the church, that was used for the body of free citizens in a town. If the people survived, then the church did, regardless of whether the building they met in was flattened or not. Of course it also depends on whether the epistle is talking about spiritual or material wealth.

→ Some commentators have suggested that the church in Smyrna may not have been established before AD 60–64, so there would not have been time for it to become a major centre. However there is little evidence for this, and it equally could have been planted by Paul around the time of his two- to three-year stay in nearby Ephesus (Acts 19), which would date it to around AD 54–57.

→ Revelation 11:1–2 seems to indicate that the Temple may still exist. At the very least, there is no mention of its destruction in AD 70, which indicates the earlier date. However, in Revelation we are dealing with signs and symbols, and the text here may not necessarily refer to the physical Temple in Jerusalem.

→ How we interpret some of the symbolism in Revelation may be affected by which Emperor it was written under. In particular, the number 666 (616 in some manuscripts), is often interpreted numerologically as 'Nero Caesar' (as we will look at in Revelation 13:18). However, this was not even one of the options Irenæus considers when he discusses what 666 represents, indicating it was not a prevalent view at that time.

→ Revelation 17:9 refers to seven mountains, usually interpreted as the seven hills surrounding Rome, which an angel says are seven kings, five of whom have fallen, 'one is, and the other has not yet come'. Nero was the fifth Roman emperor, and this fits with Revelation being written just after his reign, although the sixth emperor, Galba, only reigned briefly. However, there are questions over which ruler you start counting from and how literally we are intended to interpret these verses.

→ Clement of Alexandria (AD 150–215) wrote about John's exile: 'on the tyrant's death, he returned to Ephesus from the Isle of Patmos', and Eusebius confirmed this, adding that this 'tyrant' was Domitian. However, as already discussed, Eusebius wrote much later, but also questioned the authenticity of Revelation, listing it as a 'spurious book', and may have tried to discount it because of its 'millennialism'. As such Eusebius may well have an agenda in his writings, which it is good to be aware of.

The difficulty with either view is the number and reliability of the sources. There are only a few accounts, so it is difficult to get a comprehensive picture of events. Also, writers who were alive at the time are more credible than people writing centuries later from second-hand accounts, but even then it doesn't mean they are more accurate. Contemporary Roman writers in search of favour and recognition may have been biased, attempting to flatter the current emperor and/or write bad things about previous ones. It is also likely that highly critical accounts (and writers) would have been destroyed. Therefore we do need to take these writings in context, and with a pinch of salt!

One final consideration is that trying to assign either Nero or Domitian as the inspiration behind Revelation, may be missing the point. Revelation is written in symbols, and the Beast has 7 heads – so it is reasonable to suggest that the Beast may represent the 'Roman Emperors', not just one individual.

Does the date matter?

Does it make much difference whether you support the earlier or later date? The short answer is, probably not. In either case, the background of Revelation is the persecution of the Church by Rome, especially in the face of the pressure to come to a compromise towards the idolatry and immorality of Roman culture, particularly Emperor worship. What Revelation reveals to us about the *spiritual* backdrop to persecution is what is important, rather than which emperor was in charge. However, as we look in more depth at some parts of Revelation, the exact date of writing may have a bearing on how we interpret these passages. In particular, the Praeterist view depends upon the earlier date, as it interprets Revelation as being largely fulfilled by AD 70. People who have wished to discredit this view because of some of the theological emphases that go along with it, have championed the later date.

I do not mind which date you go with, as long as you are open to admit that the alternative may be correct! Personally I agree most with the earlier date as it fits best the theme of persecution, and because I believe in it as a prophecy. So the arguments about emperor worship and Domitian's statue can be accounted for by John's prophetic vision of the future.

Who wrote Revelation?

What about the writer? He identifies himself four times as 'John' (1:1,4,9; 22:8) but doubts have been raised as to whether this was John the Apostle, another John, or someone pretending to be John. The problem is that he seems to write in unusual Greek, very different in style from the Greek in John's gospel and epistles.

It is true that some writers of Apocalyptic literature used pseudonyms, such as 'Abraham', Moses' or 'Enoch', who were obviously not the writers – their names were attached to the books to give them authority. Even in these cases the name was used only in the title, and not first-person within the text. Some commentators suggest that Revelation is no different, and that it is a sub-Christian book or a Jewish text 'christianised' by adding in some bits about Jesus, and was not written by John the Apostle, but that his name was added to give it credence. However, unlike all other apocalyptic writings, in Revelation the writer clearly and definitely reveals himself within the text – 'I, John'.

Only a few decades after John's death, Justin Martyr, writing in AD 135 acknowledges John as the author:

> John, one of the Apostles of Christ, who prophesied by a revelation that was made to him . . . (*Dialogue with Trypho the Jew, 81.4*)

Similarly, Irenæus, who was discipled at the feet of Polycarp who was a significant figure in the Early Church and who was discipled by John himself, along with other Early Church Fathers such as Clement of Alexandria, Tertullian and Origen, all attribute Revelation to John the Apostle.

But by the middle of the third century, Dionysus of Alexandria, in support of his idea that the author of Revelation was not the same as the author of the gospel and the epistles, wrote:

> It is said that there were two tombs at Ephesus, and that each one of the two is said to be John's. (*Eus. H. E. vii. 25*)

This is hardly a strong argument. While there were other people called John around in the first century, it is a huge leap to suggest that if one person says this is John's tomb and another says that is John's tomb, that therefore there were two Johns, one who wrote the gospel and the other who wrote Revelation.

Only the Apostle John appears without any other designation. If you said to an early Christian *John wrote this*, they would think of only one – he does not need to say 'I, John the Apostle' or 'I, John the beloved disciple'. Others would have to say that they are, for example, John the Baptist, or 'John-the-son-of-whoever-and-I-come-from-such-and-such-a-place' – the identification 'John' is so vague that it has got to be the one who is the most well known.

Some liberal scholars suggest that if what Revelation records is true, the authorship is not important – does it matter if it was written by John or not? Other Bible books aren't named by the author, for example 'Esther' is just the Greek name for Adressa, the Jewish Queen – it does not mean she wrote it.

However, that John wrote Revelation *is* important because it means it is part of the apostolic doctrine, which finished when the last of the apostles died – according to Early Church tradition, this was when John died in around AD 100. The New Testament Scriptures were all approved by the apostles, who acted as a safeguard that the stories of what Jesus did and said were true and not changed or embellished. Once the last apostle had passed away, there was no one left to say, 'Yes, it was like this', or 'No, Jesus definitely did not say that'.

There are plenty of other epistles written in the Early Church period, such as 1 Clement and Barnabas, but no matter how wonderful or how true they are, they could not be part of Scripture as they were written after the apostolic doctrine came to an end.

Recurring themes

Another indication that John is the author is that Revelation contains specific concepts characteristic of both John's gospel and his epistles.

The Word

Jesus is described as 'the Word' (*logos*) in John 1:1,14, and the 'Word of Life' in 1 John 1:1; and in Revelation 19:13 we see the 'Word of God' riding out of heaven on a white horse.

Truth

Similarly, truth is emphasized: 'Him who is true . . . this is the True God' (1 John 5:20), 'This is eternal life, that they may know You, the only true God' (John 17:3), and truth also appears many times in Revelation, for example, 'Behold, a white horse, and He who sat on it is called Faithful and True' (Revelation 19:11).

Pure White

Whiteness and light appear in both the gospel and the epistles as symbols of purity – the angels at the resurrection are dressed in white (John 20:12), Jesus is described as 'the true Light' (John 1:9), just as 'God is Light' in John's epistles, and cleanses us from sin (1 John 1:8) making us pure (1 John 3:3). Throughout Revelation Christ and the Overcomers appear in white (eg 1:14, 3:4–5, 4:4).

John's gospel was written so we 'may believe that Jesus is the Christ, the Son of God; and that believing you may have life in His name' (John 20:31). John's epistles were written that we may know we 'have eternal life' (1 John 5:13). Revelation was written so that we might endure – continuing steadfastly in the face of persecution (Revelation 22).

That is a beautiful pattern – John writes first to get us to faith, then to show us that if we've got faith then we've got eternal life; so it is not surprising he then wrote Revelation so we might hang on and get right through to the End Times. What John started in his gospel, and continued in his epistles, culminates in the book of Revelation.

Recurring themes

The numbers – 3, 4, 7, 12

Revelation is full of numbers that are used symbolically and give clues to deeper meanings – numbers are included in the mode of the literature:

- 3 hints at the Trinity, and we see Father, Son and Spirit appearing throughout the book. We also see the enemy's counterfeit trinity of the Dragon, Beast and False Prophet (see Revelation 12–13).

- 4 represents the extent of the world/Creation. We see 4 Living Creatures, 4 Horsemen, 4 Angels, 4 Corners of the Earth, 4 Winds, 4 sides to the New Jerusalem.

- 7 (=3+4) is a significant number and appears throughout the book representing completeness, fulfilment, totality – it is the sum of the Trinity + Creation, so represents the totality of everything. In the first section there are 7 Churches (lampstands), and 7 Stars; in the second, 7 Seals, 7 Trumpets, 7 Signs and 7 Bowls; in the third we see 7 main characters: the Harlot, the Bride, the Beast, Christ, Babylon, Jerusalem and Satan; finally in section four, the Lamb appears 7 times.

- 12 (=3×4) is also significant and represents governing order or administration. There are 12,000 sealed from the 12 Tribes in Revelation 7, the Woman in Revelation 12 has a crown of 12 stars, and in Revelation 21 the New Jerusalem has 12 gates/pearls for the 12 Tribes, 12 foundation stones for 12 Apostles, and is 12,000 stadia long, high and wide. Finally, in Revelation 22 the Tree of Life bears 12 kinds of fruit. We also see 24 (12×2) Elders, possibly representing 12 for each covenant.

There are also hints at numerology, for example with the number of the Beast, 666. We will look at 666 more when we come to Revelation 13:17–18. In view of the importance of numbers in Revelation, throughout this book I will be using numerals for significant numbers, such as '7 Churches', '24 Elders', '4 Horsemen', and so on. While the Greek text uses words for these numbers, they did not have separate numerals. I wish to emphasise the symbolic value of the numbers.

Greek language

If Revelation was written by John, how can we account for the unusual Greek he used and the differences in style between it and John's gospel and epistles? It is true that the Greek of the book of Revelation is not very good – the verbs do not fit properly, the pronouns are often incorrect and the genders of the nouns get mixed up! The Greek in John's gospel and epistles is quite good, according to most Greek scholars, but Early Church tradition as well as internal evidence in his gospel indicate John used an 'amanuensis', a literary secretary, to whom John gave dictation. Both Peter and Paul also used amanuenses to help them write. In fact, others have doubted John wrote the gospel, because the Greek is much better than you would expect from a fisherman, but if he had a scribe to put his grammar straight, it makes sense. It would make a lot of difference between his writings when John had somebody to help him, as opposed to when he is an exile on Patmos, writing by himself.

Second, John says four times that he was 'in Spirit'. If you were filled with the Holy Spirit and witnessed an ecstatic, brilliant vision, of course you wouldn't write in the same way as you would normally, and certainly not as cool, calm and collected as if you were sitting in a study with a secretary, who was putting it quite nicely onto paper for you. So being in Spirit could have affected the way John wrote.

Third, John would have been an old man by the time he wrote Revelation (John the Aged!) and when you get old you tend to return to your earlier thought patterns. John goes back to his first language and style of speech, which was Aramaic. Revelation is written as if Greek is being used to write Aramaic, and the grammar is wrong with the verbs and cases in the wrong place, like the way you speak English when you're German. The funny thing is that despite the bad Greek, you can tell exactly what John is trying to say – it comes over with a real punch. When you break the rules of grammar that is often what happens – you get the message coming through vividly.

John may even be writing in a deliberate Hebraic–Greek style to effectively convey his message in an apocalyptic idiom. Luke also used different styles to accentuate different parts of his writing: the first four sentences of Luke's gospel are in classical Greek, chapters 1—2 about the prophesied birth of Jesus are in Septuagintal Greek (the language the Old Testament was translated into three centuries before), and then Luke 3 onwards is written in koine

Greek, which is the rough style of Greek used in the Roman world at that time. Maybe John is doing a similar thing in his writing.

One thing to note is that sometimes John uses the present tense in amongst the past tense, but most Bible versions translate everything in the simple past tense for consistency. For example, in Revelation 5:9, the Greek reads 'and they *sing* a new song' rather than 'sang'. So, to remain true to the Greek text, I have included these bits in the present tense, indicating them with '*'. Although they could be dismissed as John's bad Greek, equally they may be used intentionally to bring the text dramatically to life at certain points, so we should be wary not to ignore them.

* * *

Overall there is adequate evidence that Revelation was written by John the Apostle, not another John or a writer using a pseudonym, and the unusual Greek and differences in style from the gospels and epistles can be accounted for.

Why was Revelation written?

We have looked at *who* wrote it and *when*, but what is the purpose of Revelation? Here are four foundations for *why* it was written.

1. Theology of Power

John's gospel is known as the 'gospel of love', but what happens to love when the Church is persecuted? Will Christianity work in respect to politics, economics or war? When the Church is up against the great power movements that exist in society, will love be vulnerable and get walked over? Revelation helps us to come to terms with worldly powers and how we can deal with them without allowing them to contaminate us. In the end, God is love before He is anything else (1 John 4:8), and He loved the world so much He gave Himself for it (John 3:16).

Revelation shows us what happens at the end – ultimately the God of love triumphs over evil and destroys it, as light destroys darkness.

2. Supernatural reality

The visions in Revelation make the supernatural realm, both good and evil, very real to us. Apocalyptic means 'to reveal what is behind' – sometimes it is hard for us to see that evil is deeply entrenched not only in human beings but also in the whole spiritual substructure of the universe. Evil is serious, endemic and has got to be dealt with properly. Evil cannot just be solved with a smile and being nice to one another – it needs something far more radical than that. The book of Revelation peels the veil off the spiritual forces in the world and gives us hope that there is a solution.

3. Christian 'warfare'

Third, the book of Revelation instructs a persecuted church concerning Christian warfare. Christian warfare is not against flesh and blood (Ephesians 6:12), but is spiritual warfare and is to do with the priests, who are the soldiers.

The priests are mentioned three times in Revelation:

> He has made us to be a kingdom, priests to His God and Father. (1:6)

> And you have made them to be a kingdom and priests to our God and they will reign upon the earth. (5:10)

> They will be priests of God and of Christ and will reign with Him a thousand years. (20:6)

It is the priests who reign with God, and authority is exercised not through violence, but through priestly sacrificial serving. Priests do not take the lives of others, they give their own lives, or symbolise this as a sacrifice. Priests teach the people and pray. Interestingly in Numbers 3, while we see the people are numbered for on-the-ground warfare, the priests are numbered for spiritual warfare – consecrated to wage war in the heavens just as we see in Revelation. Indeed, Numbers 3:7 uses the same word 'guard/keep' as in Genesis 2:15, implying that there is a spiritual enemy that needs to be kept out.

However, later in Revelation there is a subtle change: 'They will be priests *of* God and *of* Christ' (Revelation 20:6). In 1:6 and 5:10 they were priests *to*

Why was Revelation written?

God but now they are priests *of* God – they are still priests with authority, but now they reign. Before the return of Jesus and the resurrection of the Overcoming Church, the priests are *to* or *for* God in their service. After the Second Coming, they have become those possessed and belonging *of* God, having served their training period of faithfulness to God while on earth.

So how do these priestly soldiers operate? What type of weapons do these priests use in their spiritual battle?

Prayer and worship

First, priests operate by prayer. The breaking of the 7 Seals in Revelation 6—8 is preceded by prayer and worship of the priests on the thrones in chapter 5. The priests pray –> trumpets get blown –> Jesus the Lamb breaks the seals –> things happen on earth.

One interesting point is that in Revelation 5:8 where it mentions the 'golden bowls full of incense, which are the prayers of the saints', the 'which' refers to the golden bowls, so it is the *bowls* that are the prayers, not the incense. Similarly, in Revelation 8:3 it is the golden censer that appears to represent the prayers of the saints, to which the incense is added, namely Christ's intercession for us (Romans 8:34, Hebrews 7:25).

To pray in the Spirit we need the incense of Jesus' intercession, who ever lives to make intercession for us (Hebrews 7:25). If we pray in our own strength we may begin to pray fleshly prayers, but if we start to pray in the Spirit and lift them up to God, they are effective. Just as with the prayers of the priests, when we pray in the Spirit seals are broken, and things happen. We are engaging in the spiritual programme of the authority of the Kingdom of God, and prayer is the first weapon of our warfare.

Blood/Martyrdom

Second, blood is a weapon. There is quite a lot about blood in Revelation, from the blood dripping through from the souls under the altar who cry out to God (6:9), to those who overcome 'because of the blood of the Lamb' (12:11), and 'the souls of those who had been beheaded because of the testimony of Jesus and the word of God . . .' in chapter 20. The blood of the Saints is part of the battle.

Revelation 14:20 talks about the winepress of God's wrath – grapes go in, blood comes out. This wine turns up again in Revelation 16 and 17, where it is given to those who shed blood; they are made drunk by it, so that they do not know what they are doing – that is how God is going to bring destruction on them. Blood is a weapon against the enemy: the blood of the Lamb and the blood of the Saints, crying out for God's intervention. Then in Revelation 19 we see Jesus as the Bridegroom 'clothed with a robe dipped in blood', which may be the blood of the martyrs.

So martyrdom and the blood shed is a second weapon. When the church is persecuted it is defeating the devil: he is destroying himself. There is an old Roman proverb: 'Whom the gods intend to destroy, they first make mad or make drunk and then destruction falls upon them.' John is writing to the whole Church to encourage them in the battle.

Word of Testimony

The third weapon in the hands of God's people is the word of testimony, which is a theme that runs all the way through the book, from Revelation 1:2 where John 'testified to the word of God and to the testimony of Jesus Christ', through to 20:4, 'and they were those who were beheaded for the witness of Jesus and the word of God'. In Greek the word for 'testimony' is the same word as 'witness' (*marturian*), from where we get the word 'martyr'.

John was exiled to Patmos 'because of the Word of God and the testimony (witness) of Jesus' (1:9). Both 'The Witness' and 'The Word' are titles of Jesus – He is the Word of God because all that God wants to say to us is 'Jesus'. He is the Witness of God, because all that we can ever want to know about God, is witnessed to by Jesus. Word emphasizes divinity: 'In the beginning was the Word, the Word was with God, the Word was God' (John 1:1). Witness emphasizes humanity: everything about Jesus, the image of God in human form, is witnessing to God. If you want to know what God is like, look at Jesus.

So the Word goes out and the witness comes back. The witness and the word has come forth from God through Jesus Christ, into the Church, which makes the word of God known to the world. When the world looks at the Church, they should see the witness to God – we as the Church need to fulfil that calling and destiny.

Those are the main weapons of the church. We pray – things happen in heaven. We give our lives – things happen in heaven. We use words and witness to Jesus – things happen in heaven.

4. Blessedness

Finally, an important theme that runs through Revelation like a spine that holds it together is 'happiness' or 'blessedness', which is the goal of its message:

> Blessed is he who reads and those who hear the words of the prophecy and heed the things which are written in it; for the time is near.
> (Revelation 1:3, see also 14:13, 16:15, 19:9, 20:6, 22:7,14).

Underlining the whole book, even the rather difficult things we will look at, is the ultimate desire of God to bring happiness to His people. He wants us to be blessed: '*Blessed* are the poor in spirit . . . *blessed* are those who mourn.' This is not a new message:

> The Lord bless you, and keep you;
> The Lord make His face shine on you,
> And be gracious to you;
> The Lord lift up His countenance on you,
> And give you peace.
> (Numbers 6:24–26)

I hope you will be blessed as we look through Revelation, and this book will bring you happiness!

* ✶ *

We have looked at how Revelation is written in apocalyptic language, using vivid imagery and strong contrasts to bring to life the reality of the spiritual battle facing the persecuted Church, in order to encourage and bless them by revealing God's glorious future. Revelation is saturated with Old Testament imagery and allusions, breathing new life and hope into the fulfilment of God's promises to His people. While John's immediate audience is the first-century church, the book is for the complete Church throughout history.

Personally, I would suggest Revelation was written by John the Apostle early in Nero's reign and before the destruction of the Jerusalem Temple, but I leave you to come to your own conclusions on those points.

With the background to Revelation firmly implanted in our minds we now turn to look at the book itself. First we will look at the structure of the book to see how it is put together, to give us a framework for getting to grips with it.

Discussion Questions

Which way do you tend to interpret the book of Revelation?

Does it matter to you who wrote Revelation, or exactly when? Would it change how you read it?

Which of the main themes resonate most strongly with you?

The 4 vision structure

We now come to one of the most important things about our study of Revelation – the *flow* of the book. What we want to discover is how the different bits of the book fit together and what the overall structure is. You will not get the totality of the message of Revelation by proof-texting – pulling out one verse from here and another from over there – you need to understand the movement of the book. This is important because if we can imagine what the flow of a book is – its order and structure – it helps us to place each verse in context.

Some scholars have claimed that Revelation is a Jewish book that has been 'christianised' – someone came along with scissors and glue, and taking some Jewish writings, snipped off one bit here, stuck on another bit from a different scroll, and so on, until they gradually built up the book of Revelation. As mentioned above, Revelation *is* packed with references to the Old Testament, but the reason many want to reduce it to a collage of Jewish writings is because of some of the horrific pictures you find in it, which they say do not sound like Jesus, who nevertheless *was* a Jew. Rivers of blood, souls crying out for vengeance, ruling with a rod of iron: these at first glance do not fit comfortably with our Western view of Jesus. It is easier for some scholars to suggest that Revelation is an example of some vengeful Jewish writing into which a few of Jesus' ideas have been added, than to try to reconcile the Jesus of the gospels to the one we see here.

As we look at the structure of the book, I think you will be captivated by the beauty of its patterns – as when you look through a microscope and see that what looked like a higgledy-piggledy mess turns out to be a wonderfully intricate and ordered structure, because nature has an order at its base which points to God as Creator. In the same way the order and pattern of the Scriptures reveal His character.

The structure I will outline is by no means the only way of dividing up the book, but to me seems the most self-consistent and helpful.

Four visions

Let's begin to unravel the structure. This is something that years ago I picked up from Merrill Tenney's book *Interpreting Revelation*, and it has been fundamental to my being able to get deeper and deeper into this book. I have taken the liberty of adapting some of the structural headings from Tenney's work. There is no better way to begin looking at the book than by using the structure which comes out of the text itself, and is not imposed upon it from outside.

As with every decent book, Revelation has a very clear introduction and a conclusion, and in between there are four major blocks of truth which are intimately integrated together. While these four main sections are very different in size, they do give a comprehensive picture of our Lord Jesus Christ. The first verse reminds us that it is the *revelation of Jesus Christ*, not only because He sent and communicated it, not only because He is also the one who owns it, but also because it is *all about Him* (see page 67) and therefore we are warned at the end of the book not to alter it, pull it to pieces or add things to it.

'In Spirit'

The four main sections of the book are found by noting a little phrase 'in Spirit' (1:10; 4:2; 17:3; 21:10), generally translated 'in the Spirit' – but there is no definite article, so I am emphasising this by just saying '*in Spirit*', which of course means 'in the Holy Spirit' (we will look at this in more depth when we get to Revelation 1:10, see page 88). Revelations that are worth anything of course are in the Holy Spirit, but come to us in *our* spirit. It is how the supernatural breaks into the natural; the spiritual into the material; the metaphysical into the physical. Because we have spirits, the Holy Spirit can reveal truth through our spirit, which is what John is experiencing.

- → Revelation 1:10 begins the first section: '*I was in Spirit* on the Lord's day and I heard a loud voice like the sound of a trumpet...' John sees a vision of Jesus, which is then applied in chapters 2–3

- → The second section begins in chapter 4:2: 'Immediately *I was in Spirit* and behold a throne was standing in heaven, and One sitting on the throne.' Here again we hear a voice like the sound of a trumpet, then John has a revelation, followed by its application, right the way through to the end of chapter 16.

The 4 vision structure

—› Chapter 17 begins: 'And one of the seven angels who had the seven bowls came and spoke with me . . . And he carried me away *in Spirit* into a wilderness . . .' This time there is not a trumpet voice, but an angel who takes John in Spirit, to see another vision. And that carries on right the way through to Revelation 21:8.

—› Then in chapter 21:9: 'one of the seven angels . . . came and spoke with me . . . And he carried me away *in Spirit* to a great and high mountain and showed me the holy city, Jerusalem coming down out of heaven from God.'

So the phrase *in Spirit* breaks the book up into four sections, as shown in the figure on page 46. The first two sections are introduced by the *voice* of a loud trumpet, the second two by the *voice* of an angel with bowls of wrath. Not only that, but in the first and third sections the Lord appears with a sword, and in the second and fourth sections He appears as a Lamb. So we are already beginning to see that there is a very clear and meticulous pattern in this book, and as we will go on to find, this pattern gets deeper and deeper.

Revelation has been constructed, not only by John the Apostle, but by the Holy Spirit, who binds it together as one complete whole. The four sections are woven together not just by the symmetry of ideas, but like a wonderful jigsaw it is dovetailed, one bit to the next bit, to the next bit, fitted together.

So let us start by looking at an overview of each of the sections to see how they fit together.

Introduction – The communication of Christ (1:1–8)

I've called the introduction *The Communication of Christ*, as Revelation 1:1 says:

> The Revelation of Jesus Christ, which God gave Him to show to his bond-servants . . . and He sent and *communicated* it . . . (NASB)

In these first eight verses a communiqué is coming to us. It's almost as if it is a letter on headed notepaper, with the secretary's initials on: 'I, John', followed by the list of titles of the one whom the letter is from, which give us a terrific description of Jesus. When we see the majesty, wonder and status of this person who is communicating with us, we begin to realise that the message coming through is absolutely momentous. This introduction sets the scene for the rest of the book – this is who is writing to us and this is why – Jesus is the *channel*, *substance* and *source* of Revelation.

Now that we know who the message is from, we can begin the first of the four main sections.

Section I – Christ Central in the Church (1:9–3:22)

In Revelation 1:9–20 we have the first vision, where John sees Jesus, the Son of Man, with a sword coming out of his mouth walking among seven golden lampstands. These 7 lampstands are the 7 Churches (v20) at Ephesus, Smyrna, Pergamum, Thyatira, Sardis, Philadelphia and Laodicea, and in chapters 2—3 this vision is applied to each of them. So the vision of Jesus is intimately related to the messages to the 7 Churches, each one of which has something of Jesus given to them so that their golden Lampstands can keep on burning brightly, even under pressure and persecution.

In the vision, Jesus places his hand on John, who was 'as dead' (v17), and says: 'I have the keys of death and of Hades [the place of those departed from this life]'. John begins to rise up and write, because all that John is beginning to see in Jesus is being ministered to him through a touch from Jesus' hand, namely the Spirit of God (see Ezekiel 37:1). Everything that we see about Jesus in the initial vision of chapter 1 is then ministered to the 7 Churches – all that they need to live and burn brightly for God is found in Jesus.

In this section, Christ is *immanent* – He is near us on earth. Immanuel, God with us. The lampstands, the churches, are on earth, and Jesus is near those lampstands to fuel them up and keep them burning brightly. He is like a High Priest keeping the lamps in the Temple burning, fuelling them with the oil of His Spirit. The immanent God, who is the One in whom we live and move and have our being (to quote the Greek poets, as Paul did on Mars Hill, Acts 17), is right near us. More than that, the **immanent** Christ knows what it is like to walk amongst us. He has feet of burnished brass, He has walked through the fire, He has been here on earth with us and before us.

When Saul was persecuting the church, Jesus said, 'why are you persecuting *Me?*' (Acts 9:4). Why? Because Jesus was in the Church; He was with them. When you are being persecuted, the first thing you need to know is that God is with you – Christ who suffered on earth, is suffering with us now. He is in us and walking amongst us and will sustain us and keep us going – anything we may need is there in Him. He is the fullness of the Godhead bodily and we are filled full in Him (Colossians 1:19).

You may not always see Him, but here is the revelation – the Lord is behind the scenes and He is with us, in the midst of the churches, keeping the lamps burning.

 ## Section II – Christ Central in Creation (4:1–16:21)

As we move into the second section, we are heading away from the earth. Revelation 4:1 says 'A door was opened in heaven . . .', and so we go up into the heavens. I've called this section *Christ Central in Creation* – not just on earth but in the universe and in the heavens – because in the vision in chapters 4 and 5 the Throne has the 4 Living Creatures around it, acting as the spiritual ambassadors of different aspects of life on earth. Together these supernatural beings: lion, eagle, ox and man, represent Creation. There is an emerald rainbow representing the life of Creation, which God will not flood again.

The whole section reveals the Creator governing His creation, and in chapter 4, we see a heavenly worship scene, as God is praised in His Creation:

> Worthy are You, our Lord and our God, to receive glory and honour and power; for You created all things, and because of Your will they existed, and were created. (v11)

In the vision, we see Jesus on the throne:

> . . . I saw between the throne and the elders a Lamb standing, as if slain . . . (5:6)

Here we are looking into the very heart of God and see an outline, a delineation – the view has got substance, pattern, order and form. We see the lion that is the Lamb. What a terrific vision! That vision is God's governmental throne over His creation, and the Lamb is in the midst of it.

The rest of the section, from chapter 6 onwards, is how God is still reigning, through rebellions, disappointments and the darkness of the earth. We get 7 Seals, 7 Trumpets, 7 Signs and 7 Bowls. The way that He reigns is like a Lamb on the throne, not like the devil – 'might is right' – but with the sensitivity and

Revelation – Approaching the text

Introduction – The communication of Christ (1:1–8)

Section I – Christ Central in the Church (1:9–3:22)

Introduced by an Angel

- 7 Lampstands
- 7 Churches
- 7 Letters
- 7 Angels

Lord appears with a sword

Section II – Christ Central in Creation (4:1–16:21)

Introduced by an Angel

- 7 Seals
- 7 Trumpets
- 7 Signs
- 7 Bowls

Lord appears as a Lamb

Section III – Christ Coming in Conquest (17:1–21:8)

Introduced by a Trumpet

7 main players in the vision: Christ, Bride, New Jerusalem, Harlot, Babylon, Beast and Satan

Lord appears with a sword

Section IV – Christ Coming in Consummation

Introduced by a Trumpet

The Lamb is mentioned 7 times

Lord appears as a Lamb

Conclusion – The Call of Christ (22:6–22:21)

The 4 vision structure

the beauty of a loving God who is seeking to lead His rebellious universe out of its own self-destruction and into the place of blessing. His *omnipotence* is so different from the dictatorial power of men and Satan.

That is His creatorial, governmental power, and He *is still reigning.*

 ## Section III – Christ Coming in Conquest (17:1–21:8)

We then come to the third section, but this time we don't get the vision at the beginning, rather it comes in chapter 19 with the Marriage of the Lamb:

> And I saw heaven opened; and behold, a white horse, and He who sat upon it is called Faithful and True; in righteousness He judges and wages war. And His eyes are a flame of fire, and upon His head are many diadems . . . (vs11–12)

The vision is Jesus leading an army, the King of Kings, and the Lord of Lords, coming from heaven to earth wearing a robe dipped in blood, with a sword in His mouth that destroys His enemies. He is coming again to collect His Bride and take her to reign with Him. This vision dominates the whole of the third section. Christ is the foremost of the 7 main players in this vision, with the others being the Bride, the New Jerusalem, the Harlot, Babylon, the Beast and Satan, who is going to be bound in a pit.

So the third section is *Christ Coming in Conquest.* He is waiting at the door, ready to come. It is not so much that He is honoured in heaven, but that heaven is open (Revelation 19:11). This is about Christ's *imminence.*

 ## Section IV – Christ Coming in Consummation (21:9–22:5)

That brings us to the final section, which starts in chapter 21:9 where we see the Bride appearing, so I have called it *Christ Coming in Consummation.* This is similar to the word used in Ephesians 1:10 when it says that Christ 'recapitulates', 'heads up again' or 'sums up all things'. The consummation is Christ coming and summing everything up into Himself – gathering all things which are redeemable and removing those things which are irredeemable.

What about this final vision? We see the Bride and the New Jerusalem, but when you look around, where is Jesus? 'The Lamb' appears 7 times in this section – everywhere you look in the New Jerusalem you see the Lamb. This vision fills the whole section, because the vision is of Christ filling everything. Even though it is the smallest of the sections, it has 'Lamb' all over it. This is the *omnipresence* of God, the omnipresence of heaven on earth. Just as everything in Eve was in Adam, because she was taken from his side, so everything in the New Jerusalem was in Christ. It is a section and a vision all in one – Christ all in all.

You don't see the Lamb of God until you look through the Bride and there, right in the middle of the New Jerusalem (because it is transparent gold) you see the Lamb. That is how we are going to display Jesus when He comes again: we don't know where or when He will come, but we do know that when He does, He is coming to be seen, and glorified, in the Church. He will come into His people and be admired in all those who believe – this is the wonder of the humble-hearted God we worship. Even when He is going to display His glory and His beauty, He does it through us to the rest of the universe. The New Jerusalem has the glory of God as her clothing and it shines out so that the world can find Jesus.

Conclusion – The Call of Christ (22:6–22:21)

At the end of Revelation we have the conclusion, which sums up why Jesus is writing to us. I've named it *The Call of Christ*: you could say that it is the *Challenge of Christ* (or even *The Challenging Call of Christ*, to get more alliteration in!).

Here is a challenge:

> Blessed is he who heeds the words of the prophecy of this book . . .
> (v7)

and a call:

> And the Spirit and the bride say 'Come'. And let the one who hears say 'come'. And let the one who is thirsty come; let the one who wishes take the water of life without cost. (v17)

The call of Christ is a call into service and obedience until He comes again, and beyond . . . There follows a warning not to remove anything out of this message, and finally Christ's promise to come quickly.

Amen. Come Lord Jesus.

The 4 vision structure

Common threads in the sections

Movement

If you look at the four sections, you will notice that we go from the closeness of Christ to the Church on earth (↰ below), up to the transcendence of Christ in heaven where He has gone to the Father, reigning through creation (↺ above). Then Christ coming, bringing heaven to earth (↯ descending), and finally Christ everywhere, in heaven and on earth, summing everything up into Himself (↻ all in all).

Greek Concepts of God

In each of the sections we see magnificent Messianic enrichments of four classic Greek concepts of God: **immanence**, **omnipotence**, **imminence** and **omnipresence**. The Greeks did not have a full revelation of the One True God, but they had developed philosophical ideas of what God must be like by looking at the world around them. The expansion of the Greek Empire had made Greek language, culture and thinking dominant in the known world, so here in Revelation John is using not only their language but their theological ideas as a platform to demonstrate who God really is in Christ. Jesus is revealed as fleshing out and beautifying these cerebral, Greek ideas of what God was like – superseding the best thoughts of men.

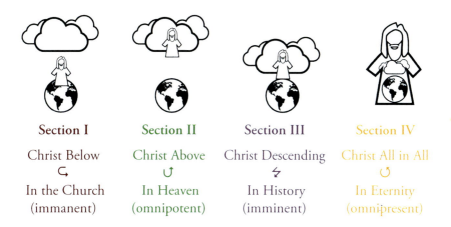

Section I	Section II	Section III	Section IV
Christ Below	Christ Above	Christ Descending	Christ All in All
↰	↺	↯	↻
In the Church	In Heaven	In History	In Eternity
(immanent)	(omnipotent)	(imminent)	(omnipresent)

Dovetailed together

As we go through the book in more depth we see that these sections are all interlinked like a jigsaw puzzle.

The first vision begins with Christ in the midst His Church and finishes in the last overcoming promise with:

> Behold I stand at the door and knock; if anyone hears my voice and opens the door I will come in to him . . . He who overcomes I will grant to him to sit down with me on my throne. (Revelation 3:20)

Moving on to the next vision, there is a door open in heaven: to those who open the door of their lives to Christ on earth, a door is opened in the heavens: it's the other side of the door – you let Him in, He lets you in.

When we rise up into heaven, we see Christ on the throne. Why is He there? Because 'the Lion that is from the tribe of Judah, the Root of David, has overcome so as to open the book and its seven seals' (5:5). When we overcome the promise is – *I am coming to you so that you can overcome and sit on my throne*. All the 7 types of overcoming in the 7 Churches we see in chapters 2 and 3 is now summed up in Jesus who has overcome and sat on the throne in the heavens, until He comes again.

The second section ends with Jesus ruling over the earth until the Final Judgement upon Babylon, that is then taken up and expanded at the beginning of the third section. After this we see the Marriage of the Lamb, the Millennium and the Great White Throne, followed by the New Jerusalem at the end of Section III. Having been introduced to it at the end of Section III, the New Jerusalem is expanded in the final section.

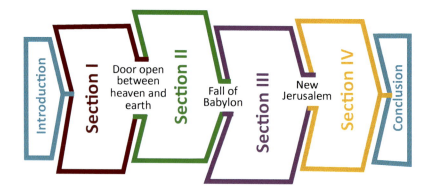

You cannot dissociate the sections – they interlink to form a whole. This dovetailing demonstrates that Revelation is not a rough cut-and-paste job of different Jewish writings. It also helps us to interpret the book within biblical parameters, not out of the feverish fantasies of our own fervent imaginations! Not only is Revelation beautifully woven together, but the vision of Christ we get builds up as we move through the book until we see its totality. That is the glorious message.

So it is sad when people entangle themselves, arguing about who the anti-Christ is and what the scorpion stings represent, when in fact Revelation presents a magnificent, fourfold vision of Jesus, giving us faith and hope and the ability to worship and love, culminating in the final picture of the Bride and the Bridegroom together forever. We will discover a lot more of the beauty of this vision as we work through these sections.

Authority

Another example of how Revelation has been so carefully constructed, is that each vision presents a different aspect of God's authority, depicted by four different thrones. Each of these thrones represents an expression of divine authority against which the hostility and rebellion of the world rise up: **Fatherhood**, **Government**, **Judgment** and all things being brought together in Christ.

There is a parallel between these thrones in Revelation and the thrones of the King or Queen of Great Britain: there is a family throne in Windsor Castle (**Father's Throne**); the sovereign's throne in the Houses of Parliament, from where the King hands over the government of the country during the State Opening of Parliament (**Governmental Throne**); judgment is carried out in their name at the High Court of Justice (**Judicial Throne**); and finally, the throne in Buckingham Palace brings order and government throughout the Commonwealth (Imperial Throne).

1. Father's Throne (3:21)

> He who overcomes, I will grant to him to sit down with Me on My throne, as I also overcame and sat down with My Father on His throne.

When God decided to make the human race, I imagine He said something to the effect of: 'What on earth shall I do with these anthropological bipeds, homo sapiens sapiens?' The Father's answer was to conform them to the image of His Son. That was the purpose for which the Father brought everything into being (see Ephesians 1, Romans 8:28–30). That is the destiny that God is working towards. If we are walking towards anything else, we are opposing the purpose of our creation.

2. Governmental Throne (4:2)

In the second vision we see God's will is not being done on the earth – so what sort of authority does He have? How can an almighty, all-powerful God allow sin and suffering to happen? And how is He eventually going to get His will done? The answer is that He is working from His governmental throne with a Lamb slain: the Cross, not sheer power, is the basis of God's government. That is why it is sometimes difficult for us to endure, but it is through the love of Christ and the blood of the martyrs that the purpose of God is being accomplished.

That God is getting His will done on earth in 'government' is apparent in the book of Job – there is a heavenly council (Job 1–2), where it is not just the Father's will, but the free will of other spirit powers that come into play. Although God is ultimately in charge of everything and does have the power to enforce His will, He chooses to rule not by might, but rather shares His reign, which of course makes it open to opposition. For more on this please see *Suffering and the Love of God*, and *God's Strategy in Human History: Vol. 1*.

3. Judicial Throne (20:11)

In the third section there is a Great White Throne, which becomes the judicial throne before which each of us will receive a verdict upon our lives. The books will be opened and the dead, both small and great, will be raised and judged. If there is no final verdict and judgment in life, then our whole existence and all our values of what is good and bad are meaningless.

In a sense, this final assize is already operating inside us – in Romans 2, Paul pictures it like a law court scene, with some of our thoughts accusing us from the Council for the Prosecution and other thoughts justifying and defending us from the Council for the Defence. Finally, the day will come when God will expose this internal judgement before the Great White Throne. When the final verdict is given, having listened to the defence and the prosecution, nobody will complain because we will know it is the truth. While in some ways this is awe-inspiring and frightening, this judicial process is not the horrific picture that some people paint of God looking around to find reasons to punish people. The judgment is simply the truth of the matter: what we have done and what we are inside one day will be brought outside, both for the saved and the lost. God is a just judge.

4. Imperial Throne (22:1–3)

Finally, we see the Emperor's throne, where we His servants will see His face and His name will be written on our foreheads. As we look into His face we shall reign with Him, implementing His will over this vast universe, of which we see only a tiny little bit: the distance to the edge of the observable universe is about 46.6 billion light-years (1 light-year = 6 trillion miles) with an estimated 30 billion trillion stars, each of which may be orbited by multiple planets. And that's just the observable universe . . . There may even be other dimensions we shall have to move into where we will reign together with Him forever and ever.

Discussion Questions

Which of these 4 visions of Christ speaks to you most?

Which of the 4 Thrones do you tend to view God as sitting on?

* ✱ *

Revelation – Approaching the text

Overview of Revelation

Revelation is a wonderfully coordinated book, with an intimately integrated structure. The following is a short schema of the structure and flow of Revelation, divided up chapter by chapter, to serve as a handy overview, including symbols which we will use as milestones throughout the book.

Chapter — **Structure**

1a — We are introduced to the author of the letter/prophecy/book/parable – Jesus Christ . . .

Introduction

1b — The first glorious vision reveals Jesus as the Almighty, First and Last, Son of Man, who was pierced, died and resurrected, and is coming again on the clouds as King and High Priest.

Section I

1st Vision

2–3 — Jesus addresses the 7 Churches in letters: each is encountering false teaching and practice from those who would compromise their witness and each is challenged to overcome. Some get no criticism while others receive serious indictments. The section finishes with the famous words of Jesus: 'Behold, I stand at the door and knock'.

7 Letters

4 — The focus now shifts from the earth to heaven, where John sees the second glorious vision of Christ – this time a Lamb as slain upon the Throne, surrounded by worshipping Creation.

Section II

2nd Vision

5 — Continuing the second vision, John sees the 7 Seals on the book of God's purposes for humanity. The Lamb, the Lion of Judah is the only one worthy to open the 7 Seals.

Overview of Revelation

6   The resurrected Lamb reigns by starting to open the seals. The first 4 Seals are broken, releasing 4 Horsemen. The 5th Seal reveals the souls of those under the Altar calling out for vindication, and the 6th Seal causes the whole earth to be shaken.

7 Seals

7   An interlude between the 6th and 7th Seals showing the 144,000 as an army on earth, followed by a vision of the innumerable followers of Jesus in Heaven to come, worshipping around the Throne.

{INTERLUDE}

8   The breaking of the 7th Seal brings silence, which leads into the sounding of the 7 Trumpets. Trumpets 1–4 are sounded and unleash fire and destruction upon the earth and sea, sun, moon and stars, like the plagues of Egypt.

7 Trumpets

9   The plagues continue with large scale destruction following the 5th Trumpet (1st Woe) – locust army, led by Abaddon/Apollyon – and the 6th Trumpet (2nd Woe) – army of horsemen, which kills a third of humankind. People are plagued by spiritual darkness – eyes are blinded to the Gospel, and there is no repentance.

10   An interlude between the 6–7th Trumpets. We see a Strong Angel, resembling Jesus, claiming the whole world and holding a Little Booklet in His hand. John is commanded to eat the book and keep preaching the Gospel.

{INTERLUDE}

11   World evangelisation is in view in this chapter, which begins with John measuring the Temple/people of God. 2 Witnesses appear who prophesy for 1260 days before being overcome by the beast. After 3½ days they receive the breath of life and go up to heaven. The 7th Trumpet sounds and we again see worship around the Throne before the Temple is opened and the Ark appears.

55

Revelation – Approaching the text

12 Two Signs appear in heaven – first, a Woman in labour and her male child, who are followed by the appearance of a great red Dragon, Satan who tries to devour the child. War bursts forth in heaven and the Dragon and his angels are thrown down by Michael and the heavenly army. The Woman is nourished in the Wilderness and protected from the Dragon.

7 Signs

13 Alongside the Dragon, Satan's counterfeit trinity is revealed in the next two Signs: the Beast from the Sea, full of blasphemies who attacks the Saints, and the Beast from the Earth, the False Prophet, who makes an image of the Beast for people to worship. The number of the Beast is revealed as 666.

14 The 5th Sign, the 144,000 Overcomers worshipping on Mount Zion are revealed as the Firstfruits, who are followed by the 6th Sign, the Full Harvest of the Earth, reaped by one like a Son of Man – both the grain, and the vine. We see the Winepress of the wrath of God.

15 As worship takes place in Heaven, we witness the 7th Sign: 7 angels with 7 Bowls of Wrath appear, in which the wrath of God will be finished.

{INTERLUDE}

16 As the 7 Bowls of wrath are poured out, one after another, Babylon, the world system, is destroyed. Jesus assures us He is coming in a short interlude between the 6th and 7th Bowls of wrath, as the enemy forces gather at Armageddon.

7 Bowls

{INTERLUDE}

Section III

17 Section III begins as we are shown the true nature of the world in the form of the Harlot of Babylon, drunk with the wine of her immorality, riding on the scarlet Beast. This is the final expression of humankind without God. God's people are to rejoice at Babylon's demise.

i) Harlot

ii) Beast

Overview of Revelation

18 Further revelation as to the true nature of the world – its politics and its inveterate hatred of God and humankind – as judgment is pronounced over Babylon.

iii) Babylon

19 The Marriage Supper of the Lamb is announced and Christ arrives on a White Horse as the King of kings and Lord of lords, while the Bride dresses in her righteous holy wedding dress. The Beast and the False Prophet are defeated and thrown into the Lake of Fire.

3rd Vision

iv) Christ
v) Bride

20 Satan is bound and in the pit for 1000 years. The Saints reign for the Millennium and at its end comes the awesome judgment of the Great White Throne with the Lamb's Book of Life. The devil, Death and Hades are all thrown into the Lake of Fire, along with any whose names are not in the Book of Life.

vi) Satan

21a The New Heaven and New Earth appear, and we see the life of the New Jerusalem coming down from heaven – 'Behold, I am making all things new'. Section III finishes with an angel taking John to see 'the Bride, the wife of the Lamb'.

vii) New Jerusalem

Section IV

21b John is carried 'in Spirit' to witness the holy city coming down out of heaven and we see a glorious vision of its beauty. There is no Temple, for 'the Lord God, the Almighty and the Lamb are its Temple.'

4th Vision fills the section

22a We see the Throne of God and the Lamb with the life-giving flow of the refreshing Spirit of God.

Conclusion

22b John concludes with final encouragements and warnings that Jesus is coming with His reward for the faithful. Even so, come Lord Jesus!

Revelation – Approaching the text

* ✶ *

Hopefully this overview gives you a flavour of how to use this structure to understand what is going on when you read through Revelation. This commentary is laid out using this colour-coded four-vision structure as a basis.

So, with the structure and flow of the book firmly embedded in our thinking, let us look at how it begins . . .

Commentary on Revelation

Revelation 1	63
Revelation 2	120
Revelation 3	151
Revelation 4	192
Revelation 5	217
Revelation 6	245
Revelation 7	281
Revelation 8	306
Revelation 9	333
Revelation 10	357
Revelation 11	384

Introduction

The Communication of Christ

The Communication of Christ
Revelation 1

Revelation 1:1–8 | The Letterhead

Text – Revelation 1:1–3

> ¹ The Revelation of Jesus Christ, which God gave Him to show to His bond-servants, the things which must soon take place; and He sent and communicated it by His angel to His bond-servant John, ² who testified to the word of God and to the testimony of Jesus Christ, even to all that he saw. ³ Blessed is he who reads and those who hear the words of the prophecy, and heed the things which are written in it; for the time is near.

Rooted in Daniel (v1, 3)

The first verse, as well as verse 3, shows us that Revelation is intimately and essentially rooted in the book of Daniel. As mentioned in the previous chapter, many people say that to understand Revelation, you need to understand Daniel – so we will look at the salient bits of Daniel when they arise.

Here from the very outset there is an important allusion to Daniel to help us begin to interpret this revelation of Jesus Christ. Seven times in Daniel 2 we get the words 'reveal' or 'revelation', which in the Septuagint (the Greek translation of the Old Testament) is *apokalupsis*, from where we get the word 'apocalypse'. 'Has made known' in Daniel 2:28 is like the word 'signify', or 'communicate', in Revelation 1:1. Secondly, verse 1 goes on to say 'the things which must soon take place'. This is a sort of substitute phrase used in the Septuagint translation of Daniel for the Hebrew words that talk about the events that are going to happen in the future.

We can see these similarities clearly if we compare Revelation 1:1 side by side with Daniel 2:28 in the Septuagint:

However, there is a God in heaven who reveals (*anakalupto*) mysteries, and He has made known to King Nebuchadnezzar what will take place in the latter days.

The Revelation (*apokalupsis*) of Jesus Christ, which God gave Him to show to His bond-servants, the things which must soon take place; and He sent and communicated it by His angel to His bond-servant John

However, in Daniel the things 'made known' will take place 'in the latter days', way in the future, but looking forward to Revelation, they are now things which 'must soon take place'. There is an increasing sense of the quickness. You get it again in Revelation 1:3 – 'for the time is near'. That is not simply a future reference because as Jesus said, 'the time *is* fulfilled, and the Kingdom of God *is at hand*' (Mark 1:15). These three things: 'revelation', things that 'will take place', and 'communicate' not only all occur in Daniel 2:27–9, but also in Daniel 2:45, 47 and Daniel 7, which parallels those events.

So the Kingdom has arrived, but it is still arriving. It is near, but it is also come – the time is fulfilled. Something has begun which was prophesied in the book of Daniel as being for the latter days, and Revelation begins by saying that *it has arrived*. In the same sort of way, the apostle Paul updates the Old Testament where many times it says 'I *will not be* ashamed' (for example Isaiah 50:7, Psalm 25:3), but Paul says 'I *am not* ashamed' (Romans 1:16). Something has changed: the death, burial and resurrection of our Lord Jesus Christ have taken hold of the whole gamut of truth and concentrated it in the person of the Son of God, and these colossal events, which transformed the universe and the destiny of the human race, have so altered things that every single word that at one time indicated a future reality has now actually been fulfilled in Christ, and the Kingdom has begun. The end of all things is at hand. That is why Peter, on the Day of Pentecost, says that we are in the last days (Acts 2:17) – we are not still looking and waiting; the End Times have begun. It does not mean that they are completed yet, but they are starting to happen because the Kingdom is here. We should not be sitting here waiting and saying, 'Well, one day the Kingdom will come', or we will be waiting another 2,000 years. It is beginning. God is getting His purposes done through Christ. Everything has been accomplished in Him, and is now being expanded into the whole of the human race, so that humankind everywhere can enter into the great Kingdom of God and His destiny for the universe, which He has planned. That is the picture we get from the first verse of Revelation!

In Revelation 1:19 there is a similar phrase: 'write the things which you have seen, and the things which are, and the things which will take place after these things' (see also 22:6). This verse shows that the whole of the book is caught up in the Kingdom to come. The 'shortly' or 'soon' in our translations of Revelation 1:1 does not confine us to a Futurist view that concentrates everything into only the last few years of this age; rather it means that something has now happened and the Kingdom *is at hand*.

This now-and-not-yet view of the Kingdom is difficult to reconcile with any of the four main schools of interpreting Revelation on their own, but is a great example of how the Gestational view draws together the best from each of them. The Kingdom started coming in the first century (Praeterist), but is still coming (Historicist), and will eventually come in its fullness (Futurist), and the things of the Kingdom we see now are glimpses of the eternal reign of Christ (Spiritual). We are already in the book of Revelation now – the Kingdom is beginning to appear, but there is more to come. Every time the Spirit of God breaks through there is some new evidence of the Kingdom, with a healing, with a deliverance, with the Gospel bringing men and women into the people of God. These are the beginnings of the pains of childbirth (Acts 2:24 (NASB margin), Romans 8:22), and the day will come when the whole child will appear and the Kingdom will be born. It is as though the Church is the vehicle to bring in the Kingdom of God, to bring the future Kingdom to birth.

Revelation opens a wonderful window for us to see that what Daniel saw is now here.

Discussion Topic: The Last Days

Studying what the Bible says will happen in 'the last days' is known as 'eschatology', from the Greek word *eschaton* which means 'the final thing'. The Old Testament looks forward to the 'latter days' (Daniel

10:14, Micah 4:1), and Revelation gives us a glimpse of what will happen at the End of the Age, when Jesus comes again:

> Write the things which you have seen, and the things which are, and the things which shall take place after these things. (Revelation 1:19)

Jesus promised He would return (eg Matthew 24:30, Mark 13:26, Luke 21:27, John 14:3), and the angels at the Ascension said He 'will come in just the same way as you have watched Him go into heaven' (Acts 1:11). The Second Coming of Christ is referred to by the word *parousia* ('presence' or 'arrival') sixteen times in the New Testament (eg Matthew 24:3,27,37,39). *Parousia* was also historically used to describe the visit of a royal person, and in 2 Peter 3:12 describes the coming of the 'Day of God'. Another word used by Paul to describe the Second Coming is *epiphaneia* ('appearing'), which appears five times (eg 1 Timothy 6:14) and is where we get the word 'epiphany' from.

Exactly what will happen when Jesus comes again is not clear, and is a matter of great speculation. What Jesus says about it is in parabolic language, for example Matthew 24—25, where His teaching on the Second Coming includes apocalyptic imagery and parables, and is also combined with prophecies about the destruction of the Temple in AD 70, which marked the end of that age.

What we can say about the End Times is that Jesus says there will be an end, and it will come when 'the Gospel of the kingdom will be proclaimed throughout the whole world as a testimony to all nations' (Matthew 24:14).

However, there is a sense in which we are already living within the End Times; just as the Kingdom is 'now and not yet', we are living in 'the end time age'. The Church is the people of the 'End Times', and the faster we preach the Gospel in all the world, the faster the 'End Times' will come in fullness.

Channel, substance, source (v1)

The phrase, 'the revelation of Jesus Christ' in verse 1 could mean three things:

i. the Revelation *comes via* Him – Jesus is the channel

ii. the Revelation *belongs to* him – Jesus is the source

iii. the Revelation *is about* him – Jesus is the substance

These ideas are closely linked: Christ, the Word, is the fulfilment of all words that are sent from God (i). Revelation is about Him (iii), and if it is about Him, it originates with Him and belongs to Him (ii). Therefore we should not misuse it, manipulate it or add to it, because it is not ours, it is His (Revelation 22:18–19). If people had been a lot more sensitive in interpreting Revelation, we may have been saved all of the rather bizarre interpretations which have been imposed upon the text. But as it is His book, if we do not understand bits of it, we can talk to Jesus about it: if any of us lacks wisdom, they should ask God (James 1:5) and the Lord will talk to us about what it means.

So the introduction reveals Jesus Christ as the channel, the substance and the source of the book.

Word and Witness (v1–2)

Jesus sent and communicated His message by His messenger (literally 'angel'), His bond-servant John (v1). John is there as a servant to put over the will of His master, not his own will – someone who 'bore witness to the word of God, and the testimony of Jesus Christ' (v2). Those two ideas – the **word of God** and the **witness of God** ('testimony' is the same word as 'witness' in Greek) – are very important, and as discussed on page 38 comprise one of the weapons in our spiritual battle.

The **word of God** sums up all He wants to say to us, which we know is Jesus: God coming to communicate to man. Jesus is revealed three times in the Bible as **the Word**: in John's Gospel (John 1:1), John's Epistles (1 John 1:1) and in the Book of Revelation (19:13). God in times past spoke through the prophets, in bits and pieces, but now has spoken to us '*in Son*' (Hebrews 1:2, literal). So the actual medium and substance of communication is 'Son'. This is the Father's word to the universe – 'My Son, Jesus'.

The Introduction – The Communication of Christ

The **witness of Jesus Christ** is that every bit of Jesus, particularly seen as the carpenter of Nazareth, a man of earth, points as a signpost, to God – 'he who has seen Me has seen the Father' (John 14:9). So whereas the **word** is God revealing Himself to man, the **witness** is man being led in to God through the one man, Christ Jesus. There is two-way communication.

But how do I speak to God? He is big, powerful, the Creator of galaxies, nature and atoms. We cannot know God personally unless He reveals Himself to us, when He lets the inside come outside, which is what He did in Jesus. If God is like Jesus then I can talk to Him, because I can understand who He is – giving friendship to the tax collector, healing the blind man. If we did not know what God was like we would not be able to talk to Him: God speaks *Jesus language* because Jesus is there in the middle. Jesus said that the Scriptures were those that witnessed to Him. We are not into *God*-ianity, we are into *Christ*-ianity: it is only through Christ that we understand who God is.

This is at the heart of our message – to get men and women into communication with God by bringing them to Jesus. So we tell people about the witness of Jesus, which is our witness to Him, and Jesus points people to who God really is. So we too, like John, should bear witness to this message: the Spirit of God has come upon us that we might be witnesses to the ends of the earth. What are we witnessing to? That God has spoken to humanity, and that humanity can speak to God.

Blessing in reading! (v3)

Verse 3 says there is a blessing in reading Revelation, presumably even when we haven't understood any of it! We are blessed if we just read it, or listen to what it says, and also blessed if we heed or take notice of the words of this prophecy, which implies in the reader a willingness to obey. Then, just as in Mark 1:15, we read 'the time is near' – the time is at hand. It is the same idea, and it all begins with Jesus and His intervention when He came as a man 2,000 years ago.

Text – Revelation 1:4–8

> [4] John to the seven churches that are in Asia: Grace to you and peace, from Him who is and who was and who is to come, and from the seven spirits who are before His throne, [5] and from Jesus Christ, the faithful witness, the firstborn of the dead, and the ruler of the kings of the earth. To Him who loves us and released us from our sins by His blood— [6] and He has made us to be a kingdom, priests to His God and Father—to Him be the glory and the dominion forever and ever. Amen. [7] Behold, He is coming with the clouds, and every eye will see Him, even those who pierced Him; and all the tribes of the earth will mourn over Him. So it is to be. Amen. [8] 'I am the Alpha and the Omega,' says the Lord God, 'who is and who was and who is to come, the Almighty.'

The 7 Churches (v4)

In the Bible, 7 is often used as a way of talking about completion and fulfilment, like the 7 days of Creation. 7 means everything is done – it is all completed. So the 7 Churches immediately gives the idea that we are talking about the whole Church. Of course seven actual churches are addressed in the letters because the revelation has got to be sent *somewhere*, but this letter is written to the totality of the Church. Just as later in Revelation 1 we will see those 7 Churches like lamps shining so that we can see Christ, our purpose as the whole Church is to shine light on Jesus.

Grace and peace (v4)

John says 'Grace to you and peace' – grace is the Greek greeting (*charis*) and peace is the Hebrew greeting (*shalom*), so we have Greek and Hebrew blessings together. The Church should be saturated with grace, not criticism, and full of peace – spiritual prosperity and wholeness – in Christ, not with strife and arguments. If we all said '*charis* and *shalom*' to each other more often, there would be a lot more grace and peace around, because they would be released from our lives by the power of the Holy Spirit: our words can release the Holy Spirit into the lives of others. Jesus said His words 'are spirit and are life' (John 6:63).

Was and is and is to come (v4,8)

In verse 4 and verse 8 we get the same phrase: 'who is and who was and who is to come'. In Greek, use of a repeated phrase like this usually acts like a kind of pull-out section, or parenthesis, called an *inclusio*, which means that like brackets, verses 4 and 8 hold together everything in between. As we will see, this *inclusio* starts with the extension of God's name (*Yahweh*) into Greek (v4) and finishes with the extension of God into *Yahweh* (v8).

In verses 4–5 we get a wonderful Trinitarian statement:

- → from Him who is and who was and who is to come [Father]
- → from the 7 Spirits who are before his throne [Holy Spirit]
- → from Jesus Christ [Son], the faithful witness, the firstborn of the dead, and the ruler of the kings of the earth.

When Moses asked who was sending him to rescue Israel, God's enigmatic reply was 'I am that I am'. In verses 4 and 8, 'who is and who was and who is to come' is clearly a play on '*I am who I am*', which is the root of the verb 'to be' – *Yahweh*, the Old Testament covenant name for God (Exodus 3:14). Here 'I am that I am' is translated and defined in a Greek verb and in different tenses – present, past and future, identifying the God of the Old Testament with God in the New.

With 7 indicating completeness, the 7 Spirits indicate the fullness of the Spirit of God. The 7 Churches are now met by the 7 Spirits: the totality of the Church is met by the plenitude of the Holy Spirit, so that the Church is filled up with enough oil to keep burning brightly. The 7 Spirits of God come from the throne because it is the Spirit who brings the will and the purpose of God: the Spirit blows where *He wills* (John 3:8); the Holy Spirit distributes gifts *as He wills* (1 Corinthians 12:4–11). The Spirit is contemporary – transcending space, coming from the throne and bringing God's purposes to humanity.

So we have the *eternal* Father, filling all of time, the Holy Spirit transcending space who is *contemporary*, and then 'from Jesus Christ', the Messiah who will save His people from their sins – Jesus, the Son, who is present in time and space, in *history*. This wonderful Trinitarian picture emphasizes Jesus' place within the Godhead, which is followed by three descriptions which highlight His place within humanity: 'faithful witness', 'firstborn of the dead' and 'ruler of the kings of the earth'. Then verses 5–6 describe Jesus as one 'who loves us, and released us . . . and made us . . .' and so we move into His relationship with the Church.

The picture we get in this *inclusio* is of Jesus, the Word and the Witness, standing in relationship to the Father and the Spirit in the Trinity. Also standing in relationship to humanity, and standing in relationship to the Church. So the titles after Jesus' name on this letterhead are: Godhead, humanity, Church.

The three great questions (v5,6)

It is important to note that the three descriptions of Jesus' relationship to the human race in verses 5–6 answer the three greatest questions that humanity can ever ask:

1) *If there is a God, what is He like?*
   If there is no God, then I can make up my own rules and choose to do whatever I like. But if God exists, whether I like it or not, I will find myself fitting in with what He wants. So how can we begin to find out what God is like, to begin to know Him? The answer is in verse 5 – Jesus is the faithful witness to all that God is. Everything about Him points you to what God is like.

2) *If there is a purpose to life, what happens after death?*
   It is all very well if we get to know God here on earth now, but what is the point if we just go back to being a handful of dust when we die, and that is the end of the story? The answer is the second title given to Jesus – 'the *firstborn* from the dead'. If Jesus is the *first*born, that means there will be more, possibly including us. Jesus is the one who has beaten death and is therefore the only one who can answer the problem of death.

3) *Where does authority come from? And why should I obey it?*
Issues with authority cause huge problems around the world today – wars, economic crises, terrorism, nation against nation – all bubbling up in the expression of the view that there is no authority except for the one who is big enough, tough enough and can stick it out long enough. If there is no God, then there is no meaning to authority, and anyone's opinions are as good as anybody else's. Without some ultimate authority rules are arbitrary and there is no definition – it just depends on who is in charge. If we throw God out, there is no solution but a sea of meaninglessness, ruled over by whoever shouts the loudest or has got the biggest fists! But if God does exist, why should we obey Him? Verse 5 reveals Jesus as 'the ruler of the kings of the earth' – earthly authority is under Jesus' authority, and should be trying to look like Him.

In Psalm 89 these three concepts of **faithful witness,** **overcoming death** and **kingly authority** are beautifully brought together to prepare prophetically the ground for the coming Messiah:

> I have found David my servant, with my Holy Oil I have anointed [literally 'messiah-ed'] Him. (v20)

It was recognised that along David's line another 'David' would come and solve the problems of the people of God. David means 'beloved', and he is a type of Jesus (eg Matthew 3:17: 'this is My beloved in whom I am well pleased').

> I shall make Him **my first-born**, the highest (or the prince) **of the kings of the earth.** (v27)

This is equivalent to Jesus, the firstborn and the ruler of the kings of the earth. And in verse 33 we see that David is faithful, as the future 'David' will be.

In verses 36–7 this covenant with the new 'David' who is going to come is prophesied:

> His seed shall **endure forever**, And his throne as the sun before Me; It shall be established forever like the moon, Even **like the faithful witness** in the sky.

As established as the sun and moon, shining and witnessing to the Godhead. So the witness, who is in the heavens, who is the Anointed One, is also the One who is faithful (v33), who is also the firstborn (from the dead) and the highest of the kings of the earth (v27, Acts 13:33). All these ideas come together in Jesus, who is the answer to the authority of the universe – He is the final authority, the ruler of the kings of the earth.

Similarly, Isaiah prophesies salvation through an everlasting covenant with a king who is faithful like David:

> Listen, that your soul may live;
> And I will make an everlasting covenant with you,
> According to the faithful mercies of David.
> Behold, I have made him a witness to the peoples,
> A leader and commander for the peoples. (Isaiah 55:3–4)

So we now have answers to the fundamental questions of the universe, and all that in the first eight verses!

Discussion Topic: King–Priests

Priests appear in three places in Revelation and each time in the context of the Kingdom:

> He has made us to be a kingdom, priests to His God and Father. (1:6)

> And you have made them to be a kingdom and priests to our God and they will reign upon the earth. (5:10)

> They will be priests of God and of Christ and will reign with Him a thousand years. (20:6)

So these priests also reign – they are King–Priests. Hebrews 5:10 says that Jesus is 'a high priest, of the order of Melchizedek', who was both king and priest (Genesis 14:18, Psalm 110:4). Melchizedek means 'king of righteousness' and he was ruler of Salem (later

Jerusalem), which means 'peace'. This gives us a glimpse of God's Kingdom, which is 'righteousness and peace and joy in the Holy Spirit' (Romans 14:17), and is the blessing of God, as we read in Galatians 3:14.

In Israel, the roles of king and priest were separate, but they did not have to be. In Exodus 19:6, God says to the whole nation, 'and you shall be to Me a kingdom of priests and a holy nation', so kings and priests were one and the same. However, in Exodus 32, following the disobedience of the people, only a limited number – the Levites – were made priests, but not King–Priests. It is only later, and begrudgingly, that God agreed to allow Israel to have a king.

It is through Christ that these two things – king and priest – are fully brought back together, although it is worth noting that king David prefigured this by dressing and acting as a priest when he wore a linen robe and the ephod and danced before the Ark of the Covenant (1 Chronicles 15:25–27).

Jesus is *the* King–Priest, and as His followers we are supposed to be both priestly and kingly in order to release God's Kingdom, to bring blessing to the world. What was lost to Israel is given now to all believers, and is called the Church (see Revelation 1:6, 1 Peter 2:9). Just as we are encouraged to act as priests now, interceding for one other (eg Ephesians 6:18, 1 Timothy 2:1–2, James 5:16), we should also be getting God's will done, by reigning with Him in the heavenly places. Priestly authority is exercised not through violence, but through sacrificial serving. In Numbers 3, while the people are numbered for physical warfare, the priests are numbered for spiritual warfare – they were consecrated to wage war in the heavens just as we see in Revelation.

Going back to King–Priests in Revelation, we may note a subtle change. In 1:6 and 5:10 they were priests *to* God but now are priests *of* God – they are still priests with authority, but now they reign. Before the return of Jesus and the resurrection of the Overcoming Church, the priests are *to* or *for* God in their service. After the Second Coming, they have become those possessed and belonging *of* God. In other words, they are King–Priests.

Jesus and the Church (v5,6)

The introduction tells us three important things about Jesus' relationship to the Church. First, Jesus *loves* the Church *now*: 'to Him who loves us' (v5) – note the present tense: it doesn't say '*loved*', but 'loves'. Jesus loves the Church and loves the people who make up the Church, so we should do the same. We are not here to put the Church down and think that we are superior to it – we are part of the Church and Jesus loves us, so we ought to love one another.

Secondly, Christ has 'released us', which is basically the word for redemption (not 'washed us', as in the King James version). The death of Jesus is the releasing power for our sins; the redemptive power of His blood has loosed us from the snare of sin.

Thirdly, Jesus has 'made us to be a kingdom, priests to His God and Father'. He gives us a purpose to live by – to be a kingdom of priests. I do not think it means we are priests *now* but not kings *yet*: while Paul does say he wishes we were reigning (1 Corinthians 4:8), there is a sense in which we do already reign in life by one man, Christ Jesus (Romans 5:17). Jesus is 'a high priest, of the order of Melchizedek', who was both King and Priest (Genesis 14:18, Hebrews 5:10) – Jesus is *the* King Priest (for more on this, see my book *The Kingdom of Jesus*).

Kings and priests were separate in Israel, but they did not have to be. In Exodus 19:6 God says to the whole nation of Israel 'and you shall be to Me a kingdom of priests and a holy nation', so kings and priests were one and the same. But in Exodus 32, following the disobedience of the people, only a limited number, the Levites, were made priests, but not king priests. We see here in Revelation 1:6 and also in 1 Peter 2:9, that what was lost to Israel – to be kings and priests – has been given to the Church. The purpose of the Church is to bring authority and rulership, as well as mediatorship; a priest takes people in to God, a king goes out to get God's will done. We need to make sure that we are doing both these things in our lives.

The Son of Man (v7)

Revelation 1:7 is a very beautiful verse and is a direct reference to Daniel 7:

> 'Behold, He is coming with the clouds' (Revelation 1:7)
>
> I kept looking in the night visions,
> And behold, with the clouds of heaven

> One like a Son of Man was coming,
> And He came up to the Ancient of Days
> And was presented before Him. (Daniel 7:13)

We will look at this 'one like a Son of Man' again in the first vision in Revelation in Section I (page 90).

The phrase 'and even those who pierced Him; and all the tribes of the earth will mourn over Him', refers to Zechariah 12:10:

> I will pour out on the house of David and on the inhabitants of Jerusalem, the Spirit of grace and of supplication, so that they will look on Me whom they have pierced; and they will mourn for Him, as one mourns for an only son, and they will weep bitterly over Him like the bitter weeping over a firstborn.

In Revelation it is *every eye* that will see Him, but in Zechariah it was just those of the tribes of Israel, and now it is not just Judah or Israel but *all the nations* who will mourn. So just as the kingdom of priests has been expanded, as a promise to Israel which is now offered to everybody else, so too the promise given to the Jews that they will look upon Him whom they have pierced (which is quoted by John at the foot of the Cross (John 19:37)), is extended to everyone on earth. The promises given to God's people are very consciously being extended.

Why did God expand these promises? Because this has been God's great rescue plan for humanity all along – God chose the Jews to reveal Himself through, so that they would then be a blessing, revealing Him, to all nations (for more on God's great plan, see *God's Strategy in Human History, vol. 1*).

God said to Israel through Hosea, 'You are not My people and I am not your God' (Hosea 1:9), but because of His heart of love, immediately promised:

> And I will say to those who were not My people, 'You are My people!', and they will say, 'You are my God!' (Hosea 2:23)

This means that God can look anywhere where they 'are not' His people and say *You are the sons of the Living God!* This is not just a promise that God would not desert Israel, but as Paul highlights when he quotes these verses in Romans 9:25–26, it is also a promise to everyone else – we can now all get in on the acts of God.

It is fascinating how these parts of Daniel 7:13–14 and Zechariah 12:10 – coming in the clouds, and every eye seeing Him and mourning as for a firstborn – are brought together in a number of places in Scripture. For example, in Matthew 24:

> Then the sign of the Son of Man will appear in the sky, and then all the peoples of the earth will mourn; and they will see the Son of Man coming on the clouds of heaven with power and great glory. (Matthew 24:30)

Then when He was before the Sanhedrin, they asked Jesus if He was the Christ:

> 'I am,' said Jesus, 'and you will see the Son of Man seated at the right hand of Power and coming with the clouds of heaven.' (Mark 14:62 csb; see also Matthew 26:64)

Although the 'piercing' of Zechariah 12:10 is not explicitly stated in Mark and Matthew, and the mourning is not included in Mark, these are surely implied by the context of the Crucifixion.

Even so, Amen (v7)

Just as we began the *inclusio* with a blessing in Greek and Hebrew, in verse 7 we have 'So it is to be' (NASB, CSB)/'Even so' (NKJV) and 'Amen', which are also equivalent in Greek and Hebrew. It is as if John is giving us a little hint that Hebrew, with the limitations on the ancient people of God, is being expanded to the nations through the international language of Greek. As the promises are expanding to the Gentiles, so is the language.

The Almighty (v8)

Verse 8 marks the end of the *inclusio* that we started back in verse 4 (page 70), which includes these wonderful Trinitarian statements sandwiched between the repeated phrase 'who is and who was and who is to come'. However, verse 8 adds '. . . the Almighty'.

The Greek word for 'Almighty' is *pantokrator*, from *panto-* 'all', *kratos* 'powerful' and is the same word used in the Septuagint to translate both *YHWH Sabaoth* – 'Lord of Hosts', and *El Shaddai* – 'God Almighty' in the Old Testament. *Pantokrator* appears nine times in Revelation (1:8, 4:8, 11:17, 15:3, 16:7, 16:14, 19:6, 19:15 and 21:22), but only once in the rest of the New Testament in 2 Corinthians 6:18, where Paul is quoting God's promises in the Old Testament:

'And I will be a father to you, And you shall be sons and daughters to Me,' says the Lord Almighty (*Pantokrator*).

God is the All-Powerful One, because: i) He is in charge of the hosts of heaven, and ii) because He is Creator, and ultimately all power in the universe comes from God.

However, it is important to understand that 'Almighty' does not mean that God is directing absolutely everything that happens, both good and evil. Rather, it means all the power in the universe comes from God, whether He delegates it or not. All of the powers depend upon His power. God is the *first cause* and keeps everything in Creation running, so indirectly He is responsible for everything that happens. However, because He has delegated some of His authority, He is not always the *immediate cause*. While at times it might look as if God Himself is causing terrible or disturbing things to happen, it is Satan who is behind these – God is love and never does evil. (Compare 2 Samuel 24:1 with 1 Chronicles 21:1.)

In a sense we can picture God as a grandmaster chess player: He is not initiating or perpetuating evil, unlike His opponent, but He will use His opponent's moves to bring about His plan. Remember, for instance, how Joseph said to his brothers: 'you meant evil against me, but God meant it for good' (Genesis 50:20). God was able to get His purposes done because He had someone like Joseph who would go on loving Him through all things. Not only does the Master Chess Player use His own moves to bring about good, but also the movements of His opponent's pieces, because He is all-knowing and understands all the possible ways to get to checkmate.

Alpha and Omega (v8)

The clear equation of Jesus with deity that we see in verse 8 has led some, who do not like this concept, to suggest this verse is not actually about Jesus, but is about 'God'. However, in the New Testament we see Jesus' divinity proclaimed in Thomas's confession (John 20:28) and in Paul's clear assertion in Titus 2:13, amongst others. The same phrase 'I am the Alpha and Omega' appears again in Revelation 21:6, where it refers to God on the Throne, and again in Revelation 22:13 where it is unambiguously Jesus speaking, so here again it is clearly referring to Jesus. Alpha and Omega are the first and last letters of the Greek alphabet, and, just like we use 'from A to Z', it signifies 'from the beginning to the end' – the totality of truth and revelation is in

God's heart and mind. Jesus is the Alpha and Omega – the *logos* Word of God:

> 'In the beginning was the Word, and the Word was with God and the word was God.' (John 1:1)

So the Alpha and Omega is God. But unless He reveals to us the truth of reality and what His purposes are – why He made the universe, who we are, what our identity is and how we relate to Him – we won't know what the beginning and end is. And so He speaks forth His Word: Jesus is *the* Alpha and Omega: He is the A to Z of all that God has to say to us. Every word that God has to communicate to us is found between A and Z, or in Greek: every jot and tittle is found between the Alpha and the Omega.

Discussion Topic: The First and the Last

The First and the Last is a title for the Lord, *Yahweh*. For instance, if you look at Isaiah, there are three places where 'the first and the last' is used:

> Who has performed and accomplished it, Calling forth the generations from the beginning? 'I, the Lord, am the first, and with the last. I am He.' (Isaiah 41:4)

This is clearly *Yahweh* speaking: '*I AM*'.

The second place, Isaiah 44:6, introduces the Lord's 'Redeemer', who is 'the Lord of Hosts':

> Thus says the Lord, the King of Israel and his Redeemer, the Lord of hosts: 'I am the first and I am the last, And there is no God besides Me.'

Finally, in Isaiah 48:12:

> 'Listen to Me, O Jacob, even Israel whom I called; I am He, I am the first, I am also the last . . .'

Here again the Lord is emphasising His uniqueness – you cannot call anybody else 'the First and the Last'. This is followed by the Messiah speaking in verse 16:

The Introduction – The Communication of Christ

> 'From the first I have not spoken in secret. From the time it took place, I was there. And now the Lord God has sent Me and His Spirit.'
>
> So here in Isaiah we have the one and only Lord God as well as His Spirit and the Redeemer; a tantalising glimpse of the Trinity, all tied up with the revelation of the First and the Last.
>
> The First and the Last also appears three times in the New Testament, in Revelation 1:17, 2:8 and 22:13, where Jesus takes up this title:
>
> 'I am the Alpha and the Omega, the First and the Last, the Beginning and the End.' (Revelation 22:13)
>
> The Alpha and Omega broadens out this title – not just the Hebrew God, but also God of the Gentiles, and *the Beginning* brings together Genesis 1:1 and John 1:1, 'In the Beginning . . .'
>
> So three times in Revelation, the unique, one and only Lord, Jesus, uses the name for *Yahweh* that appears three times in Isaiah for the unique one and only Lord God.
>
> If you would like to look at this in greater depth, please see my book *Trinity: Song and Dance God*.

Aleph and Tav

Before we finish with the letterhead, we need to go back briefly to Zechariah 12:10, where we find a little puzzle. If I were a Jewish rabbi I would be scratching my head, wondering how on earth it works: *Yahweh* is speaking, saying 'they will look on *me* whom they have pierced and they will mourn for *him*.' The 'me' that is pierced somehow becomes a 'him' whom they will mourn for as for an only son. Why mourn for *him* if you have pierced *me*? And how can *Yahweh* be pierced?

In the Hebrew, the little word between 'me' (ie *Yahweh*) and 'him' is the demonstrative particle 'whom'. Going deeper, the word 'whom' is made up of aleph (א) and tav (ת) – the first and last letters of the Hebrew alphabet, whose Greek equivalents are alpha and omega. So Zechariah 12:10 looks like this:

'They shall look upon Me (*Yahweh*) whom (aleph and tav – alpha and omega) they have pierced and mourn for Him'

The 'Me' of God becomes a 'Him' of a firstborn through the 'whom' of an Alpha and Omega. The Trinitarian God hidden in the Hebrew is revealed in the Greek. The 'whom' (aleph and tav) is the One who is both Me and Him, *Yahweh* and the Firstborn. This puzzle for the rabbis is now revealed as we begin Revelation, solved by the activity of the 'poured out' Spirit which appears earlier in Zechariah 12:10.

* ✶ *

As we go through our Christian walk, our experience and vision of Jesus should keep on expanding. When I converted to Jesus, He was to me the size of a man – He died for me and was going to take me to Heaven. As I go on living in Christ, He has grown larger and vaster, more intense and more colourful and more saturated with understanding and truth. That is the richness of who Christ is. You begin to see more and more, as detail after detail pulls in more understanding and truth, revealing the great cosmic vision of Jesus in whom all things consist: Jesus who is the King of the rulers of the earth, Jesus the ultimate expression of the divine character, who is the brightness of God's appearing and glory. That is the vision of Christ that we are meant to be living in, and it comes through breathing in the Scripture – living in prayer and worship as you read the Word of God.

Discussion Questions

What does it mean that Jesus is the First and Last?

How has your vision of Jesus changed through your Christian walk?

How does your interpretation of Revelation differ when you read it as a letter written you?

Section I
Christ Central in the Church

Christ Central in the Church

Revelation 1:9–3:22 | The First Vision

Text – Revelation 1:9

> ⁹ I, John, your brother and fellow partaker in the tribulation and kingdom and perseverance which are in Jesus, was on the island called Patmos because of the word of God and the testimony of Jesus. (NASB)

Brother and fellow partaker (v9)

As we looked at in *Who wrote Revelation?* (page 30), there is no problem with the Apostle John being the writer of the book of Revelation, especially as he starts off 'I, John, your brother' – it sounds like the John who wrote 'God is love' and 'My little children' in his epistles. It shows it is relationships which matter within the Church of Jesus Christ, and the way we see ourselves as family. It is good to belong to the Church, where we are brothers and sisters together, and here is John, writing not as some great apostle, but as our brother.

'Fellow partaker' is an interesting little phrase, and both words are again emphasizing fellowship and relationship: *brother* is family, *fellow* is together with, *partaker* is being a sharer. We are all sharing the same Jesus, not competing with one another, trying to get glory or power for ourselves, because fellow-partaking requires that we are in it together. In fact, we appropriate very little of Jesus on our own because God made human beings to exist together. One of the tragedies of modern life, as it keeps trying to reduce everything down to individual personal rights, is that it gets smaller and smaller, and life gets emptier and emptier, whereas we were meant to be experiencing things together and sharing our joy and happiness as well as sorrow and pain. The more we embrace individualism, the more we move towards emptiness and isolation. The more we open up, the more we experience the richness of living and the excitement and goodness of being human.

Tribulation, Kingdom, Perseverance (v9)

So what are we going to be fellow partakers in? The good news is, we share in the **Tribulation**, **Kingdom** and **Perseverance**! The first word 'tribulation' is the predominant one and it begins with a definite article which also governs the next two words: '*the* tribulation, kingdom and perseverance'. So these all come together as a dynamic package. It is the tribulation which is kingdom-like and through which we are persevering . . . and we find all three things in Jesus.

It is in Jesus that we share together and it is this which has brought **Tribulation** upon us. The word tribulation means 'pressure' – there are Christians in around fifty countries in the world today who are sharing in **Tribulation** which leads to death. To be in Jesus covers life, death and eternity, and imparts values on the inside that far outweigh the things that happen on the outside. To be in Jesus brings a challenge from the world, because there is a kingdom in the world in opposition to the Kingdom of Jesus. Of course being under that pressure of **Tribulation** means there is always the temptation to try and opt out, but Jesus says:

> In the world you have tribulation, but take courage; I have overcome the world. (John 16:33)

Jesus promised **Tribulation** would come, but the overcoming is in Him as well – they who have faith overcome the world (1 John 5:4–5), which is why there have been men and women who willingly laid down their lives for the Gospel throughout the centuries and who continue to do so in many parts of the world today. Why? Because Jesus is bigger than death and has overcome the world. I would rather be inspired into death and out the other side than to perspire into the meaningless existence and nihilism of the world around me.

So we share in **Tribulation** because there are two kingdoms in opposition, but when John says '. . . and **Kingdom**' he is referring not just to the fact that the **Kingdom** of God has come in Jesus and we have been brought into it, but that *we have been given* the **Kingdom**. To be given the **Kingdom** means we have been given authority, and are already beginning to reign. Of course we have not reached the place yet where we will be reigning in totality over the whole universe – that will come (see 1 Corinthians 4:8–9); but because

Jesus has come, the breaking-in of God's future age has come. We taste the powers to come now and are beginning to 'reign in life through the One, Jesus Christ' (Romans 5:17, 21 and 8:1–4). Life does not reign over us, we reign over it: we are no longer victims tossed around by every whim and fancy. The pressure of being in Jesus brings Tribulation, but also gives us the right to rule and freedom to live in reality and truth:

> If you continue in my word, then you are truly disciples of mine; and you will know the truth, and the truth will make you free. (John 8:31–2)

So what about sharing the Kingdom? Back in Revelation 1:5 we saw this Kingdom has come in Jesus, the 'ruler of the kings of the earth', and He is sharing this rulership with us: *blessed are the poor in spirit, theirs is the kingdom* – it has been put into our hands.

Thirdly, we share Perseverance. One of the characteristics of a believer is steadfastness, (see, for instance, Paul in 2 Corinthians 6:1–10). Perseverance belongs to the Christian character, and is developed through Tribulation that comes because of sharing in the Kingdom. So we have to persevere – we can do it because we are in Jesus.

John was exiled to the island of Patmos because of 'the word of God', which comes forth from God, and 'the testimony of Jesus', which is Jesus pointing us back to the Father. The Scriptures are those which testify to Jesus, and Jesus is the one who testifies to the Father. He is *the* faithful witness. Therefore when we are persecuted and under Tribulation, it is because we have been witnessing.

Text – Revelation 1:10–12

> [10] I was in Spirit on the Lord's day, and I heard behind me a loud voice like the sound of a trumpet, [11] saying, 'Write in a book what you see, and send it to the seven churches: to Ephesus and to Smyrna and to Pergamum and to Thyatira and to Sardis and to Philadelphia and to Laodicea.' [12] Then I turned to see the voice that was speaking with me. And having turned I saw seven golden lampstands.

In Spirit (v10)

Here John writes 'I was *in Spirit* . . .' – there is no 'the' in the Greek text, and as we looked at on page 42, this phrase divides the book up into four sections. John is borrowing the little phrase 'I was in Spirit' from Ezekiel (see for example seven times in Ezekiel 2:2; 3:12, 14, 24; 11:1, 24 and 43:5), another place where an echo from the Old Testament opens a door for us to understand what is going on in Revelation.

How was Ezekiel 'in Spirit'? The Spirit went into him, caught him up and took him away to where the exiles were. The Spirit was bringing revelation to him in a most bizarre and ecstatic way. Similarly, John is being caught up and overwhelmed by the vision crashing into his consciousness, and is moved by all sorts of emotions as he tries to put the revelations down on paper. What happened to John was the same sort of thing as happened to Ezekiel.

In verse 10 (see also 4:1, page 190), the 'loud voice like the sound of a trumpet' is a reference to Exodus 19—20, when the people hear 'the sound of the trumpet' as God is giving Moses the Law. Just as Moses was told to write, here John was told to write the things that God gave him.

The 7 Churches/Lampstands (v11–12)

The Praeterist view has it that the 7 Churches here merely represent the actual churches which existed at that time in Ephesus, Smyrna, Pergamum, Thyatira, Sardis, Philadelphia and Laodicea. The Historicist view suggests that these Churches represent 7 stages of the history of the Church. However, I would suggest that rather they represent the total Church, the Church 'universal', not only in the first century, but through the ages right up until this present time. Of course John needed to write to 7 Churches that actually existed and were together on a postal route, but these messages are not only pinpointed for each of these churches, they have applied continuously right through to the twenty-first century.

In verse 12, John 'turned to see the voice', which is the most natural thing to say although you do not really see a voice, you see the person who is speaking, and of course when John turns he sees Jesus, the Word of God.

John sees '7 golden Lampstands' – not just one lampstand with seven branches like the one that was used in the Tabernacle (Exodus 25:31–40) and later in the Temple in Jerusalem, but those seven branches are now separate and stand independently.

Revelation 1:11–12

If we look at Zechariah 4, there is a vision of a lampstand with seven branches in the Temple rebuilt after the Exile in Babylon, with two olive trees standing by it. These olive trees are two anointed ones who stand for the king and the priest, and who pour oil into the lampstand so that it can go on burning. The oil represents the Holy Spirit which is being poured in – 'Not by might nor by power, but by My Spirit' (Zechariah 4:6). We will look at this in more depth when we get to the 2 Witnesses in Revelation 11 (see page 397). The lamp here in Zechariah is a metonymy – it stands as part for the whole Tabernacle/Temple, which represents the people of God, who are being built up just as the Temple is being built, through the flow of the Spirit, through the light burning. You cannot build in the dark – you need light, so that when you see someone put a brick down, you can put a brick down next to it. Rather than each of us living in our own darkness trying to make our own light (or 'sparks' as Isaiah somewhat sarcastically calls them (Isaiah 50:11, NKJV)), we need instead to live and build in the light and life of the Lord Jesus, which comes by the oil of the Spirit. The oil is not directly mentioned in Revelation, but is assumed to be there to keep the lamps burning.

So the picture we get is this: for Israel there was a solid structure and organisation that held the lampstands together, called the *menorah*, but now we have 7 individual lampstands – their unity is not in their outward form, but in the oil which feeds them. As we get thousands upon thousands of lamps (churches) all over the earth, they are held in unity – not a bureaucratic or political unity, but the unity the Holy Spirit gives to the people of God.

A lamp does not burn just so you can say 'What a wonderful lamp!'; it burns so that you can look at something else (see eg Matthew 5:14–15). The 7 Lampstands are not shining so people can look at them, they are shining so that the light can fall on Jesus in the midst of them.

In the West, we spend the vast majority of church income on ourselves. If people are going to look at the Church and see Jesus, we need to spend less on ourselves, and more on reaching out to tell the Good News to others.

Text – Revelation 1:13–16

> [13] and in the middle of the lampstands I saw one like a son of man, clothed in a robe reaching to the feet, and girded across His chest with a golden sash. [14] His head and His hair were white like white wool, like snow; and His eyes were like a flame of fire. [15] His feet were like burnished bronze, when it has been made to glow in a furnace, and His voice was like the sound of many waters. [16] In His right hand He held seven stars, and out of His mouth came a sharp two-edged sword; and His face was like the sun shining in its strength.

Jesus' relation to humanity (v13)

Verse 13 gives a glorious image of Christ, which highlights three aspects of the character of Jesus in relation to humanity:

1. **Son of Man**

   I think Son of Man is the richest title for Jesus in the whole of the Bible. It emphasizes that God has become man and knows what it means to be human – Jesus understands how to help us. It was the humanity of Jesus that overcame sin and beat the devil, counted every pressure and tribulation, went through the colossal temptation in the wilderness, and the agony of Gethsemane. He overcame temptation as a human. Can you overcome temptation? Yes, because Jesus puts His hand on you. You were dead and now you are alive in Him.

Revelation 1:13–16

2. **High-priestly garment**

    The Greek word for 'robe' here, is the same one used in the Septuagint for the High Priest's garments, and the golden girdle (NASB – sash, NKJV – band) is similar to the golden girdles around the priests who come out of the temple in Revelation 15 (see also the vision of the heavenly man in Daniel 10:5). The High Priest, in his long garment acted on behalf of the whole nation of Israel in the Temple, and did things others could not do for themselves. In the same way Jesus, our great High Priest (Hebrews 4:14–16), intercedes for us in ways we cannot ourselves: He did that on the Cross, dying for our sins, but more than that, Jesus substitutes for our very life – 'It is no longer I that live, it is Christ who lives within me' (Galatians 2:20). We see Jesus, the Son of Man, as the chief priest, in the midst of the lampstands interceding for us, and making sure the lamps are burning.

3. **Maternal nourishment**

    Thirdly, Jesus is girded 'across His breast' – if you read the old King James you will see 'gird about the *paps* . . .' – rather a quaint word meaning female breasts rather than just simply 'chest'. While there are occasions in Greek literature where the word could refer to a man, the Greek word used usually means 'female breasts' (Gk. – *mastoi*), and is the most natural translation, even if a Greek would not be taken aback by a male chest being called a breast. This is a most beautiful picture – the mother's life is in the milk and with the closest possible contact she feeds her baby (see Isaiah 49:15). Peter uses the same imagery:

    > Like newborn babies, long for the pure milk of the word, so that by it you may grow in respect to salvation, if you have tasted the kindness of the Lord. (1 Peter 2:2–3)

    You cannot taste from a distance. You must be close, and in that intimacy the baby can draw the substance of the mother into its own being. Jesus feeds the Church with His own very substance: *'This is my body for you'*. The mother gives her body through her milk. Jesus gives His body through the bread. The baby is alive in the life of the mother and it is through drinking the milk of the word we are built up and nourished.

In verse 17, after seeing this vision, John falls down 'as a dead man', and Jesus reaches and puts His hand on him. Each of these three aspects of Jesus in verse 13 describes how Jesus reaches out to us: in His humanity, as a priest and to nourish us. Each of these images say the same thing: Jesus will give His life so that when we see Him, we, just like John, can rise up from the dead spiritually, psychologically and even physically (see Revelation 1:18 below).

7 aspects of Christ in the vision (v13–16)

The vision presents us with 7 aspects of Christ that build up a manifold picture of who He is in all His fullness. Each of these 7 aspects brings with it a deep Old Testament understanding and together create a rich multisensory experience. Let's have a look at each of these facets in turn.

1. Head and hair white like wool – Wisdom

As the vision progresses we see a beautiful image, with the Son of Man merging into the Ancient of Days, which is an Old Testament vision of God from Daniel 7:9:

> I kept looking
> Until thrones were set up,
> And the Ancient of Days took His seat;
> His vesture was like white snow
> And the hair of His head like pure wool.
> His throne was ablaze with flames,
> Its wheels were a burning fire.

This is a scene of judgment – the Ancient of Days is the judge who sits on the fiery throne, linked with the eyes of fire that follow in the vision of Christ (see point 2 below). In Daniel 7:13–14, one like a Son of Man is presented to the Ancient of Days and given glory and an everlasting Kingdom: this is a prophetic vision of the incarnate Jesus, the Son of Man, receiving the Kingdom from God the Father. That they merge in Revelation shows us Jesus was fully man but also fully God – when we look at Jesus, we see what God is like. More than this, it represents Christ, the Son of Man being given all authority to judge by the Father (John 5:22,27). Jesus now appears as the judge.

Revelation 1:13–16

In Daniel 7, the Son of Man was not only an individual, but also head of a whole race of people. Adam was the head and you and I were hidden in Adam – now we are in Christ we are hidden in Christ. So while an individual Son of Man is presented to the Ancient of Days in verse 13, in verse 18 it is 'the saints of the Highest One' who will receive the Kingdom. Jesus will judge our lives (Matthew 25, Romans 2:6–11), but as the Saints we will judge the world (1 Corinthians 6:2). So we need the help that God gives to judge and learn to make our lives more and more like Him.

In the Bible (unlike today!), white or grey hair is a symbol of wisdom, honour and calm dignity, for example:

> A grey head is a crown of glory; It is found in the way of righteousness. (Proverbs 16:31)

White almost always represents purity and holiness (see for example Isaiah 1:18), so Jesus' white head and hair represents full, pure, divine wisdom. Jesus is also identified as the personification of Wisdom in the book of Proverbs (see Proverbs 8:1–36). Our worldly, human wisdom generally is not very good, but Jesus *is* Wisdom, and as He lives in us, we can live in His Wisdom.

2. Eyes of fire – Searching insight and energy

The eyes of fire are also to do with judgement – light from those fiery eyes goes right into us and searches our hearts and minds. There is also something fearfully attractive about eyes with fire, they are the sparkling eyes of someone who is alive – awe-inspiring and yet attractive. They draw in and they also drive away.

When we search ourselves we may find there is not much light going on – 'Did I have the right motive or a wrong motive?' 'Was I being humble or was I being proud that I was being humble?' 'Or was I proud that I was humble about not being proud?!' It's like when you have a mirror in front of you and one behind, and when you look into one of them you see your reflection stretching on forever, and you don't really know where it ends. Investigating ourselves we get nowhere . . .

In Psalm 139, the Psalmist is not examining himself, but asking the Lord to:

> Search me, O God, and know my heart;
> Try me and know my anxious thoughts;
> And see if there be any hurtful way in me,
> And lead me in the everlasting way. (v23–24)

If you ask the Lord to show you things in your life which are not right, then He will: you can trust Him. He may show you through experiences or insight, maybe gradually or right that minute. However it happens, when we look into Jesus' fiery eyes and allow Him to search inside us, we will see things in our lives that need to change to make us more like Him. The searching insight and energy of the eyes of fire do not fade, as Jesus keeps on transforming us into His image more and more.

3) Bronze feet

We see Jesus with feet like burnished bronze when it has been caused to glow in a furnace, like Shadrach, Meshach and Abednego who were in the fiery furnace but were untouched (Daniel 3:27).

We have soft feet – in our lives we walk through many places and situations that would seek to burn and destroy us, but Jesus has bronze feet, and if we are in Christ, we can walk with His burnished feet, which have been tested in the fire and walked out the other side untouched.

We see a beautiful example of this where Isaiah says:

> How beautiful upon the mountains are the feet of *Him* who brings good news. (Isaiah 52:7)

but when Paul quotes this verse in Romans 10, he writes:

> How beautiful are the feet of *those* who bring good news of good things!

Jesus has put His feet in our feet, and now we too have His beautiful bronze feet when we walk in Him. Our feet can walk through any fire if Jesus is walking in us.

4) The voice of many waters

'Many waters' makes us think of waves or waterfalls that are continually running: they are powerful, they do not stop. But more than that, 'the voice' refers to the tone of the sound. If you go to the seaside you notice the sound of the waves for the first day or two, but after that it becomes part of the background – you stop noticing, and grow accustomed to it. If we are listening to God, sometimes we may allow the sound of His voice to become like a continual background tone, and ignore that He is constantly speaking to us. The Lord's voice is there to tune into, like a radio station. Of course, there are times when God specifically communicates something directly to us, but you can hear His voice leading and guiding all the time if you tune in.

5) Right hand

The 'right hand' represents strength and authority, and here Jesus holds 7 Stars in His hand. The Stars are heavenly bodies, presumably angels. They shine in the darkness and are sustained, fuelled and given authority by Christ's hand, that is, His power and strength. The stars are the lights each of the 7 Lampstands lift up (John 12:32).

6) Sharp two-edged sword

The Word of God is like a two-edged sword:

> He has made My mouth like a sharp sword. (Isaiah 49:2)

> For the word of God is living and active and sharper than any two-edged sword, and piercing as far as the division of soul and spirit, of both joints and marrow, and able to judge the thoughts and intentions of the heart. (Hebrews 4:12)

I cannot speak words that are going to divide between the soul and spirit, speaking incisively into people's hearts – but Jesus' two-edged sword can do that. I do not know what to say unless God so fills me with the Holy Spirit so that when I speak, His words can actually get deep down into people's lives. So we need the words of Jesus in our mouths.

7) Face like the sun in its strength

When Jesus' face is bright and shining like the sun, it is warming and you want to look into it. As the priests in the Old Testament said:

The Lord make His face shine on you, and be gracious to you;
The Lord lift up His countenance on you, and give you peace.
(Numbers 6:25–26)

After seeing God pass by from the cleft of a rock, Moses' face shone (Exodus 34:29–35), and Jesus' face also shines like the sun in the Transfiguration (Matthew 17:2).

Jesus' face is full of life and energy and warmth and acceptance. If you want to have a face like that you need to let Jesus live in you.

* ✳ *

So this vision draws together strands from Daniel, Isaiah, Psalms and Numbers: we see the Ancient of Days, sense His gaze, hear His voice, smell the smoke coming off His burnished feet and feel the warmth of His love.

Text – Revelation 1:17–18

> [17] When I saw Him, I fell at His feet like a dead man. And He placed His right hand on me, saying, 'Do not be afraid; I am the first and the last, [18] and the living One; and I was dead, and behold, I am alive forevermore, and I have the keys of death and of Hades.'

Like a dead man (v17–18)

The effect of the vision of Jesus overwhelms John: *There's no life in me, I'm finished!* Then John says Jesus 'laid His right hand upon me' – remember, the right hand signifies power and authority, and is the hand which was holding the 7 Stars. Jesus puts His hand on John, who is as good as dead, and revives him – *You feel like you are dead, but do not fear, you are alive. I know exactly what you are going through, the beginning and the end of everything is in Me, because I have been there. I was dead, and now I am alive – I am the Living One.*

Jesus is how God reached out and touched humankind – He became like us and experienced what it was to be human, sharing our pain and suffering. He understands. We, like John, are dead in our sins until one touch from the King brings us to life. We struggle to identify with someone who is poles apart from us because their life and experiences seem so different; we do identify with someone who goes through the same situations we do.

Revelation 1:17–18

Discussion Topic: Sheol and Hades

Hades is the Greek equivalent of the Hebrew *Sheol*, and both refer to the place people go after they die.

Sheol appears sixty-four times in the Old Testament, and is usually described as somewhere people 'go down to' (eg Genesis 37:35) or 'descend to' (Isaiah 5:14), sometimes literally as in Korah's rebellion (Numbers 16:33) or even as a pit, the lowest or deepest place (eg Ezekiel 31:16, Deuteronomy 32:22, Job 11:8). 'The grave' is an equivalent image, and naturally people pictured Sheol as being underground because that is where graves are. Also it stands in contrast to heaven, which is the place of light and life. *Sheol* is also personified as insatiable or greedy – see for example Psalm 49:14, Isaiah 5:14, 14:9.

Unsurprisingly therefore, *Sheol* often appears closely linked to Death. For example, 'The ropes of *Sheol* surrounded me; the snares of death confronted me' (2 Samuel 22:6). Modern translations often simply include the word *Sheol* in the text, but in the King James version about half of the instances are rendered as 'grave', and thirty-one times as 'hell'. This is a problem because *Sheol* seems to refer to the place both the righteous and unrighteous go after death, whereas 'hell' is understood as a fiery place of punishment for sinners.

We see similar things for the word *Hades*, which occurs ten times in the Gospels & Acts and Revelation. *Hades* too is somewhere people are 'brought down to' and is a place where the dead – both righteous and unrighteous go. This is exemplified in Luke 16, where both the Rich Man and Lazarus are in *Hades*, but while the Rich Man is in agony in the flame, Lazarus is comforted in Abraham's bosom. Again, while the word '*Hades*' is included in modern versions, in the King James it is translated as 'hell'. It is important to note both Old and New Testaments refer to 'valley of Hinnom'/'*Gehenna*' as a place of fire and destruction, and in the New Testament *Gehenna* is usually translated 'hell'. I would suggest we make a distinction between *Hades* and *Gehenna* as they seem to represent very different things.

> We are not given a huge amount of information about exactly how *Sheol/Hades* function, such as whether we are conscious or whether we are in a soul sleep (in the Old Testament death is often referred to as falling asleep). However, what is clear is that the popular imagery of floating up to heaven after death is not biblical – rather, souls go down to *Sheol/Hades* where they await resurrection after Jesus comes again.
>
> For more on the meanings of these words and the concepts of hell and eternity, please see our book *God's Strategy in Human History, Vol. 1*, chapter 15.

Death & Hades (v18)

Following on from John being 'like a dead man', Jesus proclaims He holds the keys of Death and Hades. Four times in Revelation we see 'Death and Hades' together (1:18, 6:8, 20:13–14).

In the Septuagint, in almost all cases, the Greek word 'Hades' is used to translate the Hebrew 'Sheol' (eg Genesis 42:38; Psalm 139:8; Isaiah 14:9), and both words refer to 'the place of the departed' so are closely linked with death:

> Shall I ransom them from the power of Sheol?
> Shall I redeem them from death?
> Death, where are your thorns?
> Sheol, where is your sting? (Hosea 13:14)

Symbolically, Death separates us from experiencing God in our lives, and Hades separates us from when we will rise again in resurrection, so although we might be able to experience something of God's presence in Death and in Hades (see Psalm 139:8), both things prevent us living in His fullness. But the good news is that He has the keys . . .

The keys (v18)

Jesus has the keys of Death and Hades, which means He will unlock them. It is like in Isaiah 22, where God speaks of how Eliakim will have the keys of the city of Jerusalem:

> Then I will set the key of the house of David on his shoulder,
> When he opens no one will shut,
> When he shuts no one will open. (Isaiah 22:22)

Jesus having the keys doesn't mean that nobody ever goes into death or into Hades. Quite the reverse: He wouldn't need the keys if nobody died, or if nobody went to the place of the departed. But the Lord does promise those who keep His word will never see Death, because when we die we will just walk right through it – when we have gone into Death and Hades, He will unlock it and we will come out again in the resurrection. Presumably, those who do not keep His word will not be resurrected at the same time, or in the same manner and therefore may 'see Death'. (We will look at this further when we get to the First Resurrection in Revelation 20:5–6.)

The Church Jesus builds will be made from those who have been unlocked from Death and Hades (compare Matthew 16:18–19) and who will then unlock Christ's Kingdom. We will come back to these keys in Revelation 3:7–8.

Text – Revelation 1:19

> ¹⁹ Therefore write the things which you have seen, and the things which are, and the things which will take place after these things.

Things seen, which are and will take place (v19)

This verse has at least six interpretations depending on what school of interpretation you follow. I am not going to go through all six in detail – rather I will tell you what I think makes most sense.

- → 'The things which you have seen' is talking about the apocalyptic vision that John is going through and experiencing at this moment (Praeterist)
- → 'Things which are' refers to the meaning of these figures that John is seeing in the vision – the truth behind the metaphors (Historicist/Futurist/Spiritual)
- → 'The things which will take place after these things' is the now and the not yet of the eschatological Kingdom, the End Times (Futurist)

As we discussed on page 64, the Kingdom has arrived but it is still coming; we taste the powers of the age to come (Hebrews 6:5), but it is not quite

Section I – Christ Central in the Church

here yet (for more on this please see my book *The Kingdom of Jesus*). While the Kingdom has arrived, it is a process by which the Last Days will come to complete conclusion. Victory over sin and evil is already happening, but the totality will not take place until Jesus comes again. With the presence of the King, the Kingdom is here, in the midst of the Lampstands.

John is writing the things he saw, what they mean, and about the coming Kingdom both now and at the end. 'Your Kingdom come, Your Will be done', is *the* prayer Jesus taught us.

Text – Revelation 1:20

> [20] As for the mystery of the seven stars which you saw in My right hand, and the seven golden lampstands: the seven stars are the angels of the seven churches, and the seven lampstands are the seven churches.

Mystery of the 7 Stars (v20)

In the Bible, 'mystery' does not mean 'mystic' or 'mysterious' as in something that cannot be understood or requires some level of special knowledge, but rather it just indicates something that needs an interpretation. So here, the 'mystery of the 7 Stars . . . and the 7 golden Lampstands' is interpreted – the Stars represent the angels of the 7 Churches, and the Lampstands are the 7 Churches.

Again there are various interpretations of this verse, so please be aware different commentaries have various nuances here, but I believe the overall picture is something like this:

Imagine the High Priest going around in the Temple, keeping the lamps burning. He trims the wicks, and pours oil into the lampstand, and the lamps shine out light. Nowadays we tend to think of a light as an electric bulb, but in those days it was a lamp which had a flame, and similarly a fire in the heavens was a star. A star is a heavenly body, as is an angel. In this verse all these ideas flow together – Jesus is holding these 7 Stars, these angels of the 7 Churches, in His right hand and He is keeping them burning in the dark, just like the High Priest did for the lamps in the temple.

You cannot see stars when the sun is out, and you do not need lamps in the daylight. The new day of the Kingdom is dawning, but until the face of

Jesus is fully revealed, shining like the sun, there will still be darkness and the need for stars to be shining. Of course we will go on shining after He comes again but we will see then our brightness is nothing compared to His (cf Hebrews 1:3).

What exactly are these angels? As we will look at when we discuss the structure of the letters to the 7 Churches, the angels represent the inner life of each church (see page 110), which are shining in the heavenly places (just as we are raised up and seated with Him in the heavenly places, Ephesians 2:6), they burn like flames and have to be kept burning. If the inner life of the church goes out, there is no light and the lampstand is not worth anything – as we will look at in the letters to the 7 Churches, Jesus warns some of them that their lampstand may be removed (see for example page 124).

So the 7 Lampstands represent the outward form of the 7 Churches, and the 7 Stars or Angels represent the inner spiritual life of each church that burns to shine into the darkness. Outwardly our church may be a smooth and polished lampstand and seem to be very successful, but if it does not contain a flaming heart for Jesus within, then there is no point in having a church – it is a lamp that gives no light.

The angel is so identified with each church, that it is the one to whom John is told to write, and through whom Christ ministers to meet each local church need. Just as Jesus puts His hand on John and ministers to him (v17), we will see in the letters to the churches that He ministers to each of the angels, pouring His Holy Spirit into the inner spiritual life of the churches.

* ✷ *

Revelation 1 and the Old Testament

This vision, together with verses 1–8, has Daniel 7 as a primary source but it is also saturated with an intricate amalgam of Old Testament concepts which show us the beauty, magnificence, superiority and priority of our Lord Jesus. Jesus said 'Do not think that I came to abolish the Law or the Prophets; I did not come to abolish but to fulfil' (Matthew 5:17) – and in this glorious vision of Christ in His Church we see the fulfilment of many of these prophecies.

The following table gives ten similarities between Revelation 1 and Daniel 7, which is the Old Testament passage Jesus quoted from most.

Similarity	Revelation	Daniel
1) God is on the throne	1:4	7:9
2) Son of Man's rule	1:4,5	7:13,14
3) Saints given the Kingdom	1:6–9	7:18,22,27a
4) Coming on clouds	1:7a	7:13
5) Books and judgement	1:11,19	7:10
6) Heavenly man	1:12–16	7:9,10
7) White hair	1:14	7:9
8) Disturbing effect of vision	1:17a	7:15
9) Interpretation is given	1:17–20	7:16–17
10) Tribulation / Persecution	1:9	7:21

It is not only chapter 7, but other parts of Daniel too that are in view in Revelation 1:

- The phrases 'the things that are' and 'will soon take place' in verses 1 and 19 come from the Septuagint version of Daniel 2
- Daniel 3 is hinted at: Shadrach, Meshach and Abednego emerging untouched from the fire parallels Jesus' feet of burnished bronze in verses 14–15
- Similar to Jesus' appearance in verses 13 and 15, the man who comes in Daniel 10 wears a golden girdle and reveals mysteries
- Daniel 12 speaks of the wise who are shining like the stars, and in Revelation 1:16,20 we see Jesus holding 7 Stars.

As you may expect, there are many other Old Testament references in Revelation 1. Here are some of the main ones:

- *Exodus:* The lampstand with 7 branches inside the tabernacle (Exodus 25:31–40) is now 7 Lampstands, and we also hear the sound of a trumpet, just as when the law was given (Exodus 20:18)

- *Zechariah:* In chapter 4 we see the 7 channels pouring oil into the 7-branched lampstand, like the 7 Spirits filling the 7 churches, and in Zechariah 12 we have the allusion to 'the Alpha and Omega' in 'they shall look upon Him *whom* (Aleph + Tav – the equivalent Hebrew letters) they have pierced'
- *Isaiah:* Similarly, Jesus as 'the first and the last' appears in Isaiah 41:4, 43:10 and 44:6. Also in Isaiah 11:4 and 49:2 we see the Messiah with a sword in His mouth, and with the keys of authority in Isaiah 22:22
- *Ezekiel:* In Ezekiel 2:2, 3:12,14,24, 11:1, and 43:5 we get the phrase 'in Spirit', just as John was 'in Spirit'
- *Judges:* Judges 5:20 refers to the stars fighting from heaven against Sisera in the days of Deborah and verse 31 sounds like the vision of Jesus with His face shining like the sun
- *1 Kings:* In 1 Kings 7:49, when Solomon built the temple, instead of one 7-branch lampstand he made 10 single lampstands, which shows that already in the Old Testament, thought was beginning to expand from just one lampstand, to multiple.

Summary of the First Vision

This first beautiful vision of Jesus in Revelation is not only for the first-century church but is also for us in the twenty-first century: Jesus in the midst of His people, putting all that He is into our hearts and lives so we can shine light through the world. That is what we are here for. It is not impossible, and it is especially when we feel dead that it becomes most possible, because we move our pride out of the way and make way for Jesus to lay His hand on us. Just as the apostle Paul says in Galatians:

> I have been crucified with Christ; and it is no longer I who live, but Christ lives in me; and the life which I now live in the flesh I live by the faithfulness of the Son of God, who loved me and gave Himself up for me. (Galatians 2:20, my translation)

Isn't it great to be in this terrific vision that God has for human beings? Compare that vision with what you see on the news!

Section I – Christ Central in the Church

This vision reveals Jesus in at least 7 ways:

1. as one like a *Son of Man*, emphasizing His humanity (v13)
2. as a *King*. He is 'ruler' (v5), He dresses like a king, and we also read about His 'kingdom'(v6,9)
3. as a *High Priest*, as He is wearing a robe and sash going around like the priests did, keeping the lampstands burning (v13)
4. as a *Judge*, particularly the white hair of the Ancient of Days on the throne in Daniel 7 where judgement is taking place (v14)
5. as a *warrior* with a sharp two-edged sword – the champion who has the victory (v16)
6. as the *Sacrifice* who was pierced and was dead (v7,18)
7. finally as the *Lord God Almighty* (v8,14)

John experiences this glorious vision of Christ, but what is the reason behind it? Why does Jesus reveal Himself in this way at this time? Throughout Scripture, visions are not just for the edification of the one seeing them, but always have a prophetic message attached. As we move into Revelation 2—3 we see the application for the vision in the form of the Letters to the 7 Churches.

Discussion Questions

Are there times you have felt 'dead'?

Which aspects of Jesus' character in the vision do you relate to most easily?

Which aspects do you find more challenging to relate to?

Letters to the 7 Churches
Revelation 2:1–3:22

In Revelation 1 we have seen a terrific vision of Jesus as the Son of Man walking amongst the lampstands, acting like a priest to keep the lamps burning – this ministry symbolises what Jesus is doing now that He has died for the sins of the world. He demonstrates this in Revelation 2—3 through the letters to the 7 Churches, as He trims the wicks and replenishes with the oil of the Spirit so that the light shines out of them, and reveals Him.

These 7 Letters are written to 7 Churches, which formed a kind of postal journey – the mail would come in to Ephesus and go round the rest in order. So it is reasonable for the Praeterist view to interpret these letters as written specifically to those 7 Churches. But given the symbolic significance of 7 as the number of completeness, I would suggest that as well as being actual churches, these 7 represent the whole Church.

These 7 Letters are fundamental to the whole book of Revelation – in them the things are prophesied which will ultimately be fulfilled by the Overcomers, as we see in Revelation 21—22 with the New Jerusalem. So the foundation of the destiny of humankind is already laid out in what is written to the 7 Churches at that time. This local setting is the start point from which comes the final completion of God's global rescue plan, because the application of the visions in Revelation is not restricted to those 7 Churches but expands through church history, and similarly is true for us as we apply them into our own situations almost 2000 years later, as well as into the future until the End of the Age when Christ returns. This highlights again just how terrifically integrated Revelation is, as the patterns and content build one upon another as you move through the book.

Themes in the 7 Letters

There are two main themes that run through these epistles and hold them together: *Witness* (or *Testimony*) and *Overcoming*.

Witness

To 'witness' (remember the Greek is *martureō*, from which we get the word 'martyr') is to recount something you have seen. If you witness a crime you will be asked to give a statement to the Police and maybe even testify in court. You could also be asked to attest to someone's reputation by being a character witness. As Christians we should be witnesses to Jesus – we should tell people who He is and the good things He has done in our lives.

In the same way, in Revelation 1:5 Jesus is called 'the faithful witness'. He witnesses in His humanity to all that is in deity – as a human He shows us what God is like. Now that Jesus has gone back to the Father, His Body, the Church are the witness to Him, who in turn is the witness to God. The Church must keep on witnessing, because the destiny of the people of God is to be:

> . . . a light of revelation to the Gentiles, and the glory of Your people Israel. (Isaiah 42:6 or 49:6, and Simeon in Luke 2:32)

The 7-branched lampstand in the Tabernacle, sometimes referred to as the lamp of the testimony, was a representative of Israel being 'a light to the nations'. It is important to see each of the 7 Letters as a message to encourage the Church to keep witnessing to the Gentiles. Indeed, the main issues raised in these epistles are to do with their witness and testimony.

When a church loses its witness, it loses its destiny, its mission, and it begins to fall apart. People may try to replace their witness with other things, like religiosity, legalism and intellectual or artistic pursuits – but ultimately, nothing else can take the place of that one great calling we have, which is to be a light and, therefore, a witness (*mártur*).

The Church is here to shine out into the Gentile world to those who do not know the Good News. So, while we can argue about the exact interpretation of the details in these epistles, overall they are all to do with getting the Church back to shining the light so that people can see Christ. The big question for the Church today is, when will we get back to being the witness to the Gentiles to the ends of the earth? As churches we need to be bright, shining witnesses to our Lord Jesus Christ.

Overcoming

Overcoming is mentioned eight times in the 7 Letters (once in each epistle and twice in the last), as well as later in the book. The phrase 'keep my deeds' (eg 2:26) is also used and means the same thing. Revelation develops the theme of enduring/overcoming that appears in the Gospels: 'The one who endures to the end, he will be saved' (Matthew 24:13). It is this persistence, this overcoming, which is the character that the Lord is looking for.

Overcoming is a fundamental characteristic of Christian life, but to be an overcomer the most important thing you need is *something to overcome*. The word 'to overcome' is the same Greek word (*níkē*) as 'to be victorious', so it means gaining the victory. We are called to be victorious Christians, that is, to overcome the world, the flesh and the devil. If one word sums up the Christian life, it is 'overcome'. Salvation should not be seen as a free ticket to heaven, where you sit down in a pew and wait to be taken to glory: it is a matter of overcoming.

So witnessing and overcoming are both important themes, but are also closely linked, going hand in hand through the letters, for example: the church in Smyrna is suffering persecution because of their witness, and some were martyred; in Pergamum, they 'hold fast the Name' and Antipas, the faithful witness, dies as a martyr; and at Thyatira, perversion and corruption are taking the edge off their testimony because they are not overcoming the world around them. It is a witnessing, overcoming message that comes through these 7 Letters to the 7 Churches.

This is vitally important. Just *being* a Christian does not bring many challenges – if we keep ourselves to ourselves, people will leave you alone, but then there is nothing to overcome. It is when we open our mouths and start witnessing that we face opposition, and this is when we really begin to fulfil our calling.

Discussion Topic: Overcoming

The Greek word translated as 'overcome' or 'conquer' is from the root *nico* (*níkē* noun; *nikáō* adj), meaning 'to gain victory'. Each of the epistles in Revelation exhorts the believers to overcome. Even when the word 'overcome' is not used, the phrase 'keep My deeds' is used to mean the same thing, for example in the letter to Thyatira (Revelation 2:26).

'Nicolaitans' also appears twice in these letters, which contains the word 'overcome' – *nico* – in it. *Laos* means people, so Nicolaitans means either 'victory over the people' or 'victory for the people'.

When the first of the 7 Seals is broken, we see a white horse whose rider was given a crown and 'went out conquering and to conquer' (Revelation 6:2). The word translated 'conquer' is the same as 'overcome', so he went out overcoming and to overcome. We will discuss whether this represents something good or bad when we look at the 4 Horsemen on page 252.

In the last epistle to Thyatira, Jesus describes Himself as having 'overcome' (Revelation 3:21) and later in Revelation we again see Christ overcoming:

> Behold, the Lion of Judah, the Root of David, has overcome so as to open the book and its seven seals. (Revelation 5:5)

Then in Revelation 12:11 we see the martyrs who 'overcame him because of the blood of the Lamb and the word of their testimony'.

The 7 Letters | Introduction

> 'Overcome' also appears twice in Revelation in a negative sense:
>
> > When they have finished their testimony, the Beast that comes up out of the abyss will make war with them, and overcome them and kill them. (Revelation 11:7)
> >
> > It was also given to him [the Beast] to make war with the saints and to overcome them. (Revelation 13:7)
>
> Here it is the beast who overcomes the saints, physically destroying them, which is similar to Daniel 7:24–25, where the powers of the little horn overcome the saints.
>
> The paradox of the Christian message is that it is when we are physically defeated that we become overcomers – when we lose, we have won. If we take up our cross and follow Him, we are actually defeating the enemy, and the triumph of the cross is taking place in our lives.

Structure: The pattern of the 7 Letters 2:1—3:22

If we look at the 7 Letters, they follow a similar structure:

   Address – 'To the Angel of . . .'

   Ministry of Christ to the Church 'says this . . .'

   'I Know . . .'

   Appeal to Mind, Conscience and Will

   Criticism (except Smyrna and Philadelphia)

   Exhortation 'To him who has an ear . . .'

   Promise to Overcomers

Address – 'To the angel of...'

Each of the 7 Letters is addressed 'to the angel of' that church. This has led some to speculate that every church has an individual angel, however, I don't think this is the point. If you look for instance at the letter to Thyatira, we read:

> ... and I will give to *each one of you* according to *your deeds* ... and I place no other burden on you. (2:23,24)

So while John writes to the angel, the letter is actually addressing the people in the church, to touch their spirits and release the Holy Spirit into their situation. So 'to the angel' is addressing the spiritual life of the members of the church.

Some people have thought that 'angel' refers to the pastor of each church, and that the letters are written to them so they can have a go at the congregation! However, the monarchical bishop, or one-man pastorate, did not exist in John's day. They would develop fairly quickly at the beginning of the second century, as we read in Ignatius, but in the earliest churches each congregation was led by a body of elders or bishops (see Philippians 1:1). In some cases this body may have had a chairman, like James in Acts 15, or a team leader, as with the apostle Paul who led a group of ministers as they planted churches, but this is not the same as having a single person in charge of the congregation.

Name and context

It is worth noting that, as so much of the book of Revelation is to do with signs and symbols, the names and situations of these 7 Churches also have significance. There were of course more than seven churches in Asia Minor, so these ones have been specifically selected.

The church names are real, but also symbolic, and each represents a desirable value we would like to see the Church expressing: comfort and strength in suffering, living in the heavenly places, living in sacrifice, renewal, brotherly love and justice.

The context of each church also is important – there are things in their histories which are known by their citizens and are being applied as part of the epistle. These are brought to bear to apply the message of Jesus to their lives: these are not circulars, but personal letters.

Ministry of Christ for the church

The Church needs Jesus. Each epistle begins with an aspect of the vision of Jesus from Revelation 1, for example 'The One who holds the 7 Stars in His right hand' (2:1). This is then ministered to that church in particular, because that is what they need more of.

This was already demonstrated when Jesus put His hand on John, who was lying as if dead: Jesus is the *living One* (1:18, see also John 1:4 & 14:6), and He ministers life into John and raises him up. In the same way, something of who Jesus is, is being placed into each of these churches, because that is what they need. The same is true today – the Church needs more of Jesus, and it is as He places His hands on us that He ministers into our lives.

'Says this...'

In each of the letters, after introducing Himself with an aspect from the vision in chapter 1, Jesus 'says this...'

This little phrase 'says this' (*tóde legei*) is used in the Septuagint to translate the Old Testament Hebrew when the Almighty says this... (eg Jeremiah 7:3; Ezekiel 25:3; Amos 1:6). This is God asserting, as the Lord of Hosts, the Almighty – *'Thus says the Lord!'* – it heralds the proclamation of prophecies and covenant statements. Revelation has already alluded to Jesus as 'the Almighty' and the 'I am' (1:8), as the Alpha and Omega (1:8), looking like the Son of Man (1:13) and the Ancient of Days (1:14), and now Jesus is revealed as the Old Testament Lord of Hosts and Almighty One, who 'says this...' Revelation has the highest Christology of all the New Testament writings. It shows Jesus without any reservation as *Yahweh,* the Beginning and the End – all titles that belong to God in the Old Testament, because He *is* God.

So even though it is just two short Greek words, 'says this...' is very provocative if you know the references in the Old Testament where God deals with His covenant people. It is strange the Jehovah's Witnesses use the book of Revelation so much, because if they studied it, instead of just picking out a verse or two here and there, they would see this and honour Jesus as He truly is!

🔍 Understanding – 'I know...'

In the vision in Revelation 1, Jesus is in the midst of the 7 Lampstands, and in each epistle there is a reminder that the Lord can perceive and understand what is going on, and he says '**I know . . .**' (in five epistles it says '**I know *your deeds***'). In most of the letters (except to Sardis and Laodicea) it follows this with a commendation.

The '**I know . . .**' is not only an assurance that the Lord knows and understands what is going on, but also that He knows what He is going to do. It is no good to trying to pull the wool over His eyes. At the same time He affirms us by what He does know.

Convince, Convict, Challenge – Mind, Conscience, Will

These epistles are aimed at the spiritual life of the people in each church. But in order to get to a person's spirit, the message needs a way in to address them either through their **mind**, their **conscience** or their **will**.

The apostle Paul refers to each of these when he writes to Timothy:

> Preach the word; be ready in season and out of season; correct, rebuke, and encourage with great patience and teaching. (2 Timothy 4:2, CSB)

When we proclaim the Gospel we need to give people cause to respond:

- we can aim at their mind by instructing them, which is sometimes translated as reprove or **convince**
- we can appeal to their conscience, by seeking to rebuke or **convict**, to touch the moral nerve of what is right and wrong and explain about sin
- or we can exhort or **challenge** them to do something about it, and aim to engage their will, so it is not just an intellectual exercise, but they will take steps to respond to God.

When we witness, most of us tend to major on one of those three things: some of us are forever giving reasons as to why people should do this, that and the other. Others hardly give any reasons, but try to convict of sin, and then there are those, like Billy Graham, who was excellent at exhorting people to make a response. Each of these letters address the mind, conscience or will of the people in that church.

Criticism

Each letter, except those to Smyrna and Philadelphia, contains a criticism, followed by a warning to 'repent'. It may dismay us that only a minority of the Church is fulfilling their calling, or it might encourage us to think that 2/7 of the Church at least are on the right track. These two representative Lampstands will come into focus again when we get to the 2 Witnesses in Revelation 11 (see page 397). Let's hope we find ourselves in that kind of church life!

There is a clear pattern to the criticisms: the first and seventh churches have very serious criticisms levelled at them ('I will remove your lampstand'/'I will spew you out of my mouth'), the second and sixth churches have no criticism, the third and fifth have minor criticisms, and right in the middle is Thyatira which receives a major criticism, followed by a grave warning.

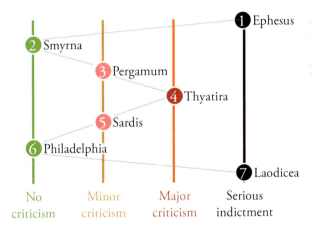

At the beginning and the end, as well as right in the heart of the letters are significant messages to all the churches, both individually, and also together as they all would have read all the epistles. These 7 Churches lead us to the total Church through history, with the Spirit dealing with churches facing the equivalent conditions and challenges we read about. But even though Jesus has significant criticisms of Thyatira, He tells them to 'repent'. Repentance is to change our mind with a view to changing our direction – we have a God of second chances, and so even if we do go off in the wrong direction, into sin, He has made a way back for us. Revelation reveals a God of forgiveness and Hope.

I am Coming . . .

Explicitly in 6 of the letters, and implied in the 7th, we see Jesus coming to the church (2:5,(10),16,25; 3:3,11,20). In some cases this looks like the Second Coming, because the same language and imagery Jesus used to talk about His *'Parousia'* are used here. Many commentators interpret these 'I am coming' statements to exclusively refer to the Second Coming, however some of them do not seem to be talking about when Jesus comes again, but rather an anticipation or foreshadowing of it.

For example, when the church in Ephesus are warned 'I will come and remove the lampstand', this would likely be in this church age now, because there would be no point removing it at the Second Coming when all the churches would be taken to be with Christ. It is as though the Second Coming is an event which is already impacting us and is being pre-empted by the Lord coming by His Spirit, until one day He *will* come again and be with us.

 ## 'To him who has an ear' – Exhortation

Each epistle includes the phrase: 'He who has ear, let him hear *what the Spirit says* to the churches . . .' However, each epistle begins with *Jesus* speaking to the angel of each church – so what Jesus says is what the Spirit says. This may not be surprising to us with our understanding of the Trinity, but of course Trinitarian doctrine was built partly upon these verses.

The only other equivalent place in the New Testament is Acts 21:11 where Agabus gives a prophecy about Paul:

> And coming to us, he took Paul's belt and bound his own feet and hands and says 'this is what *the Holy Spirit says* . . .'

So here John is in a similar prophetic ministry, seeking to reveal 'what the Spirit says'. All ministry is meant to be prophetic in the sense that it releases the spiritual power from God's heart into the lives of the people who are being addressed, so that what is being said is actually happening, or being deposited into the spirits of the people who listen.

Jesus also used the phrase '**If anyone has ears to hear, let him hear**' during His earthly ministry, when He was revealing truth to those who came to ask Him to interpret the parables. For example, in Mark 4:9 and 23 before and after the explanation of the Parable of the Sower. Here in Revelation 2–3 we get this phrase seven times, which should remind us to come to Jesus and talk about the things we don't understand, and the things we are going through. As we meditate on these things day and night, the Lord will give us more and more understanding through His Spirit.

It is interesting that what Jesus says to each church is specific and focused to that one church, but then is expanded and becomes what the Spirit is saying to *all* the churches – its first fulfilment is in an individual church situation, but it is ultimately a message for the whole of the Church.

 Promises to the Overcomer

Overcoming is one of the main themes that runs through Revelation, and is essential to see the fulfilment of the purpose God intended for His people.

God has a plan for His creation, and it goes something like this:

> And we know that in all things God works together with those who love Him to bring about what is good—with those who have been called according to His purpose. For those God foreknew He also predestined to be conformed to the image of His Son, that He might be the firstborn among many brothers and sisters. And those He predestined, He also called; those He called, He also justified; those He justified, He also glorified. (Romans 8:28–30, NIV MARGIN)

This is the pattern through which God is bringing about His purposes, but ultimately, we have the freewill to go along with God's plan in our lives and be an Overcomer, or not.

Either just before or just after 'He who has an ear . . .' each letter includes promises of blessing to 'the Overcomer'. The Christian life is about being an Overcomer. As Paul writes in Romans:

> Who will separate us from the love of Christ? Will tribulation, or distress, or persecution, or famine, or nakedness, or peril, or sword? . . . In all these things we are *more than overcomers* [overwhelmingly conquer, NASB], through Him who loved us. (Romans 8:35,37)

As we look at each in turn, we will see these blessings in Revelation 2—3 are ultimately fulfilled in the New Jerusalem in chapters 20—21. This is yet another example of the beautiful structure of this book – what is promised at the start is fulfilled at end.

Section I – Christ Central in the Church

Promise to the Overcomer in Revelation 2—3

Fulfilment in Revelation 21—22

Ephesus
- eat from Tree of Life

Revelation 22:2
- . . . the tree of life, which bore twelve fruits

Smyrna
- not hurt by Second Death

Revelation 20:15, 21:7–8
- will inherit all things, not thrown in the Lake of Fire

Pergamum
- hidden manna
- white stone
- new name on it

Revelation 21:11,14,18-21
- New Jerusalem made of crystalline stone which has the names of the 12 Tribes written on them

Thyatira
- authority over the nations
- the morning star

Revelation 22:5,16
- They will reign forever with Jesus 'the bright morning star'

Sardis
- clothed in white
- name not erased from Book of Life
- name confessed before the Father and His angels

Revelation 21:2,10,11, 19:7,8, 20:12–15, 21:27
- the Bride, the New Jerusalem comes from heaven. Those whose names are in the Lambs Book of Life are allowed in and out of the city

Philadelphia:
- pillar in the Temple of God
- name of My God, name of the city of My God, and My new name

Revelation 21:2,10,22, 22:4
- The Lord God and the Lamb are the Temple, so they are living in God, with the Lord's name on their foreheads

Laodicea
- sit with Christ on His throne

Revelation 22:5,16
- They will reign forever and ever with Jesus

Non-Overcomers

These promises to the overcomer raise other questions: Are there Christians who do not overcome? If so, what happens to them? Do they lose their salvation? The fact that Revelation keeps repeating 'To the one that overcomes' strongly indicates it *is* possible to be a Christian and not be an Overcomer. If everyone who is saved was automatically an Overcomer, then what would 'overcoming' mean?

Salvation is a free gift of grace, which cannot be earned. However the notion of overcoming is clearly that in some way you are doing / achieving something. If overcoming were the same as salvation, then we would be being saved by our deeds. Being an Overcomer cannot mean exactly the same as being a Christian – it must mean something more. If salvation is a free gift it cannot be taken away from us based on how we live our lives – if it could be taken away, it would not be a free gift. Therefore if a Christian is not an Overcomer, it should not follow they have lost their salvation.

So what happens to non-Overcomers? It is not easy to say because Revelation does not state one way or the other. Maybe this is because God wants to show us what we should be aiming for, rather than what we could get for half measures. While God has a plan for His creation, the Bible clearly shows things do not always go according to that plan. In the history of Israel in the Old Testament, and the way it is used in the New Testament, we see time and again that God's chosen people often choose to go against God's will. This is exemplified in Exodus, where God's intention was for the Hebrews to enter into their inheritance of the Promised Land, but due to their unfaithfulness they spent 40 years in the Wilderness. Eventually God's will is done, but through faithful heroes.

We are here to pursue totally what God has planned and arranged for us and He wants us to go all out for His purposes in our lives. So the emphasis in these epistles is that we should aim to keep on overcoming and then we will receive the promises. We should keep our eyes on the prize, not on wondering what we will get if we stop running! Overcoming is intimately connected to the doctrine of rewards and losses – for more on this, please see the Discussion Topic below and my book *Gold, Silver & Precious Stones*.

Section I – Christ Central in the Church

Discussion Topic: Rewards and losses

The New Testament is very clear that there are various rewards for believers. Jesus promises us blessings. rewards, treasure in heaven and an inheritance, ruling and reigning with Him. In the epistles there is a rich vein of rewards – we read about running the race set before us with endurance (Hebrews 12:1), running that we may win (1 Corinthians 9:24), and about pressing on for the prize of the upward call of God in Christ (Philippians 3:14). There are also crowns to be won (see Discussion Topic on page 214). In fact, rewards appear in almost every book in the New Testament.

These rewards are heavenly, and are based upon our actions:

> Rejoice and be glad, for your reward in heaven is great. (Matthew 5:12, also Luke 6:23)

> Your Father who sees what is done in secret will reward you. (Matthew 6:4,6,18)

> Now the one who plants and the one who waters are one; but each will receive his own reward according to his own labour. (1 Corinthians 3:8, see also Colossians 3:23–24)

In Revelation 11:18 we read that the time for the Lord to reward His bond-servants has come, and right at the end of the book:

> Behold, I am coming quickly, and My reward is with Me, to reward each one as his work deserves. (Revelation 22:12)

But as well as being gained, it seems it is possible to lose your reward

> Whoever gives you a cup of water to drink because of your name as followers of Christ . . . he shall by no means lose his reward. (Mark 9:41, also Matthew 10:42)

> If anyone's work which he has built on it remains, he will receive a reward. If anyone's work is burned up, he will suffer loss; but he himself will be saved, yet only so as through fire. (1 Corinthians 3:13–15)

This is known as the doctrine of rewards and losses.

But there is a problem. Following the Reformation, salvation was rightly emphasised as being a free gift of God's grace, rather than something we could earn by good works. However, this emphasis against good works led to rewards being dismissed or viewed as something we also receive through grace, so became merely part of salvation. The trouble is that when Jesus and Paul suggest we may lose our reward or crown, or forfeit our prize, if these are not rewards but the same as salvation, then our salvation is the only thing we can lose. If salvation is a free gift of grace, how can it be taken away or forfeited? This would mean it was not free or by grace!

In Philippians 3, Paul clearly links rewards with resurrection life: 'if somehow I may attain to the resurrection from the dead . . . Not that I have already grasped it all or have already become perfect, but I press on'. Paul was assured of his salvation (see eg Romans 5), so this cannot be what is in view here. Rather, I would suggest Paul is talking about the first resurrection of the saints, which we will look at more when we get to Revelation 20.

If we separate out salvation (free gift of grace) and rewards (earned for what we do) it makes sense of these Scriptures. Reinstating the doctrine of rewards and losses in our theology is the only way out of this tangle. For more on the doctrine of rewards and losses, please see my book *Gold, Silver & Precious Stones*.

Discussion Questions

If Jesus were writing a letter to your church, what might it say?

When you witness, do you tend to convince, convict or challenge?

What does overcoming mean for you?

The 7 Churches
Revelation 2

John writes Jesus' letters to the first 4 Churches: Ephesus, Smyrna, Pergamum and Thyatira.

Text – Revelation 2:1-7 | Letter to Ephesus

> ¹To the angel of the church in Ephesus write:
>
> The One who holds the seven stars in His right hand, the One who walks among the seven golden lampstands, says this:
>
> ² 'I know your deeds and your toil and perseverance, and that you cannot tolerate evil men, and you put to the test those who call themselves apostles, and they are not, and you found them to be false; ³ and you have perseverance and have endured for My name's sake, and have not grown weary. ⁴ But I have this against you, that you have left your first love. ⁵ Therefore remember from where you have fallen, and repent and do the deeds you did at first; or else I am coming to you and will remove your lampstand out of its place – unless you repent. ⁶ Yet this you do have, that you hate the deeds of the Nicolaitans, which I also hate. ⁷ He who has an ear, let him hear what the Spirit says to the churches. To him who overcomes, I will grant to eat of the tree of life which is in the Paradise of God.'

To the angel of the church of Ephesus (v1)

Ephesus was the port of entrance into Asia Minor and its chief religious centre – it is where the Roman Emperor would come into and depart from. So it is a natural beginning to this series of 7 Churches. Ephesus was visited by Paul and Timothy (Acts 19:1–41) – Paul lived there for 3 years, and later wrote to Timothy who had returned there (see 1 Timothy). Church tradition

Letter to Ephesus | Revelation 2:1–7

tells us that Jesus' mother Mary went to live in Ephesus with John who cared for her after Jesus committed her to his charge (John 19:26–27).

Ephesus probably means 'desirable' and is likely to have been a city full of people seeking and desiring after truth, but as we read in the letter, the church was in danger of losing its first love. It is often the way that religion and tradition takes the place of love. What has happened in the past may be fascinating, but if you love it too much and start living in it ('building up the tombs of the prophets', as in Matthew 23:29, Luke 11:47), it leads to a kind of second-hand religion based on yesterday's exploits and the spirituality of others. So there is always a danger, not just here in Ephesus as a big religious centre, but throughout church history, of glorying in the past, and not living a life of faith in the present.

Ministry of Christ for Ephesus (v1)

In Revelation 1 we see Jesus '*in the middle* of the lampstands' and 'in His right hand He *held* 7 Stars'. However, the letter to Ephesus is from 'the One who *holds* the 7 Stars in His right hand' and '*walks* among the 7 golden Lampstands'. This may seem like a small change, but it is significant – the glorious vision now becomes present and very real as it is applied by the Holy Spirit to the Church. Jesus is not just there standing in the midst of the lampstands, but *walking* among them – there is movement and life and energy. It is not just that the stars are statically being held, but that Jesus is *holding* them and is still holding them now. The Church needs to know that Jesus is walking alongside us, holding us – not in an abstract kind of way, but that His words are a living application of who He is revealed to be in the vision.

'I Know . . .' – toil and perseverance (v2)

Jesus commends the Ephesians for their toil and perseverance – living a godly life is hard work! This is even harder in modern times because we have so few boundaries. Since the time of Constantine, when the State and the Church became merged, the view has been that the Church is there to meet the needs of the people, so anyone can float in and out as they please. In more modern times there is a trend to being 'Church without Walls', demonstrating how tolerant and inclusive we are. Of course our church meetings should be welcoming and open for all those seeking the Lord, but there is a danger that some, either through sentimentality, indulgence or being frightened of confrontation, think we should therefore endure 'evil men'. However, such people will bring destruction into the church – we should not give them place or authority to corrupt it: that is not being a light and a testimony. We ought to be showing what Jesus is like, not how progressive and liberal we are. Yes, all people are loved of God, but it does not mean they can just do whatever they feel like – we need to repent. This is not about being arrogant or judging people, but if we do not point out what is evil then we are not being a light (Hebrews 1:7). Jesus loves righteousness and hates iniquity, and so we as His Body should also be lovers of righteousness and haters of evil.

So who were these 'evil men'? Some, at least, were false apostles, who had not been sent by God. The church in Ephesus tested those who said they were apostles. Being an apostle is a moral and spiritual authority that God gives to certain people who, through their teaching, are able to bring order amongst the people of God and draw others together to be able to follow them. Anybody can pop up and say, 'I am a chosen apostle', but some of them are false – we see it today just as in the Early Church. How do we know who are genuine apostles and who are not?

What is an apostle? (v2)

Apostle means 'one who is sent' specifically *with a message*. This is seen before the resurrection with the 70 sent out by Jesus (Luke 10:1). The 12 Apostles are straightforward – they were commissioned when Jesus was on earth and may be designated 'Apostles of the Incarnation'. Jesus sent them out with the Great Commission to teach all nations (Matthew 28:19) and we are meant to follow their teaching (Acts 2:42). Then there are those 500+ Apostles of the Resurrection, who saw the resurrected Jesus alive (1 Corinthians 15:5–7) – they carry the testimony that *'Jesus is alive'*. There were more of them and they also would have been known to people in the first century.

Paul had a unique apostleship: he didn't belong to the 12, he had seen only a vision of Jesus, not His resurrection presence, and specifically was sent to the Gentiles, his ministry being one of reconciling Jews and Gentiles into one Body (1 Corinthians 15:8, Romans 11:13, Ephesians 3:1–10).

Finally, 'Apostles of the Ascension' can be seen in Ephesians 4:11, who were sent to spread the Gospel, since Pentecost through to our present time.

However, outside of the 12, the 500+ and the apostle Paul, it is more difficult to know if someone is telling the truth that they are commissioned and sent from God, or if they are a self-proclaimed apostle – they need to be tested. We don't know exactly how the Ephesians went about 'testing' these apostles, and how they decided some of them were false, but we must assume it is something about their message, behaviour or authority which did not fit with apostolic doctrine.

It is interesting that in his farewell message to the elders of Ephesus at Miletus, in Acts 20:28–30, Paul warns them:

> Be on guard for yourselves and for all the flock . . . after my departure savage wolves will come in among you, not sparing the flock; and from among your own selves men will arise, speaking perverse things, to draw away the disciples after them. (Acts 20:28–30)

So the epistle in Revelation, written somewhere around 15 to 35 years later, is probably in the context of this being fulfilled. It is intriguing that Ignatius, by the turn of the century, writes that the Ephesian church took notice of this warning and got rid of the false apostles (*Epistle to the Ephesians 9:1*); they did not 'endure' them. So we can be encouraged that this letter had its own specific, first-century impact and hopefully it will have the same effect on us – we too can get things sorted out if we take Jesus' words to heart.

Commendation . . . Perseverance and endurance (v3)

Jesus commends the Ephesians for persevering and enduring 'For My Name's sake', which is for the reputation and the authority of Jesus.

Criticism – 'You have left your first love' (v4)

There are at least three ways of understanding 'you have left your first love':

i They have **stopped loving Jesus** in the way that they first began. Jesus of course should be pre-eminent in terms of our love – 'You shall love the Lord your God with all your heart, and with all your soul, and with all your strength, and with all your mind', (eg Luke 10:27).

ii They have **stopped loving each other** in the church. In his gospel, John says: 'By this everyone will know that you are my disciples, if you love one another' (13:35, CSB). If you love Jesus, you will start to love the Church.

iii They have **stopped loving the lost** . . . We can have love for Jesus, and even for the Church, but these are both part of loving the unsaved, because that is the way people know we are Jesus' disciples. Indeed this interpretation fits well with 'the deeds you did at first' we read in the next verse. A passage that backs this up is Matthew 24:

> Many false prophets will arise and will mislead many. Because lawlessness is increased, most people's love will grow cold. But the one who endures to the end, he will be saved. This gospel of the kingdom shall be preached in the whole world as a testimony to all the nations, and then the end will come. (v11–14)

Here is a witness shining out so that all the nations shall see it, but the warning is that we have to endure so that the gospel of the Kingdom will get preached. If people's love grows cold, that will not happen.

So in the light of Matthew 24, there are good grounds for saying the 'first love' being left in Ephesus is the love for the unsaved: the sinners, their enemies, the nations of the world. Rather than following the interests of Christ – that the Good News should go to everyone – the church in Ephesus have become self-centred, looking after their own interests. We are here to love every man, woman and child with the love of Christ: '. . . for God so loved the world . . .' If that lamp stops shining, then that love stops going out into the world.

In a sense, these three interpretations are all linked together, and are different aspects of the same thing: the love they had lost was a love of being pleasing to Jesus; we are pleasing to Christ by fulfilling His purpose; His purpose is that we love one another so the world might know we are His disciples, and so we shine out His love into the earth.

Again in his *Epistle to the Ephesians,* Ignatius hints that they also took notice of this part of the letter and became unified in their love for Christ, for each other and for the lost – they had rekindled their first love!

💙 Challenge – 'Repent . . . or I will remove your lampstand' (v5)

'Remember therefore from where you have fallen' sounds like a star falling and not shining brightly enough in the darkness. Here the 'repent and do the

Letter to Ephesus | Revelation 2:1–7

deeds you did at first', fits with the first love they have lost, so the warning is to turn from their self-interest to love the people of the world, going out to reach them with the Gospel. The drastic warning is that unless they repent, their lampstand will be removed, and as we have already seen, the lampstand is the outward form of the church that is preserving the light burning in it. In the parable of the talents Jesus teaches:

> For whoever has, more will be given to him, and he will have more than enough; but whoever does not have, even what he has will be taken away from him. (Matthew 13:12, 25:29, CSB)

If you don't go on adding to what you have got, it will be taken away from you – there is always a necessity to keep pressing on to get hold of more. The Lord's warning is that it can be taken away if we are not doing our job of shining out into the world. This does not necessarily mean every church which suffers a division, or closure was not doing God's will: persecution is another factor, and has destroyed many churches. What we can say is that in serious situations, Jesus will remove a lampstand.

 ## Commendation... 'You hate the deeds of the Nicolaitans' (v6)

Here we get a brief reference to the 'Nicolaitans', who also appear in the third letter to Pergamum, where we will look at them in more detail (see page 137). Here we need only note that no one knows who exactly the Nicolaitans were – what is important is that Jesus hated their deeds (NB not them), as did the church in Ephesus, so this is commended.

 ## To the Overcomer – Fruit from the Tree of Life (v7)

The first overcoming promise is 'you will eat of the Tree of Life in the midst of the paradise of God'. This is fulfilled in Revelation 22:2:

> In the middle of its street, and on either side of the river, was the tree of life, which bore twelve fruits, each yielding its fruit every month.

To eat of the Tree of Life takes us back to the Garden of Eden where we find the Tree of the Knowledge of Good and Evil and the Tree of Life (Genesis 3) – being an Overcomer means we get back to walking with God in the Garden.

The Garden of Eden (translated 'Paradise' in the Septuagint) is the original state of humanity in relationship with God, walking together in love and fellowship. This was lost through humankind's sin, but still exists in heaven. It is possible for us to momentarily experience this supernatural paradise, as Paul did in 2 Corinthians 12:4, and it will permanently be ours in the New Jerusalem when Jesus comes again (as in Luke 23:43). These are the only three times paradise is mentioned in Scripture.

Following the Fall, God put cherubim at the gate with a flaming sword so that we cannot get to the Tree of Life, at least not without dying. If we didn't die then we would live forever with our sin. The Tree of Life is very similar to, but not exactly the same as, eternal life, which refers to the quality of the life of Jesus. Rather, the Tree of Life is the gift of immortality, because you can eat and live forever.

Immortality is not something that inherently belongs to us because we are human. The idea that all souls are immortal came from Greek philosophers, not from the Bible as some people think (for more on the influence of Greek philosophy on our views of eternity, see our book *God's Strategy in Human History, Vol. 1*). The Bible clearly teaches that human souls are not innately immortal: 'The soul who sins shall die' (Ezekiel 18:20, NKJV) and God will give eternal life 'to those who by perseverance in doing good seek glory, honour, and immortality' (Romans 2:7). Only God has immortality (1 Timothy 1:17, 6:16). Genesis 2:17 shows that humankind has the capacity for dying – we were not made immortal by God. God wants to share immortality with us, but it is something we need to seek after and lay hold of.

The promise to the Overcomer, is that they 'will eat of the Tree of Life' in the midst of the paradise of God which existed when humankind were first made. We are back to where we should be – God's rescue plan has worked! The Garden of Eden (Paradise) is where we are fulfilled as humans walking with God. One question is, if you aren't one of the Overcomers, will you at any time eat of the Tree of Life? Or will you ever participate in the leaves of the tree healing the nations (Genesis 2:1–4)? It doesn't say either way, and maybe this is because God wants us to give 100% to go for that immortality and to reign with Him forever and ever, rather than doing just what is necessary to scrape through.

What is being emphasised here is that those who keep on overcoming will have the confirmed promise of God's destiny for the human race – to enjoy the fruit of immortality.

Letter to Ephesus | Revelation 2:1–7

Discussion Topic: Tree of Life

The *Tree of Life* only appears in eight places in the Bible. The first place is of course in Genesis 2 in the Garden of Eden where:

> . . . out of the ground the Lord made every tree grow that is pleasant to the sight and good for food. The *Tree of Life* was also in the midst of the garden, and the Tree of the Knowledge of Good and Evil. (v9)

Following the Fall, in Genesis 3:22–23 Adam and Eve are sent out of the garden 'lest he put out his hand and take also of the *Tree of Life*, and eat, and live forever', and a guard put on the way back to the tree:

> He placed cherubim at the east of the garden of Eden, and a flaming sword which turned every way, to guard the way to the *Tree of Life*. (v24)

Tree of Life is mentioned four times in Proverbs, and is used metaphorically, to describe God's wisdom concerning life (Proverbs 3:18, 11:30, 13:12, 15:4). Wisdom is a personification of Jesus in the book of Proverbs – see also Matthew 11:19, 23:34, Luke 11:49. When we get to the book of Revelation the Tree of Life appears once again as a symbol, clearly representing Jesus.

Since the Biblical Literalist movement of the nineteenth century, some people get hung up about having to take Genesis 1—3 completely literally, so the Tree of Life and Tree of the Knowledge of Good and Evil must be actual physical trees. We mustn't of course strip the Genesis account of meaning, but whether these 'trees' were symbols, metaphors or actual trees, the point is that there was of course a *literal* disobedience to God. Whatever the disobedience was, the Tree of Knowledge of good and evil and the Tree of Life appear as symbols – elsewhere in the Bible the Tree of Life symbolises wisdom and immortality, so we need to understand it in this way here in Revelation.

Summary – Ephesus

Ephesus is a church that needs to be renewed in its love for God's purposes in the world. They require a fresh passion to live a life of walking with Jesus – that is paradise.

Discussion Questions

In what ways is the letter to Ephesus relevant to your church?

What was your 'first love' when you were saved?

How does your view of immortality affect your life?

How do you imagine the Tree of Life?

Text – Revelation 2:8–11 | Letter to Smyrna

> [8] And to the angel of the church in Smyrna write:
> The first and the last, who was dead, and has come to life, says this:
> [9] 'I know your tribulation and your poverty (but you are rich), and the blasphemy by those who say they are Jews and are not, but are a synagogue of Satan. [10] Do not fear what you are about to suffer. Behold, the devil is about to cast some of you into prison, so that you will be tested, and you will have tribulation for ten days. Be faithful until death, and I will give you the crown of life. [11] He who has an ear, let him hear what the Spirit says to the churches. He who overcomes will not be hurt by the second death.'

To the angel of the church in Smyrna (v8)

The name Smyrna probably comes from the word 'myrrh', a rare perfume, traditionally used to embalm bodies. Not only was myrrh one of the three gifts given to Jesus by the magi, but wine mixed with myrrh was offered to Him during the Crucifixion, and was also used to wrap His body (John 19:39,

Mark 15:23). So to Christians, 'Smyrna' does not only represent death, but also anticipates resurrection. Smyrna had famously been destroyed in the seventh century BC and rebuilt – it was dead, but now lived. Indeed it was celebrated for its exceptional beauty, and its acropolis on top of a steep hill was referred to as 'the Crown of Smyrna'. Smyrna was also noted for its Olympian games which may also be behind the reference to a Crown of Life. Later, in the second century the bishop of Smyrna, Polycarp, who learnt at John's feet, was famously martyred in the arena during the games. He was told by the Proconsul that if he cursed Christ he would be set free. Polycarp answered 'Eighty-six years have I have served him, and he has done me no wrong. How can I blaspheme my King and my Saviour?' (*The Martyrdom of Polycarp*).

Ministry of Christ to the church (v8)

At Smyrna, Jesus reveals Himself to a church where people are dying for their faith as 'The first and the last, who was dead, and has come to life'. Here, 'come to life' is in the completed tense, rather than the continuous tense. Of course Jesus is continuously alive, but there was an event in which Jesus *rose again* – you could even translate it, 'I came alive again'. So the Lord here is re-emphasizing His deity as the Alpha and the Omega (see also Discussion Topic on page 79), as well as His resurrection.

'I know your tribulation' (v9)

We will look at tribulation again when we get to the Great Tribulation in Revelation 7 (see page 243). The root of the word 'tribulation' means 'pressure.' It is even used for the narrow road in Matthew 7:14 'narrow is the gate and *tribulating* is the way which leads to life' – that is the path of being a Christian. Although the church in Smyrna are suffering, they are 'rich' meaning spiritually rich, just as in the Beatitudes worldly difficulty leads to eternal blessings. Tribulation and opposition are bound to come upon the believer, as Jesus promises in John 16: 'in the world you will have tribulation', but He also provides the answer to it: 'be of good cheer, I have overcome the world' (v33).

The Christians in Smyrna are obviously under terrific pressure from people claiming to be God's people, but in reality belong to 'the synagogue of Satan'. Who are these people claiming to be Jews, but 'are not'? Were they people pretending to be Jews? – probably not. More likely they are Jewish, ie are descended from Israel, and part of the nation, but they are not following God (see also Romans 2:28–29).

Synagogue means 'coming together'/'assembly' and similarly the Greek word for 'church' – *ekklesia* – means 'called out from', both of which imply gathering together. Indeed, James uses *synagogue* to describe the Church (James 2:2). So the 'synagogue of Satan' would appear to be a rival gathering, but it is not clear whether this is inside or outside the church.

Here we must be very clear – this is not saying 'all Jews'. As Christians, anti-Semitism is completely unacceptable. Sadly, church history contains plenty of it, with notable examples such as 'Judensau' images and some of Martin Luther's writings, eg 'On the Jews and their lies'. Jesus was a Jew, and the Early Church was considered as part of Judaism. However, in Smyrna it is not Jews in general who are being highlighted, but seemingly a specific group of legalists, who are so strongly opposed to the growth of the church among Gentiles that they are causing trouble, and getting Christians arrested and even executed. Interestingly, the phrase 'Synagogue of Satan' also appears in the Dead Sea Scrolls, written by the Qumran community of Essenes, where it is used to describe a group of legalistic 'talmudist' Jews.

Discussion Topic: Who are True Israel?

'Israel' means 'perseverer of God' (Genesis 32:28). The Old Testament reveals Israel – anyone descended from the 12 Tribes – as being God's chosen people. Promises are given to them, God protects them, but there is a history of rebellion and many of them did not follow the Law or the Prophets, as Stephen summarises in Acts 7:51–53 (see for example Isaiah 1:2–4, Jeremiah 9:6, Ezekiel 44:6–7, Daniel 9:11–14).

However, Jeremiah 31:33 (quoted in Hebrews 10:16) gives us a hint that even in the Old Testament, God has a different working definition of what constituted 'Israel'. Indeed, Isaiah prophesies that they will receive a new name (Isaiah 62:2, 65:15).

One of the Old Testament promises given to Israel was that the Jews and the Gentiles would stand on the same ground (Genesis 12:1–3, Isaiah 11:1–10, 25:6–9, 55:1–13, Joel 2:28–32, Habakkuk 2:4, Amos

9:11–12 (Acts 15:16)) and that to be Jewish would be whether you are 'circumcised of the heart'(Romans 2:29) and whether your praise was of God. Also a true Israel of the Spirit is already seen in Romans 9:6. Later on in Romans 9, Paul gives an outstanding exposition of Hosea 2:23:

> And He did so to make known the riches of His glory upon vessels of mercy, which He prepared beforehand for glory, even us, whom He also called, not from among Jews only, but also from among Gentiles. As He says also in Hosea:
>
> 'I will call those who were not My people, "My people," and her who was not beloved, "beloved." And it shall be that in the place where it was said to them, "you are not My people," there they shall be called sons of the living God.' (Romans 9:23–26)

Just because you are 'of the nation of Israel', does not mean to say that you are truly 'Israel', as Jesus Himself says in Matthew 3:9–10.

Hosea, like many of the Old Testament prophets, did not just *give* a message from God, his life *was* the message. Hosea married a prostitute, and she had three children, at least two of which probably weren't his, but he has to accept them. Just as Hosea may have looked at these children and thought: *Not my kid, I don't feel like their father*, it was a picture of how Israel had been declared by God 'not My people . . .' but, as always in the Bible, there is hope. We read in Hosea 1:10:

> Where it is said to them, 'You are not My people', it will be said to them 'You are the sons of the Living God'.

If God can then say to those who are 'not My people', that they are now 'sons of the Living God', this can be applied equally to *anybody* who was not His people – both those who are of the nation of Israel and those who are not. So Jew and Gentile stand on exactly the same ground – he is a Jew who is one inwardly of the same heart (Romans 2:29).

(For a more detailed exposition of Romans 9, see our recent book *Paul's Gospel in Romans & Galatians*).

Convince – 'Do not fear' , 10 days of testing (v10)
'Do not Fear'

'Do not fear!' is the most common command of God in the whole Bible. That gives us a good idea that there are plenty of things out there seeking to harm God's people. So the Lord keeps on having to tell us: *'Do not fear!',* because of the sort of things we come up against as we resist the world, the flesh and the devil. Sin is destroying men and women and therefore inevitably fear will arise as we seek to resist it and go God's way.

One of my favourite verses for this is in Psalm 56:

> Whenever I am afraid, I will trust in You.
> In God (I will praise His word),
> In God I have put my trust; I will not fear. (v3–4)

So every time you feel afraid, there is the opportunity to 'trust in Him'.

10 days of testing

Persecution was going to hit the Smyrna church – the devil was about to cast some people into prison, but in the same way they did, we need to trust in God for justice. As we will see in Revelation 20, it is the devil who is cast into the pit – God is a just Judge! In prison there will be testing and tribulation for 10 days. So tribulation is to be regarded as a testing to make us strong and to come out victorious for the Lord.

The 10 days of testing is a little puzzle. As I have emphasised, Daniel is foundational for the book of Revelation, and in chapter 1, rather than defile themselves by eating the king's food, Daniel and his friends ask to be tested for 10 days eating vegetables and drinking water. Eating the food of the king showed a degree of commitment and reliance, so they chose this way to show to whom they ultimately belonged. Of course they were dependent upon the king in many other ways, and this is still true for us today. There are no ways in which we can completely remove ourselves from this world – we have to pay our taxes and fit in with the laws and regulations (Romans 13:1–7, Titus 3:1-2, 1 Peter 2:13-17) – but there needs to be a place where we clearly make a distinction and show that we belong to another. That kind of decision is different for different people, at different times, in different places, and even if the thing we do may not be very important in itself, it is an important step for building character and resistance against the enemy. If you give in to everything, you are too feeble, but if you make a few principled stances, you are in the place where you can resist. Fasting, like doing a 'Daniel fast' has this effect – you have a right to eat, but if you fast you are simply saying to the Lord that you are living for Him. So these 10 days of Daniel were a test, and here in the letter to Smyrna 10 days of 'testing' or 'tribulation' is mentioned twice, showing it was clearly important. As Daniel is a backdrop to so much of Revelation, it is maybe the best way of interpreting these 10 days.

Crown of Life

Those who are faithful until death will get a crown of life. So does every believer get a crown of life, or only some? A crown implies reigning, and if I reign in life by one man Christ Jesus *now* (Romans 5:17), I will receive a crown of life *then*. In 2 Timothy 4:8, Paul says in the future there is laid up for him 'a crown of righteousness'. This is to do with the doctrine of rewards, enduring and seeing the prize of the upward call that comes from that persistence and commitment.

However, if we do not endure, are we just written off? Does God have nothing for us? Of course not – we have a loving God, full of grace and truth, a Father who loves to give us good gifts, including eternal life for all who call on the name of Jesus. But we must be careful not to confuse salvation, which is a free gift that we receive by God's grace, with the reward, or prize, which we receive on the basis of how we live our lives. For more on the doctrine of rewards and losses, see the Discussion Topic on page 118, as well as my book *Gold, Silver & Precious Stones*.

 ## To the Overcomer . . . Not hurt by Second Death (v11)

The Overcomers at Smyrna will not be hurt by the Second Death. This promise is fulfilled in the New Heaven and New Earth where the Overcomers are not hurt by the Lake of Fire/Second Death:

> He who overcomes shall inherit all things, and I will be his God and he shall be My son. But the cowardly, unbelieving, abominable, murderers, sexually immoral, sorcerers, idolaters, and all liars shall have their part in the lake which burns with fire and brimstone, which is the second death. (Revelation 21:7–8)

We will look more at the Second Death and Lake of Fire when we get to them in Revelation 20, but for now we can draw a few points:

- → The second death must be distinct in some way from the 'First Death' (presumably physical death), and involves some kind of pain and testing through fire.

- → In the New Testament, *Gehenna* refers prophetically to a place of judgment and destruction, often through fire (see eg Matthew 10:28, 18:9 etc). *Gehenna* is often translated as 'hell'.

- → *Gehenna* is a Greek transliteration of the Hebrew *ge-hinnom*, meaning 'the valley of Hinnom', which appears in the Old Testament, notably in 2 Kings 23 where Josiah defiled Topheth in *ge-hinnom* so it would no longer be used for child sacrifice to Molech – this purged Judah and Jerusalem from pagan worship, and was an act of judgment and purification. Having become a rubbish tip, fires burned there continually and smoke rose, so the reference to fire is very apt. Jeremiah uses *ge-hinnom* prophetically as a place of judgment (eg Jeremiah 7:32).

But what exactly does being 'hurt' by the Second Death mean? Is being 'thrown into the Lake of Fire' (Revelation 19:20, 20:10,14–15) the same thing as being 'hurt' by it? Can Christians be 'hurt', even if they have eternal life?

If the Lake of Fire is the same as *Gehenna*, then not only is it possible that Christians will be damaged or hurt by it, but it can hurt us even now. In his epistle, James writes how the tongue is a small but powerful part of the body that 'defiles the entire body and sets on fire the course of our life and it is set on fire by Hell [*Gehenna*]' (James 3:6).

Gehenna can set our tongue on fire now – we can be defiled by it now, not only in the End Times. I would suggest that to be hurt by the fire of *Gehenna* means that we can suffer loss. But what is it that we are losing? A big problem with reformed theology is that it does not allow much room for rewards and losses. This means that because the only thing we can receive is our free gift of salvation by grace, then the only thing we can lose is that salvation. If however we also receive a reward or prize for our faithfulness and how we have lived our lives, then what we could lose may be some, or all, of this reward. It does not say that will lose our eternal life – the Lord does not take away our salvation (although we may be able to throw it away ourselves). So for example, if we backslide – yes, we will be hurt by the Second Death; there will be loss that we will experience, but not the total loss of being rejected forever.

Summary – Smyrna

Smyrna is a suffering, persecuted church – if you live godly in Christ Jesus you shall suffer persecution (2 Timothy 3:12). However, for those who come through the testing there is the assurance of a Crown of Life.

Discussion Questions

In what ways is the letter to Smyrna relevant to your church?

What have you sacrificed for your faith?

How would you feel about receiving a Crown of Life?

Text – Revelation 2:12–17 | Letter to Pergamum

> [12]And to the angel of the church in Pergamum write:
> The One who has the sharp two-edged sword says this:
> [13] 'I know where you dwell, where Satan's throne is; and you hold fast My name, and did not deny My faith even in the days of Antipas, My witness, My faithful one, who was killed among you, where Satan dwells. [14] But I have a few things against you, because you have there some who hold the teaching of Balaam, who kept teaching Balak to put a stumbling block before the sons of Israel, to eat things sacrificed to idols and to commit acts of immorality. [15] So you also have some who in the same way hold the teaching of the Nicolaitans. [16] Therefore repent; or else I am coming to you quickly, and I will make war against them with the sword of My mouth. [17] He who has an ear, let him hear what the Spirit says to the churches. To him who overcomes, to him I will give some of the hidden manna, and I will give him a white stone, and a new name written on the stone which no one knows but he who receives it.'

✉️ To the angel of the church of Pergamum (v12)

Pergamum probably means 'height' or 'elevation'. Pergamum was a religious centre and notably bore the title *Thrice Neokoros* because it had three temples where Roman emperors were worshipped as gods, which may explain why it is 'where Satan dwells'. The pro-consul seat was in Pergamum which was represented by a sword, and in this letter Jesus appears with a sharp sword.

Ministry of Christ for Pergamum – Two-edged sword (v12)

Twice in this letter the two-edged sword that comes from Jesus' mouth is mentioned, so the focus is on the spiritual battle and on using the word of truth as a weapon. In the First Vision in Revelation 1:16, Jesus has a two-edged sword in His mouth, but here He is wielding it, ready to fight.

The sword was a symbol of Roman justice, and was also the symbol of the proconsul in Pergamum – but here Jesus is the one who is holding it.

🔍 'I know … where you dwell' (v13)

In the previous letter, we had the 'synagogue of Satan', and here it talks about 'where Satan's throne is . . . where Satan *dwells*'. Pergamum was the seat of the administration in that area and there were shrines for Emperor worship, which was essential for being involved in commerce and politics. So it seems likely that this is behind the reference to 'Satan's throne'.

This is a step up from the 'synagogue of Satan', and indicates a place where the enemy has become entrenched. This seems to represent governmental or political persecution of the Church, borne out of the fact Christians would not worship the Emperor.

Jesus says '*I know* where you dwell . . .' – He understands, He is saying '*I am with you*', even when we feel in impossible situations. This is a wonderful comfort.

To 'hold fast My Name' and 'not deny My faith' mean pretty much the same thing. Our faith is in the name of Jesus (Acts 3:16) and if we confess His name we will be saved (Matthew 10:32, Luke 12:8, Romans 10:9, 1 John 4:15) – our hope is in Him and we can 'hold fast' to this confession because He is faithful (Hebrews 10:23). If we go back on our confession of Jesus as Lord we have denied our faith and not held tight to His name.

In a sense, the message Jesus came to bring us is the name 'Father'. In the Old Testament, God was seen as Father of the Nation, but Jesus now reveals God as a personal, loving Father – 'Holy Father' (John 17:11), 'Righteous Father . . . I have given them Your Name' (John 17:25). Jesus revealed God the Father to the people.

In reference to Antipas, who was martyred, 'Antipas' means 'against all' or 'all against' in Greek, which is probably describing how he felt with everybody against him. In Revelation 1:5, we saw 'Jesus Christ, *the* faithful witness' (see page 71), and here Antipas is someone who clearly had the very life of Christ in him, because he resembles Jesus: '*My* witness, *My* faithful one'.

Criticism – Balaam and the Nicolaitans (v14–15)

The criticism for Pergamum is that some of them are following the teaching of Balaam and others are following the Nicolaitans.

Balaam is in some way related to the Nicolaitans, because verse 15 says 'So you also have some who *in the same way* . . .' The names 'Balaam' and the 'Nicolaitans' may mean similar things: Balaam could be derived from the Hebrew for 'Lord over the people' and Nicolaitans means 'victory over the people'. So why do we have both names here if they are so similar? Is it more of a theological statement saying that the Nicolaitans are acting like Balaam did? Or were there two separate parties causing problems in the church there? I would think that there probably were two parties, but their actions amounted to much the same: they both put a 'stumbling block' before the sons of Israel. This stumbling block was to eat things sacrificed to idols and commit acts of immorality, both of which are closely associated with the worship of false gods of fertility, expressed as sexual promiscuity. Sexual and spiritual fornication are the common paganism of mankind, and come up again and again in the history of Israel.

The Balaamites

In Numbers 22, Balak, king of Moab employs Balaam to curse the Israelites, but he cannot – every time he opens his mouth out comes the Spirit of God's words, and he blesses Israel instead! The interesting thing is that Balaam obviously was a spiritual man and touched into the Spirit of God, because his prophecies are very clearly such (eg Numbers 22:35,38, 23:5,26, 24:2,13), but this does not mean to say he was righteous. God does not measure your spirituality by how many wonderful visions you have, but by your obedience and morality, that is, whether you are living like Jesus. Balaam still wanted his money, so he sent Midianite women to seduce the Israelite men in an orgy of fornication and idol worship involving Canaanite fertility rites (Numbers 25:1–2, 31:8,16). The aim was to compromise the people of God and reduce them to looking like the Midianites around them in order to assimilate them – there would be nothing special or 'set apart' about them, and it would take the edge off their testimony to God and His ways. This plan is prevented from spreading by Phineas, who takes a spear and puts it through a man and woman who were fornicating. While this story may upset our Western sensibilities, it shows the seriousness of idolatry and immorality.

In fact, as we go through these epistles, we will see that worldly compromise is a regular theme – there is a very important warning message here against the compromise into which the Church has always been seduced and that prevents us from doing the job that God has given us. In the Old Testament, as well as all throughout church history, right down to the present day, the enemy's main thrust has been to bring the Church into a place of compromise, both moral (inward) and also the outward impact and associations that such compromise brings with it. If there is no distinction between our lives and those of people who worship other 'gods', the Church finds itself indistinguishable from the people around it. How can we be salt and light to people if we too indulge in idolatry and immorality?

This was an issue in Acts 15, where Jewish and Gentile Christians were sitting down together to eat – the problem was the Gentiles brought along things offered to idols, but those things were abhorrent to Jews. The 'burden' laid upon the people is to disassociate from those things that could bring them into wrong associations and so cause a compromise. However, this raises some problems that come up again later in Revelation 13, where we see people without a mark on their hand or forehead who cannot buy or sell — *How are we going to trade? How are we going to live?* This again is to do with our witness to the world.

The 'Balaamites' would seem to be people who are acting like Balaam did, trying to introduce compromise into God's people in order to curse them. There is much speculation about who exactly the Balaamites were, but we do not know, and in reality it doesn't matter – it is what they *did* which is more important.

Letter to Pergamum | Revelation 2:12–17

The Nicolaitans

The Nicolaitans first appear in the letter to Ephesus (2:6, see page 125), and similar to the Balaamites, we do not know who they were exactly. In Pergamum, the main emphasis is on the *teaching* of the Nicolaitans, rather than their deeds. It seems likely there was a group which was teaching worldly compromise; that there should not be too big a distinction between them and the world.

For the last 30–40 years in Western evangelical churches, the emphasis has been to compromise: live just like the world lives; do the things the world does; share its values and then the world will listen to you. That is exactly the opposite of what is being taught here in Revelation, which is often dismissed as old-fashioned. This is why an old friend of mine, Morgan Derham wrote a little booklet entitled *Why be different?*, because if you are a Christian, you should be different! It was necessary to write it, since even in the 1950s, Christians' lives looked no different from those of their neighbours. Our lives should be absolutely different in how we conduct ourselves, our values, our language, our priorities, how we use our money, our friends and lifestyle, and so on, which is the basis of our witness. There has got to be a difference.

These two streams – the Balaamites and the Nicolaitans – will stop you overcoming. They will try to overcome you so they can lord it over you.

Convict – 'Repent... Or I will make War' (v16)

It is interesting that when Balaam finally capitulated, he was killed 'with the sword' (Numbers 31:8, Joshua 13:22), and here is the Lord with the sword coming out of His mouth, bringing judgement upon the Balaamites and the Nicolaitans – 'I will make war against them'.

To the Overcomer... Hidden manna, White stone, New name (v17)

Hidden Manna

The first promise to the Overcomer is hidden manna, which is of course something good and sweet to eat, and this is fulfilled in Revelation 22:2 with the provision of 12 kinds of fruit on the tree of life.

In Exodus 16, the Lord provided manna for the Israelites, and commanded one jarful be kept 'before the Lord', so the people 'may see the bread that I fed you in the wilderness' – manna is a testimony to God's provision. After it was placed in the Ark of the Covenant, only the High Priest would get the chance to look at it, which also leads us onto our next promise . . .

White stone

The 'white stone' with a new name written on it could represent many things, but it may be the parallel of the hidden manna as that was round and white, like 'bdellium' (pearls) or coriander seeds. Alternatively the white stone may represent one of the precious stones on the High Priest's breast plate (and shoulders), which had the names of the 12 Tribes written on them (Exodus 28). This finds its fulfilment in Revelation 21 as the crystalline stone of which the New Jerusalem is made, which have the names of the 12 Tribes written on them. We have gone from just 12 Tribes, corporately representing God's people, to each individual having a new name written on their stone.

So whichever way we look at it, we find ourselves inside the Holy of Holies in the Tabernacle/Temple where God meets intimately with the High Priest. We are hidden, either with the manna, or with the new name written on the stone, which no one else knows. To be inside with the hidden-ness is to be in the intimacy of God.

New Name

The promise of a *new* name is fulfilled in the Marriage of the Lamb, where we take on the name of the Bridegroom, and could be corporately the 'New' Jerusalem (Revelation 21:2,9–10). So what is the 'new name' that is written on the stone? The new name is almost certainly an allusion to the name that the new people of God – Israel and the Gentiles together in the Body of Christ – was going to receive:

> For Zion's sake I will not keep silent, and for Jerusalem's sake I will not keep quiet, until her righteousness goes forth like brightness and her salvation like a torch that is burning. The nations will see your righteousness and all kings your glory, and you will be called by a new name, which the mouth of the Lord will designate and you will be a crown of beauty and a royal diadem in the hand of your God. (Isaiah 62:1–3)

The Hebrew word for salvation (*yešûāh*) is 'Jesus', so Isaiah prophesies a new name will be given to God's people when the nations see salvation (Jesus) and righteousness shining brightly 'like a torch'. This is a picture of when the Gospel breaks in and the righteousness of God is revealed (Romans 1:17). At the End of the Age, a new name will be given to those who are going to be involved in bringing the glory and the righteousness of God, both the old people of God and the new who have joined that same new name.

Later in Isaiah, God is speaking to His rebellious people:

> And you will leave your name for a curse to My chosen one.
> And the Lord will slay you.
> But My servants will be called by another name.
> Because he who is blessed in the earth shall be blessed by the God of truth. (Isaiah 65:15–16)

Again, the emphasis is upon the intimacy of that name: hidden in the secret place, where we have had a hidden life with God, we have a name that only we and He know. We have a relationship which is very precious. It seems pretty straightforward that if we get to know God well when we are here on earth, the reward is that we know Him better when we see Him face to face. If we know God little when we are here on earth, then of course the result will be that we will know Him little when we see Him face to face. Why should it all suddenly change in a moment? Of course everyone who is saved will know Him better then than we know Him now, but my point is that if we develop the capacity for intimacy now, we will enjoy that greater level of intimacy when we are with Him in glory. Again, this does not write off any Christians who do not overcome, but backslide or tail off. I have known people who have backslidden but certainly were genuine Christians; they did run well for a while and then gave up. Paul wanted to keep on running so that he wouldn't be defeated and completed his course. And that is what he had done when he was approaching the end of his life in 2 Timothy 4:7: 'I have run the race, I have kept the course. Henceforth there is laid out for me a crown of righteousness.'

Summary – Pergamum

Pergamum is a doctrinally and morally pressurized church which needs to renew and intensify its teaching, out of which new depths of intimacy will be a blessing, both in this life and the age to come.

Section I – Christ Central in the Church

Discussion Questions

In what ways is the letter to Pergamum relevant to your church?

Do you recognise the teaching of the Balaamites/Nicolaitans today?

How do you interpret the White Stone and the 'new name'?

Text – Revelation 2:18-29 | Epistle to Thyatira

¹⁸ And to the angel of the church in Thyatira write:

The Son of God, who has eyes like a flame of fire, and His feet are like burnished bronze, says this:

¹⁹ 'I know your deeds, and your love and faith and service and perseverance, and that your deeds of late are greater than at first. ²⁰ But I have this against you, that you tolerate the woman Jezebel, who calls herself a prophetess, and she teaches and leads My bond-servants astray so that they commit acts of immorality and eat things sacrificed to idols. ²¹ I gave her time to repent, and she does not want to repent of her immorality. ²² Behold, I will throw her on a bed of sickness, and those who commit adultery with her into great tribulation, unless they repent of her deeds. ²³ And I will kill her children with pestilence, and all the churches will know that I am He who searches the minds and hearts; and I will give to each one of you according to your deeds. ²⁴ But I say to you, the rest who are in Thyatira, who do not hold this teaching, who have not known the deep things of Satan, as they call them—I place no other burden on you. ²⁵ Nevertheless what you have, hold fast until I come. ²⁶ He who overcomes, and he who keeps My deeds until the end, to him I will give authority over the nations; ²⁷ and he shall rule them with a rod of iron, as the vessels of the potter are broken to pieces, as I also have received authority from My Father; ²⁸ and I will give him the morning star. ²⁹ He who has an ear, let him hear what the Spirit says to the churches.

To the angel of Thyatira (v18)

Thyatira was a commercial city with many trade guilds. Lydia, the seller of purple cloth (Acts 16:14), came from Thyatira, and this letter emphasizes business compromises in particular.

In the ancient world, to work you needed to belong to one of the guilds – it was almost essential for living. Every guild, bunch of artisans and merchants had their own gods, and in addition would also worship the Emperor. Each public gathering would involve eating food offered to these gods, and all this would make it very difficult for Christians in the first century to associate purely and clearly with God and maintain any level of public life. How can you survive if you do not belong to this or that union? You would soon be in a compromised position, unable to meet or eat or drink. We will see this theme developing through Revelation, for example only those with the mark of the Beast on their hand and forehead will able to buy or sell (see Revelation 13:16–17). This may not sound too different from the business world we see around us today.

Thyatira could mean 'sacrificial offering' and is a good description for Christian life before God, particularly so for the church there.

Ministry of Christ for Thyatira (v18)

Revelation 1:13–15 depicts the Son of Man with fiery eyes and bronze feet. However, in the letter to Thyatira it talks about the Son of *God* and His eyes and feet. So far in Revelation, the Son of God has not been mentioned – how has the Son of Man become the Son of God?

Well, wonderfully, if you go back to Daniel 7 the Son of Man is presented to the Ancient of Days. If you return to Daniel 3, which has many parallels with chapter 7, there is 'one like a Son of God' walking in the midst of the fire with the three friends. Skipping forward to Daniel 10, we see the Son of Man from Daniel 7 described with imagery of the Son of God from chapter 3: 'His eyes were like flaming torches, His arms and feet like the gleam of polished (burnished) bronze' (v6). So Daniel himself makes the equation: Son of Man = Son of God (for more on this, see my book *The Kingdom of Jesus*). In fact some Jewish rabbis had already equated the Son of God from chapter 3 with the Son of Man in chapters 7 and 10, and here in Revelation John is following the same pattern – the Son of Man is thoroughly divine and equated with the Son of God.

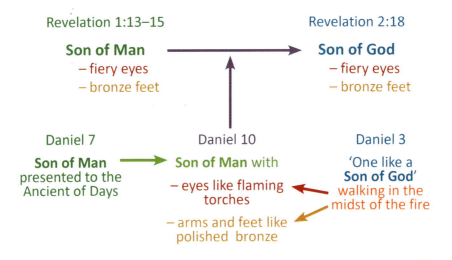

The eyes like flames of fire are eyes of incisiveness, they will search into you – 'He who searches' (v23). He is not going to be deceived. His feet of burnished bronze mean he has stood in places of challenge and difficulty, like Daniel's friends in the fiery furnace.

🔎 'I know' … your deeds (v19)

The issues at Thyatira sound much like those at Pergamum, but this time it is not the teaching, but the *practice* of the church which is in focus. Again it is the pressure of worldly compromise and conformity that is pushing in.

On one hand, Thyatira is doing quite well, and are commended for 'your deeds, and your love and faith and service and perseverance . . .' which are all things that show Christ to the world. It is interesting that the church in Ephesus have lost their first love and aren't doing as well as they had to begin with, but the church in Thyatira have improved and their deeds are a bit better than at first.

⚠️ Criticism – Jezebel (v20)

However, despite this improvement, Jesus has a very serious criticism, which is that they are giving place to 'Jezebel', a self-proclaimed prophetess who is teaching and leading people into idolatry and immorality. Jezebel, a Sidonian princess, appears in the Old Testament in 1 & 2 Kings, where she marries Israel's king Ahab and leads him and the whole nation into idolatry serving Baal and Asherah (power and sex). As well as her influence on Ahab, Jezebel 'killed the prophets of the Lord', threatened to kill Elijah who fled for his life (1 Kings 18—19) and organised Naboth's execution (1 Kings 21). Her actions against Israel and God led to her gruesome end in 2 Kings 9.

Some people have used the example of Jezebel in this letter to argue that therefore all women should not be allowed to prophesy, or teach or lead men in church – any women who tries to exercise authority is seen as a 'Jezebel'. But Jezebel was clearly *not* condemned because she was *female*, but because she was immoral and idolatrous. Both men and women can be deceitful, however we do not apply Ahab's example to say that no men can be in authority.

To prophesy simply means 'to speak forth' (see 1 Corinthians 14:3). In the New Testament age women are expected to prophesy:

> I will pour out My Spirit on *all* humanity;
> then your sons *and your daughters* will prophesy.
> (Joel 2:28, and quoted by Peter in Acts 2:17 after Pentecost)

and in Acts 21 we read about Philip's four daughters who were all prophetesses, as well as Anna in Luke 2, and Miriam, Deborah, Huldah and Isaiah's wife in the Old Testament. We also see godly women teaching others, including men – Priscilla (Acts 18:24–26) and Deborah (Judges 4). Finally, the Bible also shows women with gifts of leadership in both the Old Testament (Miriam and Deborah) and the New Testament (Phoebe, a deacon = minister, and Junia, an apostle, in Romans 16:1–16).

In fact, there are examples of women in each of the fivefold ministries and using all of the spiritual gifts listed in the New Testament, as we discuss in the book written by my wife Faith and myself: *Women and the Kingdom*.

Going back to Thyatira, obviously the church is being contaminated by this compromised teaching, leading them astray so that they are being sucked into the values of the surrounding society. As mentioned before, business meetings would take place in temples, and involve eating food sacrificed to idols. While the details may seem alien to us, the principles are the same 2,000 years later – business lunches with extravagant expenditure, parties you have to be seen at or special favours you need to give in order to clinch the deal. Not going along with this, especially if you start evangelising, will mark you out as unacceptable.

That was the pressure going on in Thyatira and just as today, acquiescing to this culture will compromise believers, who soon find they have no testimony left.

 Challenge – 'Repent...' (v21–25)

In this letter it is not only the church, but also Jezebel who are challenged to repent. The outcome of unrepentance for Jezebel will be a 'bed of sickness', which I don't think is an allusion to sexual activity, even though fornication is a result of apostasy, but more a symbol of weakness and disease. This may also be what kills her children (v23). It is the testimony of the church in Thyatira that is now on a bed of sickness, and will suffer 'great tribulation' unless they repent – our sin can make us sick and cause suffering not just to us but to others near to us. If we repent, everything can change.

It is possible that even Jezebel's future is redeemable – it says 'Behold, I *will* throw her on a bed of sickness... *unless*...' Indeed, the fact that God has given her the time and opportunity to repent shows that, despite the gravity of her wrongdoing, there is the opportunity for change.

We will be looking more carefully at what the 'great tribulation' might mean when we get to Revelation 7, but it is important to note the effect will be felt globally: it isn't just the church in Thyatira that will know about Jesus' searching eyes, but all the churches.

According to your deeds (v23)

The phrase 'according to your deeds' occurs in a few places in the New Testament, and is to do with judgement. It has both positive and negative connotations: those who do good deeds will be rewarded by the Lord according to their deeds, for example:

> [God] will repay each person according to what they have done. (Romans 2:6, NIV – see Psalm 62:12, Proverbs 24:12)

but also those who do bad deeds will receive what they deserve, for example:

> Beware of practicing your righteousness before men to be noticed by them; otherwise you have no reward with your Father who is in heaven. So when you give to the poor, do not sound a trumpet before you, as the hypocrites do... so they may be honoured by men... they have their reward in full. (Matthew 6:1–2, also v5)

> For we must all appear before the judgment seat of Christ, so that each one may be recompensed for his deeds in the body, according to what he has done, whether good or bad. (2 Corinthians 5:10)

If you desire a worldly reward, you will get what you deserve, but you won't get a heavenly reward. The good news is that not everybody in the church is like this: there are 'the rest' who do not follow Jezebel's teaching, who do not know 'the deep things of Satan'.

The deep things of Satan (v24)

These so-called 'deep things' are probably occult rites or teaching, which this Jezebel claims are some kind of special knowledge about God. This could have been the beginning of what was later called Gnosticism, which took bits of Judaism and Christianity mixed together with pagan spiritual ideas and Greek philosophy to create a heretical sect, who claimed to be superior because they had special revelations and knowledge about God (*gnosis* means knowledge). While the gnostics may have called these 'the deep things of God', in reality it is Satan who comes up out of the deep, the Abyss, and they are things that belong to him.

So what is the burden that is placed on these faithful ones in Thyatira? It is the same 'burden' as mentioned in Acts 15, which includes the main issues raised in this letter – immorality and eating things sacrificed to idols:

> For it seemed good to the Holy Spirit and to us to lay upon you no greater burden than these essentials: that you abstain from things sacrificed to idols and from blood and from things strangled, and from fornication. (Acts 15:28)

 ## To the Overcomer – Authority over the nations/Morning Star (v26–28)

The promises to the Overcomers are that they will rule over the nations with a rod of iron and will be given the Morning Star. The parallel verses where these promises are fulfilled are in Revelation 22:5,16:

> And there will no longer be any night; and they will not have need of the light of a lamp nor the light of the sun, because the Lord God will illumine them; and they will reign forever and ever . . .

'I, Jesus, have sent My angel to testify to you these things for the churches. I am the root and the descendant of David, the bright morning star.'

Authority over the nations (v26–27)

Having authority over the nations means the Overcomer will rule with Christ. However, some people struggle with the strong imagery used here of a 'rod of iron' and pottery being 'broken to pieces' – does this fit with the God of Love who is revealed in Jesus? To understand this we need to look at the Old Testament sources of these images.

First of all, Jeremiah 51:20:

> You are my war-club, My weapon of war. And with you I will shatter nations and with you I will destroy kingdoms.

The background is that God took up Nebuchadnezzar and through him used Babylon to bring judgement upon His people, Israel. This 'war club' was an instrument to bring some degree of punishment or destruction.

We then turn to Psalm 2:8–9:

> Ask of Me and I will surely give the nations as your inheritance,
> And the ends of the earth as Your possession.
> You shall break [or 'rule'] them with a rod of iron,
> You shall shatter them like earthenware.

Ancient Hebrew was written using only consonants with the vowels added in while reading. Without vowels, the word translated here as 'break / rule' is the same as the word 'shepherd' – they come from the same root. It is interesting that while most translations render it as 'break' in Psalm 2 (NASB includes 'rule' in the margin), both in the Septuagint and here in Revelation the Greek translation means 'to feed, to tend a flock, keep sheep' or 'to rule, govern'. Also 'rod' can be read as 'sceptre' or 'staff'. So verse 9 could be read 'you shall *shepherd* them with an iron *staff*'. So although God could use Babylon as a war club to shatter the nations, there is also a strong hint of a caring shepherd's heart behind this imagery: the shepherd would use his staff to keep the sheep in line, to care for them and make sure they do not go astray, as well as protecting them from being devoured by wild animals (John 10:10–12).

Here Jesus promises to share His authority with the Overcomer, who will 'shepherd/rule over the nations with a staff of iron' – if we overcome we will reign with Him (2 Timothy 2:12). It is important to note that Jesus 'received authority from My *Father*' (Revelation 2:28), and this Father-Son-ship brings us back again to Psalm 2. God is first brought before us as 'Father' in the exodus:

> When Israel was a youth I loved him,
> And out of Egypt I called My son.
> (Hosea 11:1, quoted in Matthew 2:15)

not as the Father of each of us individually, but as Father of the nation – God introduces corporate Father-and-Son-ship. However, following centuries of Israel's apostasy, eventually God declares to David:

> I will raise up your descendant after you . . . and I will establish the throne of his kingdom forever. I will be a father to him and he will be a son to Me. (2 Samuel 7:12–14)

At this point, the covenant is narrowed down, and the sonship which was first offered to Israel, is reduced to one Israelite in the line of David, to whom God says in Psalm 2:

> You are My Son, Today I have begotten You. (v7)

NB, the NIV, NLT AND CSB translations all say: 'Today I have become your father', but this is misleading as the word 'father' is not there in the Hebrew. The Hebrew actually means 'Today I have *placed you as a son*', which is to do with receiving an inheritance, not some kind of process of adoption, as some might have interpreted it.

So now the relationship is individual, not just corporate Father-and-Son-ship – but more than that: the Son-of-God-ship is realised in the one man Messiah, and as Christians we are part of His one body. God's promise is revamped on a whole new level and, because we are found in *the Son* we are sons and daughters of God and will share in His inheritance and authority. That is the process whereby God has fulfilled His prophecies and kept His promises to be a Father to Israel – it wasn't the whole body of people brought out of Egypt, it was one who went through death, burial, resurrection and now incorporates the whole church within Himself.

Section I – Christ Central in the Church

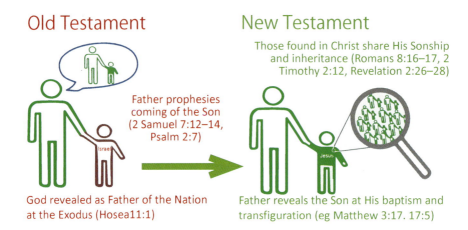

The Morning Star (v28)

'The morning star' is the first star that comes out in the morning, and here it is also an allusion to the resurrection of Jesus and the dawning of the new Kingdom Age, in which the Overcomer will share and reign with Christ. It is also another reference to Balaam, who prophesied about a coming king or Messiah, who will come with a shepherd's staff or rod (see v27):

> A star will come out of Jacob; a sceptre (staff) will rise out of Israel. (Numbers 24:17)

So to be given 'the morning star' is to receive the Messiah, and share in His resurrection and reign over the earth, as prophesied in Daniel 12:2–3.

Putting all these references together the general impression is that we will reign with Christ, but that this reign is conditional on overcoming – it is never just, *'If you are a Christian, you will reign with Christ'*, but that *'If we endure, we shall reign with Him'*. Again this does not tell us about what will happen to those who do not overcome, except that they will not reign with Christ and they will not receive the Morning Star.

Summary – Thyatira

The church in Thyatira is in serious danger of being led astray, and unless they repent, they will suffer the consequences. There is hope for the faithful remnant that they will rise and shine like a Morning Star in the resurrection.

Letter to Sardis | Revelation 3:1–6

Discussion Questions

In what ways is the letter to Thyatira relevant to your church?

What would Jesus' fiery eyes see in your life?

Are there things you tolerate which God may not?

Revelation 3

John writes Jesus' letters to the last 3 Churches: Sardis, Philadelphia and Laodicea.

Text 3:1–6 | Epistle to Sardis

> ¹ To the angel of the church in Sardis write:
>
> He who has the seven Spirits of God and the seven stars, says this: 'I know your deeds, that you have a name that you are alive, but you are dead. ² Wake up, and strengthen the things that remain, which were about to die; for I have not found your deeds completed in the sight of My God. ³ So remember what you have received and heard; and keep it, and repent. Therefore if you do not wake up, I will come like a thief, and you will not know at what hour I will come to you. ⁴ But you have a few people in Sardis who have not soiled their garments; and they will walk with Me in white, for they are worthy. ⁵ He who overcomes will thus be clothed in white garments; and I will not erase his name from the book of life, and I will confess his name before My Father and before His angels. ⁶ He who has an ear, let him hear what the Spirit says to the churches.'

To the angel of Sardis (v1)

Sardis may mean 'renewal' and was the capital city of Lydia. It was strategically important, which led to it being attacked and conquered by successive empires, such as Cyrus in the sixth century BC. It was naturally fortified, but on at least two occasions was captured because the guard did not keep a watch. It was also burnt down in the Ionian revolt and destroyed by an earthquake in AD 17 before being rebuilt. Sardis was famously the home of King Croesus who had made it rich, but by the first century AD it had grown slack and was in decline.

Ministry of Jesus – 7 Spirits & 7 Stars (v1)

This letter is from 'He who has the 7 Spirits of God and the 7 Stars', which are seen in the First Vision in Revelation 1:4,16. As we looked at in Revelation 1:20 (page 100), in that day, lights/lamps were flames, and stars were lights/flames in the sky. So here, the one who holds the burning stars is also the one who has the oil of the Holy Spirit to keep them burning, and brings the two together. Jesus is Lord over the fullness of the Church (7 stars) and supplies it with the fullness of the Spirit (7 Spirits) through being the anointed one, or 'Christ'. What Sardis needed, and what we need to keep our flame burning, is a greater flow of the Holy Spirit.

'I know ... your deeds' (v1)

There is a difference of opinion here: the church has made a name for itself with its deeds, and looks spiritually alive, however the Lord says 'But you are dead'. The criticism levelled at Sardis is they are resting on their laurels, thinking they are doing quite well, but in reality they are spiritually dead. It is a very deceptive thing to have a name that you are alive if you are not – people may keep saying you are alive, but it is the Lord's opinion that matters.

There are many who glory in church history because they have inherited a name – Wesleyan, Lutheran, Quaker, and so on – but this can lead to a kind of denominational superiority, living in what God has done in the past and not the present. We are meant to be living every second of our lives in love and obedience to Christ – then we will have a name which is alive.

Criticism – Incomplete deeds (v2)

The hope for Sardis is they can 'wake up' and 'strengthen the things that remain, which were about to die': there is hope for bruised reeds and smouldering wicks (Isaiah 42:3). It is an injunction Jesus gave again and again: the dead are only sleeping and can rise again (Mark 5:41), and in Gethsemane Jesus urged His disciples to wake up and pray for strength (Matthew 26:40–41). So we too can 'wake up' and have hope if we are weak, or even about to die, that we can be restored to full life. It is possible to be a Christian who is about to 'die'. For example, in Romans Paul says 'those that live without subduing the deeds of the body – you are about to die' (Romans 8:13).

Incompleteness is often the avenue through which the enemy can get in and attack us. Butterfly Christians who flit from one thing to the next and never see anything through to the end, are vulnerable to the enemy making all the things they are doing useless. It is not an issue of personality or disposition, it is a problem with commitment to the things God has given you to do.

Challenge – 'Repent . . .' (v3–4)

It is important for us to complete the Lord's purposes in our lives. How do we do this? It is straightforward: *Remember* what you have received and heard, and keep it. *Read* your Bible and pray, and apply it to your life. Finally and most importantly, *Repent*. Repentance is essential for continual Christian living. It means we need to keep adjusting our understanding, adjusting our actions, being willing to be challenged about the way we are living.

Like a thief in the night (v3)

Jesus refers to the Son of Man coming like a thief and taking people by surprise when He talks about His Second Coming:

> Be dressed in readiness, and keep your lamps lit. Be like men who are waiting for their master when he returns from the wedding feast, so that they may immediately open the door to him when he comes and knocks . . . But be sure of this, that if the head of the house had known at what hour the thief was coming, he would not have allowed his house to be broken into. You too, be ready; for the Son of Man is coming at an hour that you do not expect.
> (Luke 12:35–40, also Matthew 24:42–44)

Then in the following chapter in Matthew we also have the parable of the Ten Virgins: all ten are sleeping and the Bridegroom comes and takes them by surprise, but only five of them are ready and can enter the wedding feast.

The image of a thief is also used by Paul:

> For you yourselves know very well that the day of the Lord will come just like a thief in the night. (1 Thessalonians 5:2, csb)

As such, some people treat the warning to the church in Sardis as meaning at the Second Coming. However, as discussed on page 114, in six of the letters Jesus says 'I will come', and while in each case it could mean at the Second Coming, there are places where it certainly makes more sense to interpret it as a kind of foreshadowing of this, with Jesus coming by His Spirit. So 'I will come like a thief' can be seen in both ways – as anticipations of the Second Coming, which build up towards the final Day of the Lord.

The emphasis here is on being alert, watching and praying. The image of a thief appears negative, but it is not that Jesus is going to try and trick people – rather it is the devil who comes to steal and wants to snatch away all the benefits and rewards we would gain. When Jesus comes again, those who are not ready, and do not have their lamps lit, will be robbed, so this is a warning picture of what will happen if we are not alert.

Later on in Revelation 16:15 again Jesus says 'Behold, I am coming like a thief . . .' between the 6th and 7th Bowls of Wrath, followed by another warning to stay awake: 'Blessed is the one stays awake and keeps his clothes . . .' which may be an allusion to the temple guards who, it is said, sometimes had their garments burnt if they were found asleep at their post, to shame them.

 ## To the Overcomer... Clothed in White / Book of Life / Confessed (v5)

There are Overcomers in Sardis (v4) and there are three promises to them: they will be clothed in white 'for they are worthy', their name will not be erased from the Book of Life, and Jesus will confess their name to the Father and His angels.

These promises all flow together and are fulfilled together in Revelation 21, when the Bride comes out of heaven clothed in wedding garments. The New Jerusalem is the Bride and the names of those who are allowed in and out of the city are written in the Book of Life, and will be confessed before the Father.

Clothed in White (v5)

In the vision in Revelation 1, Jesus is crowned with a white head and white hair. Those who overcome will be clothed in *white* and will *walk* with the Lord, because they are *worthy*. Remember that in Revelation white represents righteousness – white garments appear seventeen times, and always symbolise righteousness or winning the victory.

Walking with the Lord takes us back to the Disciples who walked with Jesus, and these Overcomers clearly are disciples of Christ. More than that, it echoes right back to the Garden of Eden, and the restoration of what Adam and Eve forfeited – walking with God.

Jesus defines what being 'worthy' means in Matthew 10:

> He who loves father or mother more than Me is not worthy of Me; and he who loves son or daughter more than Me is not worthy of Me. And he who does not take his cross and follow after Me is not worthy of Me. He who has found his life will lose it, and he who has lost his life for My sake will find it. (Matthew 10:37–39, NASB)

Notice it is the Lord who says whether we are worthy or not. It is not biblical to say that *none* of us is worthy – it is not up to us. While it is true that we cannot make ourselves worthy, the Lord is looking for worth in our lives and some are worthy and some are not. Worthiness in Matthew 10 is in the context of being confessed before the Father, which we will look at below.

Not Erased from the Book of Life (v5)

Overcomers will not be erased from the Book of Life, but what does that mean? How and when are their names written in? And what happens to those whose names are erased?

Different theological positions take various views on who is written in the Book of Life and when, generally reflecting their stance on whether people can lose their salvation or not (see Discussion Topic below). In one view, those written in the Book of Life are predetermined from eternity – God has already chosen those whose names are written in. In the other view, the Book of Life is seen as synonymous with salvation, so your name is written in when you are saved.

However, in both cases being 'blotted out' or 'erased' from the book presents a problem. In the first case it is impossible to be erased because only 'the elect' are written in the book in the first place so therefore cannot be removed. This renders Jesus' promise of names not being erased meaningless. In the second case, someone's name being erased means their salvation is taken away, which would mean it is not really a free gift of grace. Neither of these makes sense of Scripture. Is there an alternative?

I would suggest this, as with the other promises to the Overcomer, is to do with the doctrine of rewards and losses (see Discussion Topic on page 118) – there is a difference between our salvation, which is a free gift, and our reward, which is a prize given to us based upon our deeds. If the Book of Life represents our *reward* and not our *salvation*, it means there is a prize for the Overcomer whose name is in the Book, but also those whose names are erased are not necessarily losing their salvation.

So what is the reward? As we will see when we get to Revelation 20:6, the Bible indicates there are two resurrections – the First Resurrection for those found in Christ, who will then rule and reign with Him, and then a Second Resurrection for everyone else (for more on the two resurrections see my book on rewards and losses: *Gold, Silver & Precious Stones*). If someone's name being written in the Book of Life symbolises being part of that First Resurrection of the righteous, then it being erased merely means they forfeit that reward. However, they may still receive their salvation at the Second, general Resurrection before the Great White Throne, as we will see in Revelation 20. Here the Book of Life appears again, but the picture gets more complicated as there are also other 'books':

> And I saw the dead, the great and the small, standing before the throne, and books were opened; and another book was opened, which is the Book of Life; and the dead were judged from the things which were written in the books, according to their deeds . . . And if anyone's name was not found written in the Book of Life, he was thrown into the lake of fire. (Revelation 20:12,14–15)

We will look at what the other books represent and what the Second Death/ Lake of Fire means in more detail when we get to Revelation 20. However, we now run into an intriguing problem: I have suggested those raised at the First Resurrection are those whose names are written in the Book of Life, but in Revelation 20 it seems as though the names of some of those in the Second Resurrection are *also* written in the Book of Life. 'The dead' (who cannot include those already alive in the First Resurrection) are raised before the Great White Throne, are judged, and those *not in* the Book of Life are then thrown into the Lake of Fire. It doesn't make sense of the text if *everyone* in the Second Resurrection is automatically thrown into the Lake of Fire – some *are* saved at this point. What would be the point of the Great White Throne if none are saved?

If we compare the parallel passage of Jesus' description of the final judgment in Matthew 25, we see that from among the nations there are 'Sheep' who are saved, and 'Goats' who are not, seemingly based on what they did or didn't do. Combining these passages it seems 'the Sheep' were not written in the Book of Life at the First Resurrection, but are by the Second Resurrection. This poses more questions; since they are among 'the dead' how could they have done anything to be added to the Book? When are their names added and why?

But as already mentioned, the problem is that those who did not overcome would lose eternal salvation. If at some point between the First and Second Resurrections the names of backsliders and others who did not overcome in their faith are added in to the Book of Life, it shows our Lord is a God of second chances. Even if we miss out on our reward at the First Resurrection, we still have our free gift of eternal life.

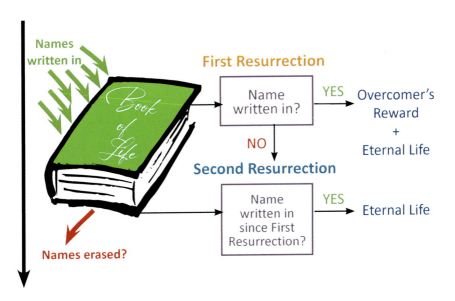

So it may be more helpful to envisage the Book of Life as a list of those who are 'ready for Resurrection' at each point – the Overcomers are in there for the First Resurrection, and 'the Sheep' are added in before or during the Final Judgment.

This is also in agreement with how the Book of Life is portrayed in the Old Testament as the situation of being in God's presence (see Discussion Topic below). In Exodus 32, to Moses being in God's Book meant being physically alive in God's presence, because God was with Israel in the Wilderness, and in Revelation we see the continuation of this into spiritual eternal life. In both cases being in the Book of Life represents the status of being one of God's people entering the inheritance.

Discussion Topic: The Book of Life

The Book of Life appears four times in Revelation (3:5, 13:8, 17:8, 21:27), but also in the Old Testament and elsewhere in the New Testament. What is the Book of Life? What exactly does it mean to be written in, or blotted out of it? As there are so few references to the Book of Life in Scripture, and those there are, are rather oblique, it is difficult to be definitive. Many see it as God's list of who is going to get in to Heaven, but does this fit with how the term is used in the Bible?

The various theological standpoints differ on who, when and how people are put in the Book of Life, largely reflecting their views on whether people can lose their salvation. Some say those 'in the Book' have been written there since eternity as part of God's perfect plan, and their salvation is inevitable (citing for example Revelation 13:8). However, this view makes Jesus' words in Revelation 3:5 about not being erased from the Book of Life meaningless – if it cannot happen, why does Jesus suggest it could? Another view sees the Book of Life as representing salvation – you are put in when you are saved, and if you are erased it means you lose your salvation. But if salvation is a free gift of grace, how can it be taken away from us? Neither of these views makes sense of the Scriptures.

Letter to Sardis | Revelation 3:1–6

The Book of Life is figurative and represents some kind of state of life or existence which is defined by God – it is not an actual book. The first allusion we get to a Book of Life is in Exodus where Moses pleaded with God:

> 'Alas, this people has committed a great sin, and they have made a god of gold for themselves. But now, if You will, forgive their sin – and if not, please blot me out from Your book which You have written!' The Lord said to Moses, 'Whoever has sinned against Me, I will blot him out of My book.' (Exodus 32:32–33)

But when Moses says 'blot me out of Your Book', he was not making a substitution of redemption, saying '*Send me to eternal punishment and let them live*' – rather he was saying, '*Let me die and let the children of Israel carry on*'. So in the Old Testament, the Book seems to be more to do with physical dying, not eternal life or death.

We also see this in Psalm 69:28, where David is asking for judgment on his enemies:

> May they be blotted out of the book of life
> And may they not be recorded with the righteous.

However, this is a Messianic psalm, with verse 21 reflecting the Crucifixion, and so there is a prophetic sense that the Messiah's enemies will be wiped out of the Book of Life.

There are various references to books in the Old Testament, but I would suggest these are not referring to the Book of Life – for example, Psalm 56:8 is talking about a record of right and wrong, the book in Psalm 139:16 is about gestation and Malachi 3:16 is a book of remembrance.

Daniel seems to refer to the Book of Life:

> And there will be a time of distress . . . and at that time your people, everyone who is found written in the book, will be rescued. (Daniel 12:1)

Moving to the New Testament, Jesus may be talking about the

Book of Life when he says 'but rejoice that your names are recorded in heaven' (Luke 10:20), and in Hebrews 12:23 it mentions the 'church of the firstborn who are enrolled in heaven' (ie Overcomers) gathering in the New Jerusalem. In Philippians, Paul talks of his fellow workers 'whose names are in the Book of Life' (Philippians 4:3) – surely Paul is not just saying they are saved, because his list would be much longer, but rather these are people who are overcoming and worthy of reward.

The Book of Life is not so much about salvation, but about participation in the full life of the paradise of God – we could call it the Book of the Redeemed. To be resurrected is to enter into full life with God. The one who overcomes will not be erased, so that is what we should aim for, rather than exploring what we could get away with.

Confessed before the Father (v5)

We saw above what it means to be 'worthy' in Matthew 10, which is in the context of confessing Jesus:

> Therefore everyone who confesses Me before men, I will also confess him before My Father who is in heaven. But whoever denies Me before men, I will also deny him before My Father who is in heaven. (Matthew 10:32–33)

Confessing His name is fundamental in our Lord's teaching, and rather than denying Jesus, we should be denying ourselves:

> If anyone wishes to come after Me, he must deny himself, and take up his cross and follow Me. For whoever wishes to save his life will lose it; but whoever loses his life for My sake will find it. (Matthew 16:24–25, also Luke 9:23–24)

If we confess Christ He will confess us to His Father – that is what it is to be worthy of Christ. An important question is whether Jesus is talking to non-believers about a confession of faith in Him at salvation, or more generally to

His followers to keep on confessing Him in their lives. In Matthew 10 & 16, and Luke 9 Jesus is addressing the 12 Disciples, so it is much more likely to do with confessing Christ as part of a life of faith. It is also important to note that if salvation were based on our confession, that could be seen as salvation by works, not by grace.

This again leads us back to the question of whether there are Christians who do not overcome, and if so what happens to them? Of course, confessing Christ is fundamental to real living faith, but if any opportunity is missed does that mean we are denied before the Father? Or taking an extreme example of a believer denying the Lord while under torture, will they be lost for eternity? If someone else, who under the same pressure and pain did still confess Christ and were saved, would they have earned their salvation?

One example of this in the New Testament is Peter – he was one of the 12 Disciples, but denied Jesus three times under duress. Was Peter lost forever? No. Jesus not only restores him as a Disciple, but commissions him as a leader to shepherd His sheep (John 21:15–19). So confession is about how we live our lives as a Christian, not what defines whether we are a Christian or not. Overcoming is essential for the full blessings that God intended for every one of us, but if we fail to reach those it does not mean that we are lost forever and ever.

Discussion Topic: Once saved always saved?

This is a very contentious topic – can a Christian lose their salvation, or once they have made a confession is salvation guaranteed, no matter what they do in life?

On one hand, Augustinian Calvinists, and others influenced by them, say 'once saved, always saved' – this is because in their view God already decided who would be saved or not. On the other hand, Arminians say you have to endure right through your Christian walk and only then you will be saved, and if you don't you will lose your salvation. Is there a third way between these polarized views?

First, salvation is a free unmerited gift of grace, which by definition cannot be taken from us. Second, God's lovingkindness endures forever (Psalm 136:1), and He will forgive us 70 × 7 times (Matthew 18:22) – He wants all to be saved and come to repentance (1 Timothy 2:4, 2 Peter 3:9). We are accepted of God in His love (Ephesians 1:6). No one will snatch us from His hand (John 10:28–29).

However I would add one qualification – while we cannot have our salvation taken from us, we may throw it away if we choose to. We can walk away from God and break that relationship by saying we do not want it any more – we can jump out of His hand, even if we could not be taken from it (John 10:28). I believe this middle ground view does embrace the whole of Scripture without having to ignore some bits or try to argue them away with special pleadings. These polarisations and arguments are unnecessary: God has given us freewill and ultimately it is our decision whether to accept or reject the gift of salvation – He will not force it upon us.

Summary – Sardis

The church of Sardis is a complacent church, but if they remember what they received, and repent, they will wake up and walk in white because they are worthy.

Discussion Questions

In what ways is the letter to Sardis relevant to your church?

Do you or your church need waking up?

Do you think it is possible to 'lose your salvation'?

Letter to Philadelphia | *Revelation 3:7–13*

Text – Revelation 3:7-13 | Epistle to Philadelphia

⁷ And to the angel of the church in Philadelphia write:

He who is holy, who is true, who has the key of David, who opens and no one will shut, and who shuts and no one opens, says this:

⁸ 'I know your deeds. Behold, I have put before you an open door which no one can shut, because you have a little power, and have kept My word, and have not denied My name. ⁹ Behold, I will cause those of the synagogue of Satan, who say that they are Jews and are not, but lie – I will make them come and bow down at your feet, and make them know that I have loved you. ¹⁰ Because you have kept the word of My perseverance, I also will keep you from the hour of testing, that hour which is about to come upon the whole world, to test those who dwell on the earth. ¹¹ I am coming quickly; hold fast what you have, so that no one will take your crown. ¹² He who overcomes, I will make him a pillar in the temple of My God, and he will not go out from it anymore; and I will write on him the name of My God, and the name of the city of My God, the new Jerusalem, which comes down out of heaven from My God, and My new name. ¹³ He who has an ear, let him hear what the Spirit says to the churches.'

To the angel of Philadelphia (v7)

Philadelphia is just the Greek words for 'love' and 'brothers' put together – 'brotherly love'. After it was conquered in the fourth century BC by Alexander the Great, Philadelphia became the doorway of Greek culture into the east, as the empire spread all the way across to India. This may be behind the images of open doors in this epistle, with Philadelphia as a missionary centre for the Gospel.

Along with Smyrna, Jesus has no criticism for the Philadelphian church.

Ministry of Christ for Philadelphia – Key of David (v7)

Here the picture of Jesus in the vision is expanded and enriched. In Revelation 1:18 Jesus is the one who has 'the keys of Death and of Hades' (see page

98), which appears negative, but if you have the keys not only can you put things in, but you can also let things out. Jesus can unlock and open up Death and Hades – this is good news!

Now we have reached Revelation 3, the keys are now called 'the key of David'. This is the more positive side of the door: if people are coming out of Hades and Death, they are going into life and the Kingdom in the New Jerusalem. David means 'beloved' in Hebrew, and is used prophetically to represent the coming Messianic Kingdom – this is the Kingdom key! So the Key of David opens up the door into the Kingdom whereas the keys were at first seen as letting us out of the place of Death and Hades. We could picture it as one door, seen from two different sides.

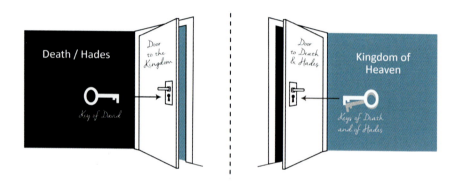

The key of David is held by the one 'who opens and no one will shut, and who shuts and no one opens'. This imagery is from Isaiah 22, where Isaiah prophesies against Shebna, the royal steward who has been exploiting his position to embezzle the king's riches seeking his own glory and building an impressive tomb for himself. God says he will depose Shebna (which means 'vigour') and install Eliakim (which means 'God establishes') in his place:

> And I will clothe him with your tunic
> And tie your sash securely about him.
> I will entrust him with your authority,
> And he will become a father to the inhabitants of Jerusalem and to the house of Judah.
> Then I will set the key of the house of David on his shoulder,

> When he opens no one will shut,
> When he shuts no one will open. (Isaiah 22:21–22)

Eliakim will be the one who opens the doors of Jerusalem to let people into the Kingdom, and open the palace doors for people to approach the throne. He will be 'a father to the inhabitants of Jerusalem', just as Jesus is a father to those who have been gathering into the new Kingdom and the reign of God (Isaiah 9:6, Hebrews 2:13b–14). Jesus has been given a key and authority to open and shut, which also resembles the apostolic authority Jesus shares with His disciples when He talks about the keys of the Kingdom of Heaven:

> I will build My church; and the gates of Hades will not overpower it. I will give you the keys of the kingdom of heaven; and whatever you bind on earth shall have been bound in heaven, and whatever you loose on earth shall have been loosed in heaven.
> (Matthew 16:18–19 and 18:18)

It is interesting that God similarly gave authority to Cyrus the Great, 'to open doors before him so that gates will not be shut' (Isaiah 45:1).

Back in Isaiah 22, Eliakim is described as like a peg or a nail, that God will drive so securely into the wall that his whole family (he is the father of the Jerusalemites) can hang onto his righteousness and authority

> I will drive him like a peg in a firm place,
> And he will become a throne of glory to his father's house.
> So they will hang on him all the glory of his father's house, offspring and issue, all the least of vessels, from bowls to all the jars.

The parallels between Jesus and Eliakim are clear. They both came to depose a liar and a cheat (the devil/Shebna), and are both given the key of David and authority to open and to shut – the way into the Kingdom and even to the King on the throne, is through them. Jesus was firmly nailed to the Cross, and carried the burden of the sins of the world, and Eliakim was nailed into a wall, and bore the weight of his people.

However, Eliakim's righteousness was not enough to keep his family lifted up forever, and we know that later on Judah and Jerusalem fell:

> 'In that day,' declares the Lord of hosts, 'the peg driven in a firm place will give way; it will even break off and fall, and the load

hanging on it will be cut off, for the Lord has spoken.'
(Isaiah 22:25–26)

This isn't saying anything bad about Eliakim or his immediate family, but that the righteousness and authority of humankind will always eventually fail and give way, as it did with Israel, whereas what Jesus did on the Cross is effective for all eternity.

🔍 'I know...Your Deeds' (v8)

Jesus says to the church: 'I know your deeds'. As there are no criticisms, only commendations and encouragements that follow, we can assume their deeds were good.

An open door (v8)

After Jesus is revealed as the one who unlocks and opens doors, He then says to the church He has opened a door before them, 'which no one can shut', because they have kept His word and not denied His name. It is not as though they are being encouraged to think they are doing wonderfully well – they only have 'a little power' – but they are holding on to the word and to the Lord's Name: 'Father'.

The Lord opened doors for Paul and Silas in Acts 16 when they were in prison. An earthquake opened the prison doors and the chains fell off, but the real open door was to demonstrate God's love to the jailer, whose whole family were saved. A number of times in his epistles, Paul talks about open doors for evangelism to preach the Gospel, with a view to getting the Good News out into all the world (see 1 Corinthians 16:9, 2 Corinthians 2:12 and Colossians 4:3). So the door Jesus is opening for the Philadelphian church may be one of evangelism.

💙 Convince – Synagogue of Satan (v9)

Here we again see 'the synagogue of Satan', which also appears in the letter to Smyrna (Revelation 2:9, see page 129). But this time the description is even stronger – it isn't just that they 'say they are Jews and are not,' but that they *lie*. Remember that Satan is the devil, 'the deceiver of the whole world' (Revelation 12:9, 2 John 1:7). Perhaps this progression indicates that here in Philadelphia there are Jews who are trying to actively pervert the work of the church, which is seeking to take up all these open doors of opportunity. These deceivers will be made to 'bow down at your feet and to know that I have loved you.'

There are three places in particular in the Old Testament, where we read that the Gentiles will come and bow down to Israel to acknowledge their God as the one true God. The first is in Isaiah 45, where slaves:

> The products of Egypt and the merchandise of Cush
> And the Sabeans, men of stature,
> Will come over to you and will be yours;
> They will walk behind you, they will come over in chains
> And *will bow down to you;*
> They will make supplication to you:
> '*Surely, God is with you, and there is none else*, No other God.'
> (Isaiah 45:14)

which is reminiscent of what Paul writes in 1 Corinthians:

> But if all prophesy, and an unbeliever or an ungifted man enters, he is convicted by all . . . the secrets of his heart are disclosed; and so he will fall on his face and worship God, declaring that God is certainly among you. (1 Corinthians 14:24–25)

So the imagery of captive slaves is now updated to those captive to the Holy Spirit, who are drawn to the Lord, coming and worshipping: '*We want to know your God*'.

We see similar prophecies in Isaiah 49:23 and Isaiah 60:14 of a coming day when people will come and acknowledge that 'God is certainly among you'. So in the letter to Philadelphia, these prophecies of people coming to Jerusalem, bowing down and acknowledging Father God are now being fulfilled.

♥ Convict – Hour of testing (v10)

It is important to interpret Revelation 3:10 with care, as there are some wildly different ideas about what 'I also will keep you from the hour of testing' means. In some interpretations it is understood as believers being taken out of the world before Jesus comes again, when there will be an hour of testing.

The phrase translated 'keep you from/out of' is *tērēō ek* and the only other place we find this in the New Testament is Jesus' High-Priestly prayer in John 17, where it is used about the Church being *in* the world, but *kept safe from* the evil one. Indeed, the noun *tērós* means a guard, so that it could be translated 'guard you'. So it does not mean we are going to be snatched out of the world secretly, or 'raptured', but that we will be in the hour of testing which is to come upon the whole world, and by God's provision and grace, kept safe.

Does it mean we will be *physically* or *spiritually* kept safe? Given that it is so full of symbolism, throughout Revelation there is a constant tension between our physical world and the spiritual realm, and we can inhabit both. I believe if we put our faith in Christ we will always be kept safe spiritually, that is, not separated from the Lord. Moreover in some instances we may be kept from physical harm, but we know this is not always the case for believers. Currently, there are testings in many parts of the world, through persecution, fear and restrictions on religious freedom. Christianity is the most persecuted religion worldwide and according to the Open Doors World Watch List, there are more than 50 countries where Christians suffer high, very high or extreme persecution. Even in many Western European nations freedom of speech and religious liberty are being eroded.

All Christians experience testing to some degree, both physical and spiritual, and we need to be kept from those 'who dwell on the earth', which is a term that will come up again and again (6:10, 8:13, 11:10, 13:14, 17:2,8), meaning those with earthly minds and worldly aspirations and values. This testing will come upon 'those who dwell on the earth', who represent those who settle for the comforts of earthly existence rather than the reality of God's Kingdom. We will look at them in more depth in Revelation 6:10 (see page 270).

Challenge – Hold Fast your Crown (v11)

Our crown represents part of our reward for being Overcomers, as we looked at with the Crown of Life in the letter to Smyrna (page 133).

Just like for Thyatira (2:25), the church in Philadelphia is also warned to 'hold fast' so that they don't lose their crown, which of course implies that somebody could take it from you. If somebody takes your crown, do you become a crownless Christian, that is, still saved but without your Overcomer's reward, or are you no longer a Christian and cast into the Lake of Fire?

If someone can take your crown, then it surely cannot represent salvation, because that is a free gift of grace, and cannot be taken from you – so it must mean something else. This makes sense in terms of the doctrine of rewards and losses (see Discussion Topic on page 118): when we are saved we have a crown set aside for us in heaven and if we 'hold fast' and overcome we will inherit the crown, which symbolises our reward of ruling and reigning with Christ. You may forfeit your crown if you let the world, the flesh and the devil lead you astray – in effect they will have taken it from you. However, losing our crown does not necessarily mean we would lose our salvation too.

 ## To the Overcomer... Pillar in the Temple / God's Name (v12)

Here the Overcomer is promised that they will become a pillar in the Temple of God, and God's Name will be written on them.

The first promise is not just to *be in* God's dwelling place, but to *be part of it* – as a supporting pillar we will never go out from it. However, when we come to Revelation 21, there is no temple in the city, 'for the Lord God the Almighty and the Lamb are its temple' (Revelation 21:22). So we will be living in God, and the whole city is now where God dwells – there are no separated parts – so there need to be plenty of pillars!

Not only will Overcomers be pillars, but these pillars will have God's name stamped upon them. Notice here that we get the same pattern as in the letter to Pergamum – if you do not deny God's Name (2:13 and 3:8) then He will write His Name upon you (2:17 and 3:12). However, here it is not just one new name that is written on a stone, but three names written on the Overcomer themselves: the name of God, the name of the city of God (New Jerusalem), and 'My new name'. It is all emphasizing this new name which will be given to His servants. I don't think we need to try to find different meanings for all these different names – some do.

In the Old Testament, the High Priestly blessing put the name of *Yahweh* upon Israel, who would then bless them (Numbers 6:24–27). To have the name of God put on us means we have: 1) the character of God, 2) the experience of God, 3) the presence of God, and 4) the authority of God. In the New Jerusalem we have been named and we are now so much in God's presence that together we form the very Temple itself.

Summary – Philadelphia

There are no criticisms for the Philadelphians, who are faithful despite their weakness. As the love of the brothers is essential for going through the open door of evangelism, they need to hold fast their name so they will receive a new name.

Section I – Christ Central in the Church

Discussion Questions

In what ways is the letter to Thyatira relevant to your church?

Are you opening doors in evangelism?

How can we be fruitful despite our weakness?

What does holding fast His name mean to you?

Text – Revelation 3:14–22 | Epistle to Laodicea

¹⁴ To the angel of the church in Laodicea write:

The Amen, the faithful and true Witness, the Beginning of the creation of God, says this:

¹⁵ 'I know your deeds, that you are neither cold nor hot; I wish that you were cold or hot. ¹⁶ So because you are lukewarm, and neither hot nor cold, I will spit you out of My mouth. ¹⁷ Because you say, "I am rich, and have become wealthy, and have need of nothing," and you do not know that you are wretched and miserable and poor and blind and naked, ¹⁸ I advise you to buy from Me gold refined by fire so that you may become rich, and white garments so that you may clothe yourself, and that the shame of your nakedness will not be revealed; and eye salve to anoint your eyes so that you may see. ¹⁹ Those whom I love, I reprove and discipline; therefore be zealous and repent. ²⁰ Behold, I stand at the door and knock; if anyone hears My voice and opens the door, I will come in to him and will dine with him, and he with Me. ²¹ He who overcomes, I will grant to him to sit down with Me on My throne, as I also overcame and sat down with My Father on His throne. ²² He who has an ear, let him hear what the Spirit says to the churches.'

To the angel of Laodicea (v14)

Laodicea means 'justice for the people', or 'overcoming for the people'. Laodicea was famous for banking, clothing and medicine, in particular for a special eye salve for treating blindness, which was renowned throughout the ancient world. But here Jesus says they are poor, naked and blind. The founder of that church was almost certainly Epaphras (see Colossians 4:12–13).

Ministry of Christ for Laodicea – The Amen (v14)

In the vision in Revelation 1, 'Amen' was not used as a name, but Jesus was called 'the faithful witness' (v5), and here is called 'the faithful *and true* Witness'. In Revelation 1:6–7, twice it suddenly says 'Amen . . . Even so, Amen' (Greek and Hebrew together), and here in the epistle to Laodicea Amen appears as the *name* of God – He is *the* 'Amen'. This almost certainly comes from Isaiah 65:15–17, which is the only place in the Old Testament where Amen is clearly used as a name for God. This is obscured in most versions, which translate it as 'the God of truth' or even 'the one true God', but literally reads:

> But My servants will be called by another name.
> Because he who is blessed in the earth
> Will be blessed by the God of Amen;
> And he who swears in the earth
> Will swear by the God of Amen;
> Because the former troubles are forgotten,
> And because they are hidden from My sight!
> For behold, I create new heavens and a new earth.

In other words, if you make an oath, remember it is by the God of Amen – God has got to agree with it: *'Let it be so'*. Interestingly the Septuagint version of Isaiah 65 translates 'Amen' using *pistis*, which means **'faith'/'faithful'** or **'truth'**. So this letter takes parts of the vision in Revelation 1:5–8 and interprets them through the lens of Isaiah 65 to give us '**the Amen – faithful and true**'.

It is important how we understand the description of Christ as 'the Beginning of the creation of God'. This does not mean Jesus was the first thing God created and therefore had a 'beginning', which is how Arius in the fourth century and more recently the Jehovah's Witnesses have interpreted it. The word for 'beginning' here is *arche*, meaning 'origin', 'source' or 'head'.

It is interesting also to look at Proverbs 8 which is the key verse used by Arius to try to argue that Jesus was a created being:

> The Lord *possessed* me at the beginning of His way,
> Before His works of old.
> From eternity I was established,
> From the beginning, from the earliest times of the earth. (vs22–23)

Wisdom is speaking, and this is widely understood as a personification of Christ, revealed as the one who says 'I will pour out my spirit on you' (Proverbs 1:23). Here some translations have, 'The Lord *created* me', but the word in Hebrew really means 'owned' or 'possessed'. As I discuss more fully in my book *Trinity: The Song and Dance God* (pages 77–82), rather than indicating Jesus, personified as Wisdom, was created, that is, had a 'beginning', it rather indicates the opposite. Jesus is 'from eternity' and was not created but conceived by the eternal begetting of the Son of God (as Origen described it) – the thoughts and wisdom of God are being constantly generated within the Godhead and this is revealed to us in the form of Jesus who communicates God's eternal thinking to us.

Jesus' everlastingness is framed in the context in which He is called 'Beginning' in the previous verse. Also in Proverbs 8:30–31, the same three Hebrew consonants are translated as 'workman' as Jesus worked in Creation, sharing in the Godhead. Jesus was there at the foundation of the world (John 1:1, 17:5, 24) and should rightly be seen as the source of Creation, not as part of it.

However, here in Revelation 3 it is not the first creation that is in view. As we have seen, the context is 'The God of Amen' in Isaiah 65, which continues 'I create a new heaven and a new earth' (v17) – we are not looking backwards but forwards to the New Creation. God is doing something totally new, and Jesus, rising from the grave, is the head of this *New Creation*, which has already begun, but will be fully revealed when we get to Revelation 21 and 22. So this is a wonderful, glorious statement: the Kingdom of God has arrived – we are in the *now* and *not yet* of the Kingdom because there is more to come.

If only the Church could get to grips with focusing on the New Creation, we would be transformed. We have already been raised together with Him in newness of life (Romans 6:4, Colossians 2:12). The life we now live in the flesh is not that dead old life we left at the Cross – 'If any man is in Christ, he is a new creation' (2 Corinthians 5:17), and Jesus is the beginning/source/head of that New Creation.

Letter to Laodicea | Revelation 3:14–22

🔍 'I know . . .' – Neither cold nor hot (v15)

I do not think we should read 'I wish that you were cold or hot' as meaning the Lord wants us to be 'cold' in our faith, it is just simply emphasizing that hot water and cold water don't make you feel sick when you drink them, unlike lukewarm water, which is an emetic. Laodicea was renowned for its sulphurous springs, which were lukewarm – it is the condition of the city and the condition of the church. The Lord would prefer us to be boiling hot for Him. Maybe even He would prefer us to be 'cold', because that would mean we didn't know Him yet, and that if we did we could become hot – however, those who are lukewarm already know the truth but are indifferent, so how can they be made hot again?

Criticism – Lukewarm (v16)

The criticism for Laodicea is perhaps the strongest and most serious statement in the Bible: 'because you are lukewarm . . . I will spit you out of My mouth' – *'You make Me sick'*. This is a terrible indictment coming from our God of Love.

In the Old Testament, God warned Israel that the Promised Land would spew them out if they lived as the Canaanites did (Leviticus 18:25,28, 20:22), and this is what happened at the Exile. The Land was Israel's inheritance, and here Jesus, who is our inheritance, is threatening to spew out the people who should be living for God, but aren't. In the land, Israel should have been flourishing and fruitful, but when sin came in they suffered drought and famine – in Jesus, we should flourish and bring forth good fruit, but sin causes that fruit to disappear, and ultimately will be spewed out. Do you think the Lord feels sick about the temperature of the Church today?

Poor, blind and naked (v17)

We then get three literal allusions to the practice and commerce of Laodicea: their wealth, their worship of Asclepius the god of medicine, and their clothing industry. Laodicea was a centre of commerce, they are 'rich and have become wealthy, and have need of nothing' – but Jesus says they are spiritually 'wretched and miserable and poor'. Laodicea had a temple to Asclepius, whose snake-entwined rod we still use as a symbol for medicine today, and was particularly renowned for an eye ointment which was used to treat blindness – but Jesus says they are spiritually 'blind'. They also produced fine cloth and clothing – but Jesus says they are spiritually 'naked'.

The church in Laodicea is materialistic and proud, and their material richness masks a spiritual shame. So what is the solution for them?

Conviction – 'Buy from Me...' (v18–22)

In each case Jesus advises them to 'buy' from Him – that is, they can trade with Him, rather than putting their faith in money, goods and reputation:

- → *'Buy from Me gold refined by fire that you may become rich...'*

  Refined by fire is seen as a description of persecution, testing or pressure – gold is refined by heating it up and the bad elements are driven out. Under testing the church can become spiritually rich and strong, when sin is driven out, like the burnished bronze feet of Jesus in the first vision.

- → *'...and white garments, that you may clothe yourself...'*

  This is so their spiritual nakedness would not be seen. These white garments are those of righteousness, and in Revelation both the Overcomers and Christ are seen clothed in white.

- → *'...and eye salve to anoint your eyes, that you may see.'*

  Their pride and reliance on themselves has blinded them, but through the Holy Spirit they will be able to see with spiritual insight, maybe even with eyes of fire, like Jesus in Revelation 1.

So although this church receives such strong criticism, we see not only an opportunity for them to repent and turn back to God, but if they 'buy' from Jesus, they can begin to look just like Him. This may be a testing and difficult process, but it is all rooted in God's love: 'Those whom I love, I reprove and discipline'. This is like Hebrews 12:6, 'Whom the Lord loves, He disciplines'.

The next verse is very well-known and loved, but, most people miss off the beginning:

> Be zealous therefore and *repent*. Behold, I stand at the door and knock...

It doesn't just say, 'Behold, I stand at the door and knock' – repentance must come first. To repent means to change your mind, so if you hear His voice, you need to repent, change your mind, and open the door.

In Song of Solomon 5:2, the loved one stands at the door and knocks, calling for his beloved to come away with him – but he is ignored and has to go away. Here Jesus is effectively quoting this. The Lord bangs on the door – when He knocks we are meant to open up to Him and fellowship together so He can serve us, just like He did with the disciples in Luke 22. We will also dine with Him – this is not just in sharing the bread and wine in communion, it also includes other times, such as Love Feasts, where believers eat together and celebrate (Jude 12). In the Early Church, every meeting was an eating meeting, so we should also take opportunities to eat together!

To the Overcomer . . . Sit on My Throne (v21)

The promise to the Overcomer here is that if they open the door to Christ they will 'sit with Me on My throne, as I also overcame and sat down with My Father on His throne'. This is fulfilled in Revelation 22:5:

> There will be no longer any night and they shall not have need of the light of the lamp nor the light of the sun, because the Lord God shall illumine them; and they shall reign forever and ever.

As well as being the last promise to the Overcomer, in a sense this is the ultimate statement of how to be an Overcomer, and sums up the other six. If we open the door of our lives and let the One who overcame into our hearts and lives, and have fellowship with Him, inevitably we will share life with Him – He has overcome already, so we will overcome also. All that Jesus is in Revelation 1 comes into us. He has already sat down on His Throne, so the life within you will also sit on His Throne.

The Christian life is not about trying to live up to certain values and rules – the Ten Commandments or the Sermon on the Mount – it is about fellowshipping with Jesus. This beautiful picture is made real simply by prayer, meditation and living in the presence of Jesus.

As with all of the overcoming promises, it raises the question of what happens if we do not open the door and let Jesus in? What is my position as a Christian? Here again, it doesn't explicitly say, but I think it is to do with the ultimate destiny that God intended for His people. We are not meant to be aiming for a second rate, sub-standard life, being dragged along into salvation – God wants us to experience the fullness of life that we were meant to enjoy.

The rewards are promised *to the Overcomer*, so we should eagerly seek those prizes the Lord wants to give us, not try to scrape by doing the minimum required. Not overcoming does not necessarily mean we are not saved, as we looked at before – however, rather than spend our time worrying about it, we should be doing all we can to be an Overcomer!

Summary – Laodicea

Laodicea is a lukewarm church, whose complacency is addressed severely by Jesus. Even though they are in danger of being rejected, the Lord is still knocking, wanting to bring overcoming back into their life together.

Discussion Questions

In what ways is the letter to Laodicea relevant to your church?

What do you think being lukewarm would look like?

How has the Lord made you rich, clothed you or helped you to see?

When have you experienced the Lord's 'knocking'?

* * *

The comprehensive Church

These 7 Letters together form a comprehensive message, not just to these 7 Churches in Asia Minor in the first century, but also to the whole Church throughout history. There are commendations and encouragements, as well as criticisms, areas for improvement and in some cases serious warnings.

Below I have brought together the main points from the letters to show the complete picture they paint of God's desire for how the Church should act, and the threats and problems that arise.

Recurrent threats to the Church

The threat to the effective witnessing and overcoming of the Church is summed up in the famous trilogy of the world, the flesh and the devil, each of which appears in these letters.

The *World* is represented by the Nicolaitans (Ephesus and Pergamum) and the closely-linked Balaamites (Pergamum). As we saw, the name 'Nicolaitans' and the story of Balaam indicate these groups are attempting to dominate and subdue God's people.

The *Flesh* is represented by Jezebel (Thyatira) who is teaching and leading people astray into idolatry and immorality.

Together, the effects of the World and the Flesh result in a slow, creeping assimilation into the ways of the world around them, compromising the witness of God's people – if the Church looks just like the world around them, then there is nothing to witness to, no message of Good News.

Almost everyone in the Roman Empire was required to pay respect and offer sacrifice to the Emperor, except for the Jews who had a special exemption. Although it was originally seen as being part of Judaism, as the Church became increasingly distinct and as such not covered by these exemptions, it came under growing pressure to show obeisance to the Emperor. Also, as the Church began to grow among the Gentiles it increasingly came up against the social pressures of Gentile society: belonging to guilds, eating food sacrificed to idols, fornication and so on. In Acts 15, this danger was recognised and averted in the Early Church to maintain their distinctiveness, and this message is reiterated in Revelation 2—3.

Finally, the devil is mentioned as in the 'synagogue of Satan' (Smyrna and Philadelphia), 'Satan's throne'/'where Satan dwells' (Pergamum), and the 'deep things of Satan' (Thyatira). These represent three different areas of the enemy's intrusion into our lives:

→ 'Synagogue of Satan' represents legalism and accusation, both from within and without, that seeks to bring down the Church. 'Satan' means 'accuser' or 'adversary' and 'devil' comes from *diabolos* which means 'liar' or 'slanderer'. This is persecution by groups or individuals in the community.

→ 'Throne of Satan' implies somewhere where the enemy rules and is firmly established, and suggests political persecution.

→ 'The deep things of Satan', indicates some kind of incipient gnosticism with their claims to have special knowledge of God, and likely represent false and heretical spirituality. Gnosticism was a very serious attack upon orthodox Christianity in the first three centuries AD.

So together, these three areas show us the kind of world into which the Revelation epistles were written, but also a full picture of the challenges faced by the Church throughout history. It is no different today.

The ninefold commendation

Each of the churches receives at least one commendation, even if they also receive serious criticism. There are nine areas of commendation:

Good works	2:2,3,5,13,19; 3:8
Patience/endurance in tribulation	2:2,3,9,10,19; 3:10
Hatred of evil/rejection of evil men	2:2,6
Faithfulness to word and name	2:10,13; 3:10
Faith	2:13,19
Love	2:4,19
Seizing opportunities	3:8
Holiness	3:4
Wholeheartedness	2:19

The ninefold condemnation

Similarly, there are nine condemnations of the churches in these epistles, although importantly two of the churches receive no criticism.

False apostles	2:2
Loss of love	2:4,5
Hypocrisy and pretence	2:9; 3:9
Deeds and doctrines of Nicolaitans/Balaamites	2:6–15
Tolerating evil people/teaching/practices	2:14,20

Lying name	3:1
Carelessness	3:3
Lukewarmness	3:15,16
Impenitence (challenged to 'repent')	2:5,16,21,22; 3:3,19

The seven values of the Church

Each epistle can be summed up in a value which the Lord is looking for in the Church, which is linked to the meaning of their name: in Ephesus, which means 'Desirable' the value is *Love*. In Smyrna ('Myrrh'), the value is *suffering endurance*. *Pure teaching* is the value in the letter to Pergamum ('Height'). For Thyatira ('Sacrifice') and Sardis ('Renewal') they are *Holiness* and *Genuineness*. Philadelphia means 'Brotherly Love' and this letter emphasizes the value of *Evangelism*. Finally, the epistle to Laodicea ('Justice for People') highlights the value of *Humility*.

When you put together the values that predominate in each of the 7 Churches they present a very strong and beautiful expression of Church: love, suffering endurance, pure teaching, holiness, genuineness, evangelism and humility. This is what we are supposed to look like.

Discussion Questions

Which of these things can your church be commended for?

In what way can we best avoid these condemnations?

How can our churches continue to grow in these 7 values?

Section II
Christ Central in Creation

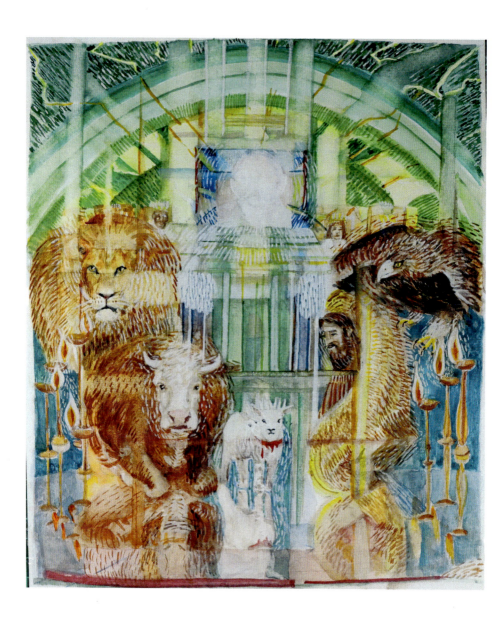

Christ Central in Creation
Revelation 4:1–5:14 | The Second Vision

The first section of Revelation ends with Overcomers on the earth opening the door to Jesus when He knocks:

> If anyone hears My voice and opens the door, I will come in to him and will dine with him, and he with Me. (3:20–21)

and the second vision begins with a door open in heaven:

> After these things I looked, and behold, a door *standing* open in heaven (4:1)

If you open the door to Christ and let Jesus into your life, you find the same thing has happened in the heavens. Heaven has come down to earth/earth has gone up to heaven – the door is two-way.

Revelation is revealing the things that lie behind the universe and behind our lives. In that spirit realm there are spiritual powers, like God Himself, who is Spirit (John 4:24), and other spiritual forces, the demonic and the angelic, as well as our own spirits, which also exert power. All of this is unseen but needs to be revealed to us, because this is where as Christians, we live and move and have our being (Acts 17:28).

Since the Enlightenment in the eighteenth century, human beings have increasingly dismissed the notion there are spiritual forces at work, but it is impossible to make sense of life unless we can get an answer to why it is that human beings are capable of some of the devilish things they do. Carl Jung, one of the founders of modern psychology, when he looked at the Holocaust, said that the only way to account for how the Jews had been treated in the Buchenwald concentration camp was to revive 'the ancient biblical concept of demons' (see Paul Tournier, *The Whole Person in a Broken World*).

If the book of Revelation does nothing else, it makes us very conscious of the realm to which we are all going, and aware of those forces that we cannot rationalise scientifically, but which seem to be at work in the world. Some of those forces are, of course, at work *through* humans, but as much as we can try to change the world at a human level, things never seem to get better. It is the powers *behind* this that we need to try to understand and contend with.

So, as grotesque and bizarre as at times it might seem, Revelation is showing us what things are really like. Rather than the well-presented politicians who are running the world at the moment, we see the horrific realities of the forces that are actually governing and being released into the world. Many of us may not like to think about this too much – we may prefer to think that everybody is quite nice really . . . but the truth is, those powers are not! We may like to think that we are immune to their deception, but unless we live in the Spirit, under the blood of Christ, we will be deceived. In Revelation, the devil is revealed to us four times as the one who deceives the nations (Revelation 12:9; 20:3,8,10) – deception is at the heart of what is going on in this background flow of energy. So what hope is there against these powers?

Major Prophets

When we look at Revelation 4—5, we see the four visions of the four major prophets all squeezed together into one magnificent, explosive vision of God. In Isaiah we see a vision of the Lord on a throne surrounded by winged seraphim:

> In the year of King Uzziah's death I saw the Lord sitting on a throne, lofty and exalted, with the train of His robe filling the temple. Seraphim stood above Him, each having six wings: with two he covered his face, and with two he covered his feet, and with two he flew. And one called out to another and said,
>
> > 'Holy, Holy, Holy, is the Lord of hosts,
> > The whole earth is full of His glory.' (Isaiah 6:1–3)

Then in the great vision that Ezekiel has of the awesomeness of God, we see 4 Living Creatures around the throne, each with four faces:

> As for the form of their faces, each had the face of a man; all four had the face of a lion on the right and the face of a bull on the left, and all four had the face of an eagle . . .

And describing the throne:

> Now over the heads of the living beings there was something like an expanse, like the awesome gleam of crystal, spread out over their heads . . . Now above the expanse that was over their heads there was something resembling a throne, like lapis lazuli in appearance; and on that which resembled a throne, high up, was a figure with the appearance of a man . . . from the appearance of His loins and downward I saw something like fire; and there was a radiance around Him. As the appearance of the rainbow in the clouds on a rainy day, so was the appearance of the surrounding radiance. (Ezekiel 1:22–28)

Then again in Daniel 7, we see the Son of Man is presented to the Ancient of Days on the Throne of God:

> And behold, with the clouds of heaven
> One like a Son of Man was coming,
> And He came up to the Ancient of Days
> And was presented before Him. (Daniel 7:13)

Remember that Daniel 7 is fundamental for understanding how Jesus understood Himself – it is how He explained Himself most often to people – so when we read Daniel and see reflections of Daniel 7 in Revelation it gives us a terrific insight into Christ. Not only that, but while in Daniel 7:14 the Kingdom is given to the Son of Man, in verse 18 it is received by the 'Saints of the High Places', which reflects the 24 Elders we see around the throne in Revelation 4.

Isaiah, Ezekiel and Daniel each get a vision, but Jeremiah doesn't get too much encouragement about anything: however, he does get himself. He is the man of sorrows and acquainted with grief. He himself was representing God's heart and mind. In fact Jeremiah is the book where you are not quite sure whether it is the prophet or God talking, because they have assimilated almost into one – that is true prophecy. Jeremiah is a forerunner alluding to the suffering of the Messiah:

> But I was like a gentle lamb led to the slaughter. (11:19)

This has echoes in Revelation 5:5–6,8:

> Behold the Lion that is from the tribe of Judah, the Root of David, has overcome so as to open the book and its seven seals. And I saw between the throne and the elders a Lamb standing, as if slain.

Jesus is seen, not as a ferocious lion, but a gentle lamb. Nothing could look more subdued and pathetic than a lamb that has just had its throat cut, but *He has overcome*. Jeremiah in turn took this picture from Isaiah 53:7, which speaks of the Messiah:

> Like a lamb that is led to slaughter, And like a sheep that is silent before its shearers, So He did not open His mouth.

The same Greek word for 'slaughtered' or 'slain' (*phagaen*) is used here in Revelation as in the Septuagint translation of Isaiah 53:7.

* ✷ *

So these majestic awesome visions of Isaiah, Ezekiel and Daniel, as well as Jeremiah and Isaiah 53, are all concentrated in Revelation chapters 4–5: Christ central in His whole Creation. It is one of the greatest assertions of the deity of our Lord Jesus. He is treated exactly the same way that the Creator is treated.

This vision is obviously a worship scene – there is a great paean of praise surrounding the Messiah sharing the Throne of God. That is why the Elders on the 24 thrones are dressed as priests, Levites who led the worship, music, poetry and prophecy in the Temple. To welcome Christ into our hearts is to open the door to communion with Him, and that communion *is* worshipping, offering ourselves to God and saying that He is worthy, He is worth it. Four times in this vision we get the word 'worthy' – what you count as worthy is what you worship.

Aspects of Christ in the Vision

Whereas the First Vision shows us Christ on the earth, the Second Vision shows us Christ in heaven on the Creator's Throne, which He shares with His Father. This is a glorious scene of worship, with the universe worshipping Christ the Redeemer, bringing together spiritual and earthly powers in His heavenly council.

Surrounded by light

The vision is suffused with overwhelming, glorious light and colour surrounding God. He 'dwells in unapproachable light' (1 Timothy 6:16), He is light (1 John 1:5) and He clothes Himself with light (Psalm 104:2). The light is not so we can see Him, but really so we can see everything else. Sometimes we call that light 'the glory'. It is very hard to define glory – honour . . . amazement . . . breath-takingly awesome. It is wonderful, this intense light which is pouring out from the Throne. How can we stand before it? Thomas Binney captured something of this when he wrote:

> Eternal Light! Eternal Light!
> How pure that soul must be,
> When, placed within thy searching sight,
> It shrinks not, but with calm delight
> Can live, and look on thee . . .
>
> There is a way for man to rise
> To that sublime abode:
> An offering and a sacrifice,
> A Holy Spirit's energies,
> An Advocate with God.

So we can dwell in the intense presence of the glory and the light of God, and that is exactly what we are going to see in this picture when we rise up through the open door into heaven.

Creator/Redeemer

In chapter 4, we see the Creator on the Throne, and in chapter 5 we see the Redeemer on the same Throne. Two things are needed by Creation: first it needs a Creator, and second it needs a Redeemer, since it has rebelled against its Creator.

Chapter 4 gives us, first and foremost, a picture of the Creator – all things were created and exist for His will. It is important that we grasp the relationship between Creator and creature: we are meaningless, purposeless blobs unless we know why the Creator created us. We are without value unless there is a God to declare why we were made. All things, including humans, were made for relationship with Him.

When we reach Revelation 5, the cry goes up for a redeemer and the answer given is 'the Lion of Judah'. However, this strong powerful champion appears as a sacrificial Lamb who still stands victoriously on the Throne.

On the Throne

In the First Vision, Christ stands amongst the 7 Churches, but here He is standing on His Throne in heaven. Whether there is a literal throne that God sits/stands on, or not, the picture we have here of a throne symbolises the literal authority of the Creator/Redeemer that lies behind this universe. The word 'throne' is used forty-seven times in Revelation and seventeen of these appear in this second section. It is God's Throne, God's authority, and it is this authority against which all hostility and disobedience fight.

We also see God on His throne elsewhere in Scripture. For example, Psalm 47:8 says:

> God reigns over the nations, God sits on His holy throne.

and 1 Kings 22:19:

> Micaiah said, 'Therefore, hear the word of the LORD. I saw the LORD sitting on His throne, and all the host of heaven standing by Him on His right and on His left'.

This throne is clearly not only where God is worshipped, but also from where judgment emanates into the earth.

Judge

Not only do we see Christ central in His Creation, but we also see Christ in judgment. In Revelation 4:3 there is an emerald rainbow around the throne and, like the rainbow in Genesis 9, this vision heralds judgment.

The Bible is incorporated between a couple of rainbows: the first was introduced as a covenant after God flooded the old creation in judgment to cleanse it. Here in Revelation the rainbow appears again, because there is another judgment and cleansing that must come upon the earth. This time God is not going to overflow it with water – the rainbow is the sign of His promise not to – but it will be judgment in a different form, which may be why it is symbolised by an 'emerald' rainbow. Out of that judgment is going to emerge a New Earth, washed clean like in Noah's day, and the emerald

The Second Vision

rainbow represents a covenant promise. We also see a rainbow in Revelation 10:1 upon the head of the Strong Angel, who resembles Christ and makes a covenant vow (see page 363). Interestingly, between Genesis and Revelation, the only other place we see a rainbow in Scripture is in the glorious vision of the Lord on His throne in Ezekiel 1.

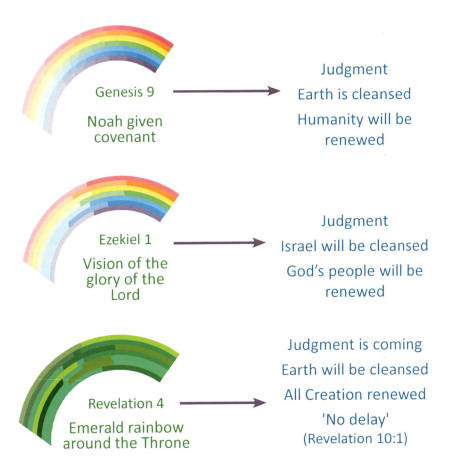

Following this Second Vision of Christ, we are going to see in chapters 6—16 God bringing a certain judgment into the earth to bring about justice, to vindicate the innocents who have been oppressed and correct all the injustices that have ever taken place. The word 'justice' comes from the word 'to right'

(*dikeaiosúnē*): it has the concept or character of being declared righteous, or something right by which you assess things, the bench-mark. God is going to bring that bench-mark in to test everything as to whether it has the right to keep existing or not. He has the right and authority to do this because all of Creation is His.

If you make something that is yours, you have a responsibility to what you have made, and equally you made it for a purpose and therefore it should fulfil your purpose – it isn't what it was meant to be unless it does what it is meant to do. The only meaning of existence is to be what you were meant to be.

The devil's deception is to delude us that true freedom is doing what you want to do. If you just do what you want, you end up destroying yourself: sin is when we act according to a way for which we were not made – the wages of sin is death (Romans 6:23). Humanity cries out for judgment (*krínō*, from which we get words like crisis): when we feel things are not what they are meant to be we yearn for them to be put right. This is what God is doing both now and at the End of the Age.

It is important to remember that judgment is not just negative, but also positive – commending and affirming. God, the Creator, who made us for a purpose, wants us to live according to what we were meant to be, and then we will find freedom.

Seals, Trumpets, Signs and Bowls

Following this glorious second vision of Christ as Creator and Redeemer, in chapters 6—16, we get 4 sets of 7 things happening:

- 7 Seals are broken and seven things happen (chapters 6—7)
- 7 Trumpets are blown and seven more things happen (chapters 8—11)
- 7 signs appear (chapter 12—15)
- 7 bowls of wrath are poured out and 7 more things happen (chapters 15—16).

All these sets of 7 are moving irresistibly towards a climax when the judgments will be finished, and all things are going to be vindicated or judged, when God will bring salvation for the whole universe.

These sets of 7 have different emphases, but each one is introduced by a gradually heightened rumbling and thundering which proceeds from the throne of God.

Seals: lightning, rumblings, thunders (4:5)

Trumpets: lightning, rumblings, thunders, earthquakes (8:5)

Signs: lightning, rumblings, thunders, earthquakes, hailstones (11:19)

Bowls: lightning, rumblings, thunders, greatest ever earthquake, extremely severe plague of huge hailstones (16:18–21)

As judgment continues everything just gets worse! However, if God does not judge, these rumblings will go on forever – there needs to be a reckoning. We can thank Him that He has not judged us immediately, because it gives us breathing space to repent and change. So we see this escalating judgment as God responds to the problem of the human race, moving through these 7 Seals, Trumpets, Signs and Bowls. It gets deeper and deeper, fundamentally transmitting God's attitude towards the things that are the deepest in the universe.

This second part of the book of Revelation is very important to grasp – God is moving like He did in the days of Noah. He is judging. He is cleaning up. He is bringing out a new earth from the old by the judgments that are being poured out.

The Second Vision
Revelation 4

The focus now shifts from the earth to heaven, where John sees the second glorious vision of Christ – this time a Lamb as slain upon the Throne, surrounded by worshipping Creation.

Text – Revelation 4:1–4

> [1] After these things I looked, and behold, a door *standing* open in heaven, and the first voice which I had heard, like *the sound of* a trumpet speaking with me, said, 'Come up here, and I will show you what must take place after these things.' [2] Immediately I was in Spirit; and behold, a throne was standing in heaven, and One sitting on the throne. [3] And He who was sitting was like a jasper stone and a sardius in appearance; and there was a rainbow around the throne, like an emerald in appearance. [4] Around the throne were twenty-four thrones; and upon the thrones I saw twenty-four elders sitting, clothed in white garments, and golden crowns on their heads.

Discussion Topic – The heavens

In Revelation 4 we get a glimpse through the door into heaven. 'Heaven' appears 52 times in Revelation, but what exactly does it mean? The Greek word translated as 'heaven/heavens' (*ouranós*) can mean a spiritual realm where God is, but can also be translated as 'sky' or 'air', so the context is important.

The Second Vision | Revelation 4:1–4

In the Old Testament a number of words are used for heaven, and similarly these may refer to God's dwelling place or more generally to 'height', 'elevation' or 'sky'. In Genesis 1, we read that God created 'the heavens and the earth' describing all of Creation, and in verse 8 'heaven' is a created expanse. Heaven can be seen as:

—› The air, where birds live (Genesis 1:20, Matthew 6:26)

—› The universe, where the stars are (Genesis 1:14–18 Deuteronomy 17:3, Matthew 24:29)

—› A spiritual realm where God is (Psalm 115:16, 1 Kings 8:27, Matthew 5:3, 2 Corinthians 12:2)

However, 2 Chronicles 18:18, indicates that it is not just God, but other spiritual powers who exist in the spiritual heaven, and some of these powers may act against God (see also Psalm 82:1, Job 1:6, 2:1). This is also clearly demonstrated in the New Testament, for example Ephesians 6:12:

> For we do not wrestle against flesh and blood, but against principalities, against powers, against the rulers of the darkness of this age, against spiritual hosts of wickedness in the heavenly places. (See also Luke 21:26, Romans 8:38, 1 Corinthians 15:24, Colossians 1:16, 1 Peter 3:22)

So even though heaven is God's 'dwelling place', it is not only God and His angels who are active there, but also forces opposed to God. It is this unseen world that is being opened up to us in Revelation. Paul also glimpsed this 'third heaven' in 2 Corinthians 12:2.

If you are not under the authority of Christ, there are other ways to break in to this spiritual realm by occult practices, but these are outside of God's security and protection – if you open the door to something else, there is no knowing where and by whom you will be led. The only safe way in to the heavenly places is in Jesus, where, under His authority we are 'seated in the heavenly places in Christ Jesus' (Ephesians 2:6).

Door of Heaven (v1)

This section begins with a door open in heaven (4:1), which reflects the door being opened on earth at the end of the first section (3:20).

In the first section, Christ was in the midst of the 7 Churches exhorting people to be Overcomers and at the end shows us how to overcome. When Jesus stands at the door and knocks, we must open the door and welcome Him into our lives. In the second section we see Jesus will not only fellowship with us, but also all He has accomplished in His life, death and resurrection will be transmitted into our lives. We can live in the power of His overcoming life – His life shall overcome again in us. His life will breathe into our lives and we will *share* life. Just as Jesus overcame and we now see Him in Revelation 4 sat on His Father's throne, He comes to live in us so that we can overcome and also sit in heavenly places in Christ Jesus (Ephesians 2:6).

As we looked at in the Discussion Topic above, here 'heavens' does not mean a place where only good things are allowed, but rather it is a glimpse into the spiritual realm, where God and His angels can act, but so can other spiritual forces (see Ephesians 6:12). While there may be other ways to engage in this spiritual realm, the only safe and secure place for a spiritual life is through the Holy Spirit – if we let Jesus into our inner life, He takes us into His authority so we enter the heavenly realm under the authority of God.

Glimpsing heaven through an open doorway has resonance with Ezekiel's vision (Ezekiel 1:1), and also Jacob's ladder:

> He had a dream, and behold, a ladder was set on the earth with its top reaching to heaven; and behold, the angels of God were ascending and descending on it. And behold, the LORD stood above it and said, 'I am the LORD, the God of your father Abraham and the God of Isaac' . . . He was afraid and said, 'How awesome is this place! This is none other than the house of God, and this is the gate of heaven.' (Genesis 28:12–13,17)

We also see heavenly doors being opened in the Psalms:

> Yet He commanded the clouds above
> And opened the doors of heaven (Psalm 78:23)

> Lift up your heads, O gates,
> And be lifted up, O ancient doors,
> That the King of glory may come in! (Psalm 24:7)

1 Kings 8:35 shows us that the heavens can also be shut.

'Come up here ...' (v1)

Here John hears the same trumpet voice as in the First Vision (Revelation 1:10, see page 88). The trumpet voice calls John up to heaven, to see 'what must take place after these things'. What exactly the 'these things' refer to is a matter of debate, as is the chronology of when 'what must take place' happens. Does it mean that at this point everything from each of the 7 Letters to the 7 Churches is now fulfilled? Or does it just mean that these things happen after the letters are written?

While it could be understood chronologically, it seems more reasonable to understand that we are called to live in the heavens, and further things will be shown to us about what is going on, and exactly when something will happen is not so important as the spiritual truths which will be shown to us.

As discussed earlier, the Gestation view can interpret 'these things' in a number of different ways, all of which have validity and build together to create a complete picture of God's plan. I would suggest 'these things' will have had specific meanings for John and his first-century readers (Praeterist), have various meanings moving through church history (Historicist) and have particular meaning for us as the End of the Age (Futurist), all of which are summed up in eternal spiritual principles (Spiritual).

There are many different interpretations from the four main theological views as to what the things are that must take place, However, what we can certainly say is that alongside John, we ourselves are called to live in the heavenlies and be watchful as to what is taking place.

In Spirit (v2)

After this, John is immediately transported to heaven 'in Spirit' (see page 42, and Revelation 1:10, 17:3, 21:10) to before the Throne, where he sees the Second Vision of Christ.

Precious Stones (v3)

John sees a Throne with One on it who looks like jasper, sardius and emerald. Why mention these three particular precious stones here? It is a picture of the totality of the beauty of the stones that God has put into the earth, the very fabric of this universe that we call beautiful. These stones are used in the breastplate of the High Priest (Exodus 28:15–21), they were there in Eden (Ezekiel 28:13), and as we will see in Revelation 21, they are amongst the 12 foundation stones of the city wall, there to sum up all the beauty and colour of Creation (21:19–20).

Socrates, when describing a great paradise, uses the same three stones, jasper, sardius (sardonyx) and emerald to represent the most beautiful precious stones that exist:

> . . . and there are hills, having stones in them in a like degree smoother, and more transparent, and fairer in colour than our highly-valued emeralds and sardonyxes and jaspers, and other gems, which are but minute fragments of them: for there all the stones are like our precious stones, and fairer still. (*Phaedo*, Plato)

Whether or not you regard Socrates as the final authority in art, he does express how people in the ancient world would talk about all precious stones coming under those three particular colours and types of stone.

- **Jasper** is opaque and can be red, yellow, green or even blue. Just as in the paradise Socrates is describing, the precious stones are 'more transparent', so too in Revelation 21:11 the jasper is not opaque as we know it, but '**crystal clear**', with light shining out from it, like diamond. So the glory of God is that which is shining in a brilliant, perfect, kind of **whiteness**. Not the 'brilliant white' of gloss paint, but whiteness that is so **intense** that it seems to go through everything, including you as you try to look at it.

- **Sardius**, also known as **carnelian**, is **red**. If we think about why we have jasper and sardius put together, we have this brilliant whiteness which moves into a brilliant red, 'like glowing metal in the midst of the fire' (Ezekiel 1:4). Our God is a **consuming fire** – to approach God without the protection of all that Jesus is, would mean that the intensity of it all would destroy us.

- An **emerald rainbow** is around the throne. The rainbow alludes to the covenant God promising not to flood the world again, and it is the **verdant green** of **life**. God is interested in His **Creation**.

The Second Vision | Revelation 4:1–4

We get a similar intense manifold picture in Exodus 24, where Moses and the elders of Israel see a vision of God on a sapphire pavement 'as clear as the sky' (v10) and 'the appearance of the glory of the LORD was like a consuming fire' (Exodus 24:17).

The 24 Elders (v4)

Who are these 24 Elders? They had 24 thrones, which indicates that whoever they are, they are sharing God's authority in heavenly administration. They look a bit like the King–Priests we will see in Revelation 5:10 and 20:6, and were mentioned in Revelation 1:6, 'He has made us to be a kingdom, priests to His God and Father'. In white garments, they look like priests, and with thrones and crowns they look like kings (see the Discussion Topic on page 73).

This brings to mind imagery of the Temple and the Tabernacle; the crowns are like the gold border around the top edge of the table of the show-bread (see Exodus 25:25) and the white garments like those the priests wore when they went into the Temple. The 7-branched lampstand from the Temple is now 7 Lampstands. The Mercy Seat on the Ark is there as the Throne, which is on a crystal sea, like the large basin outside Solomon's Temple. And the living creatures, which were in the Holy of Holies, are holding up God's throne. So as we look through the door into the heavens it is as though we are going right into the Temple, but this is a spiritual temple, and all the imagery has been changed around. It all assimilates together to give us a glorious impression of travelling into the Holy place, where we can get deeper and deeper into the heart of God.

Some suggest the 24 Elders are angels, some say they are stars, others that they are martyred saints and still others the living saints who are reigning in the heavenly places! Some say they represent the 24 books of the Old Testament in the Jewish canon (we count 39), and some that they are the 12 patriarchs and the 12 apostles = Old Covenant + New Covenant people together. All these things may have a nuance of truth, but if we look at 1 Chronicles 24:1–4 and 25:9–31 we see the priests and Levites were divided into 24 orders:

> Now the divisions of the descendants of Aaron were these . . . there were sixteen heads of fathers' households of the descendants of Eleazar and eight of the descendants of Ithamar, according to their fathers' households. (1 Chronicles 24:1,4)

They were organised that way in family lines to minister at the Temple, and represent all the people before God. These divisions were preserved throughout Jewish history, as we see with Zacharias in Luke 1:8–9:

> Now it happened that while he was performing his priestly service before God in the *appointed order of his division*, according to the custom of the priestly office, he was chosen by lot to enter the temple of the Lord and burn incense.

It was Zacharias' particular family line whose responsibility it was to work in the Temple that month when God told him Elizabeth would give birth to a son, John, 'who will go as a forerunner before Him in the spirit and power of Elijah' (Luke 1:17).

It is interesting that we are told these 24 are 'elders', not just kings or priests. Being an elder suggests wisdom. As you get older you are meant to get wiser, but true wisdom comes from those who continue to listen to God and participate in bringing in the Kingdom.

※

So these 24 Elders on the thrones are kings and priests, they are Levites in twenty-four orders. No doubt they do represent all of God's people in the days of the Patriarchs and all of God's people in the days of the Apostles, and they certainly are fulfilling the word of God, so all the things said in the Old Testament are being summed up in them. They are in the heavenly places and there is nothing wrong in talking about the Church being like the angels; the 7 Letters are each addressed to the angel of that church, we have angels representing us before God (Matthew 18:10) and after resurrection we will be like the angels (Matthew 22:30). An angel is a messenger and we are all meant to be a bit like heavenly messengers because we are sitting in the heavenly places now in Christ.

In modern political jargon, we could say these 24 elders are members of God's governing cabinet, representing the ability we now have 'to rule in life by one Man, Christ Jesus' (Romans 5:17, Ephesians 2:6), and anticipating our final eschatological reign with Christ when He returns (2 Timothy 2:12). Remember the distinction between Revelation 1:6 and 20:6 – now in this life we reign as priests *to* God and Christ, in the future we reign as priests *of* God and Christ (see Discussion Topic on page 73).

The Council of God (v4)

The 24 Elders are sharing in God's reign and the 24 thrones are a vision of God's delegated authority. It is God's council and these are His cabinet ministers – this vision reveals how God is governing the universe.

Some people talk about 'God's sovereignty', meaning He is solely and totally in charge of absolutely everything. This is not at all the picture the Bible presents – rather, God is sharing His authority, both with spiritual powers and with us. Although God is all-powerful, He has chosen to delegate some of His authority (see page 77).

We see God's heavenly council in the Old Testament: Job 1—2, Psalm 82:1, Psalm 89:5–7, 1 Kings 22:19–23 and Daniel 7:10. He delegated the power of death to Satan, the prince of death, who misused it (Hebrews 2:14).

God has also given us authority on earth to do certain things, for example Adam and Eve were given authority to rule and reign, Amos says 'surely the Lord God does nothing unless He reveals His secret counsel to His servants

Section II – Christ Central in Creation

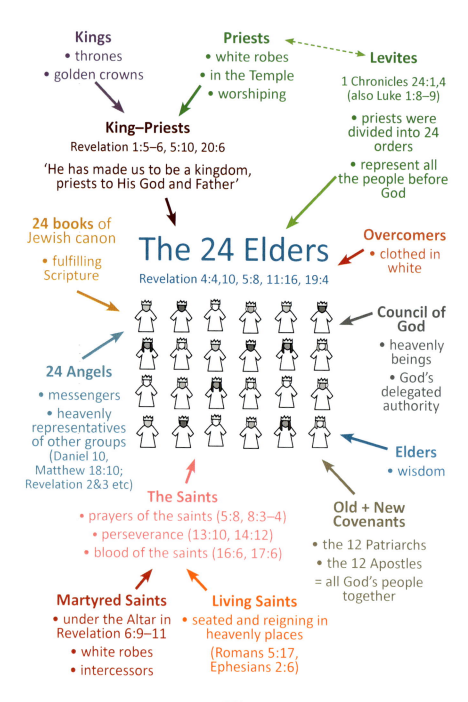

the prophets' (Amos 3:7) and Jeremiah talks about standing in the Council of God (Jeremiah 23:18). Jesus has given us authority, for example at the Great Commission (Matthew 28:18–20). For more on the council of God in Job see my book *Suffering and the Love of God*.

This is why it is important for us to rise up through this open door and start taking part in the heavenly Council – it is one way of thinking about what we are doing when we pray. Prayer is absolutely fundamental to see God's purposes brought into being (see my book *Prayer: Living in the Breath of God*). Here we are caught up to see things from a heavenly point of view, which can help us when we are praying about a situation. John Wesley said 'God does nothing but by prayer, and everything with it' – we are in participation with God concerning the bringing in of His Kingdom.

Text – Revelation 4:5–8

> ⁵ Out from the throne proceed flashes of lightning and sounds and peals of thunder. And there were seven lamps of fire burning before the throne, which are the seven Spirits of God; ⁶ and before the throne there was something like a sea of glass, like crystal; and in the centre and around the throne, four living creatures full of eyes in front and behind. ⁷ The first creature was like a lion, and the second creature like a calf, and the third creature had a face like that of a man, and the fourth creature was like a flying eagle. ⁸ And the four living creatures, each one of them having six wings, are full of eyes around and within; and day and night they do not cease to say,
>
> 'Holy, holy, holy is the Lord God, the Almighty, who was and who is and who is to come.'

Thunder, rumblings and lightning (v5)

We have seen how lightning and thunder divide up the sets of 7 in this vision (page 191), getting more intense as we move towards chapter 16 as 7 Seals are broken, 7 Trumpets are blown, 7 Signs appear and 7 Bowls are poured out. It is vital to remember this is all under the authority and expression of God's Throne – these are God's judgments that are coming out into the earth. So that, just as Noah came through the storm and flood of judgment to a new cleansed earth, we come out through these judgments of lightning, thunder, earthquakes and hail into a New Heaven and New Earth. The book of Revelation has a great ending, but we have to go through some difficult things to get there.

Thunder, lightning, rumbling and earthquakes are also reminiscent of Exodus 19—20 when the Lord visits Sinai and gives Moses the Law:

> There were thunder and lightning flashes and a thick cloud upon the mountain and a very loud trumpet sound, so that all the people who were in the camp trembled . . . Now Mount Sinai was all in smoke because the LORD descended upon it in fire; and its smoke ascended like the smoke of a furnace, and the whole mountain quaked violently. When the sound of the trumpet grew louder and louder, Moses spoke and God answered him with thunder. (Exodus 19:16–19)

God also speaks in thunder in Psalm 29:

> The voice of the Lord is upon the waters;
> The God of glory thunders,
> The Lord is over many waters. (Psalm 29:3)

Thunderings are warning that a storm is coming and produce within us a sense of awe and amazement – there is a threat. This thunder is not just a rumbling noise, it is a voice that is saying something – a warning that judgment is coming. In Revelation, it is God's word that is emanating from the throne, over the crystal sea of glass, like thunder over many waters.

What about the lightning flashes? We also see them around the throne in Ezekiel 1:

> A high wind was coming from the north, a great cloud with fire flashing intermittently and a bright light around it . . . In the midst of the living beings there was something that looked like burning coals of fire, like torches moving among the living beings. The fire was bright, and lightning was flashing from the fire. (Ezekiel 1:4,13)

These lightning flashes illuminate and execute judgment. Insurance companies describe lightning strikes, as well as earthquakes and hurricanes, as 'acts of god' and in cartoons God is often depicted as using lightning to zap people who are rude about Him! Well, it is perhaps not quite like that, but certainly a flash of lightning can signify judgment – its intense light can illuminate us and our situations, and its immense power has serious consequences.

The Second Vision | Revelation 4:5–8

So the thunder and lightning reinforces the picture of the Covenant God, who gave a promise to preserve the earth (rainbow), gave the Law to Moses (thunder and lightning) and revealed the New Covenant in Jesus, as well as depicting God as a judge, seated on His Throne.

7 Spirits (v5)

In Revelation 1:12–16, we see 7 Lampstands representing the 7 Churches surrounding and shining on Christ. Here in chapter 4, there are 7 lamps of fire, one for each lampstand, burning before the throne. These lamps are the 7 Spirits of God, which represents the fullness of the Holy Spirit. Maybe the shift we see from lampstands to lamps is due to John's change in perspective: when he is on earth John sees the 7 Lampstands, but from heaven he sees the 7 Spirits – the spiritual backdrop to the physical reality. This image of the 7 lamps is drawn from Zechariah (see also page 88):

> The angel said to me, 'What do you see?' And I said, 'I see, and behold, a lampstand all of gold with its bowl on the top of it, and its seven lamps on it with seven spouts belonging to each of the lamps which are on the top of it; also two olive trees by it, one on the right side of the bowl and the other on its left side.' (Zechariah 4:2–3)

So why are the lamps now the focus, not the lampstands? Perhaps to emphasize that while we do have the right to go into the Holy place because we belong to one of these lampstands, it is always by the power of the Holy Spirit – the fire itself – that God gets His will done in cooperation with us: "'Not by might nor by power, but by My Spirit', says the LORD of hosts" (Zechariah 4:6). We will see this again in Revelation where God's heart and mind is translated into the Church by the Holy Spirit's fire – the Spirit burns in heaven and in the Church. (NB we will come back to the 'two olive trees' in Zechariah 4 when we look at the 2 Witnesses in Revelation 11, see page 397.)

When we pray as part of the Church, we are praying in the Spirit. It is the Holy Spirit who, knowing the mind of God, intercedes for us when we do not know what to pray (Romans 8:26). You can also pray with understanding, but this should not mean you stop praying in the Spirit, because this is the fire that makes our participation in the Council of God and the worship around the Throne actually take place. We shine so that Jesus can be seen, and we can only do that if we are fuelled by the Holy Spirit.

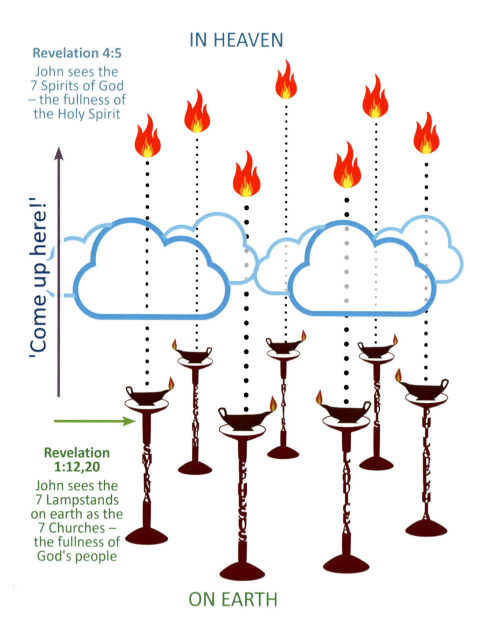

The Second Vision | Revelation 4:5–8

Sea of Glass (v6)

We have already seen how this vision is creating the experience of going into the Temple, and here the journey into the Holy of Holies continues.

In Solomon's temple, in the inner court before you entered through the doors was the 'Sea', a huge bronze basin the priests would use for ceremonial washing (1 Kings 7:23–26, 2 Chronicles 4:2). The Sea stood on 12 oxen, 3 facing outwards in each direction. From there, you would go through the Holy Place past the lampstands, and into the Holy of Holies, to the throne of God – the Mercy Seat – on top of the Ark of the Covenant. The Ark was surrounded by the Cherubim, who covered it with their wings.

In the vision in Revelation 4, it seems this 'Sea' is pushed inside under the Throne where God is sitting, surrounded by the 4 Living Creatures. Whereas in the Temple the journey to the throne was horizontal, here it is vertical as we move upwards, and the Throne is resting on the Sea, which seems to be frozen or crystalline.

We get a similar picture in the vision in Ezekiel 1, where above their heads is an expanse 'like the awesome gleam of crystal' on which is God's throne of lapis lazuli (blue), and the sound of the living beings' wings is like 'abundant waters' (Ezekiel 1:22–24). Again, in Exodus 24, Moses and the elders see a vision of God on a kind of blue, glass sea. This sea of glass appears again in Revelation 15:2, this time 'mixed with fire'.

Scripture gives us three main insights about the sea:

i. it washed and cleansed, as with Noah and the Ark (Genesis 7)

ii. it represents chaos (Psalm 46:2–3, 69:2, Isaiah 17:12–13)

iii. it was where evil powers and monsters in opposition to God lived, such as Leviathan (Isaiah 27:1, Job 41:1–34. Psalm 74:13–23), Rahab (*Egypt* – Job 26:12, Psalm 89:10, Isaiah 51:9) and the four great beasts in Daniel 7:2–8 – things that were under the earth, in the abyss.

However, the sea in the visions in Exodus, Ezekiel and Revelation appears like glass or crystal – it is under control. The authority of God is bringing disorder and chaos under control, so much so that the sea gives a sense of the distance between God and humanity.

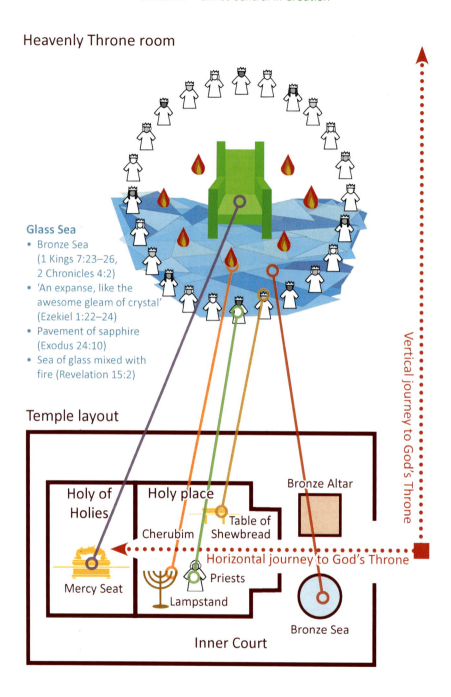

The Lord's supernatural control over the raging waters is fundamental to the Exodus story (Exodus 15:8) and Israel's entry into the Promised Land (Joshua 3:13–17), and was demonstrated by Jesus too when He calmed the storm (Matthew 8:24–27) and walked on the sea (John 6:18–20).

The Sea holds up the Throne, revealing the 'otherness' of God, showing us that the Creator is *not* the creature – He is Lord over His Creation, including chaos and evil powers. God's ability to control chaos should bring awe into our hearts.

The 4 Living Creatures – Representatives of nature (v6)

In the centre, around the throne, 4 Living Creatures now come into focus. The Hebrew word means simply 'living things'. If we look back into Isaiah 6, and his vision of the Lord enthroned in the Temple, we see seraphim, who look, and talk, quite a lot like these 4 Living Creatures:

> Seraphim stood above Him, each having six wings: with two he covered his face, and with two he covered his feet, and with two he flew. And one called out to another and said,
>
> > 'Holy, Holy, Holy, is the LORD of hosts,
> > The whole earth is full of His glory.' (Isaiah 6:2–3)

The word 'seraphim' only appears here in Isaiah 6 (v2, 6), and its root is unclear, but may come from the Hebrew root for 'to burn', or 'burning ones', maybe representing their energy and that they fly through the air.

The vision in Ezekiel 1 similarly features 4 'Living Beings', which bear strong resemblance to those in Revelation 4:

> And this was their appearance: they had human form. Each of them had four faces and four wings. Their legs were straight and their feet were like a calf's hoof, and they gleamed like burnished bronze. Under their wings on their four sides were human hands. As for the faces and wings of the four of them, their wings touched one another; their faces did not turn when they moved, each went straight forward. As for the form of their faces, each had the face of a man; all four had the face of a lion on the right and the face of a bull on the left, and all four had the face of an eagle. Such were their faces. Their wings were spread out above; each had two touching another being, and two covering their bodies. (Ezekiel 1:5–11)

In Ezekiel 10, in the vision of God's glory departing from the Temple, we again see these 4 Living Creatures, which Ezekiel now identifies as cherubim. The word 'cherubim' may originally come from an Akkadian word meaning 'to bless', or 'one who blesses', although historically it had been thought to derive from an Aramaic phrase meaning 'like a child', which is why in art 'cherubs' were often depicted with children's faces.

Cherubim first appear in Genesis 3:24, where, with the flaming sword, they are stationed to guard the way to the Tree of Life. However, there we are given no indication of who they are or what they look like. The Tabernacle and the Temple were filled with imagery of cherubim:

- There are two cherubim on top of the Ark of the Covenant, with their wings spread out to cover the Mercy Seat (Exodus 25:18–22, 37:7–9, Hebrews 9:5). This is where God spoke with Moses in Numbers 7:89.
- In the Old Testament, God is referred to as 'the Lord who is enthroned above the cherubim' (eg 1 Samuel 4:4, 2 Samuel 6:2, 1 Chronicles 13:6, Psalm 80:1, 99:1, Isaiah 37:16)
- Cherubim feature on the fine linen curtains and veil in the Tabernacle (Exodus 26:1,31; 36:8,35)
- In the Holy of Holies in the Temple, the two cherubim on the Ark are accompanied by two much larger cherubim, one on either side, made of olive wood overlaid with gold, whose wings touch and shelter the Ark (1 Kings 6:23–28; 8:6–7, 2 Chronicles 3:10–13)
- The Temple walls and doors were carved with cherubim, palm trees, and open flowers (1 Kings 6:29,31–35, 2 Chronicles 3:7)
- The Temple veil featured cherubim (2 Chronicles 3:14)
- In the Temple there were ten bronze basins, each of which had a stand decorated with lions, oxen and cherubim. These stands also had four wheels, like the cherubim in Ezekiel 1 (1 Kings 7:27–37).

Not only do cherubim appear in the Tabernacle and Solomon's Temple, but they also appear in Ezekiel's vision of the heavenly Temple in Ezekiel 40—44, where cherubim and palm trees decorate the doors and walls (eg

Ezekiel 41:18–19). We can reasonably assume that cherubim also decorated the second Temple when it was rebuilt under Ezra, and later renovated.

In both Ezekiel 1 and 10, as well as Revelation 4, the 4 Living Creatures/cherubim surround the Throne, and include the faces of a man, eagle, ox and lion. However, in Revelation they each have only one of these faces, whereas in Ezekiel each creature has all four faces. In both passages the creatures have wings – six in Revelation, compared to four in Ezekiel. I think it is clear these are the same entities in each case which are created by God to operate in the heavenly places. I do not think we have to read too much into the different numbers of wings and how many faces they had each – they are described as signs and symbols, so it is what they represent that is important, not exactly what they look like. Added to which, in the midst of an ecstatic vision, it is not surprising if John, Isaiah and Ezekiel see these spiritual beings slightly differently. Overall, the impression is of creatures clearly distinct from any form of life we see on earth – they are angelic, glorious and 'other'.

Eyes on all sides (v6)

A significant difference in description in Revelation 4 is that these 4 Living Creatures have eyes on all sides, whereas in Ezekiel 1 they move about on wheels which have rims full of eyes, and so they can see everything. Here in Revelation 4, the eyes:

- are looking forward (v6): predictive
- are looking behind (v6): reflective
- are looking all around (v8): comprehensive
- are looking within (v8): intuitive

These creatures being full of eyes is rather a strange image for us to get a grip on, and has been the basis of some fantastical artistic interpretations. However, it simply represents the all-seeing God, who can see, predict, feel and understand every factor. This represents true 'omniscience' and 'omnipresence' – it is not that God knows absolutely everything that will happen before it happens, but that He knows everything that could happen and witnesses everything that does happen. He is the infinite God and so knows every possible combination of everything.

These 4 Living Creatures represent God and His wisdom on the earth.

Section II – Christ Central in Creation

The 4 Faces (v7–8)

Taking a closer look at the faces of the 4 Living Creatures we see that they are all very strong:

 the Lion is noble and reigns as king of the animals

 the Ox is the strongest and most laborious in service

 the Human is the wisest in relationships and strong in mind

 the Eagle is strong and swift in flight, king of the birds, and sees everything below.

All these strengths of God's creation in different realms – the Lion over the wild animals, the Ox over the domestic animals, Humans over knowledge and thinking, and finally the Eagle ruling the skies – all express life. Life comes from God and He made it in these different forms, so it is not surprising that when the Creator became part of His creation (John 1:14) these four different aspects of animate life are expressed through Him.

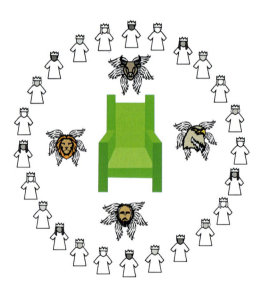

The Early Church Fathers recognised that the faces of the 4 cherubim/seraphim, are not only representative of life, but also are reflected in the different emphases of the four gospels:

 Jesus is Lion-like in Matthew – the King talking about the kingdom all the way through

 Jesus appears Ox-like in Mark – serving and persevering, doing the work of God as the Suffering Servant

 in Luke Jesus is expressing Humanity in all its relationships, one third of which are with women

 John's Gospel presents the Eagle face, the life of the divine and the prophetic.

Not only that, but there are echoes of these 4 Faces throughout the Old Testament, for example in the 4 Major Prophets, and in the 4 main Levitical sacrifices. For a deeper examination of this, see *The Four Faces of God* by John Bickersteth and Timothy Pain.

Trinitarian worship (v8)

So together these 4 Living Creatures around God's Throne represent every living, animate part of life in the universe as they worship and, as they do so, reflect the different aspects of God the Creator. They are worshipping God, which is what they were made for, and they have all the wisdom of God expressed through them. If the 24 Elders are like the cabinet of God's government, then the 4 Living Creatures are like ambassadors of all the different parts of God's Creation.

As John watches, the 4 Living Creatures worship in a beautifully trinitarian way, using three, threefold names of God.

i. **Holy, Holy, Holy**

The first name is 'Holy, Holy, Holy', also sometimes called the *Trihagion* (that is, triple-'Holy', in Greek). 'Holy, Holy, Holy' only appears here and in Isaiah 6, where we have already seen the Seraphim worshipping God (page 207). There are a few occasions in Scripture when names are said twice to indicate something important is about to happen, like with Samuel or Martha, but this is significant as it is the only time where a name is repeated three times. There is a strong hint of the Trinitarian God – 'Holy, Holy, Holy' – the Tri-Holy God.

ii. **Lord God Almighty**
The second name is 'Lord – God – Almighty' – the Lord, God, the one who is all-powerful (*pantokrátōr* – see page 77). This does not mean God is the power directly behind everything, but rather, 'Almighty' means that every bit of power in the universe comes from God, whether He delegates it or not. He is the ultimate source of all power, but this is not to say He is directing everything. 'Lord God Almighty' is the equivalent of the Old Testament title used in Isaiah 6 – 'Lord of Hosts', that is, God who is in charge of the Hosts of heaven. All of the powers depend upon His power.

iii. **Who was and is and is to come**
We have already seen God called 'Him who is and who was and who is to come', in Revelation 1:4 (see page 70) which can be seen as equivalent to the name which God revealed to Moses – 'I am that I am'. The concept is that God is eternally involving Himself in people's lives – 'I am . . . the God of Abraham . . . Isaac . . . and Jacob' (Exodus 3:6). It is interesting to notice 'Abraham', 'Isaac' and 'Jacob' do not have definite articles, and the Hebrew text could be read *'I am God–Abraham, God–Isaac, God–Jacob'*. God is defining Himself in terms of His relationships with them.

God's relationship with humanity has to happen in real-time, not in some vague timelessness, or somehow being 'outside of time', whatever that may mean. The Greek word for 'eternity' is 'ages of ages', so God should not be defined in terms of abstract Greek philosophy, but a more Hebrew relational idea of sharing life in successive ages.

Text – Revelation 4:9–11

⁹ And when the living creatures give glory and honour and thanks to Him who sits on the throne, to Him who lives forever and ever, ¹⁰ the twenty-four elders will fall down before Him who sits on the throne, and will worship Him who lives forever and ever, and will cast their crowns before the throne, saying,

'Worthy are You, our Lord and our God, to receive glory and honour and power; for You created all things, and because of Your will they existed, and were created.'

Glory, honour and thanks (v9)

The 4 Seraphim-cum-Cherubim Living Creatures give three kinds of worship to God upon the throne: 'glory and honour and thanks'.

Glory
Acknowledging that the Lord is ineffable and sublime, beyond us in ways we cannot describe.

Honour
Standing in awe of God, recognizing all the honourable things that He has done in Creation, including all that Jesus was.

Thanks
Being grateful is important to help us remember who we were made to be. On the one hand, giving thanks helps us not to think too much of ourselves: humility helps us remember we owe God everything. On the other hand it helps us not to think too little of ourselves: the fact that God cares about us individually should remind us we are loved. The opposite of thanks, ingratitude, is the heart of rebellion, bringing unhappiness for ourselves and others.

Cast their crowns (v10)

Why do the 24 Elders cast their crowns down? Rather than a sign they are repudiating their authority, because this is central to a worshipful scene, it too is an act of worship. The 24 Elders are demonstrating that whatever authority they have belongs to Christ. As they offer their crowns up before the Throne, they are showing that it is not their own glory and authority they are seeking – these are cast down out of gratitude as a way of offering the glory and honour back to the Lord. The 24 Elders are acknowledging from where the ultimate authority comes.

Discussion Topic: Crowns

The 24 Elders throw their crowns before the Throne while they worship. What exactly do these crowns represent, and why do they throw them down?

There are a number of types of crown mentioned in the Bible. In the Old Testament there is a 'crown' of anointing for the High Priest (Leviticus 21:11–12), the Lord Himself is a crown for His people in Isaiah 28:5–6 and later in Isaiah 62 it is God's people who are a crown for Him (v1–5), and finally there is a marriage crown given to the bridegroom on the wedding day in Song of Solomon (3:11).

In the New Testament, there are various crowns mentioned for believers:

- an imperishable crown (wreath) (1 Corinthians 9:24–25)

- Paul's converts are a 'crown of joy' (Philippians 4:1) and a 'crown of exultation' to him (1 Thessalonians 2:19)

- a crown (wreath) won of obedience (2 Timothy 2:5)

- later in 2 Timothy, a crown of righteousness laid up for Paul and anyone else who finishes the course and loves Christ's appearing (4:6–8)

- in Hebrews 2:5–10 (quoting Psalm 8) there is a crown of honour and glory and 1 Peter 5:4 also mentions a crown of glory for those who shepherd God's people

- both James and Revelation mention a crown of life to those who persevere (James 1:12, Revelation 2:10, see page 133)

- finally in Revelation 3:11 there is a crown of endurance (see page 168).

For a deeper look at the variety of crowns in the New Testament, see chapter 11 of my book *Gold, Silver & Precious Stones*.

> It is not clear whether each of these New Testament crowns are different entities, or more likely they are different aspects of the same crown – the authority we have in Christ. Similarly, the crowns of the 24 Elders could represent each of these different aspects of our Christian lives: joy, righteousness, honour and glory are the reward given to those who persevere.
>
> Just as the Lord is a crown for His people and His people are a crown for Him in Isaiah, the glory and honour crowning the Overcomers comes from God and reflects His glory.

Glory, honour and power (v10)

The 24 Elders now start worshipping God in almost the same way as the 4 Living Creatures: 'Worthy are You . . . to receive glory and honour *and power*'. Why do the 24 Elders say *power* instead of *thanks*? In some ways we can see them as synonyms – to give God 'power' is to thank Him for the power He has given to us, and offer it up to Him, which is equivalent to offering Him thanks.

Verse 10 says that the 24 Elders will 'worship Him who lives forever and ever'. This is a reference to what Nebuchadnezzar says in Daniel 4:34 (see also Daniel 12:7, Deuteronomy 32:40).

Creation and redemption (v11)

Notice that the word 'create' appears twice here in verse 11: 'You created all things . . . because of Your will they . . . were created'. So in Revelation 4 it is the old Creation that is in view – creat*ed*, past tense. However, as we will see when we get to Revelation 5:10 the focus changes from worshipping God the Creator, to worshipping God the Redeemer.

So the 4 Living Creatures and the 24 Elders are worshipping God for creating them. But why did God create them, and why did God create us? Genesis records God as saying: 'Let us make humankind in our Own image', so we were made in God's image to do God's will. However, we each have freewill and can choose to do God's will or not. We are not robots – if we were we could not love or relate. If we do God's will, we fulfil the purpose of our existence. But if we deny God's will for us and do what is right in our own eyes, we may end up in a sea of meaninglessness – 'All is vanity' (Ecclesiastes 1:2 and Romans 8:20). There is an English proverb: 'To err is human, to forgive divine' – this is nonsense. If we sin, we are not doing what God created us to do, and are less than human. For God to forgive us cost Him blood, which is why we should obey Him and be what God intended us to be – that is true human freedom.

Revelation 4	**Revelation 5**
Old Creation ⟶	Redeemed Creation
Worthy are You, our Lord and our God, to receive glory and honor and power; **for You created all things, and because of Your will they existed, and were created.**	Worthy are You to take the scroll and to break its seals; for You were slaughtered, and **You purchased people for God with Your blood from every tribe, language, people, and nation.** You have made them into a kingdom and priests to our God, and they will reign upon the earth.

Discussion Questions

How does the text here help us to understand the character and being of God?

Is salvation by faith sufficient, and if so what do the Crowns signify about us and about God?

Revelation 5

Continuing the Second Vision, John now sees the first of our 4 sets of 7 things – the 7 Seals. Revelation 4 finished with, 'because of Your will [purpose] they existed and were created', and here we begin to see what God's purposes for His Creation are.

Text – Revelation 5:1–5

> [1] I saw in the right hand of Him who sat on the throne a book written inside and on the back, sealed up with seven seals. [2] And I saw a strong angel proclaiming with a loud voice, 'Who is worthy to open the book and to break its seals?' [3] And no one in heaven or on the earth or under the earth was able to open the book or to look into it. [4] Then I began to weep greatly because no one was found worthy to open the book or to look into it; [5] and one of the elders says* to me, 'Stop weeping; behold, the Lion that is from the tribe of Judah, the Root of David, has overcome so as to open the book and its seven seals.'

The sealed Book (v1)

In Revelation, the right hand symbolizes power and authority, and here in the right hand of the One sat on the Throne is a small Book (or scroll – the Greek word can mean either). This Book is written 'inside and on the back', signifying that it is full, complete, and nothing more can be added to it. In some cases documents were written with a summary of the contents on the back, however this seems unlikely here as it has to be opened to be read.

This Book is important – it is in the Lord's hand, it is sealed and carries God's authority and, as we will see, significant things happen as its 7 Seals are broken. Even more revealing is that it can only be opened by one who is worthy. However, we are not told exactly what this Book is or why it is so important, so we need to do some detective work to find out. As with the other symbols in Revelation, this book has its origins in the Old Testament, in particular in the Major Prophets whose visions form the backdrop to this chapter. Drawing together these threads of Scripture will help us to build up a concept for what this book is.

God's purposes

First we need to look at the context in which it appears – Revelation 4 finishes with: 'because of Your will they existed and were created'. This begs the question: what is God's will for creation? Revelation 5 begins with the 7-sealed book, indicating it is linked somehow to what God's purpose is.

Sealed inheritance

This book is sealed with 7 Seals, which was a common way of sealing up inheritance or title deeds to property or land. Could this represent the inheritance that Adam had when he was told to fill up the earth, and to have dominion over the animals and subdue the earth? It was all his, but after the fall, Adam lost that inheritance. If this book represents the sealed up inheritance God originally gave Adam, is there any way it can be opened? Maybe we need a new Adam . . .

God's message to the people

We have looked at the similarity between the visions in Revelation 4 and Ezekiel 1, and if we read on into Ezekiel 2 we also see a hand holding a scroll, which 'was written on the front and back, and written on it were lamentations, mourning and woe' (v10). The Spirit tells Ezekiel to eat the scroll, and speak to the people, so the scroll represents God's message – the word of God.

Needing interpretation

In Daniel 7, we see the Ancient of Days on the throne and 'the books were opened' (v10). However in Daniel 12, Daniel is instructed to

> Conceal these words and seal up the book until the end of time (v4, also v9)

Similarly, in Isaiah 29 there is a vision of warning and woe to Jerusalem which:

> . . . will be to you like the words of a sealed book, which when they give it to the one who is literate, saying, 'Please

read this,' he will say, 'I cannot, for it is sealed.' Then the book will be given to the one who is illiterate, saying, 'Please read this.' And he will say, 'I cannot read' . . . On that day the deaf will hear words of a book, And out of their gloom and darkness the eyes of the blind will see. (v11–12,18)

These books of prophecy will not be understood until the End of the Age. Maybe the sealed Book in Revelation represents such warning prophecies.

Redemption deed

In Jeremiah 32:6–14, the prophet seals up the purchase deed for a field he bought even though Israel were being taken away into Exile, because 'houses and fields and vineyards will again be bought in this land' (v15). So Jeremiah's sealed scroll was a redemption deed, to be used when the people returned – a prophetic sign of God's Covenant.

This is reaffirmed in Revelation 5:9, which links breaking the seals on the book with a redemptive purchase of people from every nation, tribe and tongue.

Other books

Some have suggested it could be the Old Testament itself, others that it is the Lamb's Book of Life we saw in the epistle to Sardis (Revelation 3:5) and appears again later in Revelation (13:8, 17:8, 20:12,15, 21:27). Others think it is a book containing prophecies about the Tribulation that will precede the final expression of the Kingdom.

Each of these ideas has some Old Testament foundation, and I think there are elements of the truth in each that we can apply.

God's plan – our predestiny

As we weave together these various strands of truth, we build up a picture of the Book as representing the message of God's plan and purpose for humankind – it is sealed up and needs someone worthy to open and interpret it and bring redemption.

Section II – Christ Central in Creation

God's purposes
Revelation 4 finishes

'Worthy are You . . . to receive glory and honour and power; for You created all things, and because of Your will they existed, and were created.'

What God's will is for creation

God's Message to the people
Ezekiel 2:9–10

'a hand was extended to me; and behold, a scroll was in it. When He spread it out before me, it was written on the front and back, and written on it were songs of mourning, sighing, and woe.'

Sealed Inheritance
- sealed with 7 Seals
- inheritance/ title deeds
- Adam's lost inheritance?

The 7-Sealed Book
Revelation 5:1–5

Other books
- the Old Testament?
- Lamb's Book of Life
- books of end-time prophecies

Redemption deed
Jeremiah 32:6–14

- Jeremiah seals the purchase deed for a field
- 'houses and fields and vineyards will again be bought in this land'

Needing interpretation
Daniel 12:4,9, Isaiah 29

'Conceal these words and seal up the book until the end of time'

- visions of warning and woe to God's people
- prophecies that will not be understood until the End of the Age

The Second Vision | Revelation 5:1–5

This small Book is what God wants for us – it is what He created us for. But what exactly is God's plan and how will humanity get there? As we discuss in our book *God's Strategy in Human History*, I believe Scripture is very clear here: our destiny as God's people – the Church – is to be conformed to the image of His Son (Romans 8:29). This is the true meaning of 'predestination' – it is corporate, not individual. Predestination is often misinterpreted: it does not mean that God has already chosen who is going to heaven and who is not, rather it is that God has a purpose set before humanity that He wants us to fulfil, i) to complete creation, and ii) to defeat evil.

Satan fell before humanity was created, so part of God's plan to complete Creation is for man to defeat Satan. However, in order for us to be able to fulfil this purpose, God must redeem humanity first: at the Fall, sin entered in and humankind lost the right to fulfil the inheritance. Through His redemptive sacrifice on the Cross, Jesus made it possible for humanity to achieve its purpose – in Him we can complete Creation and defeat the disturbing elements of evil which have come in through sin and the devil. We will see his activity more clearly as we move on through Revelation, and in Chapters 11—22 – the second part of this Manifesto of Jesus written by John – we will see this come to its climax.

Who is worthy? (v2–5)

The Book of God's plan and purpose for humanity contains a perfect vision of how life should be. However, there is a problem: as we look around the world we don't see wars ceasing or everyone being conformed to the Son's image. We do not see the beautiful expression of life that God intended. The Strong Angel asks if anyone is worthy to break the seals and open the Book – *Is there anyone who can live a life worthy of God's plan?* No, no one 'in heaven or on the earth or under the earth' could live that perfect human life, and so they could not break the seals to open the Book.

This is a sobering realisation – we cannot live up to God's plan for us, we all fall short. Deep down we all feel that the world ought to be better than it is, but on our own we are powerless to improve it. The state of our world can make us despair – the wars, violence, hatred, poverty, hunger, disease, pain and brokenness we see should move us to compassion. And so we weep, just as John weeps because there is no one to open the book and read it.

Then in Revelation 5:5, 'one of the elders said to me, "Stop weeping"'. They understand something John does not – there is hope. Humankind's inheritance in God's purposes was sealed up, but 'behold, the Lion that is from the tribe of Judah, the Root of David, has overcome . . .' The Overcomer has won the right to open the book in order that it might be fulfilled. This fulfilment includes the strenuous pathway which takes us through the breaking of the 7 Seals, to arrive at the final ideal – that is, humanity made in the image of God. The Overcomer is our Saviour, who lived a perfect life. Jesus was the first to live a life worthy of God's purposes:

> The firstborn of the dead, so that He Himself will come to have first place in everything. (Colossians 1:18)

> The firstborn of many brethren.
> (Romans 8:29, see also 1 Corinthians 15:45–49, Revelation 3:21)

Lion of Judah (v5)

As the lion is the king of the animals, so the Lion of Judah is the ruler of God's people – the King of the Jews. This picture of Christ as the Lion of Judah comes from Genesis 49, where Jacob prays over his sons, and prophesies that the Messiah will come from Judah:

> Judah is a lion's whelp; From the prey, my son, you have gone up.
> He couches, he lies down as a lion,
> And as a lion, who dares rouse him up? . . .
> The sceptre shall not depart from Judah,
> Nor the ruler's staff from between his feet. (Genesis 49:9–10)

It is the overcoming Lion of God who has the right to break the 7 Seals because of His purity He was without sin (2 Corinthians 5:21, 1 Peter 1:19, 2:22, 1 John 3:5, Hebrews 4:15). The sinless One who has overcome every trial and pressure of the enemy, has lived purely and cleanly before His Father and, having overcome, is now able to open the Book to bring in the eternal purpose which God had for humanity. We will see the Strong Angel, who resembles Christ, roaring like a lion in Revelation 10:3 (see page 366).

Root of David (v5)

Israel was God's chosen people and the Messiah was prophesied to come from David's line (Psalm 89:3–4, 132:11, Isaiah 9:6–7 (Luke 1:31–33), 11:1–2, Jeremiah 33:14–17, Jeremiah 33:26, Hosea 3:5, Luke 1:68–71, John 7:42,

Acts 2:29–31, Romans 15:12). Their hope would come from Jesus, the Son of David (Matthew 1:1–2, 9:27, 22:42, Romans 1:3, 2 Timothy 2:8).

It is interesting that in Isaiah 11, the Messiah from the root of Jesse (David's father) has a 7-fold anointing of the Spirit:

> Then a shoot will spring from the stem of Jesse,
> And a branch from his roots will bear fruit.
> The $_1$Spirit of the Lord will rest on Him,
> The $_2$spirit of wisdom and $_3$understanding,
> The $_4$spirit of counsel and $_5$strength,
> The $_6$spirit of knowledge and $_7$the fear of the Lord. (Isaiah 11:1)

As 7 represents completion, this 7-fold anointing shows the Messiah is anointed with the fullness and completeness of the Holy Spirit, just as Jesus was at His baptism. David was the prototype king, a man after God's own heart (Acts 13:22) who would reign on behalf of God. However, here Jesus is called the root of David – how can He be both a root and descendant of David (see also Revelation 22:16)? This is a question Jesus himself poses to the Pharisees in Matthew 22:42–45:

> 'What do you think about the Christ, whose son is He?' They said to Him, 'The son of David.' He said to them, 'Then how does David in the Spirit call Him "Lord," saying,
>   "The Lord said to my lord, sit at my right hand, until I put
>   your enemies beneath your feet"?
> Therefore, if David then calls Him "Lord", how is He his son?'

The answer of course, is that the Lord God, would have to enter His Creation as a human, as part of David's family line. This quotation from Psalm 110:1, along with Genesis 49:9 and Isaiah 11:1 gives us hope – there is somebody who is fully anointed with the Holy Spirit and who is worthy. Why? Because He has Overcome. Adam lost the right to open the book for us all, but here is one – the second Adam – who has overcome death to regain the right to open the Book in order to fulfil it.

Redeemer

Why is it that Jesus can fulfil the purpose of God for humankind, even though humanity has gone wrong? It is because He has redeemed it, or 'purchased' it (Revelation 5:9, see also Leviticus 25:25–26, Ruth 3:9, 4:14, Isaiah 41:14,

Jeremiah 50:34) to make it right (the Greek word is *agorázo*, which comes from *agorá*, the marketplace, which may make us think of being bought back like a slave). The mortgage on Creation has now been paid and the Lord is bringing His original purpose into being out of this chaos.

God didn't give up on humanity: He could have written us off but He still works with us. He has redeemed His purpose so that at last we are back on track to fulfil God's plan for us: overcoming evil and recovering Creation as our inheritance. As Christians we should not be sitting around waiting to be taken to heaven – we are here to become like Jesus.

Text – Revelation 5:6–10

> ⁶ And I saw between the throne (with the four living creatures) and the elders a Lamb standing, as slain, having seven horns and seven eyes, which are the seven Spirits of God, sent out into all the earth. ⁷ And He came and took the book out of the right hand of Him who sat on the throne. ⁸ When He had taken the book, the four living creatures and the twenty-four elders fell down before the Lamb, each one holding a harp and golden bowls full of incense, which are the prayers of the saints. ⁹ And they sing* a new song, saying,
>
>> 'Worthy are You to take the book and to break its seals; for You were slain, and purchased for God with Your blood men from every tribe and tongue and people and nation.
>>
>> ¹⁰ 'You have made them to be a kingdom and priests to our God; and they will reign upon the earth.'

The Lamb as slain (v6)

We are now ready to see the One who is on the throne, the Creator–Redeemer, the Lion of Judah. However, rather than a fierce lion, standing on the Throne we see a Lamb as slain. Some translations put 'as though slain' or 'as if slain', but the Greek simply says 'as slain'. Jesus didn't just pretend as though He was dying on the Cross – He was slain. The Lamb is standing, because although slain He is resurrected: we have a Lamb who has gone through death and is still standing. It is important to note that 'standing' in Revelation denotes resurrection, as we see for example in Revelation 6:17 (page 279).

The Aramaic word for 'lamb' is *talia*, and this also means 'servant', which

The Second Vision | Revelation 5:6–10

takes us to the Suffering Servant in Isaiah 53, who is 'Like a lamb that is led to slaughter' (v7). A slain lamb also represents Passover and the sacrifice that brought salvation for God's people.

Jeremiah's life and ministry anticipate the Suffering Servant:

> But I was like a gentle lamb led to the slaughter;
> And I did not know that they had devised plots against me, saying,
> 'Let us destroy the tree with its fruit,
> And let's cut him off from the land of the living,
> So that his name will no longer be remembered.' (Jeremiah 11:19)

7 horns and 7 eyes (v6)

Looking closer at the Lamb, it has 7 horns and 7 eyes 'which are the 7 Spirits of God sent out into the earth'. Horns represent strength and power, and eyes represent insight, understanding and knowledge, and 7 of each indicates completeness and plenitude. So the fullness of the Holy Spirit stands for the fullness of God's power and the fullness of His knowledge (the Spirit of Truth). Here, as in Isaiah 11:1–2, the Messiah is anointed (Christ-ed) with the 7-fold Spirit. This is how the triune God is operating from the Throne: from the Creator (Father) through the Redeemer/Lamb (Son) out into the earth by His Spirit.

However, there's a problem. If God's purposes are being brought to bear upon Creation, and the Lamb is all-powerful (7 horns) and all-knowing (7 eyes) why is the universe so chaotic? Why do pain and evil exist? As we discussed for Revelation 1:8 (see page 77), while God is the ultimate source of power, He has delegated some of this power and authority, and risked giving us free will and the potential to rebel, without which we cannot love and interrelate like the Trinity.

The Lamb takes the Book (v7)

The worship is triggered off as soon as the Lamb comes and takes the Book. This is the same imagery as in Daniel 7:10,13–14, where the Son of Man comes to the Ancient of Days and is given the Kingdom. Each time Daniel 7 appears it is being reinterpreted with even greater depth and richness.

An important thing to note is that while in verses 13–14 the Kingdom is given to the 'Son of Man', in verses 18–22,27:

> . . . the saints of the High Places will receive the kingdom and possess the kingdom forever, for all ages to come . . . and the time arrived when the saints took possession of the kingdom.

> Then the sovereignty, the dominion and the greatness of all the kingdoms under the whole heaven will be given to the people of the saints of the High Places; His kingdom will be an everlasting kingdom, and all the dominions will serve and obey Him.

So when we look at the Son of Man (singular) we also see the saints or ones who are set apart (plural). In some versions it is translated Saints of the 'Highest One', but 'High Places' is what the Greek says. Of course, these saints *do* belong to God, the Highest One, but High Places indicates their sphere of operation – they are ruling and reigning in the heavenlies.

Who are these saints in Daniel 7? 'Saints' appear 13 times in Revelation and are reminiscent of, and may even prefigure or anticipate, the 24 Elders we have seen with their thrones in the heavens (Revelation 4:4), representing the authority we the Church now have in Christ, and also anticipating our reigning with Christ at the Second Coming:

> [God] raised us up with Christ, and seated us with Him in the heavenly places in Christ Jesus. (Ephesians 2:6)

This is what we have been set apart for, and through worship and prayer in the Holy Spirit we are already sharing in the reign of Christ.

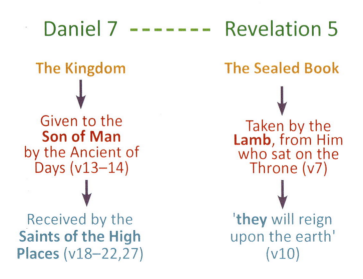

Worship and prayer (v8–10)

Worship and prayer are central to this scene. Together, both the 4 Living Creatures (ambassadors of Creation) and the 24 Elders (King–Priests, God's people) 'fell down before the Lamb', and each was holding a harp, representing worship, and bowls of incense, representing prayer.

It may seem very difficult to hold a harp and bowls and fall down as well, but we are dealing with apocalyptic language – it is communicating the idea of complete self-giving, offering themselves as a sacrifice. It paints a picture of perpetual, corporate praise – we are meant to worship together and pray together, because if we do we inspire and encourage one another.

The Church will not be effective in interceding in the heavenlies unless we do what the 24 Elders do here and fall down before the Lamb, in worship and prayer. It is the Church worshipping that stimulates the fulfilment of God's purposes – starting with the 7 Seals being broken, ultimately leading to Christ's return and the Kingdom coming in full. The more we devote ourselves to worship, the quicker these things will happen. Worship is a fundamental part of our calling.

Prayers of the Saints (v8)

As they worship, the Saints offer up prayers – as we have seen, the Holy Spirit (7 Spirits/Lamps) begins prayer from the Throne of God, takes it to the heart of His Church and brings it back again to be presented.

Either John is writing bad grammar (which some people think) or it is the golden bowls which are the 'prayers of the saints', not the incense. This is fascinating, because it is the bowl that we offer to God. Have you ever felt like an empty bowl, with nothing to give when you come to pray or worship? That is okay – if you offer it to the Lord, then incense will be added to it, as we see in Revelation 8:3. We can start to worship through the intercession of the Spirit:

> In the same way the Spirit also helps our weakness; for we do not know how to pray as we should, but the Spirit Himself intercedes for us with groanings too deep for words; and He who searches the hearts knows what the mind of the Spirit is, because He intercedes for the saints according to the will of God. (Romans 8:26–27)

So the 24 Elders presenting the prayers of the Saints are representative of how our prayers are offered up.

A new song (v9)

The harps remind us particularly of David, who was mentioned in verse 6. David, the psalmist, played the harp in worship, to ward off evil spirits (1 Samuel 16:23) and in celebration before God (2 Samuel 6:4–5).

David wrote many Psalms and here the 4 Living Creatures and the 24 Elders sing a new song. This is the first new song in Revelation (see also 14:3), as well as 7 new songs in the Old Testament.

Here they sing a *new* song (newness (*kainos*) as in fresh rather that new (*neos*) as in not existed before), because they are singing about a New Heaven and New Earth – going from Revelation 4 to Revelation 5 we are moving from the old Creation to a new Creation.

As with the new song in Revelation 4:11, it is the worthiness of our God that stimulates their worship.

Every tribe, tongue, people and nation (v9)

This is not just limited to the Jewish nation, it is the whole world now getting blessed.

King–Priests (v10)

We have already seen King–Priests appearing in Revelation 1:6 (see Discussion Topic on page 73). There is a difference in translations here – around half of the old manuscripts say 'will reign' and the other half just say 'reign', so this could be referring to them going out and reigning in the world now, or to reigning in the future age when Jesus comes again. I prefer the present tense, but in some ways both are true: we 'reign in life through the One, Jesus Christ' (Romans 5:17), but 'if we endure, we will also reign with Him' (2 Timothy 2:12). Perhaps if we left it as 'they will reign', it could refer to both ages anyway, so while it may not make much difference, it does bring home to us that the reign of God is actually already in view, with the Son of Man receiving the Kingdom.

Text – Revelation 5:11–14

> [11] Then I looked, and I heard the voice of many angels around the throne and the living creatures and the elders; and the number of them was myriads of myriads, and thousands of thousands,

The Second Vision | Revelation 5:11–14

¹² saying with a loud voice,

> 'Worthy is the Lamb that was slain to receive power and riches and wisdom and might and honour and glory and blessing.'

¹³ And every created thing which is in heaven and on the earth and under the earth and on the sea, and all things in them, I heard saying,

> 'To Him who sits on the throne, and to the Lamb, be blessing and honour and glory and dominion forever and ever.'

¹⁴ And the four living creatures kept saying, 'Amen.' And the elders fell down and worshipped.

Many angels (v11)

So far in Revelation we have seen a few angels, but suddenly here we see 'many angels . . . myriads of myriads and thousands of thousands', and they all speak together with one voice. This must have been an awesome display of glory, but the angels are not interested in their own glory – instead they glorify the Lamb. These angels add another circle of praise and worship around the Throne.

That was slain (v12)

The Lamb was 'slain', which is the same word we saw in verse 6, meaning 'slaughtered' and is the same word as 'sacrificed'. There was a price to pay to redeem people from every tribe, tongue, people, and nation – the price was His own blood. God did not pay the devil in order to redeem us, He paid the price in Himself by giving of Himself in His blood. That was the price of redemption – He has bought us and cleansed us.

7-fold praise (v12)

The 4 Living Creatures gave the Lord 'glory and honour and thanks'. The 24 Elders give God 'glory and honour and power'. Here the angels sing to the Lamb 'power and riches and wisdom and might and honour and glory and blessing'!

Every created thing (v13)

Note that in Revelation 4:11, in the vision of the Creator the 24 Elders say 'You created all things', and here we see every created thing worshipping around the Throne.

The same things were said, if not more so in verse 12, to the Lamb as were said to the Creator. Here it is to the one on the throne and to the Lamb who is the midst of the Throne – Father and Son, are given equal honour. This is perhaps the strongest identification of Jesus with deity in the whole of the book of Revelation.

So the circles around the Throne keep expanding: the 4 Living Creatures, the 24 Elders, the myriad angels and Creation itself, every single thing bouncing up and down praising God. Every little flower bursting out praising its God; every creature fulfilling its lovely purposes as the Lamb, the Son of Man has come forth, taken control again of what was lost and is bringing the Creation into its redemptive position before God.

The worship of the whole of Creation is affirmed by the 4 Living Creatures who keep saying 'Amen' – so be it! (v14)

The Second Vision | *Revelation 5:11–14*

Discussion Questions

How would you define God's plan for humanity?

Which aspect of the vision of the Lamb strikes you most?

Which 7 words of praise would you sing to the Lamb?

7 Seals, Trumpets, Signs & Bowls
Revelation 6—16

Revelation 4—5 have given us a wonderful vision of the Throne of God, but when we get into chapter 6 we start to get a very different picture; what we see is terrible and yet terribly important too. This vision reveals things which are dark and unhealthy, but these will help us to understand that a day of accountability is coming – the Day of Wrath.

Just as in the first section of Revelation, we have seen a vision of Christ, which is now applied in the rest of the section – the vision shows us what Christ is like, and then we see what the effects of that are. Christ is revealed as the Lamb slain but standing on the Throne in judgment, and judgment is the theme of the next 11 chapters.

Just as we have seen in Revelation thus far, this section is packed full of allusions and references to Scripture, and rather than interpreting these chapters in isolation, our first port of call should be to look back to what has come before. It is as if the whole of the Old Testament is flowing into this last book of the Bible, giving sense to all the threads running through it, solving the puzzles, revealing the mysteries and all the time leading us to Jesus.

It is easy to get a little lost or overwhelmed in this section as there is so much going on, with all the angels, trumpets, beasts and very unusual things happening. However, as we go through we will see there is a simple pattern of 4 sets of 7 events, which will help us navigate our way through and interpret what is going on. There are: 7 Seals being broken, 7 Trumpets being blown, 7 Signs appearing and 7 Bowls of Wrath being poured out. Before we get into the text, here is an overview of these 4 sets of 7.

In this current volume, we will cover Revelation 6—11, that is, the 7 Seals and the 7 Trumpets, with Revelation 12—16, the 7 Signs and the 7 Bowls of Wrath, appearing in the second volume.

The Second Vision | Revelation 6—16

Overview of the 7 Seals, Trumpets, Signs and Bowls

Three of these sets of 7 are easy to see, but the third is a little obscure, as John only says 'I saw a sign' three times – nevertheless there are 7 Signs in the text. There are many parallels between these sets of 7 – they cover related themes, follow a similar structure and importantly, all seem to converge at the Second Coming.

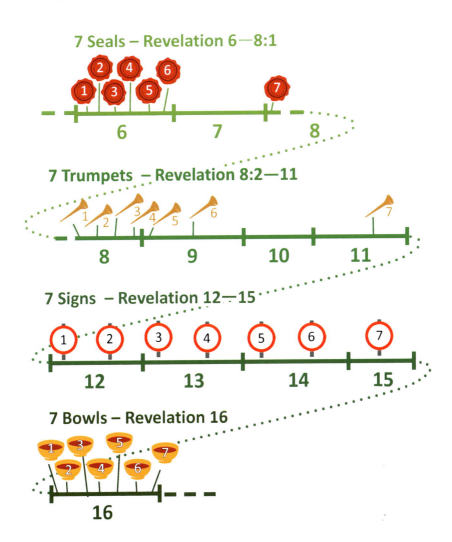

4 × 7-fold Judgments

There are important allusions here between the judgments we will see in these 4 sets of 7 events and Leviticus 26, which first outlines the blessings to Israel for obedience to the Law, followed by the penalties for disobedience. Four times in Leviticus 26 it talks about 7-fold judgements for Israel if they reject God (v18,21,24,28). Each time these judgments become more severe and are poured out until they reach their climax. This sets an Old Testament pattern for the judgments in Revelation 6—16.

The Second Coming, resurrection, judgment and wrath in the 7s

Each set of 7 seems to ultimately culminate in something that fits the description of the Second Coming; there are disturbances in the heavenly places, Christ returns, and we see wrath, resurrection and judgment. For instance after the 6th Seal is broken, there is an earthquake, the sun goes black, stars fall to the earth and the people on the earth say:

> 'Hide us from the presence of Him who sits on the throne, and from the wrath of the Lamb for the great day of their wrath has come, and who is able to stand?' (Revelation 6:16–17)

As we have seen in Revelation 5:6 (see also 6:17, 7:9, 11:11 and 20:12), 'to stand' refers to being resurrected, so the picture is of resurrection and judgment. When we get to the 7th Trumpet (see also 1 Thessalonians 4:16 and 1 Corinthians 15:52) we also see Christ's reigning, resurrection, wrath and judgment. Here the original text for 'wrath' is *orgē*, not *thumós*. Aristotle says that *orgē* is a mixture of anger and grief as a state of mind and not the transience of *thumós*. The enduring intensity of our Lord's emotions are rising at what has happened with and to Creation and humanity – the distinction between hot anger and cold fury.

> There arose loud voices in heaven saying 'the kingdom of the world has become the kingdom of our Lord and His Christ. And He will reign forever and ever' . . . the nations were enraged, your wrath came and the time for the dead to be judged. (Revelation 11:15,18)

Then there are the 7 Signs, and the last is:

> another sign in heaven, great and marvellous, seven angels who had seven plagues, which was the last, because in them the wrath of God is finished . . . and the temple was filled with smoke from

the glory of God and from His power. (Revelation 15:1,8)

Finally, in chapter 16 we get the 7 Bowls of Wrath poured out:

> A loud voice came out of the temple from the throne, saying, 'It is done'... and Babylon the great was remembered before God, to give her the cup of the wine of His fierce wrath. (Revelation 16:17,19)

Wrath appears in each set of 7, and it progresses as we go through the 4 sets:

 6th Seal – 'the wrath of the Lamb' and 'the great day of their wrath has come'

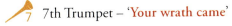 7th Trumpet – 'Your wrath came'

 7th Sign – 'the wrath of God is finished'

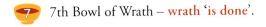 7th Bowl of Wrath – wrath 'is done'.

So what does God's wrath mean exactly? And how does it fit into our understanding of God as Love? God's wrath should not be caricatured as vengeful rage, but rather as the consequence of sin in the face of God's love – the effects of not living in God's world in God's way (see also Discussion Topic below). As we go through these 4 sets of 7, there is a greater and greater intensity of God's anger as His reaction to and rejection of evil increases.

Not only does God's wrath intensify towards its fulfilment, as the Greek reflects, but the lightnings and noises coming out of the Throne of God increase, emphasising that, whatever is happening, while not necessarily God's direct will, events are not out of His control. This does not mean God is controlling everything, including people's sin, but rather that God is at work in this process and is not going to let it be derailed. Even when we see the greatest ever earthquake or a severe hailstorm, these things emanate from the Throne: God is still in charge and ultimately, as bad as things might seem, He is getting His will done.

So as we get to the end of each set of 7, we seem to reach the Second Coming, but each time the pace and intensity seems to go up a notch. This gives the feeling that things are building up towards a great climax – Seals are broken, then Trumpets are blown, Signs appear one after another and then the Bowls of Wrath are poured out almost verse after verse – and then, 'It is done'.

Discussion Topic: The Second Coming

At His ascension, Jesus was promised to return 'in the same way as you have watched Him go into heaven' (Acts 1:11). We read about this Second Coming, sometimes called *parousia* in Greek, in Matthew 24:3,27,37,39 (NB not v30), 1 Thessalonians 4:13–17 and 1 Corinthians 15:23, among other places.

> For as the lightning comes from the east and shines as far as the west, so will be the coming (*parousia*) of the Son of Man . . . (Matthew 24:27)

> For the Lord Himself will descend from heaven with a shout, with the voice of the archangel and with the trumpet of God, and the dead in Christ will rise first. Then we who are alive and remain will be caught up together with them in the clouds to meet the Lord in the air . . . (1 Thessalonians 4:16–17)

> For as in Adam all die, so also in Christ all will be made alive. But each in his own order: Christ the first fruits, after that those who are Christ's at His coming (*parousia*), then comes the end, when He hands over the kingdom to the God and Father, when He has abolished all rule and all authority and power. For He must reign until He has put all His enemies under His feet. The last enemy that will be abolished is death. (1 Corinthians 15:22–26)

> For an hour is coming when all who are in the tombs will hear his voice and come out, those who have done good to the resurrection of life, and those who have done evil to the resurrection of judgment (John 5:28–29)

> When the Son of Man comes in his glory, and all the angels with him, then He will sit on his glorious throne. Before him will be gathered all the nations, and he will separate people one from another as a shepherd separates the sheep from the goats. (Matthew 25:31–32)

> Christ Jesus, who is to judge the living and the dead, and by his appearing and his kingdom. (2 Timothy 4:1)

We do not know exactly what the Second Coming will look like, but from these verses we can begin to build a picture of it, which will involve:

- Jesus returning to the earth in the clouds, with lightning
- Resurrection of the righteous first with recompense (cf Matthew 16:27), that is, Christ's Bride
- Resurrection of all the rest of humankind, followed by judgment at the Great White Throne.

While the word *parousia* does not occur in Revelation, the event itself is referred to throughout the book using this same imagery, culminating in His coming again in glory in Revelation 19—21.

Discussion Topic: Wrath of God

Revelation 6:16 talks about 'the wrath of the Lamb', which is a strange contrast – you may have seen an angry ram, but have you ever seen an angry lamb? We are encountering the wrath of a God of Love who died on the Cross for us – this is a serious warning, and I think this touches into some of the deepest aspects of the persons of the Godhead.

What exactly is God's 'wrath'? Wrath is often caricatured as malice, with God as a cruel and vindictive dictator, smiting everyone who does anything wrong. So much so, that some have tried to write it out of the Bible because it does not fit with a cosy view of God being our best friend. However, others seem to talk only about God's wrath and judgment, barely mentioning love or forgiveness. There needs to be a middle way, where we hold love and wrath together.

So how can we understand it? Simply put, wrath is the consequence of not living in God's universe in God's way – it is God's reaction to humankind's defection. God is light, and just as light destroys darkness, God's presence destroys sin – His wrath is the destruction of sin in our lives, merely because of who He is. This does not imply malice or hatred, but justice. We cannot eliminate the wrath of God from our theology.

Whatever else we find in this section of Revelation, we are seeing God's divine repudiation of sin – His wrath. Of course we want good news and are looking for the love of God to be revealed, but here Revelation is showing us that love can be angry. The revulsion that we see takes place because, as we have seen in Revelation 4:8, the Godhead is 'Holy, Holy, Holy' – it is this holiness which reacts against and repels the darkness and ugliness that is being revealed here.

The Greek root of the word 'wrath' – *thumós* – describes an expression of intense emotion that may spill out. For example, when one's children put themselves in harms way, say by running into the road, the rescue is often with anger and love all mixed up. It is only because God is love that He gets angry. If He did not care about His Creation, if He did not love us, then wrath would not be rational or reasonable. The closest we get to feeling wrath is when we also have great love. For example, when a parent is tragically disappointed in the way their child behaves towards them, or a husband or wife who feels the hot anger of betrayal. So there is no real contradiction between the love of God and the wrath of God – He feels anger because He is love. By becoming incarnate Jesus has experienced all the emotions we do and His anger at injustice is one of them.

There is a sense in which Christians are saved *to* some things (for example to enjoy God's approbation, fullness of joy), but we need to realise we are also being saved *from* the ugliness and horror that sin causes. The second section of Revelation heightens our awareness of what a great salvation we have in Christ, who was made a curse for us and who bore the wrath of God (Galatians 3:13, 2 Corinthians 5:21, Romans 5:9). It is as though in Jesus, i. God has reacted in anger to sin, while ii. at the same time, by becoming a man He takes the position of receiving that wrath, but as God He takes it into His own heart so that it might be exhausted. This is the wonder of the Cross.

Some Christians find the idea of the 'Day of Wrath' upsetting or scary, however, chapter 6 ends with the paradoxical assertion: 'who can stand?' The ones who can stand in resurrection are the Overcomers, so maybe we should be encouraged to look to find the hope that lies within God's wrath.

The Second Vision | Revelation 6—16

Structure of the 7s

Rather than just being discrete or sequential groups, we are meant to see these sets of 7 as integrated together: the 7 Trumpets are part of the 7th Seal being broken, and then within the 7 Trumpets are the 7 Signs, and under the 7th Sign come the 7 Bowls. While many have interpreted these 7s as a chronological sequence, maybe they would be better seen as nested one inside the other.

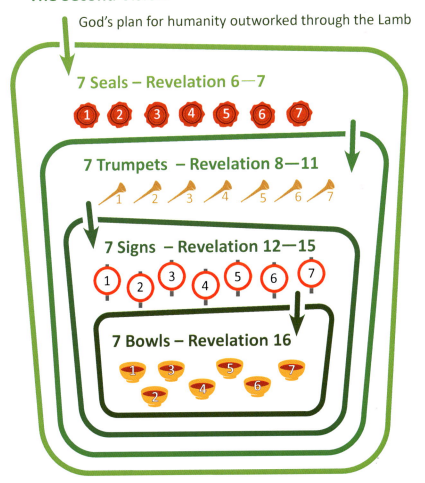

Indeed, there are pitfalls in being too literal, too prescriptive or too chronological in our interpretation – we read about these events in the order in which they were revealed to John in his vision, which may not necessarily be the same as the order they happen in. Not only the order, but the timing is open to interpretation: do they directly follow one another, or are there seconds, days, years or millennia between one event and the next?

Are these discrete events which only happen once? Or are they patterns which keep on repeating through history?

4 Spheres of existence

Even though they may roll into one other, each of these sets of 7 has its own particular emphasis and application, and represent God's judgment in different spheres of existence. We could see them as looking at the same truths from 4 different angles, similar to how the 4 gospels each record Jesus' life, but from different points of view. The 7 Seals depict judgment in the condition of humanity – politics, authority and history, whereas the 7 Trumpets when they are sounded unleash demonic forces from the Abyss. The 7 Signs show the spiritual conditions arising both of the Church and of demonic worship, and the 7 Bowls of wrath emphasize the divine – it is God who is ultimately in control.

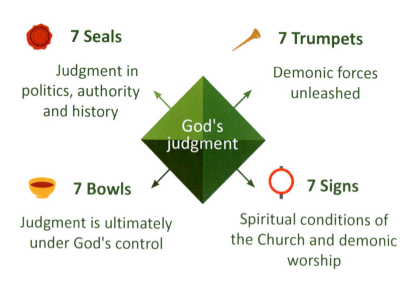

Structure within the 7s

There is also a structure that follows through each set of 7. After the first 4 of each set there is a hiatus – a break – indicating those first 4 things belong together. For instance, Seals 1–4 are all Horsemen, then it changes. The first 4 Trumpets are all to do with stars and plagues dropping from heaven into the sea and then onto the earth, and then it changes. The first 4 Signs are to do with the woman and man-child, and the next 3 Signs are different. Following this pattern indicates we should also interpret the first 4 Bowls together in the same context.

Not only that, but there is also an interlude – a breathing space – between the 6th and 7th of each set, which reveals something about the Church:

-› After 6th seal: interlude = Revelation 7:1–17
-› After 6th trumpet: interlude = Revelation 10:1–11:13
-› After 6th sign: interlude = Revelation 15:2–4
-› After 6th Bowl: interlude 'behold He comes as a thief' = Revelation 16:15

This structure of 4 + 3, with an interlude between 6 and 7 is helpful to grasp as we go through this second section.

Structure of the sets of 7

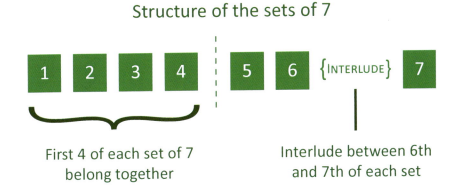

First 4 of each set of 7 belong together

Interlude between 6th and 7th of each set

Section II – Christ Central in Creation

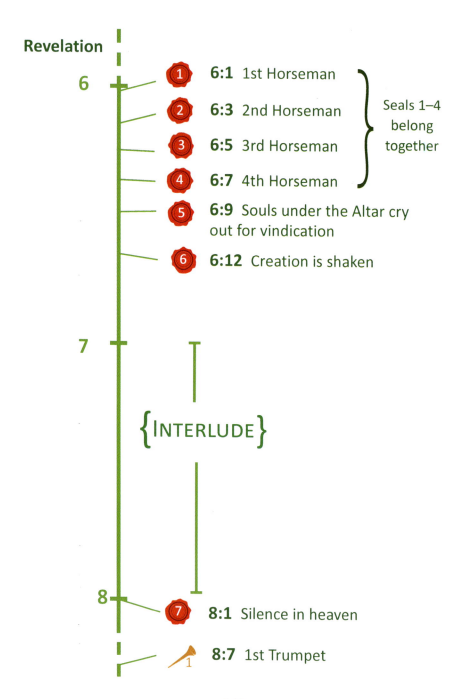

The 7 Seals

Continuing the glorious scene of Christ standing in the midst of the throne surrounded by worship in Revelation 5, in chapters 6—8 the Lamb takes the book of God's purpose for humanity and opens the 7 Seals one by one. Christ does not open the book in silence, but in a flow of praise, worship and intercession. As we worship Jesus, offering up our hearts in adoration, our praise breaks through the powers of darkness in the heavenlies, and joins the worship around the throne. The Lord has provided the basis whereby He can now act in society to bring about His purposes.

We can picture it like this: at the Fall, Satan blocked off humanity from a personal knowledge and experience of Father God – like a thick, dark blanket. It was difficult to know God or His purpose for us, but through Christ's Crucifixion God has torn through that dark shroud, symbolized by the Temple curtain. When we worship together, we can come through the tear and reach out to God, opening up a channel for God's presence here on earth – not just for ourselves, but for the whole of the human race. We are the intermediaries and we bring in the Kingdom by being priestly. Through this open channel God can begin to manoeuvre to bring about the destiny for which He made us in the first place, using the actions of the enemy as well as His own, including the things we will see appear in the 7 Seals: horsemen, thrones, dominions and powers.

The 7 Seals show us forces which represent political and international machinations, and reveal how the spiritual realm affects human structures of authority throughout history: governments, nations and wars.

The Tribulation

Traditionally, from Revelation 6:1 through to the end of the chapter has been called 'The Tribulation' or 'The Great Tribulation' – a time of widespread trouble and distress which builds up to the end of the age with a time of testing that will try the whole earth (Revelation 3:10). Many of the judgments we will see when the Seals are opened are reflections of the Old Testament, where they were prophesied about a particular nation at a particular time – 'the day of the Lord'. Those prophecies did not just have a local, Old Testament fulfilment, but also an eschatological one. While the events in Revelation 6 indicate such a time of distress at the End of the Age, I will suggest we should also see 'the Tribulation' (literally pressure or compression) as already happening now, with the whole of the Church Age in view.

The Tribulation is not confined to only the End of the Age (Futurist), nor to the first century (Praeterist), or even discrete points through church history (Historicist), neither does it merely represent a vague scheme of general distress (Spiritual) – these events are moving towards a conclusion. The danger of sticking with just one of these four main interpretations is that we may either write off the events surrounding these 7 Seals as irrelevant to our lives (they have already happened or will happen way in the future) and so do not worry us, or else by over-abstracting them we miss something specific which God is trying to point us towards.

Using the Gestational view (see page 16), we can see the Tribulation like a pebble being dropped into a pond: the ripples start in the first century with the fall of Jerusalem in AD 70 – the first fulfilment of Tribulation – we see Jesus using similar imagery in the 'Synoptic Apocalypse' of Mark 13, Luke 21 and Matthew 24. There will be travail, earthquakes, pestilence, nation against nation, kingdom against kingdom, which is what we see here, culminating with the fall of Jerusalem. However, it did not stop there and ever since other ripples of tribulation have come, with similar events happening again in the second century and again in the third century, and so on . . . and they are still happening today.

Through church history we see the same patterns of persecution reproduced as these ripples spread across the pool, until finally they reach the edge. The impact of the horsemen riding is reverberating through history, including in our present time, until at last it will spread and intensify until it engulfs the whole world. Instead of there being little mini-tribulations and expressions of 'in the world you will have tribulation' (John 16:33), there is one great maxi-tribulation – the Great Tribulation – where these prophecies will reach their ultimate fulfilment, breaking forth in the Second Coming, resurrection of the dead and final judgment.

These spiritual tribulations have been taking place through every generation, such that everyone has been warned by them – *Repent for the day of the Lord is at hand: judgment is coming*! Understanding tribulation in this way should encourage us with how it applies to our lives now. We have a choice: we can anticipate that final day of judgment now, do something about it and live our lives in a manner fit for the Lord, or we can ignore it and wait until the final judgment hits us, by which time we will not be able to do anything about it. There is going to be a day of accounting for our lives, so why not get right with God now, rather than wait and take a chance?

Revelation 6

In Revelation 6 the Lamb breaks the first 6 Seals on the Book, the first four releasing 4 Horsemen, the fifth revealing the Martyrs under the Altar and the sixth, Creation being shaken.

Seals 1–4: The Four Horsemen
Text – Revelation 6:1–8

(1) ¹ Then I saw when the Lamb broke one of the seven seals, and I heard one of the four living creatures saying as with a voice of thunder, 'Come.' ² I looked, and behold, a white horse, and he who sat on it had a bow; and a crown was given to him, and he went out conquering and to conquer.

(2) ³ When He broke the second seal, I heard the second living creature saying, 'Come.' ⁴ And another, a red horse, went out; and to him who sat on it, it was granted to take peace from the earth, and that men would slay one another; and a great sword was given to him.

(3) ⁵ When He broke the third seal, I heard the third living creature saying, 'Come.' I looked, and behold, a black horse; and he who sat on it had a pair of scales in his hand. ⁶ And I heard something like a voice in the centre of the four living creatures saying, 'A quart of wheat for a denarius, and three quarts of barley for a denarius; and do not damage the oil and the wine.'

(4) ⁷ When the Lamb broke the fourth seal, I heard the voice of the fourth living creature saying, 'Come.' ⁸ I looked, and behold, an ashen horse; and he who sat on it had the name Death; and Hades was following with him. Authority was given to them over a fourth of the earth, to kill with sword and with famine and with pestilence and by the wild beasts of the earth.

The 4 Horsemen (v1–8)

The first 4 Seals give us one of the most well-known images from Revelation in popular culture: 'The Four Horsemen of the Apocalypse' – Famine, Death, Plague and War. However, as we look in more depth we will see that there is more to this picture than the received view.

At what point in history does the Lamb break the first 4 Seals? When do these horsemen ride? As we looked at above, the Futurist view is that at a given point towards the End of the Age, the Seals will start being broken and we will see wars, famines and plagues happening. However, the problem is that these sorts of things happen today and have happened all the way through the Church Age: none of them are merely confined to some vague future time – they are with us today. The 4 Horsemen may represent ripples of similar events through history, as in the Gestational view, with the understanding there may well be an ultimate fulfilment of 'Horseman' events.

The meaning of the 4 Horsemen (v2–6)

When the first 4 Seals are broken, 4 horses with riders appear, which, as we will see represent forces in the spiritual realm that are going out and having an impact in the world. We are not meant to be looking for actual horses appearing on the earth, rather we are meant to ask ourselves what these different coloured horses and their riders represent, and why they appear here. If we look back to the Old Testament we begin to get some clues.

4 Horses – Zechariah 1 & 6

The main place to help us to interpret these 4 different coloured horses is Zechariah, which is written in the period after the Exile in Babylon, in the context of the Lord calling His people back to Him, and bringing judgment upon the nations: '"Return to Me" declares the Lord of hosts, "that I may return to you"' (Zechariah 1:3).

Zechariah has a vision of a man riding on a red horse and standing among myrtle trees, 'with red, sorrel (chestnut) and white horses behind him'. When Zechariah asks the angel, 'My lord, what are these?', the man in the myrtle

The 7 Seals | Revelation 6:1–8

trees answers, 'These are those whom the Lord has sent to patrol the earth', with the result that 'all the earth is peaceful and quiet' (verses 8–11).

Then in chapter 6, Zechariah has a vision of 4 chariots, which indicate war, pulled by different coloured horses, this time red, black, white and dappled. While the colours are not exactly the same as in Zechariah 1 and 6 or Revelation 6, the overall message of what they represent is the same:

> So I responded and said to the angel who was speaking with me, 'What are these, my lord?' The angel replied to me, 'These are the four spirits of heaven, going out after taking their stand before the Lord of all the earth, with one of which the black horses are going out to the north country; and the white ones are to go out after them, while the spotted ones are to go out to the south country.' When the strong ones went out, they were eager to go to patrol the earth. And He said, 'Go, patrol the earth.' So they patrolled the earth. Then He called out to me and spoke to me, saying, 'See, those who are going to the land of the north have appeased My wrath in the land of the north.' (Zechariah 6:4–8)

In Zechariah, these chariots and horses are 'the four spirits of heaven' (Zechariah 6:5) who patrol the earth – they are heavenly forces, whose movements are involved with the political workings of nations which take place on earth. The Horsemen here in Revelation are also 'Spirits', as we will read in Revelation 7:1 (see page 282, also Daniel 7:2). It is important to note the word for 'spirit' also means 'wind' or 'breath' both in Hebrew – *ruach* – and in Greek – *pneuma*. So these 4 spirits may be 4 winds or 4 breaths. We will see these 4 spirits reappearing when we get to Revelation 12.

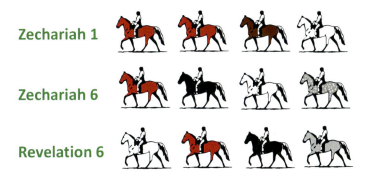

Purification and punishment

The horses in Zechariah are involved in judgment and God's wrath (6:8), themes that run through this section of Revelation, and when the 5th Seal is broken we will see the souls of the Martyrs under the Altar crying out for God to bring judgment. So in Revelation these 4 Horsemen, who are called forth by the 4 Living Creatures, similarly represent heavenly spirits whose movements impact and empower political and national powers to bring about judgment. These seem to be the same powers in their multicoloured and polymorphic manifestations in both Zechariah and Revelation.

Throughout Scripture, God's anger with His people is almost always identified with their idolatrous worship of false gods, which often expresses itself in immorality (see Romans 1:18). Time and again, Israel rejected the Lord and fell into idolatry and immorality, incurring God's judgment. Then, world forces, like Babylon, Assyria, Egypt or Persia come and rise up against the people of God. On one hand, this has a purging effect for the remnant who begin to call on the name of the Lord, while on the other it has a punishing effect because God judges evil.

The stirring up of these empires would bring judgment upon Israel because of their apostasy and idolatry, with the end result that some would repent and return to the Lord, while others would bear the punishment.

Judgment needs to be accepted before peace can ensue. Sin must be acknowledged before we can know reconciling peace – this is the effect of the horses, both in Zechariah and in Revelation. Equally, it shows that living in God's world in God's way is the best!

Fourfold judgment

The forces we see when the 4 Horsemen are unleashed in Revelation 6 closely parallel those we see in Leviticus 26 and Ezekiel 5. In Leviticus 26:14–45, we find disease, death, war and famine all mentioned as consequences 'if you do not obey Me, and do not carry out all these commandments'.

In Ezekiel 5, these same judgements are again threatened upon the apostates of exiled Israel:

> When I send against them the deadly arrows of famine which were for the destruction of those whom I shall send to destroy you, then I shall also intensify the famine upon you and break the staff of bread. Moreover, I will send on you famine and wild beasts, and

they will bereave you of children; plague and bloodshed also will pass through you, and I will bring the sword on you. I, the Lord, have spoken. (Ezekiel 5:16–17)

We see the same judgments again in Ezekiel 14:21, and another similar fourfold judgment in Jeremiah 15:2–3, which we will look at in more detail when we get to Revelation 13:10. It is important to reiterate that while in each case these judgments come from God's Throne, it does not mean He is directly orchestrating these events, however, they are consequences of His judgment.

The Old Testament often presents God as doing dark and harsh things, not because He wishes these things directly upon people, but because He 'upholds all things by the word of His power' (Hebrews 1:3), and these are the consequences of His maintaining the orderliness of the universe and its powers. For example, if a man breaks his neck while trying to deny gravity by throwing himself over a cliff; is God responsible for his injury?

We see similar things in Jesus' teaching, in what is sometimes called the 'Synoptic Apocalypse' (Matthew 24:6–8,29, Mark 13:7–9, and Luke 21:9–12,25–26). Here Jesus teaches about the Church Age and the End Times that are going to come upon us. He speaks of wars and rumours of wars, kingdom against kingdom, nation against nation, tribulation and killing, famine, earthquakes and plagues.

So in the 4 Horsemen we see what was already present in an embryonic form in Jesus' teaching, with Ezekiel and Zechariah as the background. All these warning messages in Scripture are being drawn together and concentrated in these first eight verses of Revelation 6, and their echoes will continue until we get to the final fulfilment at the End of the Age.

'Come' (v1,3,5,7)

Each of the 4 Horses/Horsemen are called forth by one of the 4 Living Creatures, who say 'Come', or 'Go' – the same Greek word is used for both.

Personally, I think it makes most sense if the Horses/Horsemen are each called forth by a different one of the 4 Living Creatures, as there are four of each. Alternatively, the same Living Creature could call each time. I will leave the detail to your imagination.

The Living Creatures speak with a voice of thunder, which hints that what they say is attached to the Throne of God – although God is not ordaining man's inhumanity to man, it is not chaotic or out of control. Indeed, the Bible shows us how God sets limits, for example in Job and with Peter's denials. God's authority is working to make even that which we ultimately intend for evil, into something out of which His good purpose will come (Genesis 50:20).

The Living Creatures and the Horsemen (v2...)

What is the link between the Living Creatures and the Horsemen? The horsemen ride forth because the Living Creatures speak.

However, as we will see, three if not four of the Horsemen are destructive forces – if the Living Creatures are speaking with a voice from God's Throne, doesn't this mean God is directly ordaining the violence, death and destruction of the Horsemen? Why are the Living Creatures, who are worshipping God and the Lamb, the means whereby these horses ride forth? Zechariah 1:10 says 'They are the ones the Lord has sent to patrol the earth.' So each of the Horsemen seems to be some sort of entity – a spirit – which is being used to get a truth over.

So how are the 4 Horses/Horsemen and 4 Living Creatures linked together? There is what you might call an apocalyptic or figurative logic, which weaves its way through all these delegated powers. The Throne of God is ultimately behind everything, but when God created the Heavens and the earth, He delegated power and gave freewill not just to humankind, but also to the angels – this is what made room for sin to take place. The Throne of God is functioning here on earth, but there are also other spiritual forces and powers at work, some for God's will and some in opposition. Not only does God work through His angels and through us, He is also working through activities that oppose His will to ultimately get His will done.

So while it may seem to be counter-intuitive that the 4 Living Creatures who worship around the Throne are responsible not only for the 4 Horsemen being released, but also for the 4 bound angels being released in Revelation 9 (see page 347), this reveals to us how 'in all things God works together with those who love him to bring about what is good' (Roman 8:28, NIV margin). This is the complex nature of the universe, but fundamentally, what God does and what He wishes are not the same thing (Matthew 23:37–39).

Of course God could choose to just scrap the whole of Creation and start again – although the same thing may happen again. Instead He has chosen to stick with the forces and powers He has made and the effect they are having on earth, and He will work with them and through them in order that, ultimately, His Will will be done. The great breakthrough, through the Cross, was to produce a people like ourselves, who, because Christ lives in us, can bring the light of heaven down onto earth – 'Your Will be done on earth, as it is in heaven' – so that ultimately God can achieve that for which He made the whole of Creation.

Discussion Topic: Crowns in Revelation

Crowns (*stephanos, stephanoi*) are mentioned eight times in Revelation and diadems (*diademata*) three times, and both basically represent having authority over something.

Most of the time we see crowns representing something good:

> Be faithful until death, and I will give you the crown of life. (Revelation 2:10)

> I am coming quickly; hold fast what you have, so that no one will take your crown. (Revelation 3:11)

> I saw twenty-four elders sitting, clothed in white garments, and golden crowns on their heads . . . the twenty-four elders will fall down before Him who sits on the throne, and will worship Him who lives forever and ever, and will cast their crowns before the throne (Revelation 4:4,10)

> A great sign appeared in heaven: a woman clothed with the sun, and the moon under her feet, and on her head a crown of twelve stars. (Revelation 12:1)

> Then I looked, and behold, a white cloud, and sitting on the cloud was one like a son of man, having a golden crown on His head and a sharp sickle in His hand. (Revelation 14:14)

As well as these 'good' crowns, there is one definite instance of bad crowns, where they appear on the heads of the locust–horse army in Revelation 9:7. The remaining crown is controversial – some interpret it as good and some as evil, as it is given to the rider on the 1st Horse.

> I looked, and behold, a white horse, and he who sat on it had a bow; and a crown was given to him, and he went out conquering and to conquer. (Revelation 6:2)

(For more on whether the Horseman on the White Horse is good or bad, see below.)

In comparison, 2 out of the 3 times diadems appear they are on the Dragon (Revelation 12:3 (7 diadems)) and the Beast (Revelation 13:1 (10 diadems)), and once on the victorious Christ:

> His eyes are a flame of fire, and on His head are many diadems . . . (Revelation 19:12)

This may represent Christ's victory over the Dragon and the Beast.

So, both crowns and diadems can be seen on 'good' or 'bad' forces, but in whichever case, they represent authority.

A number of other crowns appear in the New Testament, usually as rewards – for a more in-depth look at these, please see the discussion topic on page 118, and my book, *Gold, Silver & Precious Stones: The Doctrine of Rewards and Losses*.

1st Seal – The Horseman on the White Horse (v1)

The rider on the White Horse had a bow, was given a crown, and went out 'conquering' or 'overcoming'. Although many interpret all the Horsemen as bad, this one looks a bit like Jesus when He returns in triumph in Revelation 19:11. So who or what exactly does this horse and rider represent?

4 Horsemen, or 1 + 3 Horsemen?

Here there is controversy amongst commentators – while there is general consensus about the 4 Horsemen being spiritual powers, the popular view is that each of the four horses represent bad forces, being driven on by the horsemen, snorting to attack humanity with war, famine, plague and death.

Although these 'horse powers' which are let loose in the heavens are disturbing the earth in certain ways, we should not assume this necessarily means they are all negative or evil forces causing death.

I tend towards the view shared with a minority of commentators, that the rider on the white horse actually represents something good, whereas the next three horses and horsemen represent bad things: the red horse represents bloodshed, war and kingdom against kingdom; the black horse is famine and poverty which destroy people's lives, slowly killing them by taking away from life what God intended it to be; and the final ashen horse of pestilence and death. These latter three horses all obviously seem to be bound together in negatives, whereas the first one might not be:

Revelation 19

If we look forwards to Revelation 19:11–16, we see Jesus coming out of heaven riding a white horse, wearing many crowns, and surrounded by an army dressed in white and riding white horses:

> And I saw heaven opened, and behold, a white horse, and He who sat on it is called Faithful and True, and in righteousness He judges and wages war. (v11)

So could the Horseman on the white horse be, or at least represent, Jesus working through the Holy Spirit?

White

As we looked at on page 32, all the way through Revelation white symbolises goodness and purity, in stark contrast to the red representing bloodshed and martyrdom, and black representing darkness and evil. Later in the chapter we will see the martyred saints being given white clothing (6:11), so it would seem a little strange for the white horse to represent something bad, but the white robes to represent good, and so symbolise totally opposite things within a few verses of each other.

'Another'

The text of Revelation does seem to draw a distinction between the first horse and the next three. After the White Horse:

> And *another*, a red horse, went out. (Revelation 6:4)

After that for the third and fourth horses it merely says 'and behold, a black horse . . . and behold, an ashen horse' (6:5,8). It is as though there is a break being made between the first horse and the next three, perhaps indicating a separate group of horses.

Crown

As we look at in the Discussion Topic above, crowns represent authority, and so far in Revelation crowns have represented godly authority or reward, first for the Overcomer (2:10,3:11), and then for the 24 Elders (4:4,10). None of the other Horsemen are given a crown, so there is something different in terms of authority about the rider on the White Horse.

Conquering/overcoming

The Greek word translated in 6:2 as 'conquering' is the same one translated 'overcoming' in the letters to the 7 Churches – 'to the one who overcomes/conquers'. So the rider on the white horse is an overcomer and, up to this point at least, overcoming has always been something positive in Revelation; indeed in chapter 3 Christ says He is an overcomer (v20–21).

In the Old Testament, conquering is often seen as an attribute of the Messiah, and Psalm 45 is particularly salient here: it addresses a king riding in splendour 'victoriously', which in the Septuagint is translated using the same word as 'conquer/overcome'. This rider fires arrows, which implies they have a bow, like the rider on the white horse in Revelation.

> Gird Your sword on Your thigh, O Mighty One,
> In Your splendour and Your majesty!
> And in Your majesty ride on victoriously,
> For the cause of truth and meekness and righteousness;
> Let Your right hand teach You awesome things.
> Your arrows are sharp;
> The peoples fall under You;
> Your arrows are in the heart of the King's enemies. (v3–5)

This is a Messianic psalm: verse 6 is quoted in Hebrews 1:8 as God speaking about the Son, and verse 7 talks about Him being anointed with oil, which is a how kings and priests were commissioned, the oil representing the Holy Spirit.

The 7 Seals | Revelation 6:1–8

> Your throne, O God, is forever and ever;
> A sceptre of uprightness is the sceptre of Your kingdom.
> You have loved righteousness and hated wickedness:
> Therefore God, Thy God has anointed You
> with the oil of joy above Your fellows. (v6–7)

Psalm 45 paints a picture of Jesus, the Messiah, riding on a horse and firing arrows as He goes forth to overcome God's enemies and all that oppose His Kingdom. Is this what we are seeing in the first horseman?

4 Horses/Horsemen = negative spiritual forces

or

1st Horse/Horseman = good (the Gospel?)
+
other 3 Horses/Horsemen = negative spiritual forces

The Gospel and the counter-attack

In that case, perhaps we can see the white horse as representing the Gospel – the power of Jesus as the Good News – which goes forth into the earth overcoming, and 'must first be preached to all the nations' before the end can come (Mark 13:10).

What about the other horses? Well, as the Gospel goes out into the world, the enemy's counter-attack becomes apparent in disturbances in society, just as Jesus prophesies in the Synoptic Apocalypse (see page 248). As the Gospel goes out, overcoming:

'There will be wars, rumours of wars, kingdoms against kingdom and then there will be famine and pestilence.'

As the saints disrupt Satan's forces when they take the Gospel forward, the hit-back of the devil is to bring tribulation (John 16:33, Revelation 1:9) – this is spiritual warfare – and the impression we get from Zechariah and Daniel is that this does not just affect individuals or the Church, but these forces are at the level of nations. The disturbance caused by the Overcomers will spread to all the nations as the Gospel goes throughout the world.

The effects of these Horsemen are felt first in the heavenly places – they are spirits, and so act in a spiritual realm. However, humans are made up of mind, body and spirit together, so once these disturbances affect the spirits of humans, they will be expressed in human minds and bodies, spreading out into the world with tangible physical effects.

This leads us on to the second horseman . . .

 ### 2nd Seal: Rider on the Red Horse – War (v3–4)

Following the White Horse comes the Red Horse of warfare and bloodshed, whose rider was given 'a great sword' in order to 'take peace from the earth . . . that men would slay one another'. Whereas the Rider on the White Horse goes forth to conquer/overcome, here the Rider on the Red Horse aims to spread violence to humanity.

God does not wish war, but will use it to get His will done when it arises as part of the disturbances caused by His Kingdom.

 ### 3rd Seal: Rider on the Black Horse – Famine (v5–6)

Inevitably following war comes famine and economic hardship – the food taken by the armies, the land trampled and laid waste, and many of the labourers killed. The devastation caused, as well as heavy taxation to pay for war, leads to spiralling prices, meaning people cannot afford food to eat.

Here the Rider of the Black Horse holds scales to weigh out the food because of rationing during famine. John hears a voice talking about '1 quart of wheat' and '3 quarts of barley' for a denarius. A denarius was a typical day's wages for a labourer (see Matthew 20:2) and 1 quart was a daily ration of food. So you had to work to feed yourself, and buy cheaper grain in order to barely feed your family – with the highly inflated prices all of your money would be gone.

'Do not harm the oil and the wine' is an interesting phrase – what does it mean? Some commentators view oil and wine as luxury goods, while others regard them as part of the staple diet – either way they would be beyond the means of an average worker in a famine. 'Harming' the olive trees or grape vines, which have deeper roots than wheat and barley and can survive mild drought, could refer to farmers destroying them to avoid land taxation, or neglecting them due to the post-war conditions (compare Joel 1:10–11).

The voice John hears comes out from 'the centre of the 4 Living Creatures' – does it come from the creatures themselves, or as they are around the Throne, is it issuing forth from the Throne of God, just as the thunder and lightning do? Either way, the Lord is still on the Throne despite the chaos and destruction – God has authority and is still guiding this process, even if it is not His wish. Here the voice is expressing God's desire to alleviate the famine as a command not to harm the vines and olive trees.

4th Seal: Rider on the Ashen Horse – Death & Hades (v7–8)

Finally after war and famine come Death and disease. Death is named as the rider on the Ashen, or pale green, Horse and is followed by Hades.

Death and Hades (*Sheol* in the Old Testament) appear together in Scripture, particularly in the psalms. In some cases they are personified as they are here in Revelation:

> As sheep they are appointed for Sheol; Death shall be their shepherd. (Psalm 49:14)

> Shall I ransom them from the power of Sheol?
> Shall I redeem them from death?
> O Death, where are your thorns?
> O Sheol, where is your sting?
> (Hosea 13:14, as quoted by Paul in 1 Corinthians 15:55)

Here Death and Hades are shown not as natural physical consequences of the end of life, they are part of the supernatural forces at work, and they receive authority. The upshot is that a quarter of deaths worldwide are untimely, due to the sword (war, execution), famine, disease and wild beasts. While untimely death is seemingly contrary to the Lord's desire that His people live long in the land (see Deuteronomy 5:33, Ephesians 6:3), alternatively we could see these wars, famines and plagues as the beginning of 'birth pangs' of the coming Kingdom (see Matthew 24:6–8).

Death: spiritual or physical?

So what exactly does 'Death' represent here? Is it spiritual or physical?

In Paul's great eulogy in Romans about what would separate us from the love of God – principalities, powers, things present, things to come, death – he seems to imply death is seen, not just as physical death, but death is at work and keeps on pushing at us and challenging us, making us feel dead in our souls. In physical death we become dead to the physical world – but in spiritual death we become dead to the spiritual world and to God. It is more a figurative or metaphorical statement than literal. Similarly, we could see the other effects of the horsemen – war, famine, pestilence and wild beasts – as spiritual, and not necessarily physical. However, of course it does not preclude the literal being seen here.

Revelation is a very symbolic book, which paints very stark images, so it is certainly not unreasonable to interpret these souls not only as physical martyrs, but also those who have been persecuted for Jesus' sake.

> ### Discussion Topic: Physical vs spiritual death
>
> In Revelation we are confronted with Death, which appears in various ways: there are the keys of death and Hades (1:18), those 'faithful until death' (2:10), those who 'seek death and will not find it' (9:6), after the 4th Seal is broken Death is personified as the Rider on the Ashen Horse (6:8), and we read of the lake of fire, also known as 'the Second Death' (2:11, 20:6,14–15, 21:8).
>
> Even when not named, death appears in the form of those who are killed: Antipas (2:13), the martyred souls (6:9–11), those killed by the plagues (9:18), the earthquake (11:13) and those who do not worship the image of the beast (13:15). Also there are those killed by the fire from the mouths of the 2 Witnesses (11:5) and the sword from the mouth of the triumphant Christ (19:21). Finally, we see Death and Hades judged and thrown into the Second Death (20:13).
>
> However, what does 'death' represent in Revelation? In some cases is seems to mean physical death of the body:

> Be faithful until death, and I will give you the crown of life. (2:10)
>
> And they overcame him because of the blood of the Lamb and because of the word of their testimony, and they did not love their life even when faced with death. (12:11)

Whereas in other places it seems to represent figurative or spiritual death:

> Then Death and Hades were thrown into the lake of fire. This is the second death, the lake of fire. (20:14)

In other places it is not clear if it means physical or spiritual death or possibly even both.

We also see elsewhere in the Bible the idea of death is not always to be understood simply as physical death. For example, in Romans 8, quoting from Psalm 44:22, Paul says:

> Who will separate us from the love of Christ? Will tribulation, or distress, or persecution, or famine, or nakedness, or peril, or sword? Just as it is written,
>
> > 'For your sake we are being put to death all day long; we ere considered as sheep to be slaughtered.'
>
> But in all these things we overwhelmingly conquer through Him who loved us. (Romans 8:35–37)

Of course the psalmist here was not 'put to death all day long', as they lived to write the psalm, so it is a figurative death. It is the metaphorical death Jesus speaks about when He says:

> 'For whoever wishes to save his life will lose it; but whoever loses his life for My sake will find it' (Matthew 16:25, see also 10:39).

This is the hallmark of Christian living – if we want to be able to 'stand before the throne' (Revelation 7:9), then we must be those who are prepared to die. Jesus likens this to the dying of a seed (John

12:24), and sometimes we refer to this as 'dying to self' or 'dying to the world/flesh'. This is not a one-time event: in 1 Corinthians 15:31 Paul says 'I die daily', so whether we are physically martyred or whether it is just the description of general discipleship life, we must be men and women who are everyday laying down our lives in order that we might find them. While in the world's eyes it may seem we have lost our life, in fact we have gained it. The real life God has for us is that which comes from self-denial; not self-indulgence.

There are many who have suffered persecution and even lost their lives while remaining 'alive to the Lord' in their spirits.

While the threat of physical death or persecution may seem easy to understand, it is more difficult to comprehend what spiritual death means. We could picture it as losing the spiritual life that we have with the Lord: the actions of the world, the flesh and the devil could cause us to lose our intimacy with God. It is the reverse of 'dying to self' – dying to our spirit.

What links physical and spiritual death is that both separate us from experiencing the Lord: dying in our body or in our spirit means we are not alive in the presence of the Lord. Of course, following physical death we await resurrection, when we can once again be alive in the Lord. So I would suggest that wherever we see 'death' or being killed in Revelation it symbolises separation from God and His goodness, whether it is physical, figurative or spiritual.

Authority was given ... (v8)

While it says 'authority was given to them', it is unclear whether 'them' means 'Death and Hades' or whether the authority was given to all of the riders. In the original Greek manuscripts both are possible readings.

Whichever view you prefer to take, while it is Death that is responsible for the killing, it is the summation and climax of the effects of all the other horsemen. Whether the authority is just given to Death and Hades, or to all the horsemen, the effect is the same: in a significant proportion of the earth – 'over a quarter' – people suffer untimely, painful, physical or spiritual death.

Counterfeit white?

If you prefer to take the popular view, that all the horses represent negative forces with destructive effects, you have to take the white horse as a counterfeit white. This is not totally out of keeping with Revelation: we will see counterfeit christs, parody resurrections and false prophets appearing in chapters 12 and 13. This could echo Jesus' own warnings about false prophets as 'wolves in sheep's clothing' (Matthew 7:15 and 24:11). We also see that overcoming is not only reserved for the triumph of the saints – up to this point it has always been a positive thing, but in Revelation 11:7 and 13:7 it is the Beast who overcomes God's people. Overcoming or conquering can be a negative thing, so the conquering of the rider on the white horse could be too.

If we look back to Zechariah, all the horses are of the same nature, and even though Revelation 6:4 says 'another' horse, the Greek word used does not imply something of a different nature. Similarly, if we look at Daniel 7 and Revelation 12, the 4 Spirits of heaven there all appear to be negative forces. As for the bow and the crown that are given to the rider, it may be argued that both are symbols associated with the Roman god Apollo, and so the Roman Empire may be in view here. The crown does not necessarily represent godly authority, as crowns may appear on both good and bad forces in Revelation (see Discussion Topic on page 251).

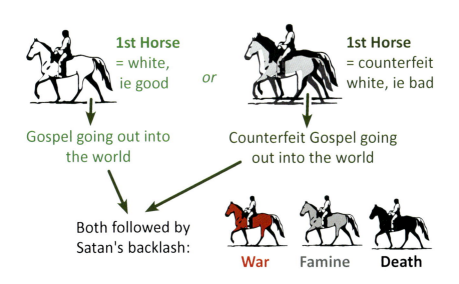

While my preferred view is that the White Horse represents the Gospel going forth into all nations as Christ prophesies, and the other 3 Horses represent Satan's backlash, the 'counterfeit' White Horse is a credible alternative. It may even be possible to have the best of both worlds and hold these views together side-by-side: there would be no point in having an imitation gospel going out into the world, unless the white horse of the Gospel is actually going out already. If the White Horse is a counterfeit, it can only be one because the true Gospel already exists and is spreading. Either way, there is a spiritual force going out into the world which is giving rise to a great spiritual reaction in the form of the last three horsemen.

The trouble with having two sides of the white horse is that there might be two sides to the other horses – somehow they would have to embody the Gospel message, such that the effects of God's judgement would bring people to repentance. The effects of the 4 Horsemen on the earth could be God shouting at us: 'Turn back to me!' The patrol of the earth may suggest that there is indeed a 'policing' to indicate limits and so on, transgression of which may have dire consequences.

The continuing decline of Western society is screaming at us that either the Gospel has not had its proper effect and this is the outcome, or the Gospel is beginning to stir up society. As we have pushed the Gospel out in recent decades, the ensuing disruptions show there is something following behind, whether that is God's judgment and call to repentance for ignoring the Good News, or the devil's backlash to try to deceive and disturb the work of the Gospel.

The effects on evangelism

So in the first 4 Seals we can see the effects on earth of these spiritual forces in heaven, but it all begins with the Rider on the White Horse riding forth. The Good News of Christ crucified, resurrected and ascended is contested, and will attract opposition in attempts to silence it. The threat of the consequences of stepping out for the Lord has been enough to stop many Christians sharing their faith, and has serious implications in our daily Christian walk. We need to be aware that as we spread the Gospel – whether sharing your faith with a friend, street evangelism, or running an Alpha Course – it will cause a reaction. The Great Commission is a serious business, and we need to be serious and strategic about how we conduct ourselves as we push the Gospel forward, and how we protect ourselves from the spiritual reactions it will trigger off.

The 7 Seals | Revelation 6:9–11

Discussion Questions

Are you comfortable with God having 'wrath'?

How do you interpret the Rider on the White Horse?

Does the threat of tribulation affect your witness?

The 5th Seal
Text – Revelation 6:9–11

> ⁹ When the Lamb broke the fifth seal, I saw underneath the altar the souls of those who had been slain because of the word of God, and because of the testimony which they had maintained; ¹⁰ and they cried out with a loud voice, saying, 'How long, O Lord, holy and true, will You refrain from judging and avenging our blood on those who dwell on the earth?' ¹¹ And there was given to each of them a white robe; and they were told that they should rest for a little while longer, until the number of their fellow servants and their brethren who were to be killed even as they had been, would be completed also.

5th Seal – The souls under the Altar (v9)

After the first 4 Seals, the focus changes – now we are looking at the Altar, but the death and destruction caused by the horsemen reappears on the lips of the martyrs underneath the Altar. They are a consequence of the destruction that followed the first 4 Seals being opened. These souls are crying out for vindication, but who are they? Why are they under the Altar? And what is 'the number' that will be completed?

Under the Altar (v9)

In the Temple, as well as in the Tabernacle, there were two altars – the Bronze Altar of sacrifice (Exodus 27:1–8, 2 Chronicles 4:1), and the Golden Altar of incense (Exodus 30:1–9, 2 Chronicles 4:19). However, in Revelation 6:9 it just says 'the Altar', so which altar is in view here?

Bronze Altar

Elsewhere in Revelation where an altar is mentioned, it sometimes refers directly to the Golden Altar of incense, for example Revelation 8:3 and 9:13, and in other places simply to 'the Altar', suggesting the sacrificial Bronze Altar (see 8:3,5, 14:18, 16:7).

In Solomon's Temple, the Bronze Altar was 20 cubits wide and long, and 10 cubits high (1 cubit = the length from the elbow to the tip of the middle finger, around 45 cm).

Golden Altar

The Golden Altar was before the veil of the Holy Place right inside both the Tabernacle and the Temple, and represents a place where prayer ascends to the Throne of God. Twice a day incense was offered on the altar by the priest after he tended to the lamps (Exodus 30:7–8).

The Golden Altar was 1 cubit wide and long, and 2 cubits high.

Bronze Altar of sacrifice

Golden Altar of incense

The Altar here in Revelation 6 is not described as 'golden' and incense is not mentioned, but blood is, so it likely refers to the Bronze Altar, which in both Tabernacle and Temple stood outside the Holy Place in the courtyard (also called the Court of the Priests, or Inner Court), and was where the majority of the sacrifices took place. The Bronze Altar fits the imagery well: the Jewish concept of the soul is that it is in your blood (Leviticus 17:11), and during sacrifices blood was shed on the Bronze Altar which would drip down underneath it. In the 5th Seal we get a similar picture to Leviticus: underneath the Altar we see the souls (blood) of those who have been slain and given up their lives in sacrifice.

However, while most sacrifices were made on the Bronze Altar, once a year on the Day of Atonement a bull and a goat were sacrificed and their blood mixed together and used to cleanse and consecrate the Golden Altar of Incense (see Leviticus 16:18–19). So while the Bronze Altar was more associated with blood and sacrifice, the Golden Altar was purified by blood on the holiest day of the Jewish calendar, *Yom Kippur*, which represents repentance and forgiveness through an atoning sacrifice. Is this what is in view here?

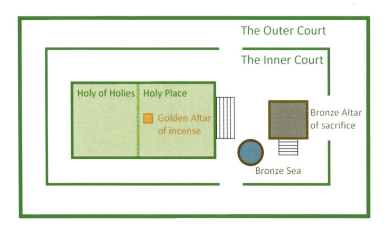

Personally, I prefer to see the Altar here as the Bronze Altar, because it links more strongly with the sacrifice of the martyrs underneath it. Similarly, later in Revelation I prefer to interpret the Bronze Altar whenever there is a context of sacrifice. On the two occasions where we clearly see incense and intercession, the altar is called 'the Golden Altar' (8:3, 9:13).

However, if Revelation 6:9 is referring to the Bronze Altar, it poses a question – why is there still a Bronze Altar if Jesus' sacrifice once for all on the Cross replaced the need for blood sacrifices? I would suggest the Bronze Altar symbolises the spiritual sacrifice of living for Christ, and here underlines the immense sacrifice of the Saints.

Bronze, golden or both?

In some ways it may not matter too much which altar is referred to here. As we saw in the vision in Revelation 4, aspects of the Temple/Tabernacle appear, but in a different form and configuration, a little mixed together, because we are looking at things from a different perspective. With the Temple door open, from the inner court you would be able to see both Bronze Altar and Golden Altar together.

The two altars were also linked together in the process of burning incense – fiery coals were taken in a censer from the Bronze Altar to the Golden Altar, in order to burn the incense before the veil.

So it is also possible that the Altar here represents a combination of the Bronze Altar and Golden Altar together, and indicates lives being given up to God in sacrifice and intercession, both physically and spiritually. Whether it is either one, or both, being under that Altar is an honour – you have become an Overcomer.

The souls (v9)

Who are these souls? Do they represent all Christians? Or only Christian martyrs – those who have been physically murdered for their faith? Or are we looking at a more general state of those, whether actually martyred or not, who have lived a crucified Christian life and suffered for their faith (Galatians 2:20)?

I have been emphasizing that so much of the imagery in Revelation is figurative, revealing spiritual truths, but how far do we take it here? There is certainly scope not to take this totally literally, but rather to see those slain as representing the faithful Church, who have lived and died holding to the Word of God and testifying to their faith, whether or not they have been martyred for it.

Martyrdom is the most extreme form of persecution, and all followers of Jesus should expect persecution of one form or another, as the New Testament makes clear:

> Blessed are those who are persecuted for righteousness' sake, for theirs is the kingdom of heaven. (Matthew 5:10)
>
> Indeed, all who desire to live a godly life in Christ Jesus will be persecuted. (2 Timothy 3:12)

So maybe the souls John sees stand for everyone who has suffered persecution for their faith. Revelation is a book of parabolic imagery and stark contrasts, so here all persecution that results from a life of discipleship is represented in its strongest form: physical death. To deny self, take up our cross and follow Christ is the heart of Christian discipleship as Jesus taught (Matthew 16:24).

We will see the same thing again throughout Revelation, culminating in 20:4, where on their thrones John sees the souls of those 'beheaded because of the testimony of Jesus and because of the word of God'. I suggest throughout we should see these souls as standing for the whole body of those who are persecuted for their faith in Christ.

Physical death versus spiritual persecution

Just as with the 4th Horseman above, the question arises as to whether these souls represent physical martyrdom – 'those who had been killed' – or whether this more broadly signifies persecution in various forms. Christian discipleship means giving up our lives for others, either as a martyr, or by dying to self. We must be men and women who are laying down our lives everyday in order that we might find them. While in the world's eyes it may seem we have lost our life, in fact we have gained it.

That is the kind of person who is under the Altar – somebody who figuratively lives on the Altar and when they die are still found there. So I would suggest the souls under the Altar corporately represent those who lay down their lives to live for Christ.

Slain (v9)

The word 'slain' in verse 9, was also used in verse 4 when humanity 'would slay one another' after the Red Horse rides forth (also in Revelation 5:6). So the same horrendous warfare and bloodshed – slaying – which affects the world in the Second Seal, also affects the Church.

However, these martyrs were slain (this word is the one used also for sacrifice) for their words and their testimony. As we saw in the *Introduction*,

Jesus is both the Word of God and the Witness (Testimony) of God (see page 67), so these martyrs were killed for Jesus. The Greek word *márturos* from which the English word 'martyr' is derived, means 'a witness' (see for example Matthew 18:16).

Why were they slain? They probably loved their enemies, cared for the poor and sought to use their lives to bless others and spread the Good News. You may have thought that godly people would be loved, and righteousness admired, but as Jesus quotes from Psalm 69: 'they hated me without a cause' (John 15:25). Jesus died because of what He was, and because of what we are as His followers, we too will be under that same pressure. The World does not want to be pointed to God, and the Church is hated when it does. It is Christ in us they are opposing: 'If the world hates you, you know that it has hated Me before it hated you' (John 15:18).

How long? (v10)

We then get another song in the book of Revelation. It is a song of worship, in which the souls cry out for vindication and judgment: 'How long O Lord . . ?' which is a quotation from Psalm 79 (see below, page 273).

Some have said this song does not sound very Christian: Jesus tells us to love our enemies and even to pray for them (Matthew 5:44), and when He hung on the cross, He said 'Father forgive . . .' (Luke 23:34). When we are persecuted, shouldn't we pray the same and forgive, rather than calling for judgment?

Forgiving an enemy is a very difficult thing to do – Jesus is not talking about some easy way to cope when someone says or does something unpleasant to you – He is talking about being able to forgive absolute brutality: murder, torture, rape. If someone hates you and really hurts you, can we say 'Father, forgive'? We certainly should pray for our enemies that they will repent and be saved. At the same time we have to understand that if the universe was created by a moral God, there has to be a day of reckoning. Injustice, persecution of the innocent, bloodshed, torture and war – all are crying out to God for vindication.

A desire for justice is paramount as part of our Christian life. It is the biblical Jesus who is the just Judge (Matthew 12:18, John 5:30, 2 Timothy 4:8) and will be given all judgment, all authority in heaven and earth (John 5:22, Matthew 28:18) and this is the foundation of the Great Commission that continues: 'Go therefore and make disciples of all the nations . . .'

(Matthew 28:19). We are told to 'do good', seeking justice for the widow and orphan (Isaiah 1:17). The Kingdom of Jesus is centred on justice – it is the very basis upon which we should spread the Gospel.

The Old Testament saints cried out to God for salvation and righteousness to appear, not because they were self-righteous – they knew they needed God's forgiveness as much as anybody else – but because there must be a day when injustice is somehow or other reversed; when God comes to declare, 'This was right' and 'That was wrong'. God being a judge is not inconsistent with God being love: the love of God is a righteous love. Without justice we would be left in the appalling condition of a God who does not care about sin. This would create a 'wishy-washy' sentimental universe, where there was no right or wrong and everybody was 'alright really'.

Just like the souls under the Altar, as Christians we too need to cry out to God, like the widow crying out to the judge, until we get justice (Luke 18:1–8). Even if we are not interested in getting justice for our own sake, we should be concerned about the appalling things done to others because of sin in the human race. The very fact that blood has been shed is an appeal to God that something should be done to redress the balance. Every martyr is an appeal to God to come with righteousness and truth to judge the earth. This should not be something that we fear, but be something we long for because we believe in righteousness and truth.

So this song of the martyrs is not unchristian – it is a cry for God to exact justice, not us to avenge ourselves:

> Never take your own revenge, beloved, but leave room for the wrath of God, for it is written, 'Vengeance is Mine, I will repay,' says the Lord. (Romans 12:19, quoting Deuteronomy 32:35)

We do not get a definitive answer here to the question 'how long?' This is not because it isn't part of God's plan – justice does come later on in Revelation. Rather, the souls of the martyrs are told to wait, which may indicate that the exact length of time is not determined.

Waking or sleeping?

The souls under the altar are singing and crying out. Does this mean these souls are actually conscious after death, and actively crying out? Or is it a figurative description that the blood which has been shed is a reminder to God, calling out for justice? This is reminiscent of Genesis 4:10, where God says to Cain 'The voice of your brother's blood is crying to Me from the ground'. Was Abel's soul conscious and crying out, or was the blood an indication of the injustice?

This raises questions about the condition in which human beings exist following death while awaiting resurrection. When we die, our soul waits in Hades, the place of the departed. As we saw in Revelation 1:18 Jesus is there, because He has the keys to Death and Hades, and went there to fill all things:

> He who descended is Himself also He who ascended far above all the heavens, so that He might fill all things. (Ephesians 4:10)

Jesus has descended under the Altar to where these, who were slain for the word of God and the testimony which they held, are waiting for the intervention of God to take place in the resurrection.

So are these souls awake or asleep? Is being under the Altar the same as resting in Abraham's Bosom, as in the parable of the Rich Man and Lazarus (Luke 16:22)? Is it what Paul talks about when he says we 'prefer rather to be absent from the body and to be at home with the Lord' (2 Corinthians 5:8)?

In general, there is very little in the Bible from which to draw definitive answers. Some Scriptures seem to suggest death is like sleep and there may be no consciousness at that time, whereas others indicate there may be some level of awareness. A fuller discussion of this is may be found in our book, *God's Strategy in Human History: Volume 1 – God's Path to Victory*, chapter 15.

Overall, I tend towards the view that it may be possible for us to have some degree of consciousness while we are waiting for resurrection, with some awareness of Christ's goodness surrounding us. Otherwise, it is difficult to explain things such as how Moses and Elijah appear at the Transfiguration, or when Samuel was brought up after death (1 Samuel 28:15–19). Also, if it is preferable to be absent from the body and 'at home with the Lord' (2 Corinthians 5:5–8, see also Philippians 1:20–22), while not necessarily conclusive, seems to suggest some kind of better consciousness awaits us even before the resurrection.

Those who dwell on the earth (v10)

Who are 'those who dwell on the earth'? The phrase occurs some eleven times in Revelation. We have already seen it in the letter to Philadelphia, where

Jesus promises those who have 'kept the word of My perseverance' that they will be kept from the testing which will affect 'those who dwell on the earth' (Revelation 3:10, see page 167).

There is a contrast drawn between those 'who dwell on the earth' and those we will read about later who dwell (literally 'tabernacle') in the heavenly places (eg Revelation 12:12) and with God in the New Jerusalem (Revelation 21:3). Those who are dwelling on the earth, are earth-bound: they are settled and stable in their lives. However, as we read on, the earth is going to be shaken and nothing unstable is going to be left.

As Christians, we should not fear suffering or even death, but rather live in light of the fact that one day we will die. Most people try to live under the illusion that they will be on the earth forever, and counter any negative thoughts with a little more entertainment or a little more affluence, so they can find their way from cradle to grave comfortably without having to think too much about death and eternity. This even includes people wishing to decide when and how they will die. I think this is what it means by those 'who dwell on the earth' – they are settling into the earth as though it is all there is, rather than as a pilgrim on a journey.

For God's children, this earth is not our final destination – we will not be stuck like this forever. We should live with the realisation we are not rooted in the earth and its materialism, but instead are learning to be those who dwell in the heavenly places, and will inherit a New Heaven and New Earth.

Many of the Old Testament references and allusions we find in Revelation come from passages where the judgments of God fall upon people because of their idolatry, and they are contrasted with 'the righteous'. Here we have a similar picture: those who follow the Word of God are under the Altar, and those who do not, are dwelling on the earth – it is likely that idolatry plays a key part in this distinction.

Idolatry in general is opposition to following God, that is, worshipping something other than God. The form of idolatry which Jesus indicated is in greatest opposition to God was worshipping Mammon – money, wealth and materialism – 'You cannot serve God and Mammon' (Matthew 6:24). So those who dwell on the earth likely worship Mammon, and spend their lives trying to gain as much as they can for themselves, whereas those under the Altar are those who worship the Lord and spend their lives dwelling in heavenly places.

White robes

In verse 2, we saw that the 1st Horse was white and discussed how the colour white in Revelation speaks of victory, righteousness and purity. A promise to the Overcomers in Sardis is that they would 'walk with Me in white' (Revelation 3:4–5).

Here these souls under the Altar are given white robes, which is a testimony of their lives – their lives have been pure and righteous – and makes them look like Jesus. This is a strong indication of a connection between the Overcomers, whom we read of in the letters (Revelation 2—3), and the souls under the Altar, as both receive white robes.

The completed 'number' (v11)

These souls in white robes are told to rest until the number of their fellow servants and brothers who were to be killed is complete. These 'future martyrs' will be killed, just as the souls under the Altar have been, and will join them in death. So whenever this scene is set, it is not all over in an instant – just as there have been overcoming martyrs throughout church history, there are more still to come, who are caught up in this Great Tribulation taking place throughout the earth.

What is this 'full number' of fellow servants that is mentioned? People have interpreted the 'complete' (NASB, NKJV, CSB) or 'full' (*plērēs*) number (NIV, NLT) differently. Does God have a threshold number in mind after which the end will come? Or does God know the number because He has already planned every aspect of the future? Or does it mean something else?

In some ways the question is misleading – the word 'number' is not actually there in the Greek text (as indicated in translations which italicise words added in to improve the understanding or flow). The Greek text has the word for 'completed/fulfilled', hence the King James Version translated it:

> Until their fellow servants also and their brethren . . . should be fulfilled.

It is not unreasonable to infer the word 'number' here – the martyrs could clearly 'be fulfilled' in a numerical sense. However, there may be other ways they could be fulfilled, possibly in terms of time, or the completion of world evangelisation. So while the way it is generally translated is not necessarily wrong or bad, introducing 'number' does change the emphasis from God rewarding any of those martyred before the End of the Age who then make up the final number, to God aiming at a particular target figure.

Some theological interpretations have taken the 'completed number' as being a literal 144,000 because that figure appears in the next chapter of Revelation. However, as we will see on page 289, not only is this figure symbolic, but this scene may chronologically come after Revelation 7.

This idea of a fulfilled number of God's people reappears in Revelation 11, where John is given a measuring rod to 'measure the temple of God and the altar, and those who worship in it' (see page 385). So I would suggest the fulfilled number is a general symbol for God's completed heaven and earth, not a specific pre-ordained number God is aiming at (see also Romans 11:12,25).

Psalm 79 and the 5th Seal

Both Revelation and Psalm 79 were written into a similar context. Psalm 79 is a lament of Asaph over the destruction of Jerusalem at the time of the Exile, and Revelation is written into a situation of invasion and occupation of the Land, destruction of the Temple, persecution and martyrdom, as well as looking forward to a future ultimate fulfilment.

Psalm 79 contains so many of the same themes as we find in the 5th Seal, it is as if Revelation 6:9–11 is a direct interpretation and exposition of it.

> O God, the nations have invaded Your inheritance;
> They have defiled Your holy temple;
> They have laid Jerusalem in ruins.
> They have given the dead bodies of Your servants for food to the birds of the heavens,
> The flesh of Your godly ones to the beasts of the earth.
> They have poured out their blood like water round about Jerusalem . . .
>
> How long, O LORD? Will You be angry forever?
> Will Your jealousy burn like fire?
> Pour out Your wrath upon the nations which do not know You,
> And upon the kingdoms which do not call upon Your name . . .
>
> Let there be known among the nations in our sight,
> Vengeance for the blood of Your servants which has been shed.
> Let the groaning of the prisoner come before You;
> According to the greatness of Your power preserve those who are doomed to die. (Psalm 79:1–3,5–6,10–11)

Israel saw their inheritance as the Land, with Jerusalem and the Temple at the centre. However, for Christians our inheritance is being conformed to Christ (Ephesians 1:11) and being part of His Body, the Church. Jesus interpreted His death, burial and resurrection as the Temple being destroyed and then rebuilt in three days (John 2:19, see also eg Matthew 26:61, 27:40). An apocalyptic interpretation of Psalm 79 is that the Body of Christ – those who keep His Word – has been invaded and killed, and we are looking for the resurrection, for the Church to rise up.

In verse 2, we see martyrs (servants) who, like in the 4th Seal, are killed, devoured by the beasts of the field, and whose blood is poured out around Jerusalem. Then in verse 5 it says 'How Long, O Lord . . .' which is quoted in Revelation 6. The psalmist is conscious that he too needs forgiveness, as do those he is calling judgment upon. Ultimately, righteousness and holiness are vindicated in the economy of God. We will look again at Psalm 79 when we get to Revelation 11:10 (see page 412).

So when the 5th Seal is broken it causes the saints to cry out from under the Altar – this call for justice takes us one step closer to being able to open up the Book of God's destiny for humanity. In order for God's plans for us to be revealed, the Church has to want justice.

While we leave the 5th Seal, with its emphasis on death and discipleship, without the prayer for justice of those under the Altar being fully answered, we will start to see the answer in the next seal.

The 6th Seal
Text – Revelation 6:12–17

¹² I looked when He broke the sixth seal, and there was a great earthquake; and the sun became black as sackcloth made of hair, and the whole moon became like blood; ¹³ and the stars of the sky fell to the earth, as a fig tree casts its unripe figs when shaken by a great wind. ¹⁴ The sky was split apart like a scroll when it is rolled up, and every mountain and island were moved out of their places. ¹⁵ Then the kings of the earth and the great men and the commanders and the rich and the strong and every slave and free man hid themselves in the caves and among the rocks of the mountains; ¹⁶ and they say* to the mountains and to the rocks,

'Fall on us and hide us from the presence of Him who sits on the throne, and from the wrath of the Lamb; [17] for the great day of their wrath has come, and who is able to stand?'

Creation shaken (v12–14)

The 6th Seal starts to bring in the Lord's response to the prayer of the 5th Seal – God answers prayer! Here we see the beginning of the emergence of the final judgment in the form of normally unshakeable parts of Creation being catastrophically shaken. We can pick out 7 things representing the fullness of Creation being completely shaken:

1. a great earthquake
2. **sun was black**
3. **whole moon like blood**
4. the stars of the sky fell to earth as the fig tree casts its unripe figs
5. the sky was split apart like a scroll
6. **every mountain was moved from its place**
7. every island was moved.

Old Testament tapestry

There are a number of parts of the Old Testament woven together into this dramatic vision as the Holy Spirit is creating a beautiful tapestry of John's understanding of Scripture, picking up threads from different places in John's mind then weaving them into a glorious picture. For example, Isaiah 34 is a prophecy about God's wrath against the nations, and provides a clear background for the events taking place after the 6th Seal is broken, as does Isaiah 13, Isaiah 24, Joel 2—3 and Habakkuk 3. Putting these together we see:

1. 'The earth is distorted . . . broken asunder . . . split through . . . shaken violently . . . reels and totters' in Isaiah 24:1,19–20, is 'shaken from its place' in Isaiah 13:13, and quakes in Joel 2:10, and 3:16.

2,3,4. In Isaiah 34:4, sun, moon and stars – 'all the hosts' of the sky – will wither away 'as a leaf withers from the vine, or as one withers from the fig tree'. We see the sun and moon grow dark (with or without blood) in Isaiah 13:10 and Joel 2:10, 30–31 and 3:15, 'the moon will be abashed and the sun ashamed' in Isaiah 24:23 and in Habakkuk 3, they 'stood in their places' then 'went away'. 'The stars of heaven and their constellations, will not flash forth their light' in Isaiah 13:10, and lose their brightness in Joel 2:10, 3:15.

5. The sky is rolled up like a scroll in Isaiah 34:4.

6. In Habakkuk 3:6 'the perpetual mountains were shattered, The ancient hills collapsed', and the mountains quaked (v10).

7. Isaiah 40:15 says, 'Behold, the nations are like a drop from a bucket, and are regarded as a speck of dust on the scales; behold, He lifts up the islands like fine dust.' At first glance, there is little other reference to 'islands' in the Old Testament, however, the word used in Isaiah 40:15 is often translated 'coastlands' in modern versions, but equally could be 'islands' as it is in the King James version (see for example Ezekiel 26:18, Psalm 97:1, etc).

It is as if God is reversing Creation days 1–3: light is taken away, the earth becomes formless again, vegetation (vine and fig tree) wither, land is no longer separated from sea, earth and sky.

This also sounds like the description Jesus gave of the fall of Jerusalem in AD 70, which of course is the affirmation of the Second Coming and Jesus' return:

> 'But immediately after the tribulation of those days the sun will be darkened, and the moon will not give its light, and the stars will fall from the sky, and the powers of the heavens will be shaken'. (Matthew 24:29, see also Acts 2:19–20)

So events of the 6th Seal look like the Second Coming and the Day of the Lord – but is it literal, or is it figurative, representing a temporal judgment in history?

Humanity Shaken (v15–16)

Not only is the whole of Creation shaken, but there is a 7-fold expression of humanity, representing 'those who dwell on the earth' (see page 270), who are also shaken:

1. kings of the earth,
2. great men,
3. commanders of thousands,

4. the rich,
5. the strong,
6. the slave, and 7. the free man.

We will see this list of people reappearing at the Great Supper of God in Revelation 19:18, where they are in judgment after Christ's return and the birds of the air are invited to eat their flesh.

Who will be judged?

Creation being shaken signifies the arrival of 'the great and awesome day of the Lord' – the coming day of judgment for the nations because of their idolatry, when the earth and everyone on it will be shaken:

> For the Lord of hosts will have a day of reckoning
> Against everyone who is proud and lofty
> And against everyone who is lifted up,
> That he may be abased . . . (Isaiah 2:12)

This judgment will come upon:

> The wicked for their iniquity;
> I will also put an end to the arrogance of the proud
> And abase the haughtiness of the ruthless. (Isaiah 13:11)

In Isaiah 24 we read about 7 groups of people who will receive judgment, made up of 6 pairs, who are summed up as 'the exalted people of the earth' in verse 4:

> . . . And $_1$the people will be like the priest, $_2$the servant like his master, $_3$the maid like her mistress, $_4$the buyer like the seller, $_5$the lender like the borrower, $_6$the creditor like the debtor . . . $_7$the exalted of the people of the earth fade away (Isaiah 24:2,4) (see also v21).

Hide us (v16)

The 7-fold expression of humanity who hide 'in the caves and among the rocks of the mountains' want to escape from God's presence, which in the Greek is literally His 'face'.

> Men will go into caves of the rocks
> And into holes of the ground

> Before the terror of the Lord
> And the splendour of His majesty,
> When He arises to make the earth tremble. (Isaiah 2:19)

They even call disaster upon themselves to try to escape:

> Then they will say to the mountains,
> 'Cover us!' And to the hills, 'Fall on us!'
> (Hosea 10:8, also quoted in Luke 23:30)

Hiding from God began in the Garden of Eden, when the man and woman hid themselves amongst the trees, and humankind has gone on hiding from God ever since. The enemy has helped us hide by putting a blanket of spiritual darkness between ourselves and the Lord, and we break through this when we give our lives to Christ. At the 6th Seal, it is as though this blanket is removed and God's presence is suddenly immanent on the earth – Creation in its fallen state is shaken, and those who have been living in darkness, either come into the light, or else try to hide in the darkest places left. It is of course pointless trying to 'hide' from God, as David writes in Psalm 139:

> Where can I go from Your Spirit?
>   Or where can I flee from Your presence?
> If I ascend to heaven, You are there;
>   If I make my bed in Sheol, behold, You are there. (Psalm 139:7–8)

However, people do try to hide themselves from God's presence: dismissing Him from their minds, ignoring their conscience.

We can also do this in our Christian lives when we know what we are doing is wrong, or we feel guilty or ashamed of sin in our lives. We know the clear purity of His light will show up things that are unacceptable to Him. God will always forgive, but we should be aware that if we try to hide from Him, we will be contributing to this picture of judgment, where one day we have to stand before Him, saying 'Lord let me hide in the rocks and the caves'. Instead, we should let Him shine upon us as we cannot hide from the magnificent supernatural presence of the Almighty.

The wrath of the Lord and the Lamb (v16–17)

Revelation contains some of the most unambiguous evidences of the deity of our Lord Jesus Christ. Here the parallel between God and the Lamb is so clear, that the two are brought together in one statement – God and the Lamb are equivalent. Whereas in the Old Testament they hide from:

> 'the terror of the Lord and the splendour of His majesty' (Isaiah 2:19)

> 'the fury of the Lord of hosts in the day of His burning anger' (Isaiah 13:13)

> 'the great and awesome day of the Lord' (Joel 2:11,31)

here in Revelation they hide from,

> 'the presence of Him who sits on the throne, and from the wrath of the Lamb, for the great day of their wrath has come.'

Where the Old Testament shows us the one true God, here it is as if the light is diffracted and we can now see Jesus as the splendour of the Lord's majesty: He is the radiance, outshining, effulgence of God's glory, and the express image of His person and character (Hebrews 1:3). Jesus expresses the splendour and the glory of who God is, reflected in the day of the wrath of the Lord and the wrath of the Lamb, calling to account the earth and its unrighteousness.

Who is able to stand? (v17)

In Joel 2, we see the same anticipation and prophecy of Revelation 6:13–17 – the heavens and the earth are shaken, and the coming judgment is in view, who is able to stand?

> The day of the Lord is indeed great and very awesome,
> And who can endure it? (Joel 2:11)

This is sometimes read as a hopeless nihilistic statement – *'who could possibly endure all that – no-one'*, but rather it is a genuine question – which of you will manage it? Reading on in Joel 2, we get the answer:

> 'Yet even now,' declares the Lord, 'Return to Me with all your heart
> . . . whoever calls on the name of the Lord will be delivered; for
> on Mount Zion and in Jerusalem there will be those who escape.'

Those who are the Lord's will be able to endure it, to stand before the Throne in resurrection life and not try to hide. As it says in Psalm 46:

> God is our refuge and strength, a very ready help in trouble.
> Therefore we will not fear, though the earth shakes
> And the mountains slip into the heart of the sea;
> Though its waters roar and foam,
> Though the mountains quake at its swelling pride. Selah
> There is a river whose streams make the city of God happy,
> The holy dwelling places of the Most High.
> God is in the midst of her, she will not be moved. (Psalm 46:1–5)

So these Old Testament backgrounds to this final day of reckoning – of vindication, of righteousness being exalted in the earth at last, and 7-fold Creation and 7-fold types of humankind – are all being shaken. The only thing that is going to stand is the Kingdom of God: we are receiving a Kingdom that cannot be shaken (Hebrews 12:28). Everything else will be shaken, in order to be brought to the test point.

It will be wonderful to enter into God's presence, but we need to be prepared for it, because otherwise, rather than a beatific vision of Christ as we stand in resurrection before the Throne of God, we could see a terrifying threat if we are not prepared to be cleansed and purged now. Being prepared to go through the fiery trial was a fundamental teaching of the Early Church and needs to be recovered and held before us in the days when the Church is being persecuted more and more throughout the earth.

1 John 2:28 gives us a last warning about judgment:

> Now, little children, abide in Him, so that when He appears, we may have confidence and not shrink away from Him in shame at His coming.

Discussion Questions

How relevant is the imagery of the Altar and sacrifice in our time?

Do you agree with the cry of the martyrs for vindication?

How can we be prepared to stand when everything is shaken?

Revelation 7

Revelation 7 is an interlude between the 6th and 7th Seals being broken. It is important to see it as an intermission rather than just a chronological continuation of events – we are taking a step back from the action, to get a broader view of what is going on. More than that, it seems to look both backwards and forwards in time, showing John a different angle on what he has just seen in the breaking of Seals 1–6.

Interlude between 6th & 7th Seals

This chapter is in two parts:

i. v1–8: the first part focuses on the 144,000, who are on earth and are sealed on the forehead. This part seems to describe the run up to the seals being broken in Revelation 6, and so is looking backwards.

ii. v9–17: The second part describes an innumerable company in Heaven. This is looking forwards, to after the 6th Seal of Judgment and on into the eternal future.

What is the reason for this interlude at this point? As mentioned on page 241, each of the 4 sets of 7 contain an interlude between the 6th and 7th events which reveals something about the life of the Church. So what does this pause in Revelation 7 show us about the Church?

The wonderful vision in chapter 5, of Jesus standing as a Lamb slain in the midst of the throne, surrounded by worship, indicates that the reign of Christ has already begun, and is going on right the way through the Church Age, and will continue for eternity.

As we worship and offer up prayers as bowls of incense to the Lamb, the 7 Seals begin to be broken, because He is the only One who can fulfil the destiny of the human race. Only through Christ can humankind come to the height of that wonderful expression of God's loving, creatorial purpose – being made in God's image – but to do this, the 7 Seals on the book have to be broken.

In Revelation 6, we saw the effects of these first 6 Seals being broken – the Gospel going out has been followed by opposition, death and destruction (Seals 1–4), as a result of which the souls of martyrs under the Altar cry out for justice (5th Seal), and then we see the whole of Creation being shaken and those who dwell on the earth trying to hide (6th Seal).

These are necessary consequences of humanity entering into God's plan for them. So what is happening to the Church while all this is going on? This is what Revelation 7 is going to show us.

Text – Revelation 7:1–3

> [1] After this I saw four angels standing at the four corners of the earth, holding back the four winds of the earth, so that no wind would blow on the earth or on the sea or on any tree. [2] And I saw another angel ascending from the rising of the sun, having the seal of the living God; and he cried out with a loud voice to the four angels to whom it was granted to harm the earth and the sea, [3] saying, 'Do not harm the earth or the sea or the trees until we have sealed the bond-servants of our God on their foreheads.'

After this . . . (v1)

The interlude begins with a visionary, or literary, division: 'after this . . .' or 'then . . .' This does not mean it follows directly on chronologically from the events of the 6th Seal at the end of Revelation 6, but rather 'after this' is what John actually saw next in the vision. This helps make sense of the text, because as we will see, John seems to be looking back to events before the first 4 Seals were broken and the 4 Horsemen released.

4 angels, 4 corners and 4 winds (v1)

These 4 angels standing on the 4 corners of the earth, symbolize the totality of the earth, and the phrase comes from Isaiah 11:12:

> And He will lift up a standard for the nations
> And assemble the banished ones of Israel,

And will gather the dispersed of Judah
From the four corners of the earth. (see also Ezekiel 7:2)

While some use this as an opportunity to suggest the Bible expounds a flat earth ideology, far more likely it refers to the four points of the compass, especially in Revelation 7:1, as these are the directions of the 4 winds. So between them, these 4 angels encompass everything to the full extent of north, south, east and west.

These 4 angels, hold back the 4 winds. The Greek word here for 'wind' means a strong, violent wind or breath – the same word is used to describe the winds that pound the house of the man who built upon the rock (Matthew 7:25) and the winds that Jesus rebuked in Mark 4:39 (also Luke 8:24). So we get a picture of powerful, spiritual forces which, while He may not be directing them, are ultimately under the Lord's control.

Elsewhere in Scripture, we also read of 4 winds of heaven, representing spiritual forces that bring about God's judgment:

- In Jeremiah 49:36, 'the four winds from the four ends of heaven' will scatter Elam.

- In Daniel 7:2, the '4 winds of heaven were stirring up the great sea'. In Daniel 8:8 when the male goat's large horn is broken 'in its place there came up four conspicuous horns toward the four winds of heaven', and in Daniel 11:4 the warrior king's kingdom 'will be broken up and divided to the four winds of heaven' (CSB).

- In Matthew 24:31, Jesus prophesies that the Son of Man 'will send forth His angels with a great trumpet and they will gather together His elect from the four winds, from one end of the sky to the other.'

Not only that but in the famous passage of the Valley of Dry Bones, in Ezekiel, the 4 winds/breaths bring life:

Prophesy to the breath, prophesy, son of man, and say to the breath, 'Thus says the Lord God, 'Come from the four winds, O breath, and breathe on these slain, that they come to life.' (Ezekiel 37:9)

In Revelation 6 we saw the 4 Horses, who are also called 'spirits' or 'winds' (compare Zechariah 2:6 and 6:5), and are called forth by the 4 Living Creatures, who ride out upon the earth when the first 4 Seals are broken. So it is reasonable to suggest these 4 winds represent or are linked to the 4 Horses.

Here in Revelation 7, we have the picture of 4 strong winds being held back from blowing 'on the earth or on the sea or on any tree' by 4 angels.

So it seems as if the events of Revelation 7 may be a precursor to Revelation 6, and rather than looking at events from the Throne of God, John is now seeing them from earth. The 4 Horsemen are 4 spiritual forces or powerful winds, that are straining to be let loose, but are being held back until they are released by the words from God's Throne.

So far in Revelation, we have seen the angels of the 7 Churches, a group of 7 angels with 7 Trumpets, and a large multitude, but not a group of 4 angels. Perhaps these relate in some way to the 4 Living Creatures surrounding the Throne, and if so would indicate the ministry of the 4 Living Creatures as seen from the viewpoint of heaven in chapter 6, and from the viewpoint of earth in chapter 7 (see for example v2,3). Along that line, as 'angel' means 'messenger', this fits with the 4 Living Creatures speaking forth God's words from the Throne.

Permission to harm? (v2)

In verses 1–3 we see that permission is 'granted' or 'allowed' to these angels and winds to cause harm, which is held back until the company of 144,000 are sealed from heaven.

Who are these 4 angels 'who were allowed to harm the earth and the sea'? Are they the ones holding back the winds, or are they the winds? Are they the 4 Horsemen, seeing as they also harm the earth?

The seal of the living God (v2–3)

An angel appears, with the Seal of the Living God, in order to seal people on the earth. In Revelation 6, we looked at 6 Seals being broken, but here, prior to this happening, the people are having the Seal of the Lord put on their foreheads. What is this Seal, and what is it for?

There are at least three aspects to the imagery of this sealing – it is for protection, possession and authentication:

i. Protection

First, we can see God's seal as a protection. There is a similar picture in Ezekiel 9, where he sees a vision of a man in linen with a writing case and five others with weapons. The Lord says to the man in linen:

> 'Go through the midst of the city, even through the midst of Jerusalem, and put a mark on the foreheads of the men who sigh and groan over all the abominations which are being committed in its midst.' But to the others He said in my hearing, 'Go through the city after him and strike . . . but do not touch any man on whom is the mark'. (Ezekiel 9:4–6)

The context is the destruction of Jerusalem and the Temple at the time of the Exile, which was God's judgment of the apostasy and unbelief of the people. God took His hand of protection off Israel and judgment fell upon them from a foreign nation, Babylon. However, Ezekiel sees this devastation is held back while a seal is put on the foreheads of a godly remnant. When Nebuchadnezzar's army take the city, the people who are preserved are those who have been sealed.

In Ezekiel, the picture is of a spiritual sealing that brings about a literal preservation of life, so that the remnant survive and eventually return to the land to rebuild Jerusalem and the Temple, as we read in Ezra and Nehemiah. However, while the same imagery is used in Revelation, I do not think it is a literal statement concerning physical life, but rather it is about spiritual preservation.

Looking back to the 5th Seal, we saw how the souls under the Altar were those who had been martyred because they were faithful to the Lord. Whether they were physically killed or just led lives of discipleship, they represent a faithful remnant who had a seal upon them that preserved them spiritually, not necessarily physically.

This spiritual sealing goes on all the way through this Church Age – God seals His people on earth to preserve them. We have been sealed by God that we might be spiritually preserved under every possible pressure from the devil and unbelief, so our spiritual lives will not cave in. We are being sealed for resurrection to eternity.

ii. Possession

If you put your seal on something, it shows you possess it – you stamp it with your mark. Later on in Revelation 14:1 we will see this seal on their foreheads becomes the name of the Father and the name of the Son, and again in Revelation 22:4 '. . . and His name shall be on their foreheads'. In the Roman Empire, owners would often place their mark on the forehead of their slaves, so it was clear to everyone to whom you belonged. Slaves are clearly in view in this passage: 'Do not harm the earth or the sea or the trees until we have sealed the bond-servants of our God on their foreheads' (v3).

The word *doulos*, often translated as 'bond-servant' in modern translations, literally means 'slave'. We are bond-slaves of the living God, and He will put His mark on us: the name of the Father and of the Son. We belong to our master. This is good news because if we belong, then we can be doubly assured that we will be preserved. God does not throw away His slaves.

Who are these bond-servants/slaves? Some commentators have suggested this passage is talking about Jews, or converted Jews at the End of the Age, largely on the basis of their being described as 'sons of Israel' in verse 4, and a couple of instances which mention 'your bond-servants the prophets' (10:7, 11:18). However, we have seen in the letterhead to Revelation (1:1) that John refers to himself as a bond-servant, who writes the book to God's bond-servants (Revelation 1:1), and in the letter to Thyatira, Christ warns that Jezebel 'leads My bond-servants astray' (2:20). While John was a Jew, and many of the Christians in the 7 Churches would have been of Jewish origin, it seems more likely that he is referring more generally to Christians here, whether Jewish or Gentile.

Being a slave is a good thing if our owner is God. The Bible has been criticized from some quarters for not being clearer in its rejection of slavery. However, the apostle Paul, as well as other leaders in the Early Church, accepted slaves in positions of leadership within the Church. By standing with slaves, as with Onesimus in Philemon, they undermined the whole brutal concept of slavery, which made it easier for Christians in many nations in later centuries to dismantle this abuse of power. Far from endorsing slavery the Bible subverts it by superseding its power structures, raising up the humble and exalting the lowly (Luke 1:52).

These slaves who are sealed refers to Christian believers, or at least includes them.

iii. Authentication

Thirdly, the Seal of the Living God represents authentication. If something has your seal of approval, you have authorized it – it is authentic. For example, the British Standards Kitemark is a sign of quality only put on products that conform to high safety standards. When God authenticates someone with His seal, it means they conform to His standards, to His Name.

* ✱ *

We can see these three elements of being sealed in the New Testament. In 2 Timothy, Paul writes about those 'who have gone astray from the truth':

> Nevertheless, the firm foundation of God stands, having this seal, 'The Lord knows those who are His,' and, 'Everyone who names the name of the Lord is to abstain from wickedness'. (2 Timothy 2:19)

This is a reference to what Moses says in Numbers 16 after Korah's rebellion:

> Tomorrow morning the Lord will show **who is His**, and **who is holy**, and **will bring him near to Himself**. (Numbers 16:5, see also James 3:13–18)

Everyone who names the name of the Lord abstaining from wickedness is a reflection of Numbers 16:26, where Moses instructs Israel – those who carry the seal of the Lord on their forehead – to separate themselves from Korah, Dathan and Abiram:

> Depart now from the tents of these wicked men, and touch nothing that belongs to them, or you will be swept away in all their sin.

Once again, we see the faithful remnant theme appearing.

The seal of the Holy Spirit

There are three times where the seal of God is mentioned as the Holy Spirit:

> Having also believed, you were sealed in Him with the Holy Spirit of promise. (Ephesians 1:13)

> Do not grieve the Holy Spirit of God, with whom you were sealed for the day of redemption. (Ephesians 4:30)

> Who also sealed us and gave us the Spirit in our hearts as a pledge. (2 Corinthians 1:22)

God has put His stamp on the things which belong to Him, and they are to be kept and preserved until the day when He comes to collect them.

High priestly seal

There was also a seal on the forehead of the High Priest when he went into the Holy Place: 'Holy to the Lord' engraved on a gold crown on his turban (Exodus 28:36–38). The names of the tribes of Israel were also engraved on two stones on the shoulder pieces of the High Priest's ephod, and on the stones of the breastplate: 'like the engravings of a seal, each according to his name for the twelve tribes' (Exodus 28:11–21), and we see the names of '12 Tribes' appearing here as a seal.

Jesus is our Great High Priest, and we are His body, so we carry the seal and the mark of God and His people. This is not just a static stamp; it is a living thing – namely the Holy Spirit – because it is the Living God who seals us.

So the sealing of the bond-slaves takes place in order that they may be preserved when the 7 Seals are broken, the Horsemen begin to ride, and tribulation is brought to bear on the earth.

The 144,000
Text – Revelation 7:4–8

> [4] And I heard the number of those who were sealed, one hundred and forty-four thousand sealed from every tribe of the sons of Israel:

> [5] from the tribe of Judah, 12,000 were sealed, from the tribe of Reuben 12,000, from the tribe of Gad 12,000, [6] from the tribe of Asher 12,000, from the tribe of Naphtali 12,000, from the tribe

of Manasseh 12,000, [7] from the tribe of Simeon 12,000, from the tribe of Levi 12,000, from the tribe of Issachar 12,000, [8] from the tribe of Zebulun 12,000, from the tribe of Joseph 12,000, from the tribe of Benjamin, 12,000 were sealed.

The 144,000 (v4)

This chapter has been interpreted literally by some groups, including the Jehovah's Witnesses, with 144,000 being the total number of saved humans on the earth. However, given Revelation's parabolic style, this is surely a symbolic figure, but what does it symbolize?

12 Tribes? (v5–8)

The 144,000 is made up from 'every tribe of the sons of Israel – but if we take a closer look, the list of the tribes is interesting. In Numbers 1—2, when the Israelites are numbered in the wilderness, it lists the 12 Tribes of Israel as follows: Reuben, Simeon, Judah, Issachar, Zebulun, Joseph (including Ephraim, as well as Manasseh) Benjamin, Dan, Asher, Gad, Naphtali, and Levi. The names of these 12 Tribes were inscribed on the 12 precious stones in the ephod (see Exodus 28:15–21). However, the list in Revelation 7 is not the same: Dan is missing and Manasseh, one of Joseph's sons, is included alongside Joseph (compare Numbers 1:32,34). The order in which the names appear is also different and not in order of birth or by mother.

Neither does the list in Revelation 7 list match up with the land allotment that we read of in Joshua 14—19: the tribe of Levi did not receive land, but the half-Tribes of Manasseh and Ephraim as Joseph's sons both received an allocation. Levi is included in Revelation 7, but Ephraim and Dan are not.

So, while at first glance this list looks something like Israel, it actually represents neither Israel as a family, nor as a nation. There are various fringe theories about why Dan is excluded, or Manasseh and Levi are included, but ultimately these are not fully convincing – the real reason I would suggest is merely to show this is not a literal historical Israel, it is a symbolic representation of God's people. There are other places in the Old Testament where 12 things symbolically represent God's people – for example, in Joshua 4 they built a memorial at Gilgal of 12 stones from the Jordan and in 1 Kings 18 Elijah built an altar of 12 stones on Mount Carmel, to which he said 'Your name shall be Israel'.

Sons of Israel Genesis 29—35	Land allotment Numbers 1—4	Moses' blessing Deuteronomy 33	The 144,000 Revelation 7
Reuben	Reuben	Reuben	Judah
Simeon	Simeon	Judah	Reuben
Levi	Gad	Levi	Gad
Judah	Judah	Benjamin	Asher
Dan	Issachar	Joseph (Ephraim & Manasseh)	Naphtali
Naphtali	Zebulun		Manasseh
Gad	Joseph (Ephraim & Manasseh)	Zebulun	Simeon
Asher		Issachar	Levi
Issachar	Benjamin	Gad	Issachar
Zebulun	Dan	Dan	Zebulun
Joseph	Asher	Naphtali	Joseph
Benjamin	Naphtali	Asher	Benjamin
	Levi		

We will see the '12 tribes of the sons of Israel' appearing again as 12 gates in the New Jerusalem in Revelation 21.

12,000 from each tribe (v5–8)

The 12,000 from each tribe mentioned are then sealed, which seems to happen as a continuation of the interlude. The sealing occurs while the 4 angels are restraining the 4 winds, which as we have seen, seems to occur before the 4 Horses are released by the breaking of the first 4 Seals. So the 144,000 are sealed, after which the events of Revelation 6 begin.

We will look at the symbolism of 12 × 12 in more detail when we get to Revelation 21, where we see the New Jerusalem has 12 gates with the names of the 12 Tribes and 12 foundation stones with the names of the 12 Apostles. Although it is lost in some translations, in Revelation 21:16 the angel measures the City as 12,000 stadia (as in the CSB, NIV). Ultimately God's measurement of choice is His people!

Who are the 144,000?

The 144,000 symbolise more than just those sealed from each of the 12 physical tribes of Israel – so who exactly do they represent? What characterizes them and why do they need to be sealed?

Warriors/Troops

The list of numbers of those sealed 'from every tribe of the sons of Israel' in Revelation 7:4–8 is evocative of Numbers 1—4. In Numbers 1—2, eleven Tribes of Israel (including Joseph as the two half tribes of Ephraim and Manasseh) are instructed to list the number of fighting men 'able to go out to war', aged twenty or over, for example:

> . . . their numbered men of the tribe of Reuben were 46,500
> . . . their numbered men of the tribe of Simeon were 59,300 . . .
> (Numbers 1:21, 23 etc)

This census of the armies leaves out the tribe of Levi because the Levites are dedicated as priests to God, and the priests did not fight. However, there is another set of lists in Numbers 3—4 where the Levites are numbered for priestly service, and allocated duties in the tabernacle by family groups:

> Bring the tribe of Levi near and set them before Aaron the priest, that they may serve him. They shall perform the duties for him and for the whole congregation before the tent of meeting, to do the service of the tabernacle. (Numbers 3:6–7)

So, there is a military numbering of how many can fight, and a priestly numbering of how many can intercede on behalf of the people of God. Importantly, these priests are also said to be doing 'warfare', but this is often hidden in our translations. In Numbers 1—2, the eleven Tribes are numbered for 'war' or 'an army', which is the Hebrew word *tsaba'* (see for example Numbers 1:20,22,24 and so on). When we look at the numbering of the Levites, we see the same word *tsaba'* used to describe the service in the Tabernacle:

> Take a census of the descendants of Kohath from among the sons of Levi, by their families, by their fathers' households, from thirty years and upward, even to fifty years old, all who enter the *tsaba'* to do the work in the tent of meeting.
> (Numbers 4:2–3, see also v24,30,35,39,43 and so on)

Spiritual warfare

So the Levites are instructed to do warfare as well, but warfare in the Tabernacle, or what we might call 'spiritual warfare'. This is an anticipation of the New Testament age when 'our struggle is not against flesh and blood, but against the rulers, against the powers, against the world forces of this darkness, against the spiritual forces of wickedness in the heavenly places' (Ephesians 6:12).

When we pray, when we worship, we can break through the shroud of the world and into the heavens and experience something of the glory of God. At other times we may be pressurised by negative spiritual powers, and feel the weight of oppression and depression as they try to take a grip on our lives. We have to throw them off our backs – these forces cannot hold us if we rise up and declare the victory of our Lord.

Spiritual opposition is the reason as to why the Church has taken so long getting through the world with the Great Commission. There are many who start to stand up to intercede and fight against those spiritual powers, but find they are overwhelmed by the pressure and instead of using the seal that God puts upon us, give in and let the enemy roll all over them. Some would rather sit down and relax into religiosity rather than standing firm and seeing the battle won. Nobody ever won a battle by sitting down – it is when we stand up that we play our part in the victory. Unlike in Numbers 3—4, where only male Levites of a certain age are numbered as spiritual warriors, any one of us – male, female, young, old, of any race or nationality – can be sealed as part of this symbolic 144,000.

This is the promise of God: where there is a desire to know the sealing of God working in our life, Jesus gathers us into His own heart as He rises again. We are sealed so we can rise up and fight! We have seen how the weapons involved in this warfare – prayer and worship, blood, testimony – appear throughout Revelation (see page 36). For a deeper look at the spiritual battle, and how we participate in it, see also our book *God's Strategy in Human History*, Vol 1.

The Old Testament precedent reveals the 144,000 as a people who are both soldiers and priests: that is the character of the sealed people we see in Revelation 7 – those with a genuine faith, sealed by the Spirit with the name of Jesus, owned, authenticated and preserved by God. While the number of those sealed seems large, the city will be even larger, so God's future for humanity is greater than just those who are overcoming here.

The 7 Seals | Revelation 7:4–8

Are the 144,000 the Overcomers/Martyrs?

I think the 144,000 are those who are brought before us as the Overcomers in the letters to the 7 Churches (Revelation 2—3), and the Martyrs under the Altar (Revelation 5:5) and now appear as troops. This army of sealed believers will form the spearhead of God's manoeuvres against the world, the flesh and the devil to bring in the Kingdom, as we will see when we get to Revelation 14.

It is interesting to note here that this body of people becomes clearer and more defined as we move through Revelation, until we see them emerge as the Bride in Revelation 19.

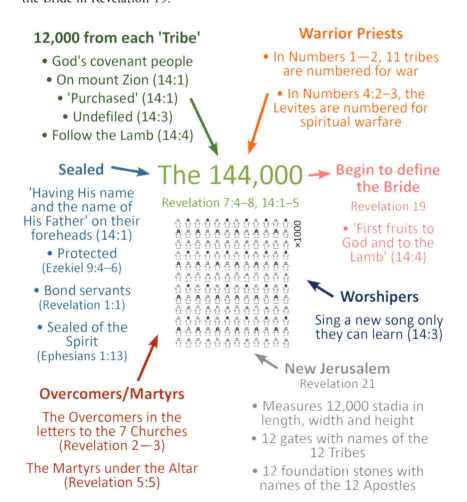

Text – Revelation 7:9–12

> [9] After these things I looked, and behold, a great multitude which no one could count, from every nation and all tribes and peoples and tongues, standing before the throne and before the Lamb, clothed in white robes, and palm branches were in their hands; [10] and they cry out with a loud voice, saying,
>
> 'Salvation to our God who sits on the throne, and to the Lamb.' [11] And all the angels were standing around the throne and around the elders and the four living creatures; and they fell on their faces before the throne and worshipped God, [12] saying, 'Amen, blessing and glory and wisdom and thanksgiving and honour and power and might, be to our God forever and ever. Amen.'

After these things … (v9)

Here there is another change in focus of the vision (see also Revelation 7:1 above). As before, this does not mean the next verses necessarily happen next in chronological time – it is just what John sees next.

While Revelation 7:1–8 seems to look at events before the 7 Seals begin to be broken in Revelation 6, this second section of chapter 7 appears to look forward to the end of the age: an innumerable number of people from every nation standing before the Throne, as in resurrection, and we read of 'wiping away all tears', which appears again in Revelation 21:4. Here we are getting a little foretaste of the worship of eternity.

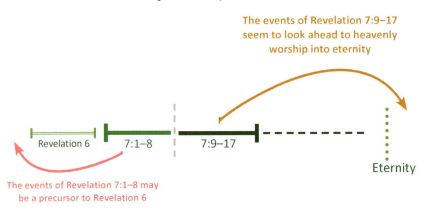

A Great Multitude (v9)

John sees a crowd that nobody could number. This is meant to stand in contrast to the 144,000 we have just been reading about, which although big, obviously can be numbered. There is a significant increase, a multiplication which is meant to take us back to the beginning of God's rescue plan for humanity with that allusion to the patriarchal promises to Abraham:

> I will make you into a great nation, and I will bless you . . . and all peoples on earth will be blessed through you. (Genesis 12:2–3)

> My covenant is with you, and you will be the father of a multitude of nations . . . (Genesis 17:4)

> I will greatly bless you, and I will greatly multiply your seed as the stars of the heavens and as the sand which is on the seashore . . . In your seed all the nations of the earth shall be blessed. (Genesis 22:17–18)

This vast company we see, presumably standing in resurrection after the Great White Throne (which we will see in Revelation 20:11), is a reminder that God's entire plan for eternity, including the whole history of God's covenant people, has been so that every person on earth can be blessed, even though some may reject it. The Bible is the story of God setting about to bring blessing to all of humankind.

It is important to see how this is reflected in the imagery of Revelation 7 – this innumerable company is the result of the 144,000 being a blessing to every tribe, tongue and nation. The Overcomers are a blessing to all the people of the earth, and the outcome is too big to measure!

So why do we see this great multitude at this point? Why does this vision seem to jump forward into the future? It is an encouragement, a ray of hope, that even after all the war, famine and death in Revelation 6, as well as all the dark events which are going to come in the following chapters, we are assured of an enormous crowd of people, saved and worshipping God for ever and ever.

We may be forgiven for sometimes thinking we the Church are poor in number and that Jesus has not got much of a victory, especially in our increasingly secular Western society. However, Revelation shows us that even when we feel like a small remnant going through tribulation, even though not everyone will be in the sealed fighting force, the picture of the end is glorious – Jesus has a massive victory.

The Great Multitude are standing, clothed in white robes and have palm branches in their hands. As we saw in verse 6 above, 'standing' in Revelation implies resurrection, so here we see a huge throng of resurrected worshippers.

White robes (v9)

White robes speak of purity and holiness, and we have seen them a few times already in Revelation – they were promised to the Overcomers in Sardis (3:4–5) and suggested to those in Laodicea (3:18), and given to the souls under the Altar (6:11). Here however there do not seem to be a limited number, but a huge crowd all dressed in white robes.

We also see white robes in Daniel 11—12, alongside many other themes which build into Revelation 6—7: the movements of nations, salvation of those 'written in the book', a book sealed 'until the end of time', resurrection and judgment of the nations, and so on. We will see those who stand in resurrection will be dressed in white:

> Some of those who have insight will fall, in order to refine, purge and make them pure until the end time. (Daniel 11:35)

Here the word often translated as 'pure', 'cleansed' or 'spotless' is literally 'white'. Being 'made white' appears again in Daniel 12:10, where 'many will be purged, purified and refined'.

Palm branches (v9)

The palm branches speak of Jesus' triumphal entry into Jerusalem where the crowds are shouting:

> Hosanna to the Son of David;
> Blessed is He who comes in the name of the Lord;
> Hosanna in the highest!
> (Matthew 21:1–11, Mark 11:1–11, Luke 19:28–44, John 12:12–19)

Hosanna is Aramaic and means 'Save now!!' – this entreaty echoes the praise of the great multitude in verse 10:

> 'Salvation belongs to our God, who sits on the throne, and to the Lamb.'

In the week before the events of the Cross, the people celebrated as Jesus entered Jerusalem, and cried out to be saved. Here in eternity, John sees the vast multitude rejoicing now they have that salvation because of the sacrifice of the Lamb.

Jesus' triumphal entry is a prefiguring of His ultimate victory over sin and death – the Cross is the beginning of the end for the devil's work, and these palm branches in Revelation 7 point towards the final destruction of evil in the Lake of Fire, which comes in Revelation 20.

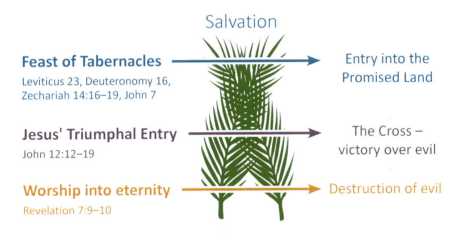

Feast of Tabernacles

As well as the triumphal entry, palm branches also speak of the Feast of Tabernacles/Booths – *Sukkot* – a 7-day Jewish festival to celebrate the harvest, when the Israelites would travel to Jerusalem and live in small shelters, or booths, which reflected the temporary dwelling of God among His people in the Tabernacle, as well as the tents the people lived in during the 40 years in the Wilderness. Not only were palm branches used to build the shelters, they were also waved and shaken about in worship and rejoicing (see Leviticus 23:39–40), just as at Jesus' triumphal entry.

The Feast of the Tabernacles represents the kind of community that God is looking for in the Church – real community, where we live side-by-side, share and care for one another. Laughing with those who laugh, crying with those who cry, and celebrating Christ's victory together in fellowship. We are meant to be building worshipful community. This does not mean interfering with one another or being nosey, or forming cliques or divisions, but sharing life together in Jesus. In his gospel, John wrote of Jesus 'the Word became flesh, and dwelt among us, and we saw His glory', where the word 'dwelt' is literally the word 'tabernacled' – Jesus *tabernacled* among us, lived temporarily on earth. The glory John talks of could well be the Transfiguration, where Peter suggests building three tabernacles for Jesus, Moses and Elijah – Peter was keen to keep on living in that kind of community!

So, just as the Israelites were travellers in temporary dwellings and God's glory accompanied them in the Tabernacle, so, like Jesus, we are only sojourners on the earth looking forward to that glorious end. It should be a longing and a willing for all of us to share Jesus together, seeking to help each other look like Him, as well as reaching out to tell others the Good News and welcoming them in. It is wonderful to belong to a community who love Jesus and have Him living among them.

Worship into eternity (v11)

This picture of the multitude adds another layer to the expanding vision of worship about the Throne we saw in Revelation 4 and 5. First we saw the 24 Elders, then the 4 Living Creatures, then countless angels followed by the whole of Creation . . . and now an innumerable company worshipping before the Throne, giving a little glimpse into the worship of eternity.

Just as in Revelation 5, the angels, 4 Living Creatures and 24 Elders praise 7 attributes of God:

> Revelation 5
> Power, riches, wisdom, might, honour, glory, blessing
>
> Revelation 7
> Blessing, glory, wisdom, thanksgiving, honour, power, might

In Revelation 5, the 4 Living Creatures kept saying 'Amen' and here we see increasing agreement as now all the angels, Living Creatures and Elders begin and end their worship with 'Amen', indicating this is an *inclusio*. The 'Amens' act as bookends, describing everything that is said in between, showing the agreement about these beautiful qualities of the Lord as worship and adoration is going on all round the Throne of God.

The 7 Seals | *Revelation 7:13–14*

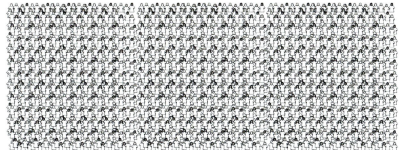

Text – Revelation 7:13–14

> [13] Then one of the elders answered, saying to me, 'These who are clothed in the white robes, who are they, and where have they come from?' [14] I said to him, 'My lord, you know.' And he said to me, 'These are the ones who come out of the great tribulation, and they have washed their robes and made them white in the blood of the Lamb.'

'My lord, you know' (v14)

When John responds: 'My lord, you know.' He is submitting his own understanding to the authority and lordship of this interpreter, saying 'You tell me.' He is not arrogantly saying he knows, or having a few guesses – there is always more to learn about God, and we are always meant to be learning, but you cannot do that unless you are humble.

This is an approach we always should use to understand the Bible – we can read all the commentaries and ideas about a passage, but we always have to submit our own understanding to God and pray 'Lord, tell me what does this mean?'

The Great Tribulation (v14)

The elder answers John that those dressed in white are the ones who are coming 'out of the great tribulation . . .' Elsewhere in Revelation we see 'tribulation' or 'great tribulation', but this time it is 'the Great Tribulation' – literally '*the* tribulation *the* great' – which is a unique and strong assertion.

This again reminds us of the end times prophecies in Daniel, where those who are 'made spotless' emerge from a persecution lasting 'times, time and half a time' (Daniel 7:23–27, 12:1–7). So, many commentators, especially those of the Futurist view, interpret the Great Tribulation as a future period of 3½ years of extraordinary persecution at the end of the Church Age. However, when we looked in Revelation 6:1–8 at what is often called 'The Tribulation' (see page 243), we saw how, rather than just being restricted to the last few years of the Church Age, Seals 1–4 being broken seem to apply throughout this time. Similarly, John talks of 'tribulation' in Revelation 1:9, 2:9–10 and 22, indicating an ongoing process. There was tribulation at the end of the Jewish Age with the destruction of the Temple, there has been and will continue to be tribulation throughout the Church Age. While I believe there will likely be a future period of increased tribulation at the end of the Church Age, tribulation is already occurring, and those John sees coming out of 'the Great Tribulation' likely comprise those from all periods of tribulation – as if all the tribulation is bundled together into one – that is, 'the Great Tribulation'.

It is probably meant to be understood that this Great Tribulation is symbolized by the 3½ years which come up later in Revelation 11 and 12.

Covenant people

Here in Revelation 7, just like in Daniel 12, the people John sees coming out of the Great Tribulation are wearing clean, white, and whitened, robes. What we see is a covenant people.

A covenant is a binding promise – a contract with conditions for both sides. God made a covenant with Noah, He made a covenant with Abraham, and with Moses, and also with David. Covenant means God is in business with us: we have a promise between us that He will accomplish all He has said, as long as we keep up our side of the agreement.

The Ten Commandments were a covenant God made with Israel during the Exodus. In Exodus 19, before Moses went up Mount Sinai:

> The Lord also said to Moses, 'Go to the people and consecrate them today and tomorrow, and let them wash their garments; and let them be ready for the third day, for on the third day the Lord will come down on Mount Sinai in the sight of all the people . . . When the ram's horn sounds a long blast, they shall come up to the mountain.' So Moses went down from the mountain to the people and consecrated the people, and they washed their garments. (Exodus 19:10–14)

This was accompanied by the long blast of a trumpet sound, anticipating the 7th Trumpet. Once God had given the covenant:

> Moses took the book of the covenant and read it in the hearing of the people; and they said, 'All that the Lord has spoken we will do, and we will be obedient!' So Moses took the blood and sprinkled it on the people, and said, 'Behold the blood of the covenant, which the Lord has made with you in accordance with all these words.' (Exodus 24:7–8)

The people needed clean clothes in preparation for God coming to give them the covenant, and once they agreed, they were sprinkled with blood, which confirmed the covenant. This dual activity is essential to approach God: it is why there was a laver outside the temple and blood was sprinkled on just about everything, because it meant that the price of those things is the blood of the sacrifice.

While to our sanitized Western minds sprinkling blood on things may seem gory and repulsive, in the ancient world covenants and contracts were often sealed with blood, hence the phrase 'to cut a covenant'. Shedding blood, whether your own, or that of a sacrifice, was a sign you were serious – it cost you something! In Revelation 7 we see the people 'have washed their robes and made them white in the blood of the Lamb' (v14) – they are a covenant people. Some may struggle with the imagery of blood making things clean, but of course this symbolizes the atoning sacrifice of Christ.

(NB, the Bible does not say we are 'washed' in blood, only 'sprinkled' or 'made white', that is, bleached. The idea of being 'washed in blood' came into Christian vocabulary because the Authorised Version translated a weak text of Revelation 1:5 as 'washed' instead of 'loosed'. No modern versions take this reading. The idea of the blood is that it bleaches or purifies the washed clothes in order that we may approach God.)

The New Covenant people – with the seal of the Holy Spirit and signs and wonders – are equally, but more fundamentally washed and then sprinkled with blood. Jesus is the mediator of a new covenant (Hebrews 9:15) which He instituted at the Last Supper:

> Jesus took some bread, and after a blessing, He broke it and gave it to the disciples, and said, 'Take, eat; this is My body.' And when He had taken a cup and given thanks, He gave it to them, saying, 'Drink from it, all of you; for this is My blood of the covenant, which is poured out for many for forgiveness of sins.' (Matthew 26:26–28)

As Christians, our clothing is our outward lifestyle – how people see us expressing our faith. We wash our spiritual clothes through the word of God and the Holy Spirit, and have the blood of Jesus' sacrifice on the Cross sprinkled on us. Together, the Holy Spirit's activity to make us clean and pure like Jesus, and the addition of the blood which is essential if we are to approach God, are the two fundamental characteristics of these people who come out of Great Tribulation.

Washing spiritual clothes

Jesus' sacrifice on the Cross was once for all, sufficient (Hebrews 7:27, 10:12). Praying a prayer of repentance may be enough to save us, but it will not keep our spiritual clothes clean forever. Just as with the clothes we wear, washing them once is not enough – they will get dirty just by us wearing them, as

The 7 Seals | Revelation 7:15–17

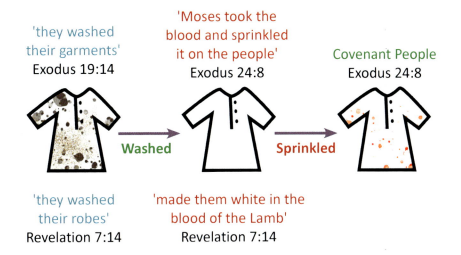

well as the dirt caused by other people and the environment we are in. It is important to acknowledge that cleaning our spiritual clothing is similarly not just a once-for-all thing, but has to be a daily exercise. Am I walking clean today? Do I need to adjust my life to keep out of the dirt?

Even when we sin and fail to keep our spiritual clothes clean, we have the blood of Jesus to bring us peace, instead of going into despair and hopelessness. The blood of Christ speaks far more wonderful things than the enemy can ever say to us, so with our lives continuously washed in the Holy Spirit and the Word (Ephesians 5:26, John 15:3) we can be a covenant people who are fulfilling the purposes of God for the human race. Like this vision of praising people, we will emerge from the Great Tribulation in worship and prayer.

Text – Revelation 7:15–17

> [15] For this reason, they are before the throne of God; and they serve Him day and night in His temple; and He who sits on the throne will spread His tabernacle over them. [16] They will hunger no longer, nor thirst anymore; nor will the sun beat down on them, nor any heat; [17] for the Lamb in the centre of the throne will be their shepherd, and will guide them to springs of the water of life; and God will wipe every tear from their eyes.

Serving in the Temple (v15)

The multitude are serving God 'day and night in His Temple', so this is a temple worship scene. We have seen how heaven is constructed in a similar way to the Temple/Tabernacle, with God's Throne at the heart (page 205).

Spread His Tabernacle (v15)

Throughout Scripture we get the imagery of God wanting to dwell with humanity – if you like, it is the meta-narrative of the Bible:

> I will dwell among the people of Israel and will be their God.
> (Exodus 29:45, see also Leviticus 26:12, Jeremiah 31:33, 32:38, Ezekiel 37:26–27)

In the Old Testament, first the Tabernacle and then the Temple were God's dwelling places among His people. As we looked at above, John describes the incarnation as Jesus coming to 'dwell' or 'tabernacle' among us.

The same thought is in Ezekiel 37, where God wants to be resident with His people in a Messianic Kingdom:

> I will make a covenant of peace with them; it will be an everlasting covenant with them. And I will place them and multiply them, and will set My sanctuary in their midst forever. My dwelling place also will be with them; and I will be their God, and they will be My people. (Ezekiel 37:26–27)

Isaiah 4 also describes God dwelling with a Messianic remnant:

> Those who are left in Zion, who remain in Jerusalem, will be called holy . . . Then the Lord will create over all of Mount Zion and over those who assemble there a cloud of smoke by day and a glow of flaming fire by night; over everything the glory will be a canopy. It will be a shelter and shade from the heat of the day, and a refuge and hiding place from the storm and rain. (Isaiah 4:3,5–6)

All this is looking forward to the ultimate revelation of God dwelling with His people: verse 15 says God 'shall spread His tabernacle over them' and Revelation 21:3–6 shows us this happens after the final judgment. This again indicates this passage is looking forward into eternity.

Verses 16–17 are a beautiful tapestry of Old Testament concepts woven together, based on Isaiah 49:

> They will not hunger or thirst,
> Nor will the scorching heat or sun strike them down;
> For He who has compassion on them will lead them
> And will guide them to springs of water . . .
> . . . For the Lord has comforted His people
> And will have compassion on His afflicted. (v10,13)

In the midst of this we see a shepherd who was once a lamb who 'will lead them' just as in Zechariah 13:7 (quoted by Matthew 26:31), Isaiah 40:11, Ezekiel 34:23, 37:24 and Micah 5:4 (quoted by Matthew 2:6).

All these Old Testament references point forward to the fulfilment of Jesus as our Shepherd, which we read of in John 10:11, Hebrews 13:20 and 1 Peter 5:4:

> He will swallow up death for all time,
> And the Lord God will wipe tears away from all faces,
> And He will remove the reproach of His people from all the earth.
> (Isaiah 25:8)

These verses create a wonderful vision of God's promises to His covenant people as He dwells with them into eternity.

* ✶ *

To sum up, Revelation 7 looks both into the past and into the future to set the scene for the answer to the prayer of Revelation 6:10 – 'How long O Lord . . ?'

The message of Revelation 6 was that the earth will be shaken and we need the Seal of God on us in order to bring us through this trial, but one day God's justice will be seen on this earth, when this prayer will be answered, after which a vast multitude will worship before the Throne into eternity.

With this reassurance in mind, Revelation 8 will begin to reveal how God is going to move His Creation towards this ultimate destiny.

Section II – Christ Central in Creation

Discussion Questions

Reflect on a time when you have asked 'How long O Lord?'

How did you get through? Has it built or weakened your faith? Has this stimulated your prayer life?

How have you addressed the question of your responsibility?

Revelation 8

Revelation 8 starts with the breaking of the 7th Seal, which leads into the sounding of the 7 Trumpets. These Trumpets will continue building up into Revelation 9, followed by an interlude and a great crescendo as the last Trumpet sounds in chapter 11, when the kingdoms of this world become the Kingdom of our Lord and His Christ.

The 7th Seal
Text – Revelation 8:1–5

¹ When the Lamb broke the seventh seal, there was silence in heaven for about half an hour. ² And I saw the seven angels who stand before God, and seven trumpets were given to them.

³ Another angel came and stood at the altar, holding a golden censer; and much incense was given to him, so that he might add it to the prayers of all the saints on the golden altar which was before the throne. ⁴ And the smoke of the incense, with the prayers of the saints, went up before God out of the angel's hand. ⁵ Then the angel took the censer and filled it with the fire of the altar, and threw it to the earth; and there followed peals of thunder and sounds and flashes of lightning and an earthquake.

Silence in Heaven (v1)

When the 7th Seal is broken, there is silence in heaven for about half an hour. After all of the intensity and energy that happened when Seals 1–6 were broken, this could seem like a bit of an anticlimax, so some people say the 7th Seal has got nothing in it. But this silence is *something*, not nothing.

In the Old Testament silence is very important, and nowhere in the Old Testament where silence is mentioned is it ever empty or void. There is always something in that silence. So what does this silence mean? Here we will look at five different ways silence appears and how it will help us understand this imagery.

1. Exodus 14 – Obedience and salvation

> Moses said to the people, 'Do not fear! Stand by and see the salvation of the Lord which He will accomplish for you today; for the Egyptians whom you have seen today, you will never see them again forever. The Lord will fight for you while you keep silent.'
>
> Then the Lord said to Moses, 'Why are you crying out to Me? Tell the sons of Israel to go forward . . . As for you, lift up your staff and stretch out your hand over the sea and divide it, and the sons of Israel shall go through the midst of the sea on dry land.' (Exodus 14:13–16)

This is Israel's salvation out of Egypt. God tells Moses to lead the people of Israel into the Red Sea, but the people were crying out and panicking: *What will we do!?*

The silence was the silence of that wonder and awe of the activity of God. It is the silence of worship: *Stand still, be silent, God is going to fight for you. Stop panicking.* The silence of obedience and salvation, knowing that God is going to do it for you.

As we continue in Revelation 8—9, the events which follow the first 5 Trumpets are reminiscent of the plagues of Egypt, and as silence appears in both places it is likely they are connected.

2. Psalm 65 – Listening for real prayer

> There will be silence before You, and praise in Zion, O God,
> And to You the vow will be performed.

> O You who hear prayer,
> To You all men come.
> Iniquities prevail against me;
> As for our transgressions, You forgive them.
> How blessed is the one whom You choose and bring near to You
> To dwell in Your courts.
> We will be satisfied with the goodness of Your house,
> Your holy temple. (Psalm 65:1–4)

Here the silence is in amazement at the wonderful things God has done, specifically in forgiving our sin and drawing us near. God wants to hear what His people have to say. Later on in this psalm, verse 13 says 'the valleys are covered with grain; they shout for joy, yes, they sing', but our God is a listening God and is longing to hear the prayers of our heart. If there is too much racket or hypocritical praying, real prayer is often drummed out, so silence is a very important part of our devotion to God – we should practice the discipline of silence so we can pray the things which lie deep within our hearts.

In Revelation 8, this silence stands in contrast to the loud noise we will soon hear when the 7 Angels start blowing their 7 Trumpets. God is bringing a silence before that so He can hear what His people are praying.

3. Ezekiel 1 – Waiting for revelation and judgment

> And there came a voice from above the expanse that was over their heads; whenever they stood still, they dropped their wings. Now above the expanse that was over their heads there was something resembling a throne . . .(Ezekiel 1:25–26)

Ezekiel describes the sound of the wings of the cherubim like 'abundant waters . . . a sound of tumult . . . like an army camp', but there are also times when they stood still, and their wings dropped and there would have been silence. This silence represents waiting for revelation and for judgement in awe. We see a similar waiting, or standing, in Ezekiel 10:

> It came about when He commanded the man clothed in linen, saying, 'Take fire from between the whirling wheels, from between the cherubim,' he entered and stood beside a wheel. (Ezekiel 10:6)

So there is a standing and waiting, followed by fire being taken from before the Throne, which is what we will also see in Revelation 8. We see the same waiting before God's Throne for revelation and judgment in other places in the Old Testament:

> The Lord is in His holy temple. Let the earth be silent before Him. (Habakkuk 2:20)

> Be silent before the Lord God! For the day of the Lord is near, For the Lord has prepared a sacrifice, He has consecrated His guests. (Zephaniah 1:7)

> Be silent, all flesh, before the Lord; for He is aroused from His holy habitation. (Zechariah 2:13)

> Coastlands listen to Me in silence,
> And let the peoples gain new strength.
> Let them come forward; then let them speak;
> Let us come together for judgment. (Isaiah 41:1)

So what is the link between silence and judgment? If we imagine standing before the Great White Throne when the Lord is about to judge, I do not think there will be giggling and chatting. An awesome silence will fall upon us and we will wait holding our breath: 'What is He going to say?' 'What will happen next?'

This sort of silence before judgment is what we have in Revelation 8 – as the Trumpets start to be blown, God's judgments against sin start to fall on the earth.

4. 'Selah' – Temple liturgy/meditation

This may also be the silence of 'selah', which you find written 71 times in Psalms, as well as three times in Habakkuk. For example:

> I was crying to the Lord with my voice, And He answered me from His holy mountain. Selah.
>
> . . . Salvation belongs to the Lord; Your blessing be upon Your people! Selah. (Psalm 3:4,8)

Nobody really knows exactly what 'selah' means, but it seems to represent some kind of pause and probably means 'be silent and listen' or 'stop breathing', so that we can be quiet and take in God's truth and understand it more deeply.

We have just seen heavenly songs being sung in Revelation 7, so maybe here we have silence appearing like 'selah' for us to pause in worship while we meditate in awe and wonder.

5. Eschatological 'primeval silence' before the New Creation

There is a further hint at the importance of silence, originating from Jewish writings. This idea is of a primeval silence, that in Genesis 1, God the Creator and His Creation were silent until verse 3 when God said, 'Let there be light!' Up until that point the heavens and the earth were formless and void, and waiting in anticipation for God to speak and bring His incredible project into being. That silence heard the voice of God, bringing the universe into the state it is in now – no longer without form, no longer empty.

In Revelation, we are looking forward to the New Creation coming into being and here is another silence until God's voice calls out. The primeval silence anticipates an eschatological silence before the New Heaven and New Earth spring into life.

Each of these elements inform the pregnant silence we get at the start of Revelation 8: obedience, salvation, God listening, anticipation of judgment, a pause for meditation and an eschatological silence before the New Creation. This silence is not empty – it is full of deep truths.

7 angels (v2)

Who are these 7 Angels who stand before God? In considering these 7 angels, we are looking both backwards and forwards. Who are they who stand before God? In Revelation 5:11 there were 'myriads of myriads, and thousands of thousands' of angels, so here why do we see just 7 in particular? There are three possibilities, each so different.

Of the 7 Churches?

We have already seen 7 angels in Revelation 1:20 and then in chapters 2—3, where there is one for each of the 7 Churches, probably representing the spiritual life of the complete Church.

Band of destroying angels?

Another place where we get a small group of angels is in Psalm 78:

> He sent upon them His burning anger. Fury and indignation and trouble, a band of destroying angels. (Psalm 78:49)

As we read on in Revelation, the angels with the 7 Trumpets also bring about some very destructive things, so could they be identified with this 'band of destroying angels' (literally 'a deputation of angels of evil')?

Not all angels in Scripture are nice 'Christmas card' ones: the devil has his angels (Matthew 25:41); one angel offers God to be 'a deceiving spirit in the mouth of all his prophets' (1 Kings 22:22, 2 Chronicles 18:21); and at Passover there was a 'destroyer' or 'angel of death', who killed the firstborn in any house not sealed with the blood of the Lamb.

In Psalm 78, the context is the Exodus and how these angels unleash plagues, just like the ones in Revelation will when they blow their trumpets. So how come these destroying angels are allowed to stand before God? This highlights once again how God, as a master chess player, can use even these 'bad' angels to bring about His purposes. The Lord may even permit evil spiritual forces to bring death and destruction, just as we see God allowing Satan to test Job (see my book, *Suffering and the Love of God: The book of Job*).

Jewish apocalyptic angels?

Jewish apocalyptic writings often featured angels, and in particular there were 7 angels designated as 'archangels': Uriel, Raphael, Raguel, Michael, Sariel, Gabriel and Jeremiel. So a group of 7 angels, representing a complete body, would be a familiar concept for a Jewish reader, especially among the Essenes, such as those in the Qumran community who we know about from the Dead Sea Scrolls. 7 angels is a formula they would understand.

Whatever they represent, these 7 angels stand before God, which is a pretty important place to be, showing they have authority. They demonstrate something of God's reaction to sin as they are let loose, so we do have to treat them with respect, even though they may not be particularly 'nice'. They are going to blow their 7 Trumpets, and when they do, significant and terrifying things are going to happen.

Another angel and the Golden Altar (v3)

In verse 3, another angel comes and stands at the Altar. We last saw the Altar in Revelation 6, where we discussed whether it represented the Bronze Altar, or the Golden Altar of incense, or possibly an assimilation of both (see page 266).

The Golden Altar stood in the Holy Place in front of the veil of the Holy of Holies, and incense was burnt as an offering each morning and evening when the lamps were trimmed (see Exodus 30). This symbolized the prayers of the people rising up to God in intercession (Psalm 141:2). The priests would transfer coals from the Bronze Altar to the Golden Altar using a censer, or firepan – a shallow bowl with a handle – and then add incense to the censers to produce an aromatic cloud of incense in front of God's Throne in the Holy of Holies (Leviticus 16:12).

The word 'altar' appears 3 times in verses 3–5: the first and last times it is just 'Altar' but the second time is 'Golden Altar'. So here we may have both the Bronze Altar and Golden Altar in view. In verse 3, we first see the angel standing at the Bronze Altar, presumably collecting fiery coals in the Golden Censer, and is given incense to burn on the Golden Altar. Then in verse 5 the Angel is back at the Bronze Altar filling the censer with fiery coals.

The incense was 'holy', made by a special recipe just for use in the Temple:

> Then the Lord said to Moses, 'Take for yourself spices, stacte and onycha and galbanum, spices with pure frankincense; there shall be an equal part of each. With it you shall make incense, a perfume, the work of a perfumer, salted, pure, and holy.' (Exodus 30:34–35)

In Luke 1:8–11, we see Zacharias the father of John the Baptist fulfilling his lot as a priest, burning the incense in just this way.

Although Jesus was not of the order of the Levites, nonetheless this priestly activity illustrates the spiritual priesthood of Christ and the Church. Jesus is our High Priest and both He and the Holy Spirit make intercession for us (1 John 2:1, Romans 8:26–27,34, Isaiah 53:10–12) and the calling of the Church is of the same priestly calling as our Lord (Acts 6:4, Hebrews 13:15, 1 Corinthians 1:2), which is greater than just the Old Testament priests, who were restricted to the Levites, but now includes everyone (1 Peter 2:5, Revelation 1:6). As Christians we can enter into the truths behind these Jewish rituals, as they reveal the importance of intercession and offering up the prayers of the saints to God.

Prayers of the Saints (v4)

A censer, or firepan, was used by the priests to carry the fire for burning incense. Here in Revelation 7, the angel by the Altar holds a golden censer, indicating he is acting in a priestly, intercessory role, and is given 'much incense . . . that he might add it to the prayers of the saints.'

As we looked at in Revelation 5:8 (see page 227), grammatically 'the prayers of the saints' definitively refers to the bowls, not to the incense. This makes sense here in Revelation 8: the incense is added to the bowls – which are the prayers of the saints – on the Altar. This is exactly what the priest would do in the Tabernacle/Temple.

However, many commentators take the position that the prayers of the saints are themselves the incense, but this is confusing as 'much incense' would be being added to incense (prayers of the saints) – why would it be called two completely separate things?

To compound this confusion, in verses 3 and 4 many translations add in the words 'with', 'mixed with' or 'together with', to make the incense equivalent to 'prayers of the saints'. For example:

> He was given much incense to offer, *with* the prayers of all God's people . . . The smoke of the incense, *together with* the prayers of God's people, went up before God. (NIV)

Such translations are misleading, as there is no word for 'mixed' or 'together' in the Greek. Indeed, the word 'with' is not present in the Greek either, although it is possible given the dative form of the verb 'to add/give'. However, while 'with' is possible, other dative prepositions are more likely and the most natural reading of verse 3, as in the NASB, is 'add it to' – the incense is added to the bowls. Similarly in verse 4 the word 'with' is a grammatical possibility, but could equally likely be another dative particle, such as 'from' or 'for' (NASB margin): the smoke rises from the bowls.

If we read the Greek text in a straightforward manner, rather than trying to fit it to some preconceived theological ideas, the incense is added to the bowls/censers/prayers of the saints on the Altar, and the smoke of incense rises from them.

What is the incense which is added to the censer? In the Old Testament the incense was an offering, a sacrifice, and burning it represented the High Priest's prayer of atonement for the people rising up to God. So here the incense is similarly an atoning offering made by the High Priest to intercede on behalf of God's people – it is Jesus' atoning sacrificial intercession for us.

> By this will we have been sanctified through the offering of the body of Jesus Christ once for all. Every priest stands daily ministering and offering time after time the same sacrifices, which can never take away sins; but He, having offered one sacrifice for sins for all time, SAT DOWN AT THE RIGHT HAND OF GOD . . . For by one offering He has perfected for all time those who are sanctified. (Hebrews 10:10–14)

> [Jesus] himself is the atoning sacrifice for our sins, and not only for ours, but also for those of the whole world. (1 John 2:2)

The picture is very beautiful – we come before God as an open censer, and Jesus will add in His intercession through the Holy Spirit to make our prayers rise up to the Throne of God as a pleasing aroma. While sometimes we may not know what to pray, if we come to the Lord with open hands, the intercession of the Spirit is put into your heart and will flow through us 'with groanings that cannot be uttered'. The Holy Spirit brings us into the prayer life of Jesus.

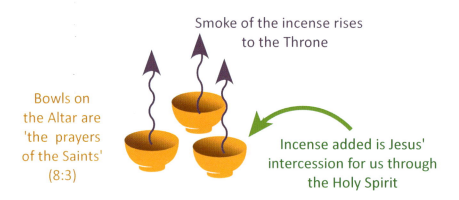

Fire thrown down (v5)

The angel fills the golden censer with fire and throws it to the earth, which is followed by thunder, lightning and an earthquake. These all represent wrath from the Throne of God.

This seems to be the direct response to the prayer going up before God the verse before, so it is the prayers of the saints which are calling down God's wrath, echoing the call of the Martyrs under the Altar for vengeance in the 5th Seal.

This is a good verse for anyone who struggles in their prayer life and thinks their prayers maybe do not accomplish much. We may not see the direct effects of praying, but it is our prayers for justice and God's Kingdom to come that will ultimately lead to people having to face up to what it means to be righteous and pure. Our prayers will call people to account, with God speaking through their consciences as they feel the pressure of God's reaction to their actions. If the Church is prayerless, the fire is not sent forth: we need the church to pray!

Sealing fire

We have seen how the sealing of God's people in Revelation 7 parallels the sealing of the saints in Ezekiel 9, where an angel put a mark on the foreheads of the people of God so they would be preserved as judgment fell upon Jerusalem. This is followed in Ezekiel 10 with a vision of an angel being instructed to:

> . . . enter between the whirling wheels under the cherubim and fill your hands with coals of fire from between the cherubim and scatter them over the city. (Ezekiel 10:2)

After this, the glory of the Lord departs from the Temple.

In Revelation 8, just as in Ezekiel 10, the sealing of God's people is followed by fiery coals from the Altar being thrown down on the earth as a sign of God's judgment.

Looking ahead to Revelation 9:4, we see the locusts are not allowed to hurt those with the seal of God on their foreheads, and these ones are preserved. We will see a similar development as we go through the 7 Trumpets of judgments that resemble the plagues of Egypt, falling upon those who do not have the seal upon them. In a similar way the blood on the door posts sealed the children of Israel when they came out of Egypt during the Exodus.

Thunder, lightning and an earthquake (v5)

Here again we see an escalation in the seriousness of the events, which worsen as we go through the 7s. We have not only thunder, rumblings and lightning, but also an earthquake.

Section II – Christ Central in Creation

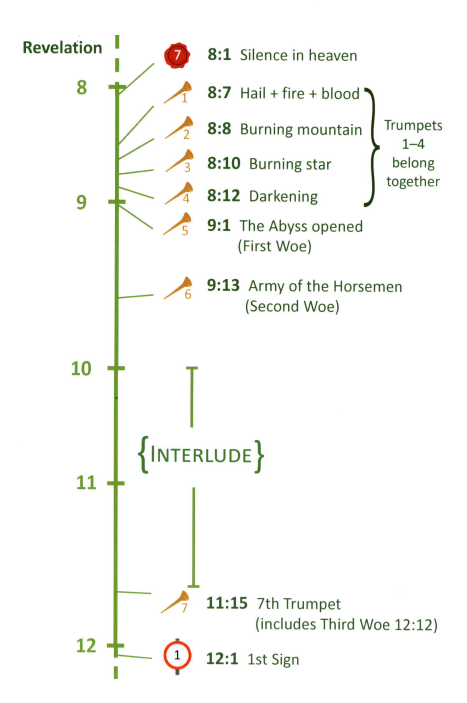

The 7 Trumpets

Text – Revelation 8:6

> [6] And the seven angels who had the seven trumpets prepared themselves to sound them.

Prepared to sound (v6)

The 7 Angels with the 7 Trumpets now prepare to sound them, and this set will take us up to Revelation 11, which culminates in the last Trumpet bringing judgment upon the whole earth. But what do these Trumpets signify?

To start to grasp the significance of the 7 Trumpets, we need to understand what trumpets meant to people reading in the first century.

End of the Age

In the New Testament, trumpets symbolise the End of the Age. There is a great trumpet in Matthew 24:30–31 which signifies the end of the Jewish Age when Jerusalem falls in AD 70. In 1 Corinthians 15:52 and 1 Thessalonians 4:16, a trumpet will sound and the dead in Christ will rise and in the twinkling of an eye we shall be changed, which represents the Second Coming and the end of the Church Age. So here in Revelation, the first 6 Trumpets point to and prepare us for the sounding of the 7th Trumpet that Paul writes about to bring in the End of the Age.

Trumpets in the Old Testament

Trumpets appear at important junctures throughout the Old Testament, where they usually speak of judgment and battle. We will look at some of these trumpets to see what they can tell us about the 7 Trumpets in Revelation.

Seven trumpet blasts at Jericho – Joshua 6

The first Old Testament picture to get hold of is the Jericho trumpets. The people went around the city once a day for six days, with the priests blowing their trumpets before the Ark of the Covenant. On the 7th day they went around 7 times (a 7 within a 7).

> At the seventh time, when the priests blew the trumpets, Joshua said to the people, 'Shout! For the Lord has given you the city'... and when the people heard the sound of the trumpet, the people shouted with a great shout and the wall fell down flat. (Joshua 6:6,20)

The 7th Trumpet heralded the Ark appearing and revealed God's presence among His people – at this the resistance of the city disintegrated.

In Revelation 11:15–19 we also see the 7th Trumpet blast, followed by loud voices worshipping, and the Ark of the Covenant appears signifying God's presence among His people. So the picture of Jericho lies behind whatever these trumpet sounds in Revelation are about.

Trumpets at Mount Sinai – Exodus 19

There are also trumpets blown at Sinai, when the Ten Commandments are given to Moses.

We have already seen the theme of Exodus appearing in Revelation 7—8: in the covenant as the people had to wash their clothes and be sprinkled with blood like at the atonement (Revelation 7:14/Exodus 19:14, 24:8); a silence before the 7th Seal like that before the Red Sea (Revelation 8:1/Exodus 14:14); and now we will see the plagues appearing in the first 6 Trumpet blasts (Revelation 8:7–12/Exodus 7—12).

In Revelation, the sounding of the 7 Trumpets is preceded by thunder, lightning and an earthquake, and in Exodus 19 we also get thunder, lightning and 'a very loud trumpet sound, so that all the people who were in the camp trembled', just like an earthquake. Not only does the trumpet sound get louder, but God talks to Moses *in* thunder (Exodus 19:19). It must have been an awesome sound!

So we can take the imagery of the Old Covenant people in Exodus and build it into our vision of the New Covenant people.

Moving the People Forward – Numbers 10

In Numbers 10, Moses is instructed to make two silver trumpets, and these were blown to move the people of God forward and to assemble them. They were blown during Holy warfare, in celebration and in victory. All of these concepts are brought together in this chapter.

- Summoning the whole congregation to the tent of meeting (v3)
- Assembling the leaders (v4)
- Setting out the camps of the people to journey (v5–6)
- Interceding and warning when going into battle (v9)
- Rejoicing at celebrations and sacrifices (v10)

Notably, it is the priests who blow the trumpets (v8), so it is a priestly activity of assembling and guiding the people, worship and warfare. In Revelation 8—11, these 7 angels are acting in a priestly way.

Victory and celebration

In addition to Numbers 10:10, Psalm 150 shows very clearly that trumpets (among other instruments) were used in worship in the temple:

> Praise the Lord!
> Praise God in His sanctuary;
> Praise Him in His mighty expanse.
> Praise Him for His mighty deeds;
> Praise Him according to His excellent greatness.
> Praise Him with trumpet sound . . . (Psalm 150:1–3)

In 1 Chronicles 16:4–6, we again see Trumpets being blown before the Ark of the Covenant

> And he appointed some of the Levites as ministers before the ark of the Lord, even to celebrate and to thank and praise the Lord God of Israel . . . and the priests Benaiah and Jahaziel blew trumpets continually before the ark of the covenant of God.

Judgment

In Joel 2, we see a trumpet (*shofar*) bringing in judgment:

> Blow a trumpet in Zion,
> And sound an alarm on My holy mountain!
> Let all the inhabitants of the land tremble,
> For the day of the Lord is coming. (Joel 2:1)

The many Old Testament uses and meanings of the trumpets, mean it is unlikely that Revelation exclusively represents just one idea here, but is bringing various aspects together: ₁Bringing defeat to the enemy, like at Jericho; ₂heralding a covenant people, like at Sinai; ₃bringing a warning of warfare and ₄to be alert; ₅for worship, ₆delighting in God's victory; and ₇for guiding the whole company through the desert. The 7 Trumpets in Revelation encapsulate these ideas.

It is important to note these trumpets will elicit different responses from different people – God's people will be reassured by them, but they will bring fear to God's enemies. The key is that the Trumpets anticipate God's presence – just as they were blown before the Ark and were used to summon the people to God's tent, as well as to summon God to the battle. To His people, the Lord's presence will bring victory and rejoicing, but to those in opposition it will bring defeat and pain.

Trumpets and the plagues of Egypt

Trumpets 1–6 show significant parallels to the Plagues of Egypt, and we will look at these in more detail as we go through:

Trumpet	Plague	Exodus
1 (8:7)	Hail	9:22–25
2 3 (8:8–11)	Water turned to blood	7:20–21
4 (8:12)	Darkness over the land	10:21–23
5 (9:1–11)	Locusts Horses prepared for battle Abaddon/Apollyon – Destroying angel	10:12–15 14:5–9 12:23
6 (9:13–21)	Chased by army on horses and chariots 'Three Plagues' (v18)	14:5–9

The 7 Trumpets | Revelation 8:7–12

What is the overall significance of these parallels with the plagues of Egypt? Just as in Exodus, John is writing to believers who are being afflicted and persecuted, and these Trumpets will encourage them not to be dismayed by the threats and plagues of the world and its hardened heart of opposition to the people of God, but to keep on following the Lord until the final Trumpet sounds, and the Kingdom of God comes.

With this overview in mind, let us go through these 7 Trumpets in depth.

Trumpets 1–4
Text – Revelation 8:7–12

 ⁷ The first sounded and there came hail and fire, mixed with blood, and they were thrown to the earth; and a third of the earth was burned up and a third of the trees were burned up and all the green grass was burned up.

 ⁸ The second angel sounded, and something like a great mountain burning with fire was thrown into the sea; and a third of the sea became blood, ⁹ and a third of the creatures which were in the sea and had life, died; and a third of the ships were destroyed.

 ¹⁰ The third angel sounded, and a great star fell from heaven, burning like a torch, and it fell on a third of the rivers and on the springs of waters. ¹¹ The name of the star is called Wormwood; and a third of the waters became wormwood, and many men died from the waters, because they were made bitter.

 ¹² The fourth angel sounded, and a third of the sun and a third of the moon and a third of the stars were struck, so that a third of them would be darkened and the day would not shine for a third of it, and the night in the same way.

First 4 Trumpets

Just as with the first 4 Seals, Trumpets 1–4 be999long together as a group. These 4 Trumpets reveal the consequences of sin in our lives – this is what idolatry does to humanity. As we well see, it destroys the foundations of our life, it surrounds us with death, no matter what we do we will burn with a lack of satisfaction, and our inner lives will be darkened.

1st Trumpet – Loss of foundations

As you know by now, we are not meant to interpret Revelation totally literally, so rather than exactly one third of the earth, it indicates a significant portion being destroyed. A significant portion of the trees were burned up and as well as all the green grass. Why these things? They are foundational – the earth, trees and grass formed the background to their life and existence, and their destruction represents our lives being thoroughly disturbed. When Jesus fed the 5,000 they sat down 'on the green grass' (Mark 6:39, also Matthew 14:19, John 6:10), so this Trumpet is taking away comfort. In our modern society we may find this difficult to relate to, but in the first century, people's lives were far more agrarian and linked to nature than our increasingly urban ones. So the impact of the hail and the fire does not just affect grass and trees, but the foundations of the earth as well as society.

It is worth mentioning here that in the next chapter, the locust army is told not to harm the grass (Revelation 9:4), but if all the grass is burnt up now, there would be none left to harm! This just reaffirms that in Revelation we are dealing with highly symbolic language.

Plague of hail

This Trumpet is a clear allusion to the plague of severe hail in Exodus 9:22–25:

> . . . the Lord sent thunder and hail, and fire ran down to the earth. And the Lord rained hail on the land of Egypt . . . The hail struck all that was in the field through all the land of Egypt, both man and beast . . . struck every plant of the field and shattered every tree of the field.

Not only is there hail, but fire too, likely from the lightning. We see burning both here and after the next two trumpet blasts. This fire not only consumes the earth, crops and trees which have been destroyed by the hail, but in so doing it produces famine. Without homes, without trees for fruit and wood, and without grass to feed animals and sit down on, there is nothing to rely on. People's lives lose their security and their provision.

There is a clear allusion here to Ezekiel 4—5, which prophesies the siege and destruction of Jerusalem. For example:

> One third of you will die by plague or be consumed by famine among you, one third will fall by the sword around you, and one

third I will scatter to every wind, and I will unsheathe a sword behind them. (Ezekiel 5:12, see also v2)

God is bringing about this shaking to demonstrate to people that the consequence of their sin – their lives lived without God – is they have no foundations. If God allows the things which make life easy to be taken away, that is, what you are used to living on, what do you have left? God's wrath can be seen as what happens when you don't live in God's world, God's way. We will see the final fulfilment of this when we get to Revelation 18:8.

2nd Trumpet – Loss of communication

Following the second Trumpet a great burning Mountain is thrown into the sea, a third of which turned to blood. This image is of death and disorder. Again we must not take it so literally that we have to argue one third of the sea is kept from filtering into the other two thirds, and so on. The blood is caused by death in the sea – huge numbers of creatures die and a significant number of ships are destroyed, presumably with all those on board. This signifies terrific disruption as ships were very important for trade and communication.

This mirrors the first plague of Egypt, with the Nile turning to blood:

> The fish that were in the Nile died, and the Nile became foul, so that the Egyptians could not drink water from the Nile. (Exodus 7:21)

This is what sin does; not just to us, but to those around us. It stops us being able to make contact with one another. We become unable to interact, talk and share with one another. Not only do the fish die, but their blood makes things foul for those who survive – their life is surrounded by blood. Sin creates a deadly kind of existence.

The image of the destroying Mountain is important. In the Old Testament mountains are sometimes used to signify a city or a kingdom, for example in Jeremiah 51:25:

> 'Behold, I am against you, mountain of destruction
> That destroys the whole earth,' declares the Lord,
> 'And I will stretch out My hand against you,
> And roll you down from the rocky cliffs,
> And I will make you a burnt out mountain.'

Who is this destroying mountain? We see from verse 14 it is the nation or the city of Babylon. Continuing in Jeremiah 51 it says:

> And it will come about as soon as you finish reading this scroll, you will tie a stone to it and throw it into the middle of the Euphrates and say 'Just so shall Babylon sink down and not rise again, because of the calamity that I am going to bring upon her'. (v63–64)

When we get to Revelation 18:11–21, Babylon's trade is completely disrupted and finally the city is tied up like a stone and thrown into the sea. So this mountain burning with fire is speaking of the end-time kingdom which is going to be destroyed, or possibly the kingdoms that have existed through the Church Age, whom God is threatening with destruction.

3rd Trumpet – Loss of satisfaction

Great Star

When the 3rd Angel sounds, we again have burning – this time 'a great star' falls from heaven. While after the second Trumpet, the burning mountain represents an earthly a destructive kingdom in opposition to God's people, here we have a burning Star, signifying a spiritual entity.

Jude talks about woe for men who reject the Lord – 'Woe to them! . . . wandering stars for whom the black darkness has been reserved forever' (v10,11,13). These stars may represent the heavenly counterpart of the inner spiritual life of these men.

As we looked at in Revelation 1, stars speak of heavenly, supernatural entities. Each of the 7 Churches in Revelation 2—3 had an angel who was addressed in the letters, and who was also a star held in Jesus' right hand (Revelation 1:20). Here, this great Star also likely represents an angel, possibly the spiritual counterpart to the city of 'Babylon' from the 2nd Trumpet, which would be thrown down. In the Old Testament, Isaiah talks about the king of Babylon who wanted to make himself as high as God:

> How you have fallen from heaven,
> O star of the morning, son of the dawn!
> You have been cut down to the earth,
> You who have weakened the nations!
> But you said in your heart,

> 'I will ascend to heaven;
> I will raise my throne above the stars of God,
> And I will sit on the mount of assembly . . .
> I will ascend above the heights of the clouds;
> I will make myself like the Most High.' (Isaiah 14:12–14)

This person represents the leader of Babylon, but at the same time reflects a supernatural power, who resembles the devil, thrown down from heaven.

In the New Testament, Jesus says he saw 'Satan fall from heaven like lightning' (Luke 10:18). Putting these together with 1 Corinthians 6:3 (we will judge the angels) and 2 Peter 2:4 and Jude 1:6 (some angels have sinned and await judgment), we get a picture of angels (stars) who have sinned and fallen from heaven. So the fallen Star here represents an evil angel, emulating Satan.

This is different from angels 'descending' (eg Genesis 28:12, John 1:51), and Jesus Himself who will descend (1 Thessalonians 4:16), meaning He will come down to the earth. 'Fallen' means this Star/Angel, while created good, now has no foundation in the heavens – there is nowhere for them to stand, like the Nephilim in Genesis 6 (*nephilim* means 'fallen').

Whoever this Star exactly represents in Revelation 8, it is speaking of a spiritual entity, in contrast to the mountain of the Second Trumpet, which speaks about a kind of political, earthly entity. The Star and the Mountain are linked though, and, as we saw in Isaiah 14, however we interpret the one who is 'fallen from heaven', suffering affects the Star and the nation together – judgment falls on both the angel and the people.

The burning Mountain and burning Star together embody twin aspects of the earthly and spiritual forces of the kingdoms of the world who oppose God's Kingdom. Both resemble the plague of the Nile turning to blood: in the Second Trumpet trade and communication are disrupted as death affects the seas, and here the freshwater – the rivers and springs – become contaminated and polluted.

Wormwood

The name of the Star is 'Wormwood', or in Greek *ápsinthos*, meaning 'undrinkable'. It is a bitter herb that can cause hallucinations and is even toxic at high doses. We read about wormwood in Jeremiah:

> Thus says the Lord of hosts concerning the prophets. 'Behold, I am

going to feed them wormwood. And make them drink poisonous water. For from the prophets of Jerusalem, pollution has gone forth into all the land.' (Jeremiah 23:15, also 8:14, 9:15)

These false prophets of Jerusalem have bitterness going into them and coming out from them – they speak false prophecies and so will eat wormwood and drink poison water. We also see poisoning in Revelation 8:10–11, where a significant proportion of the rivers and springs become wormwood – they are not just 'bitter', but toxic, as many die after drinking from them. There is no fresh water, and the situation is so desperate that people will drink bitter, poisonous water.

Wormwood is also mentioned in Deuteronomy 29 in connection with idolatry:

> Moreover, you have seen their abominations and their idols of wood, stone, silver, and gold . . . so that there will not be among you a man or woman, or family or tribe, whose heart turns away today from the Lord our God, to go and serve the gods of those nations; that there will not be among you a root bearing poisonous fruit and wormwood. (Deuteronomy 29:17–18)

Possibly we are meant to understand widespread idol worship is going on here in Revelation. Wormwood is known for causing hallucinations and was used in idol worship and witchcraft – it is interesting that the Greek word for witchcraft is *pharmakeía*, literally 'drug taking'. Here is a warning that if you start to worship false idols, they will contaminate you, and you will become like a poison weed, contaminating and defiling others:

> See to it that no one comes short of the grace of God; that no root of bitterness springing up causes trouble, and by it many become defiled. (Hebrews 12:15)

The Church should be a place that has clean fresh water, not the contamination and bitterness of worshipping idols such as money, sex, and power. James 3:11 alludes to this activity which spreads bitterness in the Church.

Whereas with the 2nd Trumpet the consequence of sin is to become cut off and surrounded by death, this is followed in the 3rd Trumpet by bitterness and a lack of satisfaction. No matter what we do, we will not find satisfaction in our lives if they are given over to worshipping idols.

4th Trumpet – Loss of illumination

The 4th Trumpet sounds and the lights start to go out, with the sun lost for a third of the day, and the moon and stars lost for a third of the night.

In Scripture, the sun setting early is a sign of judgment. For example, Amos 8:9 and Jeremiah 15:9 (see also Joel 2:10, 3:15, Jude 13):

> 'It will come about in that day,' declares the Lord God,
> 'That I will make the sun go down at noon
> And make the earth dark in broad daylight'. (Amos 8:9)

These are all evidences of God acting with judgment and causing sin to have its final outworkings; sun, moon and stars going out are all harbingers of 'the great and dreadful day of the Lord'.

The consequence of sin is that light is taken away. Jesus not only said He was the light of the world (John 8:12), but we *the Church* are the light of the world (Matthew 5:14–16). The cumulative effects of sin are to cut people off from Jesus and His Church, so they will get less of the light shining in their lives.

While some interpret this Trumpet as a literal diminution of light at the End of the Age, I suggest it is better understood as a loss of understanding. Is our society losing its sense of meaning? Are nations losing their ability to communicate with one another, increasingly unable to appreciate one another? These are movements we can see as we look around the world today, and these are likely to happen more and more.

Below is an overview of the consequences of sin we see in the first 4 Trumpets.

Trumpet		Consequence of sin	Caused by
1	(v7)	Loss of Foundation	Burning famine
2	(v8–9)	Loss of Communication	Burning mountain
3	(v10–11)	Loss of Satisfaction	Burning star
4	(v12)	Loss of Illumination	Darkening

The first 4 Trumpets sound warning notes that look like the judgments that fell on Egypt. The promise to those who have been sealed by God in Revelation is the same as it was to the Hebrews in Egypt – they will be preserved and protected when these updated plagues come upon the earth, building up towards the great last Trumpet when God's judgment will come to a final conclusion. This is also an encouragement that injustice and unrighteousness will not win forever, and in that sense we are meant to be on the side of the angels, crying out to God.

This means we cannot be wishy-washy in our thinking concerning what is right and what is wrong, as well as demonstrating righteousness in the way we live before others who are vulnerable to the deception of fake news. Jesus speaks much about false language and deception, while exhorting us to absolute truth in our lives.

De-Creation

There is a fascinating reflection of the creation account in Genesis with the things which are afflicted by the first 4 Trumpets, though not in the same order:

- Day 1   Light is afflicted (v12, 4th Trumpet)
- Day 2   Sea turned to blood (v8, 2nd Trumpet)
- Day 3   Vegetation burnt up (v7, 1st Trumpet)
- Day 4   Sun, moon and stars smitten (v12, 4th Trumpet)
- Day 5   1/3 sea creatures die (v9, 2nd Trumpet)
- Day 6   Humans are affected, in the ships sunk and also those who try to drink the water (v9–11, 2nd/3rd Trumpet)

So, there is a kind of six days of 'de-creation' as opposed to the six days of Creation, hinting that these disturbing events are taking place in preparation for the New Creation, or re-Creation, which is going to emerge by the end of Revelation. Given all the pollution and destruction we see around us in our world, it feels we are in desperate need of the New Heaven and New Earth. However, this does not mean we should continue plundering and abusing our world just because it may all be done away with and replaced anyway – God's Creation is *good* (Genesis 1:4,10,12,18,21,25) and after the 6th Day, 'God saw all that he had made, and it was *very good*' (v31). We were given authority to rule over Creation, but it was in terms of working in the garden and taking care of it (Genesis 2:15).

3 Woes
Text – Revelation 8:13

> [13] Then I looked, and I heard an eagle flying in midheaven, saying with a loud voice, 'Woe, woe, woe to those who dwell on the earth, because of the remaining blasts of the trumpet of the three angels who are about to sound'

Eagle flying in midheaven (v13)

Why is it an eagle flying who speaks here? It could represent God moving through and speaking from the heavens, because in Deuteronomy, when talking about Israel coming out of Egypt, Moses says God is:

> . . . like an eagle that stirs up its nest and hovers over its young, that spreads its wings to catch them and carries them aloft. (Deuteronomy 32:11, see also Exodus 19:4)

In Scripture, God is also depicted as an eagle when He is coming to take vengeance. So the cry of the swooping or searching eagle is a warning as to what is coming next – the threat of God's judgment. For example, in Deuteronomy where judgments were prophesied against Israel if they disobeyed God:

> . . . the Lord will bring a nation against you from afar; from the end of the earth. As the eagle swoops down, a nation whose language you don't understand. (Deuteronomy 28:49, see also Hosea 8:1)

This eagle activity is translated into movement of an army coming in judgment upon Israel because they have broken their covenant with God. Eagles also declare judgment against Moab and Edom in Jeremiah 48:40 and 49:22. So the eagle seems to represent some form of godly activity.

Nowhere else in Revelation do we see God represented as an eagle, however we will see the wings of 'a great eagle' are given to the woman to fly into the wilderness in Revelation 12. Also one of the 4 Living Creatures is 'like a flying eagle' (Revelation 4:7, see also Ezekiel 1:10). Whether or not the eagle directly represents God, the words it speaks show that it knows what will happen next, so may reflect God's will. This flying eagle is a spiritual being, who is prophesying the 'Woes' – the damage the next 3 Trumpets are going to bring.

Midheaven (v13)

Where is midheaven? This presumably is referring to the 'heavenly places', as opposed to the sky/atmosphere (the heavens) or the heaven of heavens where God permanently dwells. It makes sense that *mid* heaven is somewhere between the two – separated from the earth, but not the highest heaven. The heavenly places are where God is active and to which we have access.

Woe, Woe, Woe (v13)

Here we see the 4 + 3 pattern of the 7 trumpets: the first 4 belonged together, and the last 3 are also linked, as each contains 'Woe' for those who dwell on the earth.

We have met these earth-dwellers before – they are those who are rooted into the earth and live in materialism, and are contrasted with those who dwell in the heavens (see for example Revelation 6:10, page 270).

These 3 Woes will come from the blasts of the 3 remaining trumpets, which the angels are about to sound. The Woes at the 5th and 6th trumpet sounds are easy to see, and basically the whole of each blast is a Woe:

> The first woe is past; behold, two woes are still coming after these things (Revelation 9:12)

> The second woe is past; behold, the third woe is coming quickly. (Revelation 11:14)

However, the 3rd Woe does not seem to start at the beginning of the angel sounding the 7th Trumpet – in fact, some of the things that happen are very good – and the Woe does not appear until Revelation 12:12, after the 1st and 2nd Signs have appeared:

> Woe to the earth and the sea, because the devil has come down to you, having great wrath, knowing that he has only a short time.

The third Woe is not the whole of the 7th Trumpet, but some part of that trumpet's development becomes a Woe. So of the three Woes, two are Trumpets and the third is part of a Trumpet, which is expanded and elucidated in Revelation 12. Understanding these Woes will help us see how they fit into the overall structure.

The 7 Trumpets | Revelation 8:13

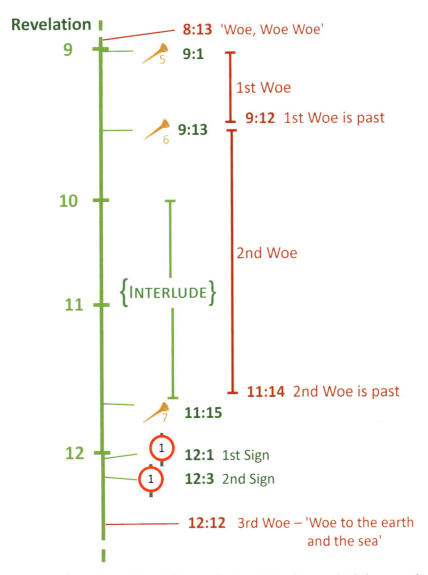

What defines these 'Woes'? We might think the things which happened in the first 4 Trumpets were full of woe, but here we see a significant increase in the length and intensity of the events following the last 3 Trumpets. The events become more weighty as we will see when we move into the next three chapters.

Discussion Questions

How do you interpret the silence after the 7th Seal is broken?

What impact does the imagery of the bowls of incense have on you?

How literally or otherwise do you think these first 4 Trumpets are felt?

Revelation 9

The parallel we have seen between the first 4 Trumpets and the 10 Plagues of Egypt, which began in Revelation 8, continues through chapter 9. The sounding of Trumpets 1–4 resulted in partial disruptions of material Creation, but when we come into chapters 9 and 11, we are clearly dealing with large scale Satanic intrusions. God, Satan, and of course human beings, are all interacting in these events, and we will see that people are afflicted and plagued by spiritual darkness – eyes are blinded so they cannot see the Gospel.

The 3 Woes correspond to Trumpets 5 and 6, and part of Trumpet 7. Here in Revelation 9 we begin the first Woe.

The 5th Trumpet – The First Woe
Text – Revelation 9:1–6

> ¹ Then the fifth angel sounded, and I saw a star from heaven which had fallen to the earth; and the key of the bottomless pit was given to him. ² He opened the bottomless pit, and smoke went up out of the pit, like the smoke of a great furnace; and the sun and the air were darkened by the smoke of the pit. ³ Then out of the smoke came locusts upon the earth, and power was given them, as the scorpions of the earth have power. ⁴ They were told not to hurt the grass of the earth, nor any green thing, nor any tree, but only the men who do not have the seal of God on their foreheads. ⁵ And they were not permitted to kill anyone, but to torment for five months; and their torment was like the torment of a scorpion when it stings a man. ⁶ And in those days men will seek death and will not find it; they will long to die, and death flees from them.

Fallen Star and the key (v1)

When the angel sounds the 5th Trumpet, John sees a Star fallen from heaven. We saw a great Star called 'Wormwood' that fell after the 3rd Trumpet in Revelation 8:10–11 (see page 324), and here we see a Star 'which has fallen', so this may be the same Star, or at least of the same nature. Either way, this fallen Star is following Satan, who has also fallen from heaven (Luke 10:18).

In Revelation 9, this particular star which is fallen from heaven to earth is given a key. Keys represent power and authority – the ability to open things that are shut or shut things that are open. Even though this is a fallen angel, it has authority and is used as part of God's plan. This again raises the question of whether God endorses or is responsible for evil by allowing it to have authority. In the book of Job we see God's Heavenly council, which includes Satan – it is how God has set up the universe. So while the fallen angel is given authority in the form of a key, it does not mean God is directly commanding the events which follow.

Bottomless pit (v2)

The key given to the fallen angel is to the bottomless pit, which he then opens, presumably because it had been locked. 'Bottomless' is the word *ábussos* in Greek, from which we get the word 'abyss', meaning 'immeasurably deep', 'without a foundation', and this is sometimes translated 'shaft of the abyss'.

We will see the Abyss and the key again in Revelation 20:1–3 at the Millennium, when Satan is bound and sealed in the Abyss for 1000 years (see also Revelation 11:7, 17:8).

'Abyss' appears twice in the rest of the New Testament. In Luke 8, where Jesus casts out the 'Legion' demons 'they were imploring Him not to command them to go away into the abyss', and instead pleaded to be sent into the pigs. So the Abyss is a place where the evil spirits would presumably be trapped or possibly even destroyed.

Paul mentions the abyss when paraphrasing Deuteronomy 30:

> Do not say in your heart, 'Who will ascend into heaven?' (that is, to bring Christ down), or 'Who will descend into the abyss?' (that is, to bring Christ up from the dead) . . . (Romans 10:6–7)

The Abyss is a place of death. In Acts 2:31, Peter attests that Jesus went to Hades, the place of the departed – is this bottomless pit the same as Hades, or are they two separate places that Jesus entered? In Luke 16, the rich man and Lazarus clearly have two separate experiences of Hades, separated by a chasm – could the Abyss be the side of torment? Maybe the Abyss is 'the lower parts of the earth' Paul mentions in Ephesians 4:9? Or the prison of disobedient spirits in 1 Peter 3:19–20?

In many ways, it does not matter whether the Abyss/bottomless pit is describing Hades or not – whatever it refers to, Paul is confident that from the lowest places to the highest, Christ will 'fill all things'. In Revelation 1:18 Christ has the Keys of Death and of Hades because He has conquered death (2 Timothy 1:10) – Jesus has the keys and is in control.

If we assume this were the same key we read of here, why would Jesus be giving it to a fallen angel? The Bible does not explain, but presumably it must be part of God's plan for wrath – in some way He is bringing about His purposes, even if that mean using Satan's moves as part of that plan. In Revelation 20, we will see the key is in the hands of an angel coming from heaven, so the authority of the devil will not last forever.

Smoke and locusts (v2–3)

Smoke comes up out of the pit, and out of the smoke come locusts. Locust swarms can be made up of many millions of insects and from a distance can look like smoke. Locusts move across the land, completely stripping vegetation and destroying crops, and this would have been a familiar scene to early readers of Revelation, and still is in many areas today. This passage paints a powerful picture of invasion, of being overrun by a sudden attack which is impossible to prevent or fight, leaving you helpless in the face of devastation. A swarm of locusts not only leads to destruction of crops, but just like a real army, may be followed by famine, disease and death.

Smoke in the Bible is often linked to the idea of judgment and falling in destruction, and is the consequence of fire and brimstone:

> . . . and he looked down toward Sodom and Gomorrah, and toward all the land of the valley, and he saw, and behold, the smoke of the land ascended like the smoke of a furnace. (Genesis 19:28)

Later in Revelation we read of 'the smoke of their torment goes up forever and ever' (14:11), and of the smoke of Babylon (18:9) when it is destroyed. Just like smoke from a fire, a swarm of locusts shows that destruction is going on.

Here the smoke is probably made of the locusts themselves and when they fly together there are so many of them they can even darken the sun and the sky. Smoke that blocks out the light brings us into darkness where demonic hordes, like a whole cloud of locusts, sweep into a society or into a community, or upon a person – they will darken understanding so people will not be able to think or see straight.

This reminds us of where Paul says:

> The god of this world has blinded the minds of the unbelieving so that they might not see the light of the gospel of the glory of Christ, who is the image of God. (2 Corinthians 4:4)

Satan's smoke brings the darkness of deception and misunderstanding, and also creates the conditions where spiritual destruction and death may follow.

Locust army (v3)

The way this image of a locust army weaves together Old Testament Scriptures is fascinating. Exodus 10 is an obvious source. The plagues of Egypt have been a background for the first 4 Trumpets and here we continue with the plague of locusts and the darkness over the land:

> [Locusts] covered the surface of the whole land, so that the land was darkened; and they ate every plant of the land and all the fruit of the trees that the hail had left. Thus nothing green was left on tree or plant of the field through all the land of Egypt . . .
>
> There was thick darkness in all the land of Egypt for three days. They did not see one another, nor did anyone rise from his place for three days, but all the sons of Israel had light in their dwellings. (Exodus 10:15,22–23)

Joel 2—3 describes a locust army, who will bring judgment on the land, and centuries later Jeremiah describes another army, who will bring judgment upon Babylon, who themselves had been the instrument through which God brought judgment upon Israel:

> The Lord of Hosts has sworn by Himself: surely I will fill you with a population like locusts, and they will cry out with shouts of victory over you. (Jeremiah 51:14, see also v27)

Are these armies of men which resemble swarms of locusts? Or are these swarms of locusts like armies of men? Especially in Joel it is not clear, and the two merge together. In either case, they are devouring, greedy, destructive.

Both places also have Trumpets being blown:

> Blow a trumpet in Zion,
> And sound an alarm on My holy mountain!
> Let all the inhabitants of the land tremble,
> For the day of the Lord is coming;
> Surely it is near,
> A day of darkness and gloom,
> A day of clouds and thick darkness. (Joel 2:1–2)
>
> Lift up a signal in the land,
> Blow a trumpet among the nations! (Jeremiah 51:27)

These passages set the scene for the 5th Trumpet in Revelation, where God's judgment is anticipated by a Trumpet bringing an army of locusts and devastation. That is not to say God is directly behind these locust armies – they are the consequence of people not living before God in the power of His righteousness, as we read in Deuteronomy 28:

> If you do not obey the Lord your God, to observe to do all His commandments and His statutes with which I charge you today, all these curses will come upon you and overtake you . . . You shall bring out much seed to the field but you will gather in little, for the locust will consume it. (v15,38)

Amos 7 is interesting because it also speaks about a destroying army of locusts, but Amos prays and God changes His mind and holds it back. So could this locust army in Revelation be held back by prayer? Repentance and protection are still possible, so we should emulate Amos and pray for God's outcome.

Power of Scorpions (v3)

The locust army are given the 'power' or 'authority' of scorpions, and we see in verse 10 this refers to their stings, which can 'hurt men'. So these locusts now have the ability to act as scorpions – not only can they cause destruction, famine and darkness, but also disease and pain.

Do not hurt ... (v4)

... the grass, nor any green thing, nor any tree

When the locusts are told not to hurt the grass it may seem redundant, as back in Revelation 8:7 'all the green grass was burned up' after the 1st Trumpet sounded. However, we are of course dealing with apocalyptic literature and we need to look beyond literary conventions to the inner meaning. As discussed following the 1st Trumpet (8:7), grass represents something that gives us comfort and satisfaction on the earth.

Similarly, green trees give us fruit and provision, and we rely on other 'green things' for crops for food. Following the 1st Trumpet only a figurative third of the trees on earth were burned up, so there are trees around, but the locusts may not harm them. It is clear these cannot merely be actual locusts, but represent something else, as all locusts naturally do is to eat grass, trees and 'any green thing...' Whereas in Joel we are left wondering if the army is of men or locusts, here there is a distinction – it is clearly something supernatural.

... the Sealed Ones

Here is the one little bright ray of hope in Revelation 8 and 9. Those who have the Seal of God cannot be hurt by these scorpion–locusts. This is not to say we should rejoice in the suffering of those who are not sealed, rather we should take it as an encouragement to press on to get God's seal over our lives.

We first looked at the Seal of God in Revelation 7 (page 285) – it is the name of the Father and His Son, which is stamped on the forehead of the bond-slaves of God – there are 144,000 who are sealed and represent the overcoming people of God (see Revelation 14:1–5).

What does this mean for us? As Christians are we part of the Sealed Ones, or part of those who dwell on the earth? Can we be hurt by this locust army? It seems very unlikely that all Christians are in the 'Sealed Ones' – not all Christians will be Overcomers. Being a Christian may not guarantee you will not be harmed, but being sealed does, so like Paul we need to aim to be Overcomers. Thus it may be possible for someone to live an overcoming life to a point, but then backslide and therefore be hurt by these scorpion stings. Conversely, it follows that someone who has been living an ungodly life and was stung a lot may become an Overcomer and be protected from these stings. We could step in and out of God's protection for us.

Again, we need to think about what being harmed means here – is it physical or spiritual? These supernatural scorpion–locusts could cause spiritual harm, bringing discouragement or destroying ministries, but equally we see in Job that Satan causes Job not just emotional and spiritual anguish, but also applies pressure through physical suffering. So it could be either, or like Job, both.

It is important to add, that while ultimately all sickness and suffering does trace back to the Fall, it does not mean it is all directly caused by the enemy's attack through these scorpion stings – otherwise we end up in a theological tangle where being ill or in pain has to be a sign you are not sealed of God.

In Luke 10, we see a parallel to verse 4 in what Jesus' says to the 70 when they return:

> The seventy returned with joy, saying, 'Lord, even the demons are subject to us in Your name.' And He said to them, 'I was watching Satan fall from heaven like lightning. Behold, I have given you authority to tread on serpents and scorpions, and over all the power of the enemy, and nothing will injure you. Nevertheless do not rejoice in this, that the spirits are subject to you, but rejoice that your names are recorded in heaven.' (Luke 10:17–20)

Star falling

Either Jesus is recounting having seen Satan fall from heaven at the beginning of the world, or more likely is saying He figuratively saw it as the spiritual backdrop to what was going on while the 70 went out, preaching and healing the sick. Similarly we could see the Star falling in verse 1 as a result of the Gospel going out, like with the rider on the White Horse in Revelation 6:2 (see page 244).

Those sealed of God

Not only is the Greek word for 'injure' in Luke 10 the same as 'hurt' in Revelation 9:4, but we also see a parallel between those who have 'authority' whose names are 'written in Heaven', and those who have been sealed in Revelation 7 and are protected from torment. God will fulfil His promises to His people – this is worth rejoicing about!

Protection from the enemy

If we have the Seal of God we can put our feet on scorpions and on all the power of the enemy – not just some of it, but all of it. Satan does not reign over us! The more we assert the authority given to us in Christ, the more we will see the enemy ultimately having to flee (James 4:7). (NB in Luke 10 Jesus talks about serpents as well as scorpions, and we will see these appear when we get to Revelation 9:19, as snake-like tails of the horses (see below).)

5 months of torment (v5)

These scorpion–locusts are not allowed to kill anyone, but are permitted to torment them for 5 months by 'stinging' (v5,10). The 5 months could mean the life span of the locusts, or the length of the plague, or how long the sting lasts – although it may not matter which.

Longing to die (v6)

Above we looked at whether the pain and torment caused by these scorpion–locust 'stings' is physical or spiritual – in the world around us we see that either is enough to push people to their limit. Physical pain certainly can lead people to 'long to die' (v6), but so too mental and emotional torment can cause mental health problems and depression, leading to people giving up hope. These locusts are clearly not just normal insects, but represent spiritual powers, and I would suggest these stings represent all of these different ways in which the devil tries to get in and destroy lives.

Once again we need to consider what 'kill' and 'death' mean in this context – are they physical or spiritual? The primary focus of Revelation is on spiritual death, which pervades the lives of men and women. However, here in Revelation 9 'death' looks more physical, and it is hard to understand otherwise. The people are so dying inside that they want to physically die. However, they cannot, because then they will be judged, which is the tension in this passage – if you do not want to be judged you had better not die. You don't really escape anything by dying, so you have to endure your deathly life.

Text – Revelation 9:7–12

> [7] The appearance of the locusts was like horses prepared for battle; and on their heads appeared to be crowns like gold, and their faces were like the faces of men. [8] They had hair like the hair of women, and their teeth were like the teeth of lions. [9] They had breastplates like breastplates of iron; and the sound of their wings was like the

sound of chariots, of many horses rushing to battle. [10] They have tails like scorpions, and stings; and in their tails is their power to hurt men for five months. [11] They have as king over them, the angel of the abyss; his name in Hebrew is *Abaddon*, and in the Greek he has the name *Apollyon*.

[12] The first woe is past; behold, two woes are still coming after these things.

Not Locusts … (v7)

As John looks more closely, we now see this army not only resemble locusts and scorpions, but they also look like horses, have men's faces, women's hair, lion's teeth and wear crowns and iron breastplates.

As discussed in *Approaching the Text* (page 19), Revelation is written in dream language, and this is a particularly nightmarish image. Not only are these things not what they first appeared to be, they keep getting worse! They are destructive and overwhelming like a swarm of locusts, and can sting like scorpions, but what do their other attributes represent?

Horses – War (v7)

They are like horses, prepared for battle. This draws in a number of Old Testament passages. As we saw above an army of locusts appears in Joel 2, and there too they are likened to horses:

> Their appearance is like the appearance of horses;
> And like war horses, so they run.
> With a noise as of chariots
> They leap on the tops of the mountains,
> Like the crackling of a flame of fire consuming the stubble,
> Like a mighty people arranged for battle. (v4–5)

In the Old Testament, horses represent war, so when we see them we should think: 'Battle!' rather than ploughing. For example, we see the two equated in Proverbs 21:31 as well as in Jeremiah 8:16–18:

> From Dan is heard the snorting of his horses;
> At the sound of the neighing of his stallions
> The whole land quakes;

For they come and devour the land and its fullness,
The city and its inhabitants.
'For behold, I am sending serpents against you,
Adders, for which there is no charm,
And they will bite you,' declares the Lord.
My sorrow is beyond healing, My heart is faint within me!

You can imagine the sound of war horses charging faster and faster and the earth beginning to shake with the thunder of hooves – it must have been an overwhelming, intimidating noise. Jeremiah is using this warning imagery to encourage the people to repent. It is worth noting that these horses appear alongside snakes in Jeremiah, because as we will see in Revelation 9:19 below, the locust–horse army also have tails like serpents.

In the New Testament, horses represent power, and in Revelation 6 in particular, they symbolise spiritual power.

Crowns – Authority (v7)

Crowns represent authority, so these locusts have some form of authority. That does not mean they are righteous or doing God's will – just as the fallen Star receives the key in verse 1, or when we read about the council of God in Job 1 where Satan has a level of authority. By their actions we will see these locust–scorpion–horses are evil spiritual forces, but nevertheless they have authority.

While their crowns are 'like gold', this does not always reflect God's glory in Revelation. For example, in Revelation 17:4 the Great Harlot is 'adorned with gold', but the Greek literally is 'gilded', and similarly here the crowns are not gold but 'like gold'.

How do these locusts use their authority? Everyone, including Christians can feel plagued by guilt, with their sin seemingly having authority over them: *You are just a sinner – you cannot change.* That is the authority with which the devil tries to control people.

Human Faces – Intelligence (v7)

These locusts have 'faces of men', which indicates intelligence: they do not just have locusty brains – they see and think as humans. This means their attacks, while sometimes aggressive, may also be calculating and targeted. One of the ways Satan uses to attack people is through deceiving them into thinking the exact opposite of the truth about who God is and who they are.

Women's hair – Seduction (v8)

In many cultures in the ancient world, women covered their hair in public, and showing their unloosed hair was a sexual symbol. While this still occurs in some parts of the world, it may be hard for us to appreciate nowadays, as there are ever diminishing limits on sexual expression in Western culture. To John's readers however, a woman's uncovered hair would most likely indicate self-glorification and was therefore seductive or vain. This is not simply sexual temptation, but more encompasses the idea of being enticed along. This is another way the enemy works: a little bit of temptation here and a little bit there, and gradually people are beguiled along a seductive path.

Teeth of lions – Savage (v8)

One of the 4 Living Creatures is 'like a lion' (Revelation 4:7) and Jesus is called the Lion of Judah in Revelation 5:5, but here the locust army have teeth like lions. Lions are strong and majestic, but when they open their mouths they present a threatening sight with savage, rapacious teeth that can tear humans to pieces and devour them. Christ roars with authority like a lion, but the devil trades in the animal terror and savagery of a lion.

Breastplates of iron – Undefeatable (v9)

Iron breastplates indicate the locusts are prepared for warfare. Armour makes the wearer seem invulnerable, giving the implacable appearance they cannot be defeated. Iron is unrelenting and dismay paralyses resistance in people, causing them to submit. The devil often seeks to dominate people by a show of force to make them give up hope.

Sound of their wings like chariots – Overwhelming (v9)

The sound of chariots is that of a team of horses charging together and so not only represents approaching war, but the noise itself is a frightening thing which brings fear and panic. If everything is quiet, you can cope with some problems, but when there is a terrific noise going on – when threats and pressure build up – it disturbs your spirit: not enough time to contemplate, not enough time to rest. It is reminiscent of how the Israelites might have felt with Pharaoh's army of horses and chariots bearing down on them in Exodus 14:5–12.

Sometimes people can feel overwhelmed by the devil, especially when all sorts of things start to go wrong one after the other – not only feeling attacked in their minds or emotions, but also suffering physically. Patrick, in his 'Confession' describes such an experience of spiritual attack at the beginning of his Christian life:

> While I was sleeping, Satan strongly put me to the test – I will remember it as long as I live! It was as if an enormous rock fell on me, and I lost all power in my limbs. Although I knew little about the life of the spirit at the time, how was it that I knew to call upon Helias [ie, 'The Lord is God']? While these things were happening, I saw the sun rise in the sky, and while I was calling 'Helias! Helias!' with all my strength, the splendour of the sun fell on me; and immediately, all that weight was lifted from me. I believe that I was helped by Christ the Lord, and that His Spirit cried out for me. I trust that it will be like this whenever I am under stress, as the gospel says: 'In that day, the Lord testifies, it will not be you will speak, but the Spirit of your Father who speaks in you.'

This is an example of spiritual warfare and how it can affect people in their body and mind. The enemy's pressure, like the approaching thunder of charging horses' hooves, may make you feel crushed or powerless, not just in spirit or soul, but in your whole being. At those times, like Patrick, we need to call on the Lord. These onslaughts are not continuous, but may come at particular times, as exemplified by Satan's attack on our Lord – 'When the devil had finished every temptation, he left Him until an opportune time' (Luke 4:13).

Tails like scorpions – Deceptive s(v10)

As we saw in verse 5, the horse–locusts have scorpion stings, which are at the end of their tails. We will see in verse 19 that their power is in their mouths and in their tails, which are like serpents and have heads.

There have been many very fanciful and imaginative ideas about these 'stings in the tail' in the **Historicist** view. From the Saracens being adept at fighting rearward on their horses, to the Turkish cavalry towing rear-facing guns behind their horses, to the rear-facing guns on some Luftwaffe aircraft, these interpretations have often tried to tie this imagery to a particular historical event, in order to suggest we are approaching the end of the age. What they have in common is that, like these tails, they are deceptive: locusts and horses do not have stings, but this vision reveals something which lies behind. People may think there is no danger once the threat has passed, but there is and it may sting them after they have passed it. The enemy strikes them when they are not looking.

* ✳ *

This fascinating description of the spiritual army of 'locusts' reveals a variety of ways the enemy uses to attack people – as Christians we can do our best to stay out of these troubles by keeping our lives clean and pure and open before God.

King/angel of the Abyss (v11)

The locust army is led by a king, the 'Angel of the Abyss'. This angel is likely the Star who dropped out of heaven in verse 1, and was given the key to the Abyss (note that Proverbs 30:27 says: 'The locusts have no king, yet all of them go out in ranks', confirming these creatures are not literal locusts). Why does this army need a king? Kings provide a spearhead of authority and leadership, without which an army may disintegrate. This locust army is not swarming around aimlessly like insects, driven by the wind – they are organized, strategic.

The angel's name in Hebrew is *Abaddon*, which means 'destruction', and *Apollyon* in Greek, which means 'destroyer'. *Abaddon* also appears 6 times in the Old Testament, in Job, Psalms and Proverbs, where it means destruction and is always seen as accompanying death (Job 26:6, 28:22, 31:12; Psalm 88:11; Proverbs 15:11, 27:20). *Apollyon* is used to translate *Abaddon* in the Septuagint. *Apollyon* – the Destroyer – also may remind us of Exodus, and the final plague:

> When He sees the blood on the lintel and on the two doorposts, the Lord will pass over the door and will not allow the Destroyer to come in to your houses to smite you. (Exodus 12:23)

While a different Hebrew is word used here for 'Destroyer', we do get a similar picture of the embodiment of destruction. *Abaddon* and *Apollyon* signify destruction leading to death, so while the locust army can only torment people, they are led by 'deathly destruction'.

The name 'Apollyon' is also reminiscent of the main god of Rome, Apollos: most Roman emperors worshipped Apollos and also thought they were sons of Apollos. This may well be a further allusion to the situation of Roman persecution into which this book was written.

God is a Creator, and loves to build ('I will build my church', (Matthew 16:18)), but Satan loves to tear down and destroy. I believe there is something which the Spirit of God imparts into our lives, which means that as Christians we too become builders – we should be creating and building in all areas of our lives, and this will mean we are working against the forces of *Abaddon* and *Apollyon*. These destructive powers can affect us as individuals, and also affect the Church, for example deconstructionism, church splits and divisions have all tried to pull the Church to pieces; the opposite of building it up.

The first Woe is past … (v12)

Verse 12 marks the end of the first of the 3 Woes, the other two Woes end in Revelation 11:14 and 12:12.

Just as the first 4 Trumpets apply throughout the Church Age and in our lives today, so I would argue does the 5th Trumpet. The devil seeks to attack people in many different ways, and if we are not constantly living under the Seal of God, we are leaving our lives vulnerable to attack and destruction.

The 6th Trumpet
Text – Revelation 9:13–16

[13] Then the sixth angel sounded, and I heard a voice from the four horns of the golden altar which is before God, [14] one saying to the sixth angel who had the trumpet, 'Release the four angels who are bound at the great river Euphrates.' [15] And the four angels, who had been prepared for the hour and day and month and year, were released, so that they would kill a third of humankind. [16] The number of the armies of the horsemen [lit. 'horseman'] was two hundred million; I heard the number of them.

The 6th Trumpet (v13)

In verse 13, the 6th Trumpet sounds, and we can see its effects as including the answer to the prayer of the Martyrs in the 5th Seal: 'How long O Lord . . ?' (Revelation 6:10). The prayers of the saints are bowls on the Golden Altar of incense in Revelation 8:3–5 before the trumpets sound, and here in the 6th Trumpet the voice comes 'from the four horns of the Golden Altar'.

In Revelation 6, the Martyrs are told to rest a little while longer, but here in chapter 9 we seem to have arrived at the time when the Lord will begin judging 'those who dwell on the earth' and avenging the blood of the Martyrs.

4 bound angels (v14)

The voice from the Golden Altar says to release the 4 angels bound at the Euphrates. This is a similar picture to Revelation 7:1, where the 4 angels standing on the 4 corners of the earth are holding back the 4 winds – the angels seem to be good, the winds appear to be bad. Similarly, here the 4 bound angels are bad, presumably being restrained in some way by good angels, just as the locusts/demon army had been bound in the bottomless pit in verse 2. Perhaps these bound angels are the winds themselves because when they are released they swirl around like smoke and unleash terrible destruction (see Psalm 78:49).

Euphrates (v14)

The 4 angels are bound at 'the great river Euphrates', which comes into view here and will reappear when the 6th Bowl is poured out in Revelation 16.

The Euphrates is a river of great geographical and theological importance. It runs south from Turkey then southeast through modern day Syria and Iraq. It is one of the four rivers named in the Garden of Eden in Genesis 2 and was also part of God's covenant with Abram:

> To your descendants I have given this land, From the river of Egypt as far as the great river, the river Euphrates. (Genesis 15:18)

The Promised Land extended from Egypt to the Euphrates (see also Exodus 23:31, Deuteronomy 1:7, Joshua 1:4 etc), beyond which to the east lay Babylon. The river was the life-blood of the Babylonian Empire, and in the first century AD formed the boundary between the Roman and Persian empires, so it still held great significance in John's day.

Army from the north or the east?

As we will see below, when the 4 bound angels are released, a huge army is unleashed. What is the significance of this army originating from the Euphrates? Later on in Revelation, we see Babylon as the great rival city to Jerusalem – this was also true in the Old Testament, as well as in the first century AD, where the Persian empire were a threat to the Romans.

The Euphrates runs from the north of Israel, and some parts of the Old

Testament prophesy about an army coming from the north. For example, the locust army we looked at in Joel 2 comes from the north (verse 20), as does the army in Ezekiel 38:6. Jeremiah wrote:

> Then the Lord said to me, 'Out of the north the evil will break forth on all the inhabitants of the land. For, behold, I am calling all the families of the kingdoms of the north,' declares the Lord; 'and they will come and they will set each one his throne at the entrance of the gates of Jerusalem . . . (Jeremiah 1:14–15)

Later in chapter 46, Jeremiah prophesies, 'To Egypt, concerning the army of Pharaoh Neco king of Egypt, which was by the Euphrates river . . . in the north beside the river Euphrates', and again in verse 10 'in the land of the north by the river Euphrates'.

However, in Jeremiah 46:24–27, the 'people of the north' are revealed as Babylon, which lies to the east, and in Revelation 16 we will read the Euphrates is dried up to prepare the way 'for the kings from the east.'

So does this army come from the north or the east? We can understand this seeming discrepancy by looking at the geography. From Jerusalem, although Babylon lies to the east, there is a desert in the way, so rather than march an army straight across, a better route for the Babylonians was to travel in the fertile crescent around the top of the desert. This detour around the desert means they would come into Israel from the north. So while the kings are from the east, their armies attack from the north.

As their release brings about an attack from an army, maybe these angels represent 'angels of nations', like the Prince of Persia or the Prince of Greece, whom we read about in Daniel 10:13,20–21.

Prepared for the hour, day, month and year (v15)

This verse can be interpreted in various ways depending upon your theological flavour. If you believe God has already decided and planned every aspect of the whole of history, you may read this as saying there is an exact hour, on an exact day in the future when this will happen. Or does Satan have plans in mind for certain days in the future? Alternatively, could it mean there is no specific time set, but these angels are prepared and ready to go whenever the hour arises? Or could this be an ongoing event, which happens throughout the Church Age, and these angels are ready all the time?

The 7 Trumpets | Revelation 9:13–16

However you like to interpret the timing of it, the main point is that killing humans is what these 4 angels are prepared for, and this is what they will do. A third of humanity will be killed in this way, as the angels let loose their forces.

Armies of the Horseman? (v16)

These 4 unbound angels seem to head up, or even become, great armies, which now come into focus. Interestingly, the word translated 'horsemen' or 'mounted troops' appears to be in the singular, so should read 'horseman'. As we read about multiple armed horsemen in the next verse, we may just put this down to John's bad Greek, or possibly he is trying to indicate that these vast numbers of troops come from one source and all act as part of one body.

Another possibility is that, as we have seen, there is some sort of relationship between these 4 unbound angels, the 4 winds in Revelation 7:1 and the 4 Horsemen riding forth in Revelation 6:1–8. So maybe this is referring to one 'horseman' or some of the horsemen from the first 4 Seals.

200 million

John hears the number of the armies of the horsemen, just as he heard the number of the Sealed Ones back in Revelation 7:4. This number is usually translated as 2 million, or 'twice ten thousand ten thousands' – this is understandable as John says he heard a number, just as he heard the precise number of 144,00 servants of God. However, the Greek word is the same word used back in 5:11 for the angels around the throne and can mean 'myriad of myriads' or 'an innumerable multitude'. In any case, it is not likely to be an exact number, but give the impression of an army so large the only way you can know how many of them there are is to hear it from an angel!

We also see myriad angels around the throne in Daniel 7:10 (see also Jeremiah 46:23, Judges 6:3–5, 7:12). So we can be assured that even if there are millions of evil forces prepared to destroy us, there are also myriads of myriads, ten thousands of ten thousands who are before the throne of God, worshipping Him.

Text – Revelation 9:17–21

> [17] And this is how I saw in the vision the horses and those who sat on them: the riders had breastplates the colour of fire and of hyacinth [or jacinth]* and of brimstone; and the heads of the horses are like the heads of lions; and out of their mouths proceed fire and smoke and brimstone. [18] A third of mankind was killed by these three plagues, by the fire and the smoke and the brimstone which proceeded out of their mouths. [19] For the power of the horses is in their mouths and in their tails; for their tails are like serpents and have heads, and with them they do harm.
>
> [20] The rest of mankind, who were not killed by these plagues, did not repent of the works of their hands, so as not to worship demons, and the idols of gold and of silver and of brass and of stone and of wood, which can neither see nor hear nor walk; [21] and they did not repent of their murders nor of their sorceries nor of their immorality nor of their thefts.
>
> (*NB *While most translations include the word 'hyacinth' here, as in the colour of the dark blue/purple flower, the King James version says 'jacinth'. The Greek word is the adjectival form of the word translated by most versions as 'jacinth' in Revelation 21:20, so maybe here it should be 'jacinth-y'. Some believe 'jacinth' was a transparent orange-red gemstone, like amber, while others suggest it was a blue or purple gemstone like amethyst.*)

Fire and brimstone

As John looks on, the 4 bound angels become a vast army of horsemen, who have breastplates *of* fire, jacinth/amber (or hyacinth) and brimstone.

Strangely, many translations add extra words in to make these adjectives merely the colours of their breastplates, whereas there is no word for 'colour' there in the Greek, so I would suggest this is more to do with their nature. These breastplates are fiery, amber-like (or smokey?), and brimstone-y!

Fire is destructive, it burns and destroys, and is difficult to control. Jacinth may refer to amber, which has electrical properties, and whose name may derive from an ancient Phoenician word *elēkrōn*, meaning 'shining light', from which we get our word 'electricity'. Brimstone is burning sulphur, it is bright yellow and gives off noxious vapours. So rather than red-, purple- and yellow-coloured breastplates, we may rather imagine them as fiery, flaming or smoky, sparking, crystalline and glowing. They are certainly a few steps up from the iron breastplates of the locust army in the 5th Trumpet (verse 9).

The word 'breastplate' only appears in two other places in the New Testament:

- in Ephesians 6, the armour of God includes a 'breastplate of righteousness' (see also Isaiah 59:17)
- in 1 Thessalonians 5:8, Paul encourages us to put on 'faith and love as a breastplate'.

This is how God's people should dress for battle – in faith, love and righteousness, which is in stark contrast to the destructive army we see in Revelation 9:17.

Not only are their breastplates fiery, but in the same verse, fire, smoke and brimstone come out of the mouths of the horses (v17–18) – their breath is fiery, brimstone-y and smoky too!

Heads and tails (v17,19)

These horses have the 'heads of lions', and their tails 'are like serpents and have heads'. This again is a level above the locust army who only had the teeth of lions and tails like scorpions – the whole head of a lion implies they are even more savage, even more vicious, and a tail which is a snake indicates it is more cunning and deadly. The locust–scorpion–horses only stung, but this army kills – and they kill a third of humankind.

Their mouths and tails are where their destructive power lies, so whether you are in front of them, or behind, there is nowhere to escape from these armoured fire-breathing horse–lion–serpents.

Three Plagues (v18)

Verse 18 describes the fire, smoke and brimstone as three destructive plagues. We have seen how the events brought about by sounding these first 6 Trumpets resemble the plagues of Egypt (see page 320), and here the effects of the 6th Trumpet are called 'plagues'. There are a number of plagues in Revelation (see 6:8, 11:6, 15:1–8, 16:9,21, 18:4,8 and 21:9) and they reappear right at the end of the book, where it says that if anyone adds to this prophecy God will add to them 'the plagues which are written in this book' (Revelation 22:18). This would seem to indicate these plagues are actually operative during the Church Age, not just reserved for some future time. The fire, smoke and brimstone are active today, and impact our lives and the world around us. I would suggest these 6 Trumpets and the plagues they release upon the earth are happening all the way through the Church Age. But if this is the case, what do they represent? How do we experience them?

Smoke – Deception

Putting all the images in the 6th Trumpet together – angels, horses, lions, serpents and smoke – the impression we get first and foremost is that we are looking at a deception. Smoke is deceptive – it blinds you, so you cannot see or understand. This spiritual army presumably breathes out smoke which dulls our spiritual senses. Satan took the form of a serpent to deceive Adam and Eve, and he is the father of lies (John 8:44) and deceives the nations (Revelation 20:3,8).

Lies and deceptions are the ways in which the enemy works.

Fire and brimstone – Death and damnation

'Fire and brimstone' often appear together and symbolize God's judgment and wrath. We see fire and brimstone, as well as smoke, at the destruction of Sodom and Gomorrah in Genesis 19:

> the Lord rained on Sodom and Gomorrah brimstone and fire from the Lord out of heaven . . . and [Abraham] looked down toward Sodom and Gomorrah, and toward all the land of the valley, and he saw, and behold, the smoke of the land ascended like the smoke of a furnace. Genesis 19:24,28

God's judgment on these cities came because not even 10 righteous people could be found in Sodom (Sodom is mentioned 'spiritually' later on in Revelation 11:8). When Jesus sent out the 12 Disciples, He said if anyone did not welcome or listen to them: 'it will be more tolerable for the land of Sodom and Gomorrah on the day of judgment than for that town'. So maybe the fire and brimstone these horses breathe out cause people to not welcome or listen to God's witnesses, and hence will bring wrath upon them.

Fire and brimstone appear again later on in Revelation 14:10–11, and in particular as the Lake of Fire and Brimstone in 19:20, 20:10 and 21:8, which is the place of the ultimate destruction of the Beast and the False Prophet (Revelation 19:20), the devil (20:10), and Death and Hades (20:14). So are these plagues of fire and brimstone a foretaste of God's judgment and wrath? If, as I suggest, we understand wrath as the consequences of not living in God's world in God's way, the horses may be causing people to turn away from God's truths and purposes for their lives by tempting them into idolatry and immorality, which will lead to judgment falling on them. While all the nations will ultimately face judgment at the Great White Throne, God's wrath – the consequences of our sin – can affect our lives today.

They did not repent … (v20–21)

In verses 20–21, the remainder of those who dwell on the earth and were not killed by the army from the north, are unrepentant. In verse 20 they do not repent of their idolatry, and in verse 21 they do not repent of their immorality.

Idolatry and immorality sum up the totality of human rebelliousness. What you worship eventually will affect your morals: if you worship the one true God you will live in God's goodness and truth, but if you worship a false god you will develop false beliefs and wrong morals (see Psalm 115:8, Psalm 135:18).

We can see a further reflection of Exodus imagery here, as idolatry and immorality are the antithesis of the two tablets of the Ten Commandments given to Moses in Exodus. The first tablet is primarily to do with commands against idolatry: 'Have no other gods before Me', 'Do not worship idols', 'Do not take the Lord's name in vain' and 'Keep the Sabbath day holy'. Each of these commands gives us the opportunity to worship God: if we replace this with something else – money, power, violence, intellectualism, ourselves – that is idolatry. This encapsulates the lack of repentance in verse 20. The second tablet of commandments is to do with immorality – 'Do not murder . . . commit adultery . . . steal . . . bear false witness . . . or covet your neighbour's house'. This sums up what the people do not repent of in verse 21.

This lack of repentance brings to mind the hardening of Pharaoh's heart in Exodus during the plagues. Although he had ample opportunity to change his mind, Pharaoh hardened his heart to such a degree that God had no choice but to strengthen his stubborn resolve. (For further discussion on the hardening of Pharaoh's heart, including the various Hebrew words used, please see chapter 11 of *God's Strategy in Human History: Volume 1 – God's Path to Victory*).

Here, John is using the Old Testament in much the same way as it was used by first-century Rabbis and Jewish commentators, such as Josephus. He is taking prophecies that appear to be literally described, in Exodus, Isaiah and Jeremiah, and reapplying them to the spiritual condition of the first-century church under persecution by Rome.

Does no one repent?

Why do we have so much in Scripture about judgments of God being poured out which only seem to harden people's hearts? Four times in Revelation we read of those who 'did not repent' (9:20,21, 16:9,11). Here, Revelation 8—9 draws much from negative Scriptures in Deuteronomy, Exodus, Ezekiel, Jeremiah, Isaiah and Joel. What is the point of these prophecies if in the end nobody repents?

Often in Scripture the effect of God's wrath is to lead people to repentance, so that they might return to Him. However, here the people 'did not repent' of their immorality and idolatry. Whereas in the Old Testament there are warnings before judgment, here is a warning that there will come a point where there will be no warning, but a final demonstration of the effects of sin and idolatry on humanity.

Does this mean that no one, not one single person, will repent? While some commentators take verse 21 as such an absolute statement, I don't think we should understand it that way. Revelation is not meant to be read as a textbook of the future, but as a figurative description of spiritual truths. We often use exaggeration and hyperbole when we talk, and Hebrew writers were no different, making sweeping comprehensive statements – but there were always qualifications. For instance, the hearts of the Egyptians were hardened . . . but there were still a mixed multitude who came out of Egypt with Israel (Exodus 12:38). Jesus 'came to His own and His own received Him not' (John 1:11) . . . but some did. So if the text says 'they did not repent', overall they may not, but there will very likely be some who do respond and turn to Christ. Later, in Revelation 14, we see an angel preach 'the eternal Gospel' to 'those who live on the earth', followed by the Harvest of the earth – which indicates there are those who clearly turn to the Lord. While this is not explicitly stated in the text, it is assumed given the numerous exhortations to repent and overcome.

However, repentance is not the focus of this passage, but rather the aim is to encourage the Church to keep going even in the face of plagues and persecution! John may take it as read that there will be those who respond and repent.

Blessing and judgment

The overall emphasis of Revelation 8—9 is that the ministry of the Church is not only to bring blessing to the world, but also to begin to bring the judgment of God against those who oppose Him and His Kingdom. Throughout the centuries, people are judged by the way they treat the people of God, which is a foretaste of the ultimate judgment, when all are called before the Great White Throne – 'Whatever you did for one of the least of these brothers and sisters of mine, you did for me' (Matthew 25:40, CSB).

God is love still, and the very fact He can love so intensely means He also hates evil intensely. If we learn nothing else from Revelation 8—9, we know that God is a serious judge and in particular He judges those who persecute the Church. In so doing, the effect of these judgments is at the very least to restrain those who are persecuting God's people, who are calling good 'evil' and evil 'good' (see Isaiah 5:20). God's warning trumpet notes are to remind humankind there is a final judgment coming, and to some degree this restrains them. The first 6 Trumpets are a prelude to the 7th sounding in chapter 11, and their effects show God's judgment is a reality, and operates in the Church Age now, giving us a foretaste of that coming, great, final 7th Trumpet, which marks the end of judgment. That is the reason for this warning – it does not happen sometime in the distant future which has nothing to do with us, nor is it just a theoretical paradigm, but rather, these plagues of spiritual death, darkness and depression are happening today.

New Creation

In Exodus, Israel coming out from Egypt following the plagues represents a new creation – from slave people to the people of God. Here in Revelation, out of these plagues that are falling upon the earth will come another New Creation – these judgments are all in preparation for the coming of a new people. When we look back at the Old Testament texts that flow into and saturate this passage, these judgments which follow are all in relationship to idolatry.

Experiencing God's wrath during our lives may lead us to repentance, but that is only part of the purpose of Revelation – the prime reason is to show that, even as judgment descends upon the earth, the suffering of the Church itself is part of the redemptive process of bringing Creation to its final destiny.

This New Creation is not something we can achieve ourselves as human beings, by using an ideology or a political system to bring about a new society. Such efforts, however well meaning, will inevitably try to change God's moral laws with our own ethics, which will cause knock-on effects upon the laws that govern Creation and society, leading to their breakdown. This New Creation is God's Kingdom being released.

With this in mind, we now turn to Revelation 10, the interlude before the 7th Trumpet sounds.

Discussion Questions

What should our response be to the events of the 5th Trumpet?

Which aspects of the locust–horse army do you find most disturbing and why?

How do you feel about the rest of the people who 'did not repent' of their idolatry and immorality?

The Angel and the Little Booklet
Revelation 10

Revelation 10 is an interlude between the 6th and 7th Trumpets. We see a Strong Angel. who looks like Christ, claiming the whole world and holding a Little-little Book, or as I will call it: the Little Booklet, in His hand. John is commanded to keep preaching as he eats the book.

The heart of Revelation

The next section, from chapter 10:1–11:13, forms the heart of the book of Revelation. It is not just physically in the middle, but it also forms the very core of its message.

We have reached this point after coming through the horsemen riding, trumpets blowing and terrifying judgments descending upon the earth. This is all part of God's purpose in bringing judgment into our experience now as an anticipation of the final judgment. Ever since the glorious vision of the Lamb on the Throne in chapter 5, it has been getting steadily more negative and dark, except for the interlude of Revelation 7 between the breaking of the 6th and 7th Seals.

Here in Revelation 10, the light seems to start shining a little more brightly again, and like chapter 7 this is also an interlude, this time between the 6th and 7th trumpets. Once again we have the tension: are these trumpets chronological? If so, does the 7th Trumpet come seconds, days, or centuries after the first? Or do they happen at the same time? Is it simply a literary device?

The 6th Trumpet finishes on a very gloomy note, with the people not repenting of their idolatry and immorality, or 'ungodliness and unrighteousness' as Paul says in Romans 1:18. However, chapter 10 starts with a vision of something wonderful and reveals true worship, and even though the emphasis of the chapter is still that of judgment falling upon the earth, we begin to see some hope. There are some very dark and dismal chapters to come, but here we have a light shining – Jesus' face shining out into the world.

The Gospel for all nations

Right in the middle of this central section is a clear reminder of the worldwide message of the Gospel to all nations:

> Then I was told 'Once again you must proclaim God's message about many nations, races, languages and kings. (Revelation 10:11, see also 11:9)

The whole of the earth is to be confronted with a message from God, a prophecy. But what exactly is it?

We know God's aim for His people is that 'all the nations of the earth might be blessed' (Genesis 12:3, 14:3, 18:18, 22:18; Galatians 3:9), and this interlude is all to do with the universal Gospel. We will see before the 7th Trumpet sounds, that 'the mystery of God is finished' – what is this 'mystery'? and what are its implications for how we understand the prophecy? Whatever the mystery signifies, it is to do with the Gospel, and here the spreading of this good news is coming to an end.

Interlude between 6th and 7th Trumpets
Text – Revelation 10:1–4

> [1] I saw another strong angel coming down out of heaven, clothed with a cloud; and the rainbow was upon his head, and his face was like the sun, and his feet like pillars of fire; [2] and he had in his hand a little book which was open. He placed his right foot on the sea and his left on the land; [3] and he cried out with a loud voice, as when a lion roars; and when he had cried out, the seven peals of thunder uttered their voices. [4] When the seven peals of thunder had spoken, I was about to write; and I heard a voice from heaven saying, 'Seal up the things which the seven peals of thunder have spoken and do not write them.'

Discussion Topic: The Angel of the Lord

The Angel of the Lord is one of the ways in which the Old Testament prepares us for an understanding of the Trinity. When we read through Scripture, we begin to see there is an implicit distinction and yet an identification with God, which points us towards the Trinity. There is a closeness, but also a separation – a unity within a variety.

Far from being anti-Trinitarian as is sometimes claimed (for example by the Jehovah's Witnesses) the Old Testament is saturated with ways which gradually bring out the necessity for a triune God. While the Old Testament boldly asserted there is one true God into the midst of the polytheism of the surrounding nations – 'the Lord your God is one God' (Exodus 6:4) – there is a plurality implied within that oneness, with various appearances of the Lord: the Word of the Lord, the Angel of the Lord, the Spirit of the Lord, and so on.

This is a mystery which puzzled Jewish scholars, such as Philo. We see God being represented in different forms, such as an angel, or three men – but are these actually God Himself, or angelic representatives acting on His behalf? Sometimes the Angel of the Lord speaks God's words, or does things only God can do. For example, In Exodus 23:20, God says:

> Behold, I am going to send an angel before you to guard you along the way and to bring you into the place which I have prepared. Be on your guard before him and obey his voice; do not be rebellious toward him, for he will not pardon your transgression, since My name is in him.

Under those kind of terms, who could this 'angel' be if not God? 'Who can forgive sins but God alone' (Mark 2:7–11).

–› In Genesis 16:10, the angel speaks to Hagar and she calls the angel, 'The God who sees me.'

–› In Genesis 22:11–18, the Angel of the Lord calls to Abraham and stops him offering up Isaac, and then says: 'now I know that you fear God, since you have not withheld your son, your only son, from Me'. Then the angel calls again saying 'By Myself I have sworn, declares the Lord . . . I will greatly bless you, and I will greatly multiply your seed . . . because you have obeyed My voice.' So the voice of the Angel and God's voice are mixed up together.

→ In Genesis 24:7, Abraham reiterates that it was 'The Lord, the God of heaven' who spoke to him in Genesis 22 and guided him, and then tells his servant that God 'will send His angel before you'.

→ In Genesis 31:11–13, Jacob says 'The Angel of God said to me in the dream . . . I am the God of Bethel, where you anointed a pillar and where you made a vow to me.' So the angel is in effect saying, 'I am God . . .'

→ In Genesis 48:15–16, Jacob talks of:

> The God before whom my fathers Abraham and Isaac walked, the God who has been my shepherd all my life to this day, the angel who has redeemed me from all evil.

So God and the angel appear equivalents, and moreover this angel brings redemption, so is a redeemer.

→ In Judges 2:1, the Angel of the Lord speaks to Gideon and says: 'I brought you up out of Egypt and led you into the land which I have sworn to your fathers; and I said, "I will never break My covenant with you . . ."' – it is clearly the covenant God who is speaking.

→ In Judges 13, the Angel of the Lord tells Manoah and his wife they will conceive Samson. When they ask him his name, he replies 'My name is wonderful/beyond comprehension' (v18), so his name is a mystery to them. In the New Testament, Christ is the mystery of God (Colossians 2:2), whose love and peace are beyond understanding (Ephesians 3:19, Philippians 4:7). After the angel ascends in the altar flame, Manoah realizes it was the Angel of the Lord and says: 'We will surely die, for we have seen God'.

- In Zechariah 3:1–3, Joshua is standing before the Angel of the Lord, but it is the Lord Himself who is speaking. The Angel takes away Joshua's iniquity, so here again is a redeemer.

- In Malachi 3:1–4, we read about the Angel (messenger) of the Covenant, who is promised to come, and turns out to be Jesus:

> 'The angel of the covenant, in whom you delight, behold, He is coming' says the Lord of hosts. 'But who can endure the day of His coming? And who can stand when He appears? For He is like a refiner's fire . . .'

This sounds just like the picture of the Second Coming and judgment we saw in the 6th Seal – 'for the great day of their wrath has come, and who is able to stand?' (Revelation 6:17). So it is not difficult to see the Angel of the Covenant as Jesus.

- In Acts 7:30, Stephen says 'an angel appeared to [Moses] in the wilderness of Mount Sinai, in the flame of a burning thorn bush'. However it was God – I AM – *YHWH* – who met Moses in the bush in Exodus 3. So here again the Angel is identified with God.

We see a mysterious but close relationship developing between the 'Angel of the Lord' and God Himself. Added to this we must also note Isaiah 48—49, where Isaiah 48:16 shows the Lord God acting together with His Spirit in sending 'Me'. Then in Isaiah 49:1–6, the 'Me' is revealed as the incarnate Servant (v2–3,6), the Redeemer of Israel (v5–7), the Holy One (v7) – which is Christ, the anointed. In addition, His name, *Yeshua*, which is Hebrew for 'salvation', appears in verse 6.

Section II – Christ Central in Creation

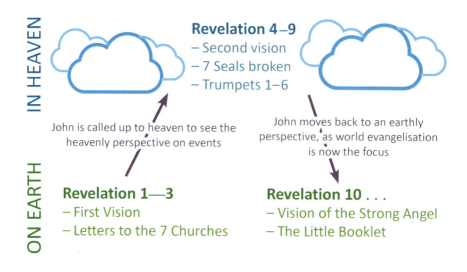

Coming down out of heaven (v1)

This chapter starts with an angel coming down from heaven, which should make us pause a moment, because ever since Revelation 4:1–2, we have been up in heaven through the 7 Seals and first six Trumpets. As this angel is 'coming down', it indicates our focus has changed – we are now viewing things from the earth. If there is any implication involved in us changing to an earthly perspective, it may be to challenge us to work towards completing world evangelisation, which is the focus of this section.

Another Strong Angel (v1)

There are three strong angels in Revelation – we saw the first one in 5:2 who asks 'Who is worthy to open the book', and we will see another in 18:21 who throws a great stone into the sea.

However, this Strong Angel is a little different: the first and third strong angels do not particularly resemble Jesus, but the description of the second one here in Revelation 10 looks remarkably like our Lord. Some people have suggested this is a vision of Jesus, and others suggest it may be the Angel of Jesus – His representative – which is why he looks like Him.

There is no problem using the word 'angel' for Jesus, because if we look back to the Old Testament, we find 'the Angel of the Lord' is easily identified with the Lord Himself (see Discussion Topic above). The word 'angel' simply means 'messenger', and was used for example of John the Baptist (Mark 1:2) – maybe Jesus as the 'Angel of the Lord' reflects His title: the Word of God (John 1:1).

Ways the Strong Angel resembles Christ

Here are 7 ways in which this 'Strong Angel' resembles Christ:

1. Coming down from Heaven (v1)

At the incarnation Jesus came from heaven to earth, though not in a visible way. At the ascension He went up into the clouds to heaven and at the Second Coming, Christ 'will come in just the same way as you have watched Him go into heaven' (Acts 1:11). The Strong Angel coming down from heaven resembles this same transition. As such, this vision may represent a prelude to the Second Coming.

2. Clothed with a cloud (v1)

It is almost always God who dresses in clouds (eg Exodus 16:10, 19:9, Leviticus 16:2; compare Job 38:8–9). John writes 'God is spirit' and 'no man has seen Him at any time' (John 1:18, 1 John 4;12), so the clouds are like God's clothing which He puts on so we can see He is around. In Daniel 7, Christ appears as 'one like a son of man, coming with the clouds of heaven' (Daniel 7:13), He ascends in a cloud in Acts 1:9 and in Revelation 1 we read, 'Look, he is coming with the clouds . . . one like a son of man' (Revelation 1:7,13).

What is the Strong Angel doing wearing clouds unless He is the Lord?

3. Rainbow (v1)

The Strong Angel has a rainbow on his head. Maybe this is like a crown, or maybe above his head – either way this rainbow over him signifies who he is. Back in Revelation 4:3 we saw an emerald rainbow encircling the Throne of the Creator God (see page 188) and in Genesis 9, where the rainbow is first mentioned, it is God's covenant promise with Noah to not flood the earth again. In between, in Ezekiel 1 we get a vision of the glory of the Lord, which is in the shape of a man full of fire and glowing metal, sitting on God's throne: '. . . and there was a radiance around Him, as the appearance of the rainbow in the clouds on a rainy day, so was the appearance of the surrounding radiance. Such was the appearance of the likeness of the glory of the Lord' (v27–28).

You don't get a rainbow without some clouds, and we have already seen clouds clothing the Strong Angel, and here this rainbow is also associated with the glory of the Lord. As we will see in Revelation 21:9–11, the Bride, who is the New Jerusalem, is also clothed with glory. We can picture the rainbow as a covenant promise – like an engagement ring – sealing the assurance that there will be a New Jerusalem where we will dwell with God in His glory.

4. Face like the sun (v1)

In the vision of Christ in Revelation 1, 'His face was like the sun shining in its strength' (verse 16, see page 95), and at the Transfiguration, Jesus' face 'shone like the sun, and His garments became as white as light' (see Matthew 17:2). In Numbers 6, the blessing the Lord gave to Aaron to speak over the people is:

> The Lord bless you, and keep you;
> The Lord make His face shine on you, And be gracious to you;
> The Lord lift up His countenance on you, And give you peace.
> (Number 6:24–26)

This Strong Angel also has a face shining like the sun, so in this way too resembles Jesus.

5. Feet like pillars of fire (v1)

In Ezekiel 1, we also see the figure on the throne:

> From the appearance of His loins and upward something like glowing metal that looked like fire all around within it, and from the appearance of His loins and downward I saw something like fire. (Ezekiel 1:27)

We have seen this already in Revelation 1:16 and Daniel 10:6, where both visions of Jesus have feet of burnished bronze, indicating they have been through fire (see page 94). When we are faced with difficult situations Jesus can identify with us because He knows what it is like to walk through fire.

The 7 Trumpets | Revelation 10:1–4

The Strong Angel resembles The Angel of the Lord, who resembles Christ

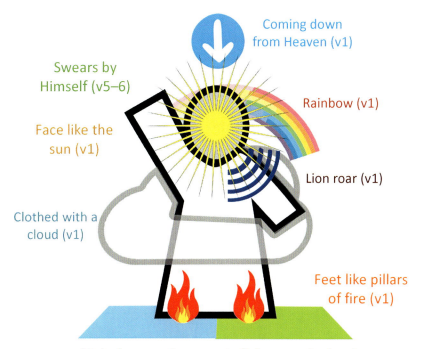

The Strong Angel being clothed with cloud and having feet like pillars of fire takes us back to Exodus 14, where Israel was led through the wilderness by a pillar of cloud in the day and a pillar of fire at night. God promised Moses 'I will send my angel before you', and it was the Angel of the Lord who led them out of Egypt towards the Promised Land. Importantly, the movement of the Angel of the Lord was the same as the movement of the pillar of fire and cloud, not only going ahead to lead the people, but also standing behind to protect them (Exodus 14:19). So in Revelation 10, the Strong Angel is ready not only to lead God's people, but also to protect them. Although persecution and pressure will come against the Church, this Strong Angel is there, leading us towards the inheritance of the Saints, as well as protecting us from the dark forces we are going to face.

The 7th and final Trumpet is just about to blow, which will mark the final, anticipated end of world evangelisation, as the Church is guided through the earth waiting to enter into the 'Promised Land'. If we are going to engage in this Great Commission we need to know God is going before us, and will stand behind us.

One further echo of Exodus comes in the next verse where the Strong Angel puts one foot on the sea and the other on the land, once again bringing to mind God's people crossing the Red Sea.

6. Lion roar (v3)

In Revelation 10:3, the Strong Angel 'cried out with a loud voice as when a lion roars'. Lions are a symbol of power and authority. We saw twice in Revelation 9 how the destroying armies had teeth like a lion, symbolizing power, but here we have the voice of a lion, symbolizing authority. The voice of the lion could have come from Revelation 5:5 where Jesus, the Lion of Judah, opened the book (see page 222).

In Amos there is an interesting allusion to the Lord as a lion:

> The Lord roars from Zion
> And from Jerusalem he utters his voice. (Amos 1:2)

Then later in Amos 3:

> If a trumpet is blown in a city will not the people tremble?
> If a calamity occurs in a city has not the Lord done it?
> Surely the Lord God does nothing
> Unless He reveals His secret counsel
> To His servants the prophets.
> A lion has roared! Who will not fear?
> The Lord God has spoken! Who can but prophesy?
> (Amos 3:6–8)

The Lord's voice roars like a lion and the prophets who hear it prophesy and they too will sound like a lion. God's plans are secret, mysterious, but revealed to 'His servants' who roar them out!

Who are these prophets? Amos was a prophet, and John was a prophet, and so is anyone who hears what God is saying and speaks it out. 'The prophets' could and should include all followers of Christ.

We should not be apologetic about proclaiming the kingship of Jesus: He is Lord whether you like it or not, and this roar is a declaration of His divine authority of God: Christians have something to roar about!

If we are so politically correct we never open our mouths, but instead tiptoe around the truth that Jesus is Lord, we are not really being evangelical (which means 'bringing good news'). Supposing we don't roar, or evangelise? How will God's will be done?

7. Swears by Himself (v5–6)

The resemblance between the Strong Angel and the Angel of the Lord as a pillar of cloud and a pillar of fire, should remind us of the covenant God made with Moses to guide the people through the Wilderness to the Promised Land. We see God swearing an oath by Himself a number of times in the Old Testament, for example:

> . . . Indeed, I lift up My hand to heaven,
> And say, as I live forever . . . (Deuteronomy 32:40)

In Revelation 9:5–6 we see Jesus, as the Strong Angel, doing the same. We will look at this in more detail on page 372, below.

* ✷ *

All these different facets of this Strong Angel draw together a wealth of Old Testament imagery into a beautiful understanding of our Trinitarian God, which should inspire and encourage us to speak out the things He has revealed to us.

Right foot on the sea, left foot on the land (v2)

In verse 2, the Strong Angel holds a 'Little Book' and stands astride the sea and the land. In fact, it is stated three times in this chapter (see also v5,8), so this seems to be an important point. Before we look at the Little Book, what could be the significance of the Strong Angel's two-footed stance?

A first impression is that this takes us back to Genesis 1:10, where the sea and the dry land are separated – in a sense this is a reversal of that, as they are being drawn together beneath the feet of the Strong Angel.

In ancient cultures, the sea was often seen as a place of chaos, disorder and death. We should be very conscious there is a lot of evil in this world, and elsewhere John says 'the whole world lies in the power of the evil one' (1 John 5:19). However, there are also many good and beautiful things in Creation, and indeed in humans, which we can enjoy and celebrate – as it says in Psalm 24, 'The earth is the Lord's, and all that is in it' (KJV) (see also 1 Corinthians 10:26). How can we reconcile the earth being the Lord's while also being in the power of the evil one? God has promised to bring the earth back to its full glory, hence the covenant He gave to Noah, and the rainbow we see in this vision speaks of God restoring His dominion through Jesus. In the bold stance of the Strong Angel we see the essence of what this chapter is about: God regaining authority over the earth in order to restore it.

In the Old Testament, Canaan was Israel's inheritance – 'everywhere the sole of your foot has trodden I have given to you' (Joshua 1:3, Deuteronomy 11:24). Again in Psalm 72, the righteous king reigns 'from sea to sea, and from the river to the ends of the earth (Psalm 72:8, see also Zechariah 9:10). However, whereas even the most righteous earthly ruler can only reign over land – that is, from sea to sea – not over the sea, the Strong Angel is claiming rulership over the land and the sea. Jesus twice showed His authority over the sea, once when He calmed the storm (see eg Matthew 8:23–27), and second, like here, when He walked on the water (see eg John 6:16–21). In the Sermon on the Mount, Jesus says 'the meek shall inherit the earth' (Matthew 5:5), but if the earth is our inheritance, we need Christ to win it back for us first, before he can give it to us. There is a sense in which Joshua 1:3 is true for us today – we could imagine it like the Kingdom breaking through wherever the soles of our feet tread as we serve Christ and take the Gospel to the ends of the earth.

However, some theologies have interpreted the Kingdom reign as meaning we should forcibly 'take the land' for Jesus, in the form of politics, business, the arts, and so on, in order for Christ to come. This so-called 'dominion theology' is prevalent in the Western church although it is not always clearly stated. The concept is that if we claim our part of the earth for God, we are helping Him to regain it, furthering the Kingdom and expediting the end. But dominion theology misinterprets not only the Kingdom, but our role within it: while we may be raised up and seated with Him 'in the heavenly places in Christ Jesus', we do not reign over the earth before Christ comes.

Here we are looking forward to when the great and glorious Strong Angel finally reclaims the earth, bringing order to the land and the sea. But how does He do it? What is the instrument the Strong Angel uses? It isn't might or power or armies of angels, or even the splendor of His coming (2 Thessalonians 2:8) – it is a Little Booklet . . .

The Little Booklet (v2)

The Strong Angel of the Lord is holding a 'Little Book' (or scroll), but in fact in the Greek it is a double diminutive, so it actually says a 'little little book' – βιβλαρίδιον – which is why I use the term 'Little Booklet' in referring to this. It seems that John may even have made this word up, taking two diminutive versions of 'book' and combining them to emphasise that this book is small (like 'mini-booklet' in English). Some commentators argue you should just translate the word as 'book', however, there is clearly a significance to it being called a 'little little book', distinguishing it from the one in Revelation 5:1, which is called just a 'little book' (βιβλίον, see page 217). There are some close similarities between these books and, as we shall discuss below, also with the scroll in Ezekiel 2—3: clearly the relationship between them is significant.

Opened

In Revelation 5, we learn it is the Lamb on the Throne who is the only one worthy to open the book, and we see the effects of Him breaking the 7 Seals in Revelation 6 and 8. Here in chapter 10 the Little Booklet ' . . . was open' (v2).

Held by Christ

In Revelation 5, the Lamb 'came and took the little book out of the right hand of Him who sat on the throne' and in Revelation 10 the Little Booklet is in the hand of the Strong Angel, who we have seen may be identified as Christ. Both books appear to be His.

Like a Lion

The Lamb in Revelation 5 is also 'the Lion of Judah' and in Revelation 10 the Strong Angel has the voice of a lion.

These similarities have led some commentators to identify the two books as the same, however, I believe John is clearly indicating a difference by calling the one in Revelation 10 a Little Booklet. So what is different about it? Why is it smaller?

We will investigate what this Little Booklet signifies when we look at verse 8, but whatever it may represent, its key distinguishing feature is the contrast between its size and its impact – it may be 'little–little' but it will take command of the whole earth.

7 Thunders (v3)

The effect of the lion roaring is that 'seven peals of thunder uttered their voices', which reflects Psalm 29, where 7 times we read 'the voice of the Lord':

> The voice of the Lord is upon the waters;
> The God of glory thunders (v3)

This is followed by six more descriptions of the awesome power of the Lord's voice, which is not only destructive but also creative, ministering life (see v9). It is strength that is being eulogized, not violence.

Thunder features prominently in Revelation, sometimes before the release of destructive powers (8:5), but also emanating from the Creator's throne (4:5), and in 6:1 one of the 4 Living Creatures speaks 'as with a voice of thunder', presumably because it speaks forth what God is saying.

Thunder is God's voice, and this reminds us of God speaking in thunder to Moses on Mount Sinai in Exodus 19:16–19, and in John 12:29 people thought it thundered when it was actually the voice of God. This thundering is God *speaking* – not just making a loud noise to frighten people. In Psalm 29, the end product of this 7-fold thundering is

> The Lord will give strength to His people;
> The Lord will bless His people with peace. (v11)

Similarly at Sinai, the Lord's aim was to bring strength and peace to Israel such that through them following His commandments they would make it into the Promised Land. Here in Revelation 10:4, John hears the Lord's thunderings, but is told not to record them – but presumably, whatever these words were, these too would have had the ultimate aim of bringing strength, blessing and peace to God's people, the Church.

Not all revealed (v4)

In verse 4, John is about to write what the 7 Thunders said, but is told to 'seal up' the things he heard and 'do not write them down'. There are other occasions in Scripture where God commands things not to be revealed; for example, Daniel is commanded to do a similar thing:

> But as for you, Daniel, conceal these words and seal up the book until the end of time. (Daniel 12:4)

There are times when words are not appropriate to be revealed. Sometimes the Lord speaks personal and intimate things to us, which are not meant to be related to others. There are things God says which we will never fully fathom, or cannot be interpreted – 'inexpressible words, which a man is not permitted to speak' (2 Corinthians 12:4). Sometimes God gives us a message, but a mystery remains, which we will not understand until later (for example Jesus' words in John 13:7). This was true for 'the previous generations' (for example in Ephesians 3:5), which reminds us we do not know everything in the universe, in particular about the End Times, so we never will have the complete picture. This will help us to stay humble, saving us from arrogance and encouraging us to keep listening to God (as with Paul's thorn in the flesh in 2 Corinthians 12:7).

Here in Revelation, John does not write down these thunders but they remain 'sealed up' or 'shut up' in his heart. Maybe they were words just for him, or alternatively may be released at the End of the Age, as in Daniel 12:4.

Some commentators suggest these thunders may have been judgments too horrific to record, others that they are encouragements to John, and others a prophecy for the End of the Age, but as John gives no indication even as to whether they were positive or negative, there is nothing to be gained from making strong assertions. What we can say for sure is that God does not always want everything to be revealed, at least not until the appointed time comes (see Deuteronomy 29:29 and 1 Corinthians 13:9–12).

There is an important contrast here between these 'sealed up' words, which were not to be written or spoken, and the contents of the Little Booklet, which, as we will see, are what John is meant to speak out.

Text – Revelation 10:5–7

> [5] Then the angel whom I saw standing on the sea and on the land lifted up his right hand to heaven, [6] and swore by Him who lives forever and ever, who created heaven and the things in it, and the earth and the things in it, and the sea and the things in it, that

there will be delay no longer, ⁷ but in the days of the voice of the seventh angel, when he is about to sound, then the mystery of God is finished, as He preached to His servants the prophets.

Swearing by Himself (v5–6)

The Strong Angel lifts his right hand to heaven and swears 'by Him who lives forever and ever'. Swearing an oath is a covenant process, and the idea of covenant is important in understanding this passage. Christ (as the Strong Angel) is making a promise by swearing by Himself, because there is nobody else more important to swear by.

Why does God need to swear by Himself? Is it for His own benefit, or for ours? Or as a challenge to the devil? There are nuances of each of these in other Old Testament examples of God swearing by Himself (Genesis 22:16, Exodus 32:13, Isaiah 45:23, Jeremiah 49:13, Ezekiel 20:5 and Amos 6:8). In each of these oaths the one basic principle is His unchangeable faithfulness, as the writer to the Hebrews writes:

> For when God made the promise to Abraham, since He could swear by no one greater, He swore by Himself . . . For men swear by one greater than themselves, and with them an oath given as confirmation is an end of every dispute. In the same way God, desiring even more to show to the heirs of the promise the unchangeableness of His purpose, interposed with an oath, so that by two unchangeable things in which it is impossible for God to lie, we who have taken refuge would have strong encouragement to take hold of the hope set before us. (Hebrews 6:13–18)

The emphasis on a covenant oath is important because it means God is saying: 'These promises *are* going to be fulfilled'. While this may not be surprising in the final book of the Bible, nonetheless it is important to have this affirmation in the middle of Revelation. Despite all the destruction and judgment going on, God's covenant to bless all the peoples of the earth will actually be accomplished.

Universal claim for inheritance

In Genesis 1:26–28, God made humankind, male and female, in His image, and then He blessed them to rule and reign over Creation:

Be fruitful and multiply, and fill the earth, and subdue it; and rule over the fish of the sea and over the birds of the sky and over every living thing that moves on the earth. (see also Genesis 19:2)

So humanity has a universal claim for inheritance of the earth – every person is made in God's image, and so each one has a potential part in the commission to be fruitful, in the responsibility to look after the earth, and in the blessing. This claim to the inheritance is mirrored here in Revelation 10, where the Strong Angel shows His heavenly authority over land and sea, and swears an oath by the Creator God (v2,5,6,8).

No delay (v6)

We saw how John, being told to 'seal up' what he heard, pointed back to Daniel 12. The parallel continues in the following verses:

> I heard the man dressed in linen, who was above the waters of the stream, as he raised his right hand and his left toward heaven, and swore by Him who lives forever that it would be for a time, times, and half a time; and as soon as they finish smashing the power of the holy people, all these events will be completed. (Daniel 12:7)

I would suggest Daniel is prophesying about the End of the Age, which in this case is the Old Testament Jewish age. The man dressed in linen resembles the Strong Angel, standing over the waters as he swears by the Lord that the events would be completed, but here in Revelation it is not for 'time, times and half a time' – instead the Strong Angel swears 'that there will no longer be a delay'. Given the similarities, it seems likely this also is a prophecy about the end of the age, but this time the end of the Church Age at Jesus' Second Coming.

When does this part of the Revelation take place? As we will see below, the end of the mystery implies the completion of world evangelisation, and if there will be no delay, it seems we are looking forward here to the future, to 'the days of the voice of the 7th Angel'. Again, we need to be careful not to overinterpret the chronology, or impose an interpretation dependent upon a particular timepoint – John is experiencing a sequence of visions and scenes one after the other, but their order does not necessarily mean they follow one another in time. A vision of the future may be followed by one of something that had happened previously – the link may not be temporal, but causal (ie a cause and its effect), or even vice versa. Hence, where John writes 'days', he implies a period of time, not an instant in time, or even for that matter a sequence, but instead a process in which he may even be moving back and forth in his visions.

In verse 7, we see the thing which will be delayed no longer is the mystery of God being finished. So what is this 'mystery'? And what does it mean that it 'is finished'?

> ## Discussion Topic: The Mystery of God
>
> In the New Testament, the word 'mystery' (*mustērion*) is not to be seen as mysterious, rather it means a secret, but one which will be revealed. We require revelation to bring the meaning of the secret to light (Ephesians 3:3). These mysteries do not refer to simply anything we do not know now but will find out, rather they concern God's covenant promises and how they will be fulfilled.
>
> 'Mystery' is mentioned three times in the synoptic gospels, four times in John's gospel and twenty times by Paul. Jesus, in Matthew 13:11, Mark 4:11 and Luke 8:10, says that His task is to show, or reveal, the mystery of the coming Kingdom of God. The mystery is how God will fulfill Old Testament prophecy, and the answer is that it has begun in Christ Himself – that is the Gospel! Paul also reveals the good news of Jesus as the answer to the mystery, for example:
>
>> But we speak God's wisdom in a mystery, the hidden wisdom which God predestined before the ages to our glory. (1 Corinthians 2:7)
>
>> I was made a minister of this church according to the commission from God granted to me for your benefit, so that I might fully carry out the preaching of the word of God, that is, the mystery which had been hidden from the past ages and generations, but now has been revealed to His saints, to whom God willed to make known what the wealth of the glory of this mystery among the Gentiles is, the mystery that is Christ in you, the hope of glory. (Colossians 1:25–27, see also Romans 16:25–26, Ephesians 1:9, 3:4, Colossians 2:2, 4:3, 1 Timothy 3:16).

The revelation of Jesus is not the end of the mystery. There are many who have not heard the mystery, and we are not to keep it to ourselves or treat it as some kind of special knowledge. We as the Church have a responsibility to steward and reveal this mystery, and we need revelation in order to help us do this:

> This is the way any person is to regard us: as servants of Christ and stewards of the mysteries of God.
> (1 Corinthians 4:1)

> To me . . . this grace was given, to preach to the Gentiles the unfathomable riches of Christ, and to enlighten all people as to what the plan of the mystery is which for ages has been hidden in God, who created all things; so that the multifaceted wisdom of God might now be made known through the church to the rulers and the authorities in the heavenly places. (Ephesians 3:8–10)

> If I have the gift of prophecy and know all mysteries and all knowledge, and if I have all faith so as to remove mountains, but do not have love, I am nothing.
> (1 Corinthians 13:2, also Ephesians 6:19, 1 Timothy 3:9)

In Romans, 1 Corinthians and 2 Thessalonians we read of further mysteries including End Time events of trumpets and resurrection:

> Listen, I tell you a mystery: We will not all sleep, but we will all be changed—in a flash, in the twinkling of an eye, at the last trumpet. For the trumpet will sound, the dead will be raised imperishable, and we will be changed.
> (1 Corinthians 15:51–52)

> For I do not want you, brothers and sisters, to be uninformed of this mystery—so that you will not be wise in your own estimation—that a partial hardening has happened to Israel until the fullness of the Gentiles has come in. (Romans 11:24–26)

> For the mystery of lawlessness is already at work; only

He who now restrains will do so until He is removed.
(2 Thessalonians 2:7)

In Ephesians, Paul describes Christian marriage as reflecting the relationship between Christ and the Church, giving us a foretaste of the Marriage of the Lamb in Revelation 19:

> Husbands, love your wives, just as Christ also loved the church and gave Himself up for her, so that He might sanctify her, having cleansed her by the washing of water with the word, that He might present to Himself the church in all her glory, having no spot or wrinkle or any such thing; but that she would be holy and blameless . . . This mystery is great; but I am speaking with reference to Christ and the church. (Ephesians 5:25–27,32)

Already in the vision in Revelation 1 we have seen the mysteries of the 7 Lampstands and the 7 Stars, which are revealed as the 7 Churches and the angels of the 7 Churches (see page 100). Later in Revelation 17 we will see another mystery – that of the Harlot of Babylon (Revelation 17:5,7).

However, we will reach a time, as in Revelation 10:7, when the mystery is fulfilled or completed, when all revelation is given – at the End of the Age there will be no mystery left.

Discussion Topic: The Gospel in Revelation

There are only two places where 'gospel' occurs in Revelation. It appears as a noun, 'evangel', in Revelation 14, where the 'eternal Gospel' is preached to those who live on the earth. The other instance is here in Revelation 10:7, where it appears in its verbal form – 'which He preached [literally 'evangelised'] to His servants the prophets'.

The Gospel appearing as a verb emphasises there is some good news around to share and it is the job of the prophets to evangelise. People need to have Jesus revealed to them – Christ is the mystery of God (Colossians 2:2), a secret to be revealed, and we need the Holy Spirit to get that vision into people's hearts (see also Matthew 16:15–17). That is why we need to pray for people to be saved.

However, the day will come when the mystery will come to an end as Christ is revealed to all from heaven – this will be the end of the Gospel.

The Mystery (v7)

In the Bible, a 'mystery' is not something that is unknowable, but something that will be revealed (see Discussion Topic above). Just as in a murder mystery we expect the culprit will be revealed, in biblical terms, mysteries are revealed when prophecy is fulfilled. A mystery does not remain mysterious.

So what is 'the mystery' that we find in Revelation 10? In the New Testament the 'mystery' is revealed by Jesus in the Gospels, as well as by Paul, as being Christ Himself – He is the way in which God is fulfilling the Old Testament prophecies and bringing in His Kingdom. There are five things that I want to pick out from Revelation 10 which appear in Romans 16:

> In the days when the seventh angel is about to sound his trumpet, $_1$the mystery $_2$of God will be accomplished, just as he $_3$evangelised to his servants $_4$the prophets . . . Then I was told, 'You must prophesy again about $_5$many peoples, nations, languages and kings.' (Revelation 10:7,11)

> Now to him who is able to establish you in accordance with my gospel, the message I proclaim about Jesus Christ, in keeping with the revelation of the mystery hidden for long ages past, but now revealed and made known through the prophetic writings by the command of the eternal God, so that all the Gentiles might come to the obedience that comes from faith. (Romans 16:25–26)

This wonderful statement at the end of Romans is a mandate that all the nations of the earth might be brought to the obedience of faith – the Gospel is not just 'Believe in Jesus Christ and be saved', but 'Believe in Jesus Christ and be saved *in order to obey* Him'. The bottom line of any relationship is faith, and the whole point of having a relationship with Jesus through faith is in order to follow Him – both now in this life and on into eternity. So **the Gospel** leads to the obedience of faith, and this is now being offered to **all the nations**.

The mystery is something that needs revealing, and as we have seen this *is* Christ (see Discussion Topic above). **This Gospel** of Jesus is something that has to be preached, using the Scriptures of **the prophets** by 'the command of **the eternal God**'.

Simply put, when Jesus comes again He will be revealed to all men – there will be no ignoring Him, and no one can claim they did not know about Him – there will be no 'mystery' left.

There is an urgency about the coming end of this mystery: *Get ready, the trumpet is about to sound – the end of the good news is coming, get your hearts and lives right.* This is a universal message and Revelation is trying to put it over to us before it is too late. There is an imperative that every nation of the earth must hear before the final trumpet blows.

Text – Revelation 10:8–11

> [8] Then the voice which I heard from heaven, I heard again speaking with me, and saying, 'Go, take the book which is open in the hand of the angel who stands on the sea and on the land.' [9] So I went to the angel, telling him to give me the little book. And he says* to me, 'Take it and eat it; it will make your stomach bitter, but in your mouth it will be sweet as honey.' [10] I took the little book out of the angel's hand and ate it, and in my mouth it was sweet as honey; and when I had eaten it, my stomach was made bitter. [11] And they say* to me, 'You must prophesy again concerning many peoples and nations and tongues and kings.'

Sealed Book versus Little Booklet (v8–9)

We can see a development here between Jesus, the Lamb of God, taking the Book and breaking the 7 Seals to open it in Revelation 5 (see page 225), and John being asked to take the open Little Booklet, eat it, and then prophesy.

In Revelation 5, the 7-sealed Book represents God's purposes for humanity (see page 217), and through the Cross, Jesus inaugurated a whole new age, whereby God's plan for His people can now be worked out as the Seals are broken and the book is opened. Given the similarities we saw above to this Book, the Little Booklet, probably represents something along those lines too. But why is one a 'Little Book' and the other a 'Little Booklet'? What is the link between them?

Simple message

Is the book in Revelation 10 described as 'little–little' because it contains a simple message? Maybe it simply represents the Gospel and the scene is a reenactment of the Great Commission, with John receiving the message of salvation to speak out to the nations. Here we may see John as representative of the whole Church – what he does in taking and eating the Little Booklet, and then prophesying, is what we all must do as the body of Christ to spread the Gospel.

Christ's death, resurrection and ascension to sit on His Father's throne mean He is able to break the Seals upon the book in Revelation 5, which opens up God's plan for humanity. While the totality of God's plan is too much for any of us to comprehend, what every person *can* get to grips with and share is the abridged version, the Gospel: Jesus died for our sins to bring us back into relationship with God.

Individual message

Another possibility is that the Little Booklet may be an individual message for the apostle John – his little individual portion of God's purposes for humanity and living it out. As Christians, this is what we are all meant to do with our own calling, our little part of God's bigger purpose. We must take it into our lives and get on with doing our bit.

Each of our Little Booklets is a tiny part of God's bigger plan: a fragment of His purposes for humanity. Together they build up like millions of tiny pixels to create the full picture. We may each have different bits to do, and we may not always see the outcome or effect of us doing our bit . . . but one day we will.

Whether the Little Booklet represents the Gospel message, our own individual parts in God's bigger plan or possibly a combination of these, the Lamb has broken the Seals and opened the Book so that each of us may play our part in living out our portion of that terrific work. Jesus has won it, but now it has got to be won out in us and our experience of dying to self and rising again. We are involved and necessary for God's purposes for humanity to be realised, until ultimately He can pursue that purpose of destroying evil and beginning the fullness of His Kingdom. That is all contained in this Little Booklet!

Sweet as honey, then bitter

We saw how the Book in Revelation 5 is similar to that in Ezekiel 2—3 (see page 217): both are written on front and back, so that nothing else can be added. In Revelation 10, John is told to take the Little Booklet and eat it, and then prophesy, and that it will taste sweet as honey in his mouth but will make his stomach bitter.

The parallel imagery in Ezekiel 2—3 says:

> 'Open your mouth and eat what I am giving you.' Then I looked, behold a hand was extended to me and lo, a scroll was in it. When He spread it out before me, it was written on the front and back, and written on it were lamentations, mourning and woe.
>
> Then He said to me, 'Son of man, eat what you find; eat this scroll and go speak to the house of Israel.' So I opened my mouth, and He fed me this scroll. And He said to me, 'Son of man, feed your stomach and fill your body with this scroll which I am giving you.' Then I ate it and it was sweet as honey in my mouth.
>
> Then He said to me, 'Son of man, go to the house of Israel and speak with My words to them . . .' (Ezekiel 2:8–3:4)

Ezekiel, 'embittered in the rage' of his spirit (3:14), then goes to the Exiles and speaks God's warnings to them; so, just as in Revelation 10, the scroll is sweet in his mouth but bitter as he speaks it out.

Why does the book taste sweet when John eats it? If, as I have suggested, we see the Little Booklet either as the Gospel, or as our individual part of God's destiny for humanity, these are God's words for us, to take into ourselves and speak out:

> How sweet are Your words to my taste!
> Yes, sweeter than honey to my mouth! (Psalm 119:103)

We can only receive God's purpose for us because of Jesus – *the* Word of God – who is the only one worthy to break the 7 Seals and reveal God's plan for humanity. What Jesus did for us brings sweetness to our lives.

Why does it then become bitter in John's stomach? Despite the joy and sweetness of following Christ, it comes at a cost. Jesus is clear that his followers should expect persecution:

> In the world you will have tribulation. But take heart; I have overcome the world. (John 16:33, see also 15:20, Matthew 5:3–12)

And similarly, Paul writes to Timothy that 'all who desire to live godly in Christ Jesus will suffer persecution' (2 Timothy 3:12), and Paul and Peter say we will share in Christ's sufferings (Philippians 3:10–11, 1 Peter 4:2–5).

John wrote Revelation in exile for the sake of the Gospel, and doubtless had seen much suffering and persecution not only personally, but also against his fellow disciples and the Early Church. Maybe this is what Paul is talking about in Colossians 1:24 when he says:

> Now I rejoice in my sufferings for your sake, and in my flesh I do my share on behalf of His body, which is the church, in filling up what is lacking in Christ's afflictions.

Not only that, but 'prophecy' includes negatives as well as positives. Just as Ezekiel had a message of 'lamentations, mourning and woe' to speak to Israel, some of the things we have to proclaim to the world and to the worldly people of God are very painful for us, such as the sin of the Church and its failure to be obedient.

'Prophesy again' (v11)

Up to now in Revelation 10 we have only seen the Strong Angel – so who are the 'they' who speak to John, encouraging him to preach the Gospel again?

Maybe they are the 7 angels with the trumpets, or the 4 Living Creatures, or the 24 Elders, of the 144,000 Overcomers or the voices of the Souls under the Altar who cry out in Revelation 5 . . . we can only speculate. I like to see them as our colleagues in the Gospel – the Church – which brings a number of these ideas together. Whoever these voices belong to, they are like a great 'cloud of witnesses' surrounding John and encouraging him to 'lay aside every encumbrance and the sin which so easily entangles us, and let us run with endurance the race that is set before us, fixing our eyes on Jesus, the author and perfecter of faith' (Hebrews 12:1–2).

John might be excused for thinking he had already done his bit for the Gospel, having spent most of his life proclaiming Christ, being exiled, as well as writing his gospel and epistles. Maybe he was feeling he had fulfilled his work for the Lord. We might even imagine John's actions here as being reluctant, but clearly God still has more for him to do – if even John needs a bit of encouragement from time to time, then so might we!

The nations (v11)

There is a further similarity between Revelation 5 and 10 – in both places the destiny of the nations is in view:

> 'Worthy are You to take the book and to break its seals; for You were slain, and purchased for God with Your blood men from every tribe and tongue and people and nation.' (Revelation 5:9–10)

> 'You must prophesy again concerning many peoples and nations and tongues and kings.' (Revelation 10:11)

Whereas, when he eats the scroll and speaks, Ezekiel is prophesying to exiled Israel, John's remit is much broader: peoples, nations, tongues and kings. The number 4 represents the extent of the world, and here we have a 4-fold list of humanity, indicating John's role is expanded to the inclusiveness and comprehensiveness of all the peoples of the world. John was there at the Great Commission in Matthew 28:16–20, and here he is being re-commissioned.

There are 7 places in Revelation, including here, where we see 'every tribe, tongue, kindred and nation (*ethnos*)' (5:9, 7:9 10:11, 11:9, 13:7 14:6, 17:15) – Revelation is an international message about God's destiny for the whole of humanity.

Discussion Questions

What strikes you most about the Strong Angel in the vision?

What does the 'Little Booklet' represent to you?
What would your part of God's plan for humanity be?

How would 'the mystery' being finished affect you?

Which parts of your walk with the Lord have been sweet as honey? Are there bits which have made your stomach bitter?

Section II – Christ Central in Creation

Revelation 11

World evangelisation is in view in this chapter, which begins with John measuring the Temple/people of God. 2 Witnesses appear who prophesy for 1260 days before being overcome by the beast. After 3½ days they receive the breath of life and go up to heaven. The 7th Trumpet sounds and we again see worship around the Throne before the Temple is opened and the Ark appears.

Measuring the Temple and the 2 Witnesses

In Revelation 10, we saw John being given the Little Booklet to eat and then told to prophesy into world evangelisation. As we move into chapter 11, we will see this global movement which began in the small microcosm of occupied Israel in the first century being fulfilled by the 2 Witnesses, as the Gospel is taken to 'many peoples and nations and tongues and kings'. So these two chapters, so far, cover almost 2000 years of Church witness and evangelism.

Once again, Revelation 11 is saturated with Old Testament imagery, with multiple levels of symbolism layered one upon another. As he is writing down this vision, God is speaking through John's mind and imagination, using his knowledge of the Old Testament, highlighting associations, bringing

together ideas into wonderful configurations. Hopefully we can rediscover some of John's sense of wonder as we peel back these layers of prophecy.

Text Revelation 11:1–2

> [1] Then there was given me a measuring rod like a staff; and someone said, 'Get up and measure the Temple of God and the altar, and those who worship in it. [2] Leave out the court which is outside the temple and do not measure it, for it has been given to the nations; and they will tread under foot the holy city for forty-two months.'

The Temple appears (v1)

In chapter 11, the Temple begins to come into focus. So far in Revelation we have seen some elements of the Temple appearing, as well as a couple of mentions about serving in it, but here we see the whole thing. Why does the Temple appear at this point? Which Temple is it, and why does John need to measure it? Why is the outside court trampled?

The Temple was the centre of Jewish faith – it was where the glory of the Lord descended (see 1 Kings 8:11, 2 Chronicles 5:14, Ezekiel 43:5, see also Exodus 40:34–35), and where the priests offered sacrifices and interceded on behalf of the people. Not only that, but it was the glory of the nation, famed throughout the known world for its beauty and magnificence. So when the Temple appears here it is a symbol of God being with His people.

John's measuring (v1)

John is instructed to measure 'the temple of God and the altar, and those who worship in it' – we will look at each of these in turn:

i. The Temple

There are a number of different versions of the Temple in the Bible:

- The Tabernacle was built in the Wilderness under Moses (see Exodus 26) and was precursor to the Temple, and contained similar elements in a similar layout
- Solomon's Temple, built around BC 957 (1 Kings 6, 2 Chronicles 3), was destroyed by the Babylonians in BC 586 (2 Kings 25:9–14)
- Ezra's Temple, built after return from the Exile in BC 515 (Ezra 3, 6:15)

- → In Jesus' day, Ezra's temple had been expanded and renovated under Herod (starting around BC 19, see John 2:20), and was eventually destroyed by the Romans in AD 70
- → Ezekiel 40—48 reveals a vision of a heavenly (spiritual) temple.

Which, if any of these, is the Temple we see in Revelation 11?

As we have seen earlier in Revelation, God's heavenly throne room seems to be laid out a bit like the Temple (see page 197) – the Bronze Altar, Golden Altar or both combined, the Lampstands and the Throne, not to mention all the angels, cherubim and seraphim. Although the Temple John would have been familiar with was the renovated Herodian Temple, the Temple he measures here is clearly a spiritual one. It is a symbol of worship, sacrifice and God's glory.

ii. The Altar

The Altar is a metonymy for the Temple – that is, it stands for the whole thing – one part of the Temple which embodies all of it. The Altar is the place of priestly ministry, and as we will see, links this verse to Revelation 6:11. In Revelation, as we saw on page 266, it is not necessarily clear whether 'the Altar' represents the Bronze Altar for burnt offerings, situated in the inner court of the Temple, or the Golden Altar of incense, which was inside the Temple in the Holy Place. Or maybe it is a merger of both.

While, in verse 2, the Outer Court is trodden underfoot, the Altar remains unscathed – there is nothing that earthly pressures and persecution can do to us that can affect the sacrifice and desire to worship seen at the Altar. Jesus Himself is *the* great sacrifice and it is through this we have communion with God (Hebrews 10:10–14).

We can read many testimonies of Christians who have been jailed, persecuted and even tortured: but not only do their inner lives with the Lord grow, but their ability to worship grows too.

John measures the Altar to reveal how much God's people have sacrificed through prayer and worship at the Altar.

iii. Those who worship in it

According to the New Testament, the Temple is made up of the holy people of God – it is a living, breathing, worshipping Temple:

> Or do you not know that your body is a temple of the Holy Spirit who is in you, whom you have from God. (1 Corinthians 6:19)
>
> So then you are . . . of God's household, having been built on the foundation of the apostles and prophets, Christ Jesus Himself being the corner stone, in whom the whole building, being fitted together, is growing into a holy temple in the Lord, in whom you also are being built together into a dwelling of God in the Spirit. (Ephesians 2:19–22)
>
> You also, as living stones, are being built up as a spiritual house for a holy priesthood, to offer up spiritual sacrifices acceptable to God through Jesus Christ. (1 Peter 2:5)

This is reflected in the writings of Ignatius:

> You are stones for the Father's temple, prepared for the house-building of God the Father. You are raised high up by the hoist of Jesus Christ, which is the cross, while the Holy Spirit is your rope. Your faith is your windlass. Love is the path that leads up to God. You are all traveling companions, God-bearers, temple-bearers, Christ-bearers, bearers of holy things, in everything adorned with the words of Jesus Christ. (*Letter to the Ephesians*)

* * *

So the three things John is told to measure are actually the same thing: the Altar symbolizes the whole Temple, which is made up of the priestly people of God.

The Holy City (v2)

Not only is the Temple made up of God's people, but in verse 2 we read of 'the Holy City' – the New Jerusalem, Zion – that stands in contrast to the Great City – Babylon – the persecutor of God's people (see Revelation 11:8, 16:19, 17:18 and so on). The Holy City is made up of the holy ones, the Saints, who are being built together:

> But you have come to Mount Zion and to the city of the living God, the heavenly Jerusalem, and to myriads of angels, to the general assembly and church of the firstborn who are enrolled in heaven. (Hebrews 12:22–23)

So here is a multifaceted image emerging of the Temple and the Holy City, both of which are made of God's people. As we go from the Temple (worship), to the Altar (sacrifice and priestly ministry), to those who dwell with the Lord, they are all built of the people of God. We get different views from different angles, but we are still dealing with the same group of people. As the Gospel goes out into the earth, and the people of God increase, so does the Temple and so does the worship of God in the heavenly places, as we see in Hebrews 12. The measurements of the Temple, the Altar and the worshippers will keep increasing as more and more come to a knowledge of Christ.

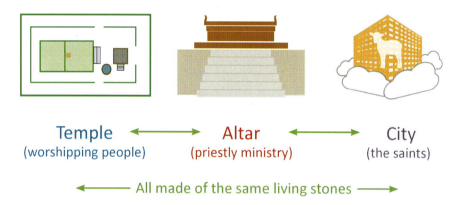

Measuring rod (v1)

John is given a 'measuring rod like a staff' – it is interesting that the word translated 'staff' here is the word used for 'rod of iron' in 2:27, 12:5, 19:15. In Revelation 2 we saw that this 'rod of iron' was less a depiction of autocratic rule, and more an indication of shepherding and protection (see page 148).

We see a measuring rod appear again in Revelation 21:15–16, where it is now made of gold, and measures the New Jerusalem.

Measuring the Temple in the Old Testament

Measuring the Temple occurs a number of times in the Old Testament and indicates one of three things:

1. Measuring with a view to destruction/judgment

> Thus He showed me, and behold, the Lord was standing by a vertical wall with a plumb line in His hand. The Lord said to me, 'What do you see, Amos?' And I said, 'A plumb line.' Then the Lord said,
> 'Behold I am about to put a plumb line
> In the midst of My people Israel.
> I will spare them no longer.
> The high places of Isaac will be desolated
> And the sanctuaries of Israel laid waste.
> Then I will rise up against the house of Jeroboam with the sword.' (Amos 7:7–9)

2. Measuring up in order for protection

In Micah and Zechariah, a measuring rod/line is something that is for protection:

> Behold, I am planning against this family a calamity
> From which you cannot remove your necks . . .
> On that day they will take up against you a taunt
> And utter a bitter lamentation and say,
> 'We are completely destroyed!
> He exchanges the portion of my people;
> How He removes it from me!
> To the apostate He apportions our fields.'
> Therefore you will have no one stretching a measuring line
> For you by lot in the assembly of the Lord. (Micah 2:5)

Here God is warning His people that judgment is going to come upon them, but this wouldn't have happened if they had somebody stretching a measuring line: nobody is protecting the people.

> Then I raised my eyes and looked, and behold, there was a man with a measuring line in his hand. So I said, 'Where are you going?' And he said to me, 'To measure Jerusalem, to see how wide it is and how long it is.' And behold, the angel who had been speaking with me was going out, and another angel was

going out to meet him. And he said to him, 'Run, speak to that young man there, saying, "Jerusalem will be inhabited as open country because of the multitude of people and cattle within it. But I," declares the Lord, "will be a wall of fire to her on all sides, and I will be the glory in her midst."'

So from the point of view of spiritual protection, 'measuring up' is to see that we, the Temple, are reaching a certain point where the Lord can say, 'That is the right size'.

3. Measuring up to move in

We also measure up a building when we are going to move in – what furniture will go where, how big the carpets need to be, and so on. There is a sense that when Jesus comes again there is going to be an expression of His house on the earth – 'the Tabernacle of God is with men' (Revelation 21:3).

This seems to be the setting for the most well-known passage about measuring the Temple in the Old Testament, in Ezekiel 40 – 43. In his vision, Ezekiel was taken to a very high mountain:

> And behold, there was a man whose appearance was like the appearance of bronze, with a thread of flax and a measuring rod in his hand. (Ezekiel 40:3)

Ezekiel meticulously details the measurements the bronzen man makes of the Temple: the outer courtyard, the inner courtyard, the inner temple, the chambers, before, in Ezekiel 43, God moves in . . .

> Behold, the glory of the God of Israel was coming from the way of the east. And His voice was like the sound of many waters; and the earth shone from His glory . . . And the glory of the Lord entered the house by way of the gate facing east. And the Spirit lifted me up and brought me into the inner courtyard; and behold, the glory of the Lord filled the house . . . And He said to me, 'Son of man, this is the place of My throne and the place of the soles of My feet, where I will dwell among the sons of Israel forever. (Ezekiel 43:2,4–5,7)

Ezekiel's vision continues, describing new rules for worship, land divisions and the dimensions of 'the city', as well as famously the water flowing from the Temple (Ezekiel 47). This vision happened during the Exile, and on one level prophesies the return of Israel return to the land to rebuild the Temple, but the dimensions of Ezekiel's Temple are much grander than either Solomon's or Ezra's. Instead, Ezekiel is witnessing a visionary Temple – some suggest it is one that will be built during the Millennium (the Third Temple) and others that it spiritually or figuratively represents the New Jerusalem, the worshipping people of God, which we will look at in Revelation 21—22. Either way the vision ends with the name of this heavenly city – 'The Lord is there'.

God measures the Church to see how far it has to grow: has it reached every nation, tribe and tongue? It is getting larger as more and more martyrs are added . . . but the time has not yet arrived. One day the Temple will be ready for the capstone, the final stone, as we read of in Zechariah 4:7.

When will the Temple of God's people reach the right size? This takes us back to the question in Revelation 6:11: 'How long, O Lord?' . . . and the answer, 'Wait until the rest of your brothers who will be martyred is fulfilled.' At some point we are expecting the number of the martyrs to be 'complete' – until then, the souls of the Martyrs under the Altar must wait. Here John gets a visual representation of how big the Temple – the People of God – is, and a sense that more are needed.

The 'Outer Court' (v2)

John is told not to measure 'the court which is outside the Temple'. It seems that this Outer Court being given to the nations is the equivalent of the holy city being trodden underfoot.

- → 'The nations' refers here to those who are not God's people, and who seek to attack and bring down those who are.
- → 'Trample under foot' is a strong term, literally meaning stamping or treading on, and is the same word used in Luke 21:24, where Jesus prophesies the fall of Jerusalem and destruction of the Temple: Jerusalem will be trampled on by the Gentiles until the times of the Gentiles are fulfilled.

There are many varied interpretations of what the Outer Court is and why God allows it to be trampled underfoot.

Temple Courts

Around the Temple building was the 'Inner Court' (or 'court of the Priests') which contained the Bronze Altar and the Bronze Sea, and is where the priests would gather. Given its name and position it is not likely to be the 'Outer Court'.

Solomon's Temple seems to have included an outer court, and during the later renovations of Ezra's Temple, Herod introduced additional courts. Outside the 'inner court' was the Court of the Israelites, the Court of the Women, and another outer court, the Court of the Gentiles – maybe, as it is the nations who are doing the trampling, this is the one that is symbolically mentioned.

Ezekiel's vision of the Temple also includes an 'outer courtyard' surrounding the inner courtyard (see Ezekiel 40:17–27). There are even rules that the Levitical priests cannot enter this outer court without removing their priestly robes 'so that they will not transfer holiness to the people with their garments' (Ezekiel 42:14, 44:19). Given that, like Ezekiel, John sees a visionary Temple, maybe this is in view in Revelation 11, and the Outer Court represents something which is not set apart for the Lord.

* * *

The 7 Trumpets | Revelation 11:1–2

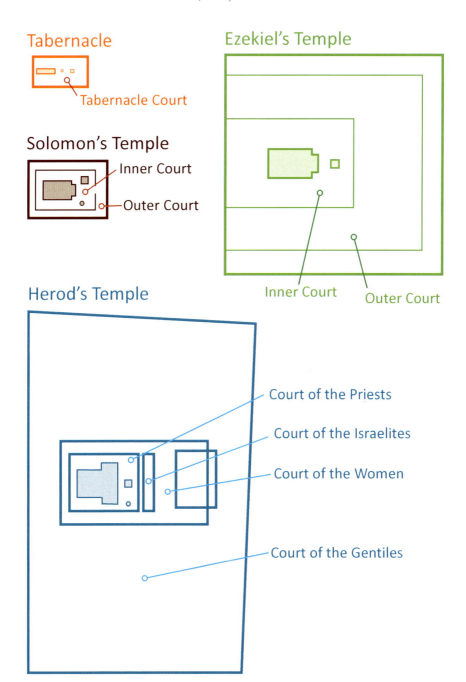

Whether this Outer Court refers to a particular court in a particular Temple or not, as we looked at above, the Holy City, Jerusalem, and the Temple are equivalents: they are all made up of the people of God, and are to a degree used interchangeably. So one way or another, some part of God's people, or some aspect of their lives, is being trampled underfoot, signified as this court outside the Temple/the Holy City.

This trampling probably represents something to do with the persecution of believers, most likely to do with freedom to worship. There are various interpretations as to its meaning, for example:

- Maybe the Outer Court is the Court of the Gentiles, so these are Gentile Christians, just as in the Old Testament God allowed Israel to be trampled by other nations.
- Maybe this is a symbol of persecution that will fall upon some areas of the Church, and shows that some believers will come under judgment – possibly, the non-Overcoming Church, those whose faith has faded, or those with the wrong theology!
- Or maybe the trampling by the nations signifies persecution, which may come upon the outer, physical aspects of our lives – our health, our circumstances – but the Temple itself, our inner spiritual life, is protected.

My view is that the Holy City/Outer Court being trampled by the nations represents the earthly side of the heavenly Temple. It represents that which is abandoned to the physical destruction and persecution coming on the Church.

Whoever or whatever it represents, this is a significant change: in Revelation 9 the locusts were not allowed to harm those who are sealed of God, but here it is part of the Temple which is being attacked by the armies of the Horsemen – God's people are now the target.

Why does God allow this court to be trampled? Again, the fact that God allows it to happen does not mean it is His desire, but nevertheless He will use it to further His purposes. Here, the Lord is revealing that nothing will violate the Temple itself – nothing will damage our inner spiritual life with Him, nothing will prevent the Overcomers from overcoming. Whatever persecution or abuse is done to the Church from outside, it cannot stop God from ministering to us in our inner life. He Himself is there to sustain and strengthen us in our inner being by His Spirit, and this is true for us as individuals and together as a body. Our worship of Jesus and our adoration of the glory we see in Him is in no way able to be touched by the trampling of the nations of this world.

> If any man destroys the temple of God, God will destroy him, for the temple of God is holy, and that is what you are.
> (1 Corinthians 3:17)

To summarise, God's people are represented here as the Temple/Altar/City. They need to be measured because there is growth with the addition of more and more believers, who are now living in heavenly places in Christ Jesus. The nations will attack the outer body but, the Temple itself – our inner spiritual life – will be protected.

3½ Years – 42 months – 1260 days (v2)

The nations are allowed to trample the City/Outer Court, for the next 42 months. This is equivalent to 3½ years, which is the same as a 'time' (1 year), 'times' (2 years) and 'half a time' (½ year), which we read of in Daniel 7:25 and 12:7, and we will see again in Revelation 12:14. Later in this chapter we also see 3½ again as the number of days the nations look at the body of the 2 Witnesses (v9,11).

42 months will reappear in Revelation 13:5 and is also equivalent to 1260 days. As we will see in the next verse, this is for how long the 2 Witnesses will prophesy. 1260 days is also how long the Woman is nourished by God in the Wilderness in Revelation 12:6,14.

42 months seems to be used when describing the times of persecution of God's people (Temple courts trampled/Beast given authority to act), and 1260 days is used when describing God's protection of His people (2 Witnesses, the Woman nourished in the Wilderness). What is the link between these things?

Is this describing the same period of time in each case, or is the number in itself representative of something else? To understand the significance of this period of time, first we will look at these 2 Witnesses – who they signify and why they appear here. Then, we will return to look at the meaning of the 42 months (see page 406).

The 2 Witnesses

Text – Revelation 11:3–6

> ³ And I will grant authority to my two witnesses, and they will prophesy for twelve hundred and sixty days, clothed in sackcloth. ⁴ These are the two olive trees and the two lampstands that stand before the Lord of the earth. ⁵ And if anyone wants to harm them, fire flows out of their mouth and devours their enemies; so if anyone wants to harm them, he must be killed in this way. ⁶ These have the power to shut up the sky, so that rain will not fall during the days of their prophesying; and they have power over the waters to turn them into blood, and to strike the earth with every plague, as often as they desire.

Without reading too much into this picture, it appears that while God allows the Outer Court of the Temple (His people) to be trampled, at the same time He also grants these 2 Witnesses to appear. Since they are called 'two olive trees and two lampstands that stand before the Lord', they would have been found inside the Temple, and come out of it to do their witnessing and prophesying. It is an important aspect of the people of God that they live in the Temple, in the presence of God, but then go out into where things have been trampled down, where the nations are, and bring their testimony and a witness in that place, and this is what the 2 Witnesses do.

Who are the 2 Witnesses?

Who are these 2 Witnesses? What do they represent? There are many varied interpretations, some wilder than others, but rather than look at all of these, we will instead get to grips with these questions by drawing together various symbols and threads from Scripture.

Many interpretations of the 2 Witnesses suggest they are resuscitations or resurrections of two literal people, usually involving Enoch or Moses and Elijah because of the similarities between these biblical characters and the activities of the Two Witnesses, as we will look at below. Some suggest they symbolise biblical concepts, like the Law and the Prophets, or Old and New Testaments. Others suggest they represent a corporate aspect of the God's people, such as Jewish and Gentile Christians, or the Church and Israel.

As we look through various aspects of the 2 Witnesses below, I will suggest that instead of individuals, or abstract concepts, or the whole Church, rather, the Two Witnesses typify what the Church ought to look like – they are the embodiment of the Overcoming Church, which is living out God's plans and purposes for them.

Prophetic

The Two Witnesses are, first and foremost, prophets – they are given authority to prophesy (v3) and are clothed in sackcloth (v3), which was one symbol of being a prophet. Sackcloth, along with ashes, signifies mourning, regret and repentance. It is a visual demonstration on the outside of how the people are (or should be) feeling on the inside. Many Old Testament prophets wear or declare sackcloth to be worn, for example Isaiah 22:12, Jeremiah 4:8, Ezekiel 7:18, Daniel 9:3, Joel 1:13, Amos 8:10, Jonah 3:5–8. So these Witnesses embody the need to rethink, acknowledge sin and turn away from it.

Let's look in more detail at the various indications we get about these 2 Witnesses to to help us gain an understanding of their character:

The character of the 2 Witnesses

1. Two olive trees – Anointed King/Priests

In verse 4, the 2 Witnesses are identified as two olive trees, which is a reference to Zechariah 4 where there is a vision of a golden lampstand with 7 lamps (which we have looked at already on page 88 and 203):

> 'Behold, a lampstand all of gold with its bowl on the top of it, and its seven lamps on it . . . also two olive trees by it, one on the right side of the bowl and the other on its left side.' Then I said to the angel who was speaking with me saying, 'What are these, my lord?' . . . Then he said to me, 'This is the word of the Lord to Zerubbabel saying, "Not by might nor by power, but by My Spirit," says the Lord of hosts' . . . Then I said to him, 'What are these two olive trees on the right of the lampstand and on its left?'

And I answered the second time and said to him, 'What are the two olive branches which are beside the two golden pipes, which empty the golden oil from themselves?' ... Then he said, 'These are the two anointed ones who are standing by the Lord of the whole earth.' (Zechariah 4:2, 3–4,6,11–12,14)

Where it says 'the two anointed ones' this is literally 'the two *sons of fresh oil*'. In Hebrew, being a 'son of' something, means being full of that thing, so 'son of blood' is someone full of murder, a 'son of perdition' is brimming with lostness, Jesus called James and John 'sons of thunder'. Here 'sons of oil' means they are overflowing with oil. Lamps need oil to burn, and olive trees produce oil from their fruit. As well as fueling the lampstand in the Temple, oil was used for healing, to anoint priests and kings, and also is a symbol of the Holy Spirit (see for example Isaiah 61:1 and Acts 10:38). So these two olive trees can be seen as pouring out the Holy Spirit.

Zechariah prophesied to the remnant returning from Exile about the rebuilding of the Temple (see Ezra). As John is measuring the Temple, we are looking inside it at the 7-branched lampstand, which is symbolic of the whole people of God. The rebuilding is headed up by the leaders of the people: the spiritual leader Joshua (who appears in Zechariah 3) and the governor Zerubbabel. Together, Joshua and Zerubbabel are the two anointed ones – the 'sons of fresh oil'.

Both kings and priests were ceremonially anointed, and the Hebrew word for 'anointed one' is 'messiah' – so here we have a kingly messiah and a priestly messiah. Jesus assimilated both roles into one – He was the King–Priest Messiah, of the order of Melchizedek (Genesis 14:18, Psalm 110:4, Hebrews 5:6,10, 6:20, 7:11–17, see also the Discussion Topic on page 73).

Both Zechariah and Haggai prophesy to keep the Temple being built – this has to be done in the Spirit, because the flesh is lazy and people soon want to give up. This is the backdrop to the well-known verse 'not by might, not by power but by My Spirit says the Lord' (Zechariah 4:6). In Revelation 11:4, the 2 Witnesses also 'stand by the Lord of the whole earth' as they pour out their oil. The message is clear: if we are going to see the people of God grow to the full dimensions of the Temple, we need a ministry that pours the oil of the Holy Spirit into the Church to shine light onto Jesus.

People who are filled with the Holy Spirit do you good by pouring the Holy Spirit into your life. They have the calling of King–Priests: kingly because they carry His authority, and priestly because they go into God's presence on your behalf. When we spend time with these people we come away wanting to do more for the Lord: they are sons and daughters of oil.

As well as the olive trees, we will see other imagery from Zechariah 3—4 appearing elsewhere in Revelation: stones with eyes on them (3:9), a plumb line (4:10), and we have already seen the horsemen from Zechariah 1 and 6 in Revelation 6 (see page 246).

2. Two Lampstands (as opposed to 7) – Overcoming Church

Not only are the 2 Witnesses olive trees, but also 'two lampstands' (verse 4). In Revelation 1—3, we see 7 Lampstands, which are 7 Churches, representing the whole Church. However, in the letters, only two of those churches were not criticised: Philadelphia (3:7–13) and Smyrna (2:8–11). It is significant that 2/7 are overcoming churches (lampstands) and here the 2 Witnesses are 2 lampstands – only 2/7ths of the Church is providing oil and has the type of ministry required in the last days.

This already begins to hint that, even though the 2 Witnesses could be seen as two separate individuals, as lampstands – like churches – they more likely signify movements or whole bodies of people. While in Jesus' day there was a popular belief that a prophet like Moses or Elijah would return in person (see eg Matthew 17:10–12, Mark 15:35–36, Luke 9:19, John 1:21, and so on), it is the Church which is meant to be corporately fulfilling what these men stood for, as prophesied in the Old Testament (see point 4 below).

3. Moses and Elijah

The 2 Witnesses display attributes which make us think of Elijah and Moses:

> Elijah – Fire consumes the enemies of the 2 Witnesses (v5) like Elijah calling down fire (on Mount Carmel in 1 Kings 18 and on the soldiers in 2 Kings 1:9–12), and they 'shut up the sky' just as Elijah prophesied it would not rain for 3½ years. (1 Kings 17:1)

> Moses – Moses is also in view, as the 2 Witnesses can turn waters into blood and 'strike the earth with every plague' (v6), just like Moses unleashed the plagues upon Egypt, including turning the Nile to blood. As we read on, Egypt appears symbolically as a name for the great city, Babylon (see verse 8).

However, it does not say that one of them was like Moses and the other like Elijah, but the characteristics of both Elijah and Moses are ascribed to them together. This is not the same as at the Transfiguration, where Moses and Elijah are recognized individually by Peter. So it seems both the 2 Witnesses are mosaic and both are elijaic (or whatever the adjectival form of Elijah is!) – we may not be dealing with two distinct individuals, but people who share the same qualities.

4. A corporate body – groups of people

In point 2 above, we saw how the 2 Witnesses are called lampstands, which in Revelation 1 represent churches – if we apply these symbols consistently, the 2 Witnesses stand for 2 groups of believers. There are a number of further indications that the 2 Witnesses, rather than simply two individuals, actually represent two corporate bodies.

> Make war – Revelation 11:7 says the Beast from the Abyss 'will *make war with them*, and overcome *them* and kill *them*'. While you may fight against two people, you would not say you 'make war' with them – rather you make war with a whole body of people, like an army or a nation. This may also inform how we interpret what this Beast signifies.
>
> If we look ahead to Revelation 13:7 we see the Beast given power to 'make war against the saints and to conquer them'. Both Revelation 11 and 13 parallel Daniel 7, where the Horn wages war against the saints and defeats them (eg Daniel 7:18,21), so we can see a precedent.
>
> Mouth, body/bodies, tomb – In verse 8, we read 'their dead bodies', but the margin notes says some ancient manuscripts read 'dead body', singular. Then in verse 9, in the Greek we get one single 'body' and then plural 'bodies':
>
>> Those from the peoples and tribes and tongues will look upon their *dead body* . . . and will not permit their *dead bodies* to be laid in a tomb.
>
> So we have a 'them' (plural) who are overcome and killed, and then 'a body' (singular) which suddenly becomes 'bodies' (plural) and laid in 'a tomb' (singular). Somehow, the 2 Witnesses are actually *one body* and represent *many bodies* – who knows how many, but enough to make war against – so, you could say a whole army.

However, back in verse 5 it says that if anyone desires to harm them 'fire proceeds out of their *mouth*', singular. So the multiple bodies of the 2 Witnesses have only one mouth between them. This mixture of plurals and singulars indicates we are dealing both with specific individuals and a corporate entity, ie the Church as a body of believers' bodies.

Worldwide – We will see another indication that the 2 Witnesses represent corporate bodies of people in verse 9, where their bodies will be seen by 'those from the peoples and tribes and tongues and nations' – so the whole earth can see this, it is global. If we are talking about the bodies of two individuals, the only way to make sense of it is suggest (as some have) that this prophesies the invention of television or the internet – how else can two individual bodies be seen worldwide in 3½ days?

If instead, we understand the 2 Witnesses to consist of a worldwide remnant people of God, when they are overcome and killed (whether physically or spiritually) all over the earth, their bodies will be able to be seen by all peoples, tribes, tongues and nations. This indicates they are a significant group of people.

5. Two Witnesses in Scripture – Truth

Pairs of Witnesses are also mentioned elsewhere in Scripture. For example:

> A single witness shall not rise up against a man on account of any iniquity or any sin which he has committed; on the evidence of two or three witnesses a matter shall be confirmed. (Deuteronomy 19:15)

Jesus affirms this in His teaching (Matthew 18:16) and demonstrated it when He sent out the 70 in pairs as witnesses (Luke 10:1–24). Jesus also stresses the importance of being an eye witness and uses this to minister life to the woman caught in adultery (John 8:17). In contrast, Jesus was found guilty by Caiaphas on the basis of two false witnesses (Matthew 26:59–61).

Having two witnesses was very important in establishing truth, and truth is a very significant aspect when it comes to the 2 Witnesses in Revelation 11.

6. The return of Elijah – Prophetic fulfillment

The final verses of Malachi are the last words of the Old Covenant, and cry out for something new:

> Behold, I am going to send you Elijah the prophet before the coming of the great and terrible day of the Lord. He will restore the hearts of the fathers to their children and the hearts of the children to their fathers, so that I will not come and smite the land with a curse. (Malachi 4:5–6)

In the New Testament, these verses are applied to John the Baptist, first by the angel who visited Zacharias (Luke 1:17) and also by Jesus (Matthew 11:14). People were also speculating that Jesus was Elijah (eg Matthew 16:14). Then in Matthew 17, we get the Transfiguration, where Moses and Elijah appear and talk with Jesus. As they come down the mountain, the Disciples ask Jesus, 'Why then do the scribes say that Elijah must come first?' (v10), presumably because now they have seen Elijah, they are wondering when the 'great and terrible day of the Lord' will follow. Jesus answers:

> 'Elijah is coming and will restore all things; but I say to you that *an* Elijah [NB there is no definite article] already came, and they did not recognize him, but did to him whatever they wished. So also the Son of Man is going to suffer at their hands.' Then the disciples understood that He had spoken to them about John the Baptist. (Matthew 17:11–13)

The story of Elijah was one of conflict: Jezebel was always trying to trap him and bring him down, and a very similar thing happened to John the Baptist. The spirit of Elijah rested on Elisha, and maybe it passed down the line of prophets all the way to John the Baptist. Elijah typified prophetic ministry, and just as John the Baptist was 'an Elijah', the same prophetic theme and spirit would pass on to Jesus, the Messiah. Jesus sent His Holy Spirit so that the fulfillment of Malachi 3 will be seen in the 2 Witnesses – that is, those who testify about Christ and prophesy His return.

7. Law and prophets – Pointing to Christ

We have seen how the 2 Witnesses together resemble Moses and Elijah, who are the figureheads of the two streams of Scripture, summed up as the Law (Moses) and the Prophets (Elijah). Jesus refers to Scripture as 'the Law and the Prophets' a number of times, including after His resurrection on the Emmaus road (see Luke 24:27,44–45).

However, in John 5:39 Jesus says: 'You search the Scriptures because you think that in them you have eternal life; it is these that testify about Me'. The Law and the Prophets do not give eternal life in and of themselves – but together they bring you to Jesus, who is the source of eternal life. This is what was enacted at the Transfiguration, when Peter wants to make three tabernacles and the Father speaks and says: 'this is My Son, listen to Him' . . . (ie *not* Moses, *not* Elijah). Scripture means nothing unless it leads us into a living relationship with God through Christ.

* * *

Overall, the picture we get of these 2 Witnesses is that of a significant portion of God's people fulfilling the prophetic testimony of the Church, witnessing, and bringing the oil of the Spirit to shine upon Jesus. The evangelistic witness will build the temple of living stones to its fullness, at which point the end will come (Matthew 24:14).

Consuming fire (v5)

In what kind of spirit are the 2 Witnesses acting when **fire** comes out of their mouth and devours their enemies? As mentioned above, in 2 Kings 1:9–12, Elijah called down fire from heaven on the soldiers sent to capture him and in 1 Kings 18 he called down fire on Mount Carmel, and afterwards slaughtered the priests of Baal. However, in the New Testament when James and John suggest calling down fire upon a Samaritan village who would not receive them, Jesus rebukes them, saying: 'You do not know of what kind of spirit you are; for the Son of Man did not come to destroy people's lives, but to save them.'

How is it alright for the 2 Witnesses to destroy people with **fire** but not James and John? Some have suggested the 2 Witnesses may be meeting fire with fire, invoking the *lex talionis*, or law of retaliation from the Pentateuch:

> . . . if the witness turns out to be a liar, giving false testimony against his brother, then do to him as he intended to do to his brother. (Deuteronomy 19:18–19)

> Anyone who kills a person is to be put to death as a murderer only on the testimony of witnesses. But no-one is to be put to death on the testimony of only one witness. (Numbers 35:30)

Section II – Christ Central in Creation

The 2 Witnesses
Revelation 11:3–12

Law and Prophets ←---→ Moses and Elijah

2 streams of Scripture, summed up as:
- the Law (Moses)
- the Prophets (Elijah)

(see Luke 24:27, 44–45)

Moses: turn waters to blood, unleash plagues
Elijah: call down fire, shut up the sky

- like the transfiguration

In Scripture
Deuteronomy 19:15

". . . on the evidence of two or three witnesses a matter shall be confirmed."

Fulfillment of Prophecy
Malachi 4:5–6

'Behold, I am going to send you Elijah the prophet before the coming of the great and terrible day of the Lord.'

(also Matthew 17:11–13)

Overcoming Church
- 2 of the 7 Churches in Revelation 2—3 have no criticism
- what the Church should look like

Prophetic
- authority to prophesy
- wear sackcloth

Corporate body/group

Lampstands signify churches, which are groups of people, not individuals

- the Beast will 'make war' with them, ie not individuals, but a big group

Mixture of singulars and plurals:
- they have 1 mouth (v5)
- have a dead body/dead bodies (v9)
- laid in a tomb (v9)
- dead bodies are seen worldwide (v9)

Two olive trees – Anointed King/Priests
Zechariah 4:9–10

'These are the two anointed ones who are standing by the Lord of the whole earth.'

- two 'sons of fresh oil'
- pour out the Holy Spirit

404

The fire comes against those who intend to harm the 2 Witnesses. While there is no indication the Samaritans wished to harm James and John (although they *were* two witnesses), it is difficult to imagine that even if they had, Jesus would have called down fire on them in retaliation – it does not fit with the Jesus who teaches us to turn the other cheek and who heals Malchus' ear.

So here in Revelation if this isn't retaliatory fire from heaven, what is it? As it seems to bring destruction and death, we could interpret it as simply being fire, physically burning things up, possibly as a parallel to the fire hurled to the earth at the 1st and 2nd Trumpets, seen as a plague on the breastplates and coming out of the mouths of the lion-headed horses after the 6th Trumpet sounds (Revelation 9:18).

However, many of the references to fire so far in Revelation indicate it as coming from God – in the First Vision, Jesus has eyes of fire as well as feet like pillars of fire in Revelation 10. There is fire on the 7 Lampstands before God, as well as in the Golden Altar, and gold being refined by fire (3:18). Elsewhere in Scripture, fire represents an attribute of the Lord's discernment and judgment:

> And the foundations of the mountains were trembling
>   And were shaken, because He was angry.
> Smoke went up out of His nostrils,
>   And fire from His mouth was devouring.
> (Psalm 18:8, see also Isaiah 11:4)

> Then that lawless one will be revealed, whom the Lord will eliminate with the breath of His mouth and bring to an end by the appearance of His coming. (2 Thessalonians 2:8)

Another possibility is that this fire from heaven is refining fire, which uses the imagery of removing impurities to purify gold and silver as a representation of the action of God amongst His people to remove sin and make them pure in righteousness:

> And I will bring the third part through the fire, Refine them as silver is refined, And test them as gold is tested. They will call on My name, And I will answer them; I will say, 'They are My people,' And they will say, 'The Lord is my God.' (Zechariah 13:9)

> Examine me, Lord, and put me to the test;
> Refine my mind and my heart. (Psalm 26:2)

> And He will sit as a smelter and purifier of silver, and He will purify the sons of Levi and refine them like gold and silver, so that they may present to the Lord offerings in righteousness. (Malachi 3:3)

We have already seen 'gold refined by fire' in Revelation 3:18, and the same imagery is used elsewhere in the New Testament:

> If anyone's work is burned up, he will suffer loss; but he himself will be saved, yet only so as through fire. (1 Corinthians 3:15)

> So that the proof of your faith, being more precious than gold which perishes though tested by fire, may be found to result in praise, glory, and honour at the revelation of Jesus Christ. (1 Peter 1:7)

Are the 2 Witnesses calling down fire to purify those who are against them, whose hearts are sinful and unrighteous? If so, the refining fire would bring destruction of evil and death to sin, so in that sense, could represent an aspect of salvation:

> - So you too, consider yourselves to be dead to sin, but alive to God in Christ Jesus. (Romans 6:11)

Another aspect of fire we see in Scripture is in representing the Holy Spirit. We see flames of fire on the heads of the disciples at Pentecost, and John the Baptist said of Jesus: 'He will baptize you with the Holy Spirit and fire' – so here in Revelation 11 does the fire represent the Holy Spirit?

In summary, the fire from the Witnesses seems to be a combination summed up in the Holy Spirit bringing conviction of sin and purification through the fire of God's judgment.

1260 Days (v3)

How should we interpret the 1260 days for which the 2 Witnesses prophesy? This is the same as 3½ years, 42 months, 'time, times and half a time', which is the same length of time the nations are allowed to trample the City/Outer Court, in verse 2. What does it signify? Are these literal days, or if not what do they mean?

We should remember that sometimes the number is far more important than the unit of measurement. The 3½ or 42 may be symbolic, but not necessarily about literal years, or days, or even about time. We see another example when we look at the symbolism of the number of Sealed Ones in Revelation 6 (12 × 12 × 1000) and the dimensions of the New Jerusalem (12 × 12 × 12) – they are linked by the numbers, but not exactly what is measured.

Here are 6 ideas of how to approach the 1260 days/42 months/3½ years:

1. Elijah – Rain restrained for 3½ years (1 Kings 17—18)

Elijah clearly informs the meaning of the 2 Witnesses: fire consumes their enemies like Elijah on Mount Carmel (v5, 1 Kings 18), and they 'shut up the sky' just as Elijah prophesied it would not rain in 1 Kings 17:1. The Old Testament says there was no rain for over 3 years until Elijah prayed (1 Kings 18:1), and Jesus confirms it was 3 years 6 months (Luke 4:25, see also James 5:17).

So the 3½ years may indicate a time of prophetic judgment on those who oppose God's people.

2. Moses – 42 encampments (Numbers 33:5–49)

Moses is also in view as we look at the 2 Witnesses. In verse 6 we read they can turn waters into blood and 'strike the earth with every plague', just like Moses struck Egypt with plagues, including turning the Nile to blood. As we read on, Egypt appears symbolically as a name for the great city of opposition – Babylon (see verse 8).

It is fascinating that following the Exodus, as Moses led the people of Israel through the Wilderness, they were divided into 42 encampments, as we read in Numbers 33. So the 42 months could correspond to 42 encampments of Israel before they got to the Promised Land.

The 42 months may represent God leading His people through a difficult period.

3. 42 wilderness years?

While we are thinking about the Wilderness, there has also been the suggestion it really took Israel 42 years to get from Egypt to the Promised Land, rather than the 40 we tend to think of. Numbers 32:13 says the Lord 'made [Israel] wander in the wilderness forty years', however this period only starts in Numbers 14, after the people rebelled and refused to enter Canaan. Before this they had journeyed to Sinai, where they stayed for over a year (Numbers 10:11) and

Section II – Christ Central in Creation

constructed the Tabernacle (Exodus 25—40). So if we assume it took them a couple of years overall to get from Egypt to Canaan the first time, a total of 42 years, while speculative, is reasonable.

So again, 42 may symbolize God leading His people through the Wilderness towards their inheritance in Him.

4. Temple tribulation – Daniel 7:25,12:7

Daniel is never too far away in the background of Revelation, and in chapters 7 and 12 we see 'a time, times and half a time', that is, 3½ years. In Daniel 7:23–27, we get the interpretation of the 'little horn' of the fourth beast which was prophesied in verse 8, who dominates and suppresses God's people. Historically this 'little horn' seems to correspond to Antiochus Epiphanes, a Greek ruler who conquered Israel in the second century BC and defiled the Temple by sacrificing a pig on the altar. It is fascinating that this persecution lasted 3½ years, from 168 to 165 BC. The desecration of the temple stimulated the revolt by Judas Maccabees that brought the people 90–100 years of freedom, which was the only time they were not under occupation since being taken into exile by Nebuchadnezzar in the seventh century BC.

In Daniel's vision in 12:1–4, the man dressed in linen prophesies a future time of distress before what resembles the End of the Age, with coming judgment. In verse 7, he reveals it would be for 'a time, times and half a time'.

Both Daniel 7 and 12 mirror Revelation 11, where the court outside the Temple is trodden underfoot and the 2 Witnesses prophesy under persecution for 3½ years.

5. Siege and fall of Jerusalem, AD 70

The siege of Jerusalem ended in AD 70, but began 3½ years before in AD 66. Eventually the Romans overwhelmed the Zealots, the city fell and the Temple was destroyed. This strongly mirrors the Temple being trodden underfoot and God's Witnesses being killed.

It is possible that John either witnessed this, or knew others who had, and is drawing upon that experience, especially if we go with the earlier date for writing Revelation, as it would have happened recently.

The destruction of the Temple marks the End of the Age following 3½ years of persecution.

6. Duration of Jesus' ministry

Finally, our Lord's ministry parallels that of the 2 Witnesses: both were around 3½ years in length, at the end of which they were attacked and killed, but resurrected 3½ days later.

While the synoptic Gospels do not give many clues about the length of Jesus' ministry, we get a more comprehensive timeline from John, who notes the festivals Jesus attends, showing it was over 3 years long.

So, this 3½ years or 42 months or 1260 days, in various ways represents the ministry and persecution of the Church. Here the Futurist view emphasizes it as a literal time period at the End of the Age. However, in reality, such persecution has been ongoing for nearly 2000 years of the Church Age, and looks likely to continue, although it may well become increasingly concentrated as we approach the End of the Age.

Text – Revelation 11:7–14

⁷ When they have finished their testimony, the beast that comes up out of the abyss will make war with them, and overcome them and kill them. ⁸ And their dead bodies will lie in the street of the great city which mystically is called Sodom and Egypt, where also their Lord was crucified. ⁹ Those from the peoples and tribes and tongues and nations will look at their dead bodies for three and a half days, and will not permit their dead bodies to be laid in a tomb. ¹⁰ And those who dwell on the earth will rejoice over them and celebrate; and they will send gifts to one another, because these two prophets tormented those who dwell on the earth.

¹¹ But after the three and a half days, the breath of life from God came into them, and they stood on their feet; and great fear fell upon those who were watching them. ¹² And they heard a loud voice from heaven saying to them, 'Come up here'. Then they went up into heaven in the cloud, and their enemies watched them. ¹³ And in that hour there was a great earthquake, and a tenth of the city fell; seven thousand people were killed in the earthquake, and the rest were terrified and gave glory to the God of heaven.

¹⁴ The second woe is past; behold, the third woe is coming quickly.

Finished their testimony (v7)

The 2 Witnesses, the epitome of what the Church should look like, 'finished their testimony', which seems to indicate the fulfillment of global evangelisation. Everyone in the world has now heard the Gospel message and been able to choose whether to accept or reject Christ. Ultimately, this brings about what the souls of the Martyrs under the Altar are waiting for in the 5th Seal (Revelation 6:9–11): the time for judgment has arrived . . .

The Beast from the Abyss (v7)

We last saw the Abyss in Revelation 9:11, where the king of the locust army is 'the Angel of the Abyss' – aka *Apollyon/Abaddon*. Here we see 'the beast that comes up out of the Abyss'. How are these related? – are they the same entity?

Later on, in Revelation 13 we will see 'a beast coming up out of the sea' (v1) and 'another beast coming up from the earth' (v11). As they all have their own spheres of operation they could be different beasts, or alternatively different aspects of the same beastly force. In each case, the word 'beast' is the same as that in Revelation 6:8, where it is usually translated 'wild animals' or 'beasts of the earth'. In Revelation 13 it is clear the beasts who appear are not just wild animals, but beings with authority to rule, the ability to blaspheme and deceive, and the first beast 'was permitted to go to war against the saints and conquer them', which is what we see here with the beast and the 2 Witnesses.

This is again reminiscent of Daniel 7, where in verse 3, four great beasts come up out of the sea, and in verse 21 the little horn is 'waging war with the saints and overpowering them'. I made the point above that the warring is unlikely to be between individuals, but large bodies of people, so does this mean that the Beast from the Abyss and the Little Horn are also groups of people?

Up to this point in Revelation, overcoming has always been a positive thing, but here it is the Beast from the Abyss who overcomes and kills the 2 Witnesses. If the 2 Witnesses represent corporate bodies of people, we are looking at the persecution or martyrdom of God's overcoming servants.

The 'Great' city (v8)

This is the first time we get a glimpse of 'The Great City', which in Revelation always refers to Babylon. Although it was alluded to in Revelation 9 where the great armies came from the Euphrates (see page 347), Babylon itself is not named until chapter 14 (Revelation 14:8, also 16:19, 17:18, 18:10,16,18,19,21).

Babylon represents the antithesis of Jerusalem – it is the ungodly world of the Exile (see Daniel 1—6) and persecution, and as we go through Revelation we see Babylon, the 'Great City' standing in opposition to Jerusalem, the Holy City. The great city is then symbolically called 'Sodom', 'Egypt' and 'the place where their Lord was crucified'. Here we get a triplet of places where God's chosen people were persecuted and His judgment was revealed:

- Sodom, as we looked at on page 352, is suggested by the fire, brimstone and smoke in Revelation 9:18
- Egypt has been alluded to many times in Revelation through the themes of plague and exodus
- The place of crucifixion was outside Jerusalem

While none of these 3 places actually is the city of Babylon, they are all 'symbolically' (ESV)/'mystically' (NASB)/'figuratively' (NIV, NLT) Babylon. The Greek word here is 'spiritually' (*pneumatikōs*) as in the King James version, and indicates those with spiritual discernment see these three places as being of the same spirit as Babylon.

Physical or spiritual death? (v9,10,11)

In Revelation, persecution is often depicted as physical death, like the souls of the Martyrs under the Altar in Revelation 6, but in most cases it is not clear if the death it represents is spiritual or physical (see Discussion Topic on page 258).

When the 2 Witnesses are killed, assuming they do represent the Overcoming Church, is this physical death or spiritual death? Will a representative 2/7 of the Church be martyred, or will their testimony be suppressed in other ways, so it is as though they had died? There are many ways the world seeks to stop the Gospel being spoken, for example, by subjecting the Church to public humiliation, discrimination, economic pressures, and so on. We do not need to look too hard to see that aspects of this imagery apply to our situation today.

Peoples, tribes, languages, and nations (v9)

At the end of Revelation 10, John prophesies concerning a fourfold representation of all humanity, which sets the scene for the 2 Witnesses to complete world evangelisation. Here we see a similar fourfold aspect of humanity who look at the corpses of the 2 Witnesses – the peoples and tribes and tongues and nations – these are 'those who dwell on the earth' (see Revelation 6:10, page 270).

They look at the bodies in satisfaction and rejoicing, sending each other gifts. They do not let the bodies go into a tomb maybe as an act of humiliation and a warning – victims of crucifixion were often left on display to dissuade other potential offenders.

Psalm 79 and the 2 Witnesses (v10)

On page 273 we looked at how Revelation 6 is virtually an exposition of Psalm 79, and here again in Revelation 11 it is interesting to compare it with Psalm 79.

We see the Temple defiled by the nations (as in Revelation 11:2), the faithful servants (v3–6) are killed (v7) and their bodies left unburied (v8–9), and God's people being made a reproach (v10) by those who dwell on the earth (v9–10):

> God, the nations have invaded Your inheritance;
> They have defiled Your holy temple;
> They have laid Jerusalem in ruins.
> They have given the dead bodies of Your servants to the birds of the sky as food,
> The flesh of Your godly ones to the animals of the earth. They have poured out their blood like water all around Jerusalem;
> And there was no one to bury them.
> We have become a disgrace before our neighbours,
> An object of derision and ridicule to those around us.
> (Psalm 79:1–4)

Dead for 3½ days (v9,11)

The bodies of the Two Witnesses are left for 3½ days, perhaps a comparative representation of 3½ years (/1260 days/42 months/times, time and half a time) which we saw in verse 2, as well as elsewhere in Scripture. This generally stands for a time of persecution of God's people, as well as His provision.

Resurrection (v11)

When the 2 Witnesses spring to life and stand on their feet, they are fulfilling what Ezekiel prophesied to the valley of dry bones:

> Then He said to me, 'Prophesy to the breath, prophesy, son of man, and say to the breath, "Thus says the Lord God, 'Come from the four winds, O breath, and breathe on these slain, that they come to life'."' So I prophesied as He commanded me, and the breath came into them, and they came to life and stood on their feet, an exceedingly great army. (Ezekiel 37:9–10)

When Israel thought they were totally finished – conquered, exiled and the Temple destroyed – just like a bunch of dead bones with no flesh, God breathed and they stood up. God's breath, or spirit (same Hebrew word – *rûah*) brings life, just as in Genesis 2 where God formed 'man' and 'breathed into his nostrils the breath of life' (Genesis 2:7).

At different points throughout church history it has looked like everything may be finished for God's Overcoming Church, for example the Roman persecution of the Early Church under Nero, and countless times when groups of true believers were persecuted by the state church, such as the persecution of the Anabaptists by Zwingli. In the modern era, the persecution of Christians has continued in many nations by totalitarian regimes rooted for example in Communism and Islam. In the End Times, there will be a final expression of this, when the nations will trample over the Overcoming Church, so that it will look completely defeated, but suddenly the breath of God will spiritually resurrect it as a great army. On the other hand, we do also get physical resurrections in the Bible – both Elijah (2 Kings 4) and Elisha (2 Kings 8) raise children from the dead. In the New Testament, not only is Jesus resurrected but other individuals like Lazarus and Jairus' daughter are raised from the dead, and there is also a mass resurrection of sorts at the Crucifixion, where those who were in the grave came back to life. Even if the 2 Witnesses represent corporate groups of people, there is a biblical precedent for physical resurrection as well as spiritual resurrection from dry bones.

I would suggest the 2 Witnesses are not suffering a physical, but a spiritual death followed by a resurrection, brought about by the Holy Spirit. Their witness is thought to be lost, but the testimony is spiritually recovered in order to make one final huge impact on the world.

'Come up here' (v12)

A loud voice from heaven calls the 2 Witnesses to 'Come up here', and they go up in a cloud. This should remind us of Revelation 4, where there was a door open in heaven and John heard a voice 'like a trumpet' which said: 'Come up here . . .', using the same words in Greek.

Given the similarities between them and the 2 Witnesses, it is interesting to note that both Moses and Elijah have mystery surrounding their bodies. Elijah did not die but was caught up to heaven in a whirlwind with a fiery chariot, which is similar to Ezekiel 1 and the vision of the figure of a man filled with fire surrounded by the glory of the Lord. Moses died on Mount Pisgah and was buried by God (Deuteronomy 34), but in Jude we read there was a dispute between Michael and Satan over his body.

Both Moses and Elijah appear at the Transfiguration (Matthew 17:1–8, Mark 9:2–8, Luke 9:28–36) – they were recognisable and presumably their bodies were changed into another form, however, this is before the general resurrection. At the Transfiguration they are surrounded by a cloud, which holds significance for both figures: Elijah when he was 'taken up', and when Moses led Israel out of Egypt the Angel of the Lord went before them as a pillar of cloud, and also moved behind them to protect them from Pharaoh's army.

Verse 12 says the 2 Witnesses are taken up in *the* cloud – not *a* cloud – but which cloud is this? At the beginning of this interlude in Revelation 10, we saw the strong angel 'coming out of heaven clothed with a cloud', and now these 2 Witnesses are caught up in this cloud.

Their enemies watched (v12)

It is interesting that the 2 Witnesses go up to heaven while their enemies watch: those who dwell on the earth are present, but unable to intervene, and this is reminiscent of Psalm 23 where the Lord prepares a table 'in the presence of my enemies'.

Great earthquake (v13)

There is a great earthquake that destroys 1/10th of the Great City – is this a response to the 2 Witnesses, or a consequence? There is a parallel here with Jesus' resurrection, when there was a 'severe earthquake' and the guards at the tomb were terrified (Matthew 28:1–4). These are cosmically significant events which are shaking the heavens and the earth, as we saw in the 6th Seal.

Regarding the 7000 who are killed in the great earthquake, this could possibly point us back to Elijah:

> Yet I will leave 7,000 in Israel, all the knees that have not bowed to Baal and every mouth that has not kissed him. (1 Kings 19:18)

Paul quotes this in Romans 11:4 and calls this 7000 a remnant of God's grace. There was also a remnant of 7000 'men of valour' who were taken to Babylon in Exile (2 Kings 24:16).

However, aside from the numerical value, the link between these references and the 7000 in Revelation 11 is not clear: those who die in the earthquake are in Babylon, so do not seem to represent a faithful remnant.

The rest of the people were terrified and gave glory to God – some of these may be repentant, so may have been saved, but it does not say definitely that they are all saved. One can give God glory and not necessarily be born of God (see for example Matthew 7:21).

The Second Woe is past (v14)

The Second Woe began with the 6th Trumpet sounding back in Revelation 9:13, after which bound angels are freed, who release an army from the East to kill 1/3 of humankind, but the other 2/3 do not repent. Following a change of perspective we see a glorious vision of the Strong Angel, resembling Jesus, coming down from Heaven with a Little Booklet, who swears that there will no longer be a delay to the mystery of God – Christ – being revealed. John takes the Little Booklet, eats it and prophesies. He then measures God's people depicted as a Temple, whose Outer Court will be trampled for 3½ years. 2 Witnesses appear who minister for 3½ years before being killed, resurrected after 3½ days and called up to heaven in a cloud, while the nations look on. There is a great earthquake and 7000 people die.

We might be forgiven for thinking the events of the 6th Trumpet (2nd Woe) might signify the End of the Age and now we get the Second Coming and judgment – however, there is more still to come!

This is the end of the Second Woe, and although it says the Third Woe is coming quickly, we do not see it appearing until halfway through Revelation 12. While Trumpets 5 and 6 are the first 2 Woes, not all of the 7th Trumpet is a Woe.

Section II – Christ Central in Creation

7th Trumpet
Text – Revelation 11:15-19

 [15] Then the seventh angel sounded; and there were loud voices in heaven, saying,

> 'The kingdom of the world has become the kingdom of our Lord and of His Christ; and He will reign forever and ever.'

[16] And the twenty-four elders, who sit on their thrones before God, fell on their faces and worshiped God, [17] saying,

> 'We give You thanks, O Lord God, the Almighty, who are and who were, because You have taken Your great power and have begun to reign. [18] And the nations were enraged, and Your wrath came, and the time came for the dead to be judged, and the time to reward Your bond-servants the prophets and the saints and those who fear Your name, the small and the great, and to destroy those who destroy the earth.'

[19] And the temple of God which is in heaven was opened; and the ark of His covenant appeared in His temple, and there were flashes of lightning and sounds and peals of thunder and an earthquake and a great hailstorm.

The Kingdom coming (v15)

Whose are these loud voices in heaven? As we discussed in Revelation 10:11 (page 382), where John heard 'they' speaking, these voices could be those of the Martyrs coming from under the Altar, the voices which welcome and greet the Lord as He ascends and takes the throne in Revelation 5, or the great multitude from chapter 7. Or are they the voices of the 2 Witnesses who were carried up to heaven in verse 12. Remember these 2 Witnesses seem to be corporate bodies representing many people, so all together they could have a loud voice.

Whoever they belong to, these voices are euphoric:

> 'The kingdom of this world has become the kingdom of our Lord and His Christ!'

We may think this is describing the Second Coming, when Christ's Kingdom will come in its fullness, and indeed the events after the 7th Trumpet sounds look as though this is the final judgement at the End of the Age (see Discussion Topic on page 234). However, as we have seen, the message of the New Testament is that while the Kingdom *is coming*, it has *already come*. The Kingdom has arrived and we have a preliminary experience of it as those who reign in life through Christ Jesus (Romans 5:17), before the Kingdom finally arrives in its fullness.

The Kingdom is where the King is rejoiced in, and we can join in with the loud voices rejoicing in these words even now, and continue doing so until we reach the climax, when the Second Coming dawns upon the earth.

The worship of the 24 Elders (v16–18)

The last time we saw the 24 elders was in chapter 7, and here they reappear and fall on their faces as they worship, as we saw them do in Revelation 4:10, 5:8 and 7:11. Our response to the Kingdom reign of God should be the same as theirs: humility – '*Your* kingdom come, *your* will be done'. . . The Kingdom advances where there are those who are worshipping and acknowledging the Lord's reign.

As the 24 Elders worship, they reveal 7 things brought in by the 7 Trumpets. However, again we face the conundrum of how much of this is in the future and how much has already begun and is happening now.

1. Taken your great power (v17)

Verse 17 says God has taken His great power, but hasn't Jesus already taken His great power? There is a foretaste of this in Matthew 28, when Jesus appears to His disciples on the mountain:

> When they saw Him, they worshiped Him . . . And Jesus came up and spoke to them, saying, 'All authority has been given to Me in heaven and on earth. Go therefore and make disciples of all the nations . . . I am with you always, even to the end of the age.' (Matthew 28:17–20, see also 1 Peter 3:22)

So Revelation 11:17–18 could set at be any time from the ascension to the final judgment.

2. Begun to reign (v17)

When Jesus ascended and sat down at the right hand of God, He not only has taken His great power, but He also has begun to reign (Luke 22:69, Romans 8:34 , Colossians 3:1, Hebrews 12:2). Again this could be talking about any time from the ascension onwards.

3. The nations were enraged (v18)

In John 15:25, quoting Psalm 69:4, Jesus said:

> 'They hated me without a cause'.

You would have thought people would welcome goodness and maybe even exploit it – however, goodness is not popular, and the world often despises good deeds and those who do them. Jesus was hated when all he did was good, and Christians who seek to follow His example have invoked a response of hatred throughout church history from Acts onwards.

Here it says 'the nations' were enraged, which implies most or even all of the world, indicating this is set at a time when the Gospel must be spread fairly well globally.

4. Your wrath has come (v18)

We looked at God's wrath back in Revelation 6:16 (see Discussion Topic on page 237) and how it should not be caricatured as vindictive rage or spitefulness, but is rather the consequence of not living in God's world in God's way. The consequence of sin is wrath, which is God's just judgment.

The wrath of God is not confined only to when Jesus comes again. For example, the apostle Paul wrote to the Thessalonians about a group opposing the spread of the Gospel, 'But wrath has come upon them to the utmost' (1 Thessalonians 2:16). In Romans, Paul writes:

> The wrath of God is revealed from heaven against all ungodliness and unrighteousness of men who suppress the truth in unrighteousness . . . (Romans 1:18–19)

Part of this wrath culminated in AD 70 with the destruction of the Temple in Jerusalem and has been present through history – so this statement of God's wrath coming could apply to people today.

However, there will be an ultimate expression of God's wrath at the final judgment, so this could be looking forward to that event:

> You are storing up wrath for yourself in the day of wrath and revelation of the righteous judgment of God, who will render to each person according to his deeds: to those who by perseverance in doing good seek for glory and honour and immortality, eternal life; but to those who are selfishly ambitious and do not obey the truth, but obey unrighteousness, wrath and indignation. (Romans 2:5–8)

5. The time for the dead to be judged (v18)

Verse 18 says it is 'the time for the dead to be judged', but it doesn't say they *have been judged yet* . . . so the dead may not yet be resurrected. Judgment comes after death, as Hebrews 9:27 says:

> It is appointed for men to die once and after this comes judgment.

This does not state definitively whether you are judged immediately or if you have to wait until the last assize. While the final judgment comes at the Great White Throne (Revelation 20:11), there are indications an assessment may already be made of your life. For example, in the parable of the Rich Man and Lazarus, there is a great gulf between those like the Rich Man who is awaiting trial and those like Lazarus who know they have passed through judgement into life and are resting in 'Abraham's bosom'. In Revelation 5, we saw the souls of the Martyrs underneath the Altar – presumably there must be some form of selection when they died? So this 'time for the dead to be judged' may be referring to the time when someone dies, or looking ahead to the final judgment at the Great White Throne.

6. Rewards to prophets, saints, God-fearers (v18)

Verse 18 continues by saying the time to give rewards has arrived, but it does not say they *have been received yet*. The word 'reward' appears only twice in Revelation – here and in 22:12, where Christ says 'Behold, I am coming quickly, and My reward is with Me'. Whatever this reward is, it is not the gift of eternal life, which is a free gift of grace, not earned according to our works. The reward is surely the prize that is won by the way that we live and serve (see for example Philippians 3:14, 1 Corinthians 9:24).

If we look back to the letters in Revelation 2—3, we see there are rewards awarded to the Overcomers, and the Bible is clear that every believer is meant to be an Overcomer. History is full of men and women who have gone through persecution, torture and even martyrdom for Christ's sake – they deserve to be rewarded. However, just as every Israelite who came out of Egypt was meant to enter into the Promised Land, in practice we know that many fail along the way and do not gain their reward. They do not overcome to attain all that God intended them to. We looked at the doctrine of rewards and losses in the Discussion Topic on page 118 – for a more in depth look at this subject, see my book *Gold, Silver & Precious Stones*.

In Revelation 11, these rewards are for:

i. The Prophets/Bondservants

Who are the prophets mentioned here? The Greek word we translate as 'prophecy' is *prophetes*, which means 'to speak forth', so a prophet is someone who speaks God's message to people. I would suggest any witnesses to Jesus – even the most timid 'I believe in Jesus' – in the power of the Holy Spirit, is speaking forth God's message of truth and can pierce the heart of the unbeliever as a prophetic word. Witnessing is prophetic. As Jesus said to His disciples:

> You will receive power when the Holy Spirit has come upon you; and you shall be My witnesses . . . (Acts 1:8)

and when they received the Holy Spirit at Pentecost, Peter quotes from Joel 2:28:

> 'And it shall be in the last days,' God says,
> 'That I will pour forth of My Spirit on all mankind;
> And your sons and your daughters shall prophesy . . .
> (Acts 2:17)

Prophecy and witness are inextricably linked. These prophets are also called 'Your bondservants' indicating they are working for the Lord by speaking out what He wants them to.

ii. The Saints
The saints are those who seek to live in a holy way, regardless of what the world around thinks of them. As we have seen earlier in Revelation 5:8 and 8:3–4, 'Saints' is literally 'holy ones' or 'set apart ones' and in Revelation 11 we have already seen the Holy City (v2), which is presumably the home of these Holy Ones (see also Daniel 7:18, 21–22). Purity and holiness itself is a witness into the earth:

> Blessed are the pure in heart, for they will see God. (Matthew 5:8)

> Pursue peace with all men, and the sanctification without which no one will see the Lord. (Hebrews 12:14)

This holiness does not originate in us but has been made available so that we can live in Christ and share that sanctification – Christ is made holiness for us (1 Corinthians 1:30).

iii. Those who fear Your Name
We read about the God-fearers in Acts:

> God is not one to show partiality, but in every nation the man who fears Him and does what is right is welcome to Him. (Acts 10:34–35)

Peter is talking about people, in this case Cornelius and his household, before they have actually received the Holy Spirit. There are those in past generations, before Jesus came, who were God-fearers, as well as people today who have not heard the Gospel, but have awe for their Creator. The tragedy is that we have not managed to get the Gospel to all peoples, tribes, tongues and nations in over 2000 years – this is not the fault of those who have not heard, but a failing of the Church. It does not say that you need the right theology, or even to have heard about Jesus, in order to be God-fearing. However, those who fear God and do what is right, will not be ignored – God will reward them.

God is just. He will reward those who have been His witnesses, those who have given up everything for Him, and those who have put their trust in Him. Even those who might never have heard, but when they stand before Him choose to say: 'I don't deserve to be anywhere near you'. Those are the rewards that are coming, the small and the great.

The Old Testament backdrop to the Lord bringing a reward is in Isaiah 40:

> Behold, the Lord God will come with might,
> With His arm ruling for Him.
> Behold, His reward is with Him
> And His recompense before Him. (Isaiah 40:10)

But when is this happening? The beginning of Isaiah 40 clearly refers to the First Coming of Christ, and is quoted at the start of each of the four Gospels:

> 'A voice is calling, clear the way for the Lord in the wilderness; make smooth in the desert a highway for our God . . .' (Isaiah 40:3, quoted in Matthew 3:3, Mark 1:3, Luke 3:4, John 1:23).

However, the verses that follow could be interpreted as being either the First or the Second Coming. 'Here is your God' (v9) could refer to the incarnation, or to Jesus coming in the clouds at the Second Coming, whereas tending His flock 'like a shepherd' (v11) seems more like the First Coming, but could be either. In between it says, 'His reward is with Him', which points forward to the Second Coming (Revelation 22:12).

In Isaiah 40, the First and Second Comings seem to coalesce, in much the same way as the Kingdom having come in Jesus' life and ministry, will come fully in its final expression when Jesus returns. Therefore, we cannot be too dogmatic about confining this 'time for reward' to the First Coming or the Second Coming.

7. Destroy the destroyers (v18)

Who are 'those who destroy the earth'? Today it may be obvious for us to apply this to those who have a cavalier attitude towards the wonderful beauty of God's Creation. Misuse and abuse of our planet and the life which inhabits it, by habitat destruction, exploitation and pollution are very much on our agenda in the twenty-first century, and may be in view in this passage. However, climate change and species extinction would not have been a concern in the first century – so what would this have meant to John and his readers? Jeremiah 51 helps give a definition:

> 'But I will repay Babylon and all the inhabitants of Chaldea
> for all their evil that they have done in Zion before your eyes,'
> declares the Lord.
> 'Behold, I am against you, O destroying mountain,
> Who destroys the whole earth,' declares the Lord,
> 'And I will stretch out My hand against you,
> And roll you down from the crags,
> And I will make you a burnt out mountain.'
> (Jeremiah 51:24–25)

In the Old Testament, mountains were sometimes used as metaphors for great kingdoms or rulers, and here God is addressing Babylon.

The destroyers of the earth are those great and mighty ones who despise and devastate the land, who destroy people's lives, those who ignore the beauty and the form and the wonder of the world and try to crush them. It is not just their actions, but their attitude which demonstrates they are destroyers of the earth. It is not just that they pollute the environment, but that this reflects what is in their souls.

Whereas such 'destroyers' usually seem not only to get away with their destroying but prosper from it, here at the 7th Trumpet the time has come for them to be destroyed. This is a clear picture of judgment, but again it does not say they *have been destroyed* yet.

We can see each of these 7 things at work to a degree through church history and today, but of course they will be perfectly expressed when Jesus comes again at the last Trumpet. We can sum them up as reward, requittal, and retribution – Jesus comes with His reward for His bond servants, with His requittal to those on the earth, and His retribution to those who are destroying the earth. Until we get to that time, as believers we need to live in the knowledge and light of these, because if they are just relegated to the future we will miss the impact these words are meant to have on us now.

What we should take from this passage is this: *Jesus is reigning so let's get as much done for the Kingdom as we can!* Ultimately, the Kingdom will come and all things will be brought under Christ's feet, but until that time there is a responsibility for the Church to act, and, as we do, 'the God of peace will soon crush Satan under your feet' as Paul says in Romans 16:20.

The general impression is that the 3½ years/42 months/times, time and half a time, seems to apply right the way through the Church Age, instead of being squeezed into the last 3½ years at the end.

We will not understand some prophecies until after they have happened, just as many of the Jews did not recognize Jesus as fulfilling the messianic prophecies. We should avoid drawing overly hard conclusions on such points – it will do us no good. In the past, disagreement over such points has caused tremendous damage to the Church, resulting in divisions and schisms, robbing us of our witness of being one in Christ.

Revelation of God's presence (v19)

In verse 19, we seem to reach a great climax when the Temple is opened in heaven and the Ark of the Covenant appears. There are strong parallels between this imagery and 1 Chronicles 15, when David moves the Ark to Jerusalem – there were 7 trumpets blown by 7 priests:

> Shebaniah, Joshaphat, Nethanel, Amasai, Zechariah, Benaiah and Eliezer, the priests, blew the trumpets before the ark of God.
> (1 Chronicles 15:24)

The conquest of Jericho (Joshua 6) is also in view. For 7 days the people marched around Jericho with the priests blowing their trumpets and on the last day they went round 7 times. In both cases, the Ark appeared after the sound of 7 trumpets, followed by a demonstration of God's power through His people: the walls of Jericho fell and the people entered the land; with the Ark in Jerusalem, David's kingdom was strengthened.

That 7-fold trumpet is both a celebration and a warning – God is with His people, which is good news for God's people, but a challenging note for anyone who stands against Him. Here in Revelation, as we hear the 7th Trumpet sound and see the Ark appear, we anticipate breakthrough for God's people to enter the new 'Promised Land'.

However, there is a little puzzle here – if the 7th Trumpet brings in what looks like the final judgment, rather than the Ark appearing up in the heavenly Temple, we may have expected to see Christ coming on the clouds, or even the Ark coming down to the earth. That would make interpretation simpler! However, the Ark still being in heaven instead indicates there are still things yet to happen before the Second Coming, and we will go on to look at these through the 7 Signs and 7 Bowls.

The 7 Trumpets | Revelation 11:15–19

Again we see the growing intensity of action from God's throne: lightning, sounds, thunder, an earthquake and a great hailstorm as we head towards a fuller revelation of truth.

The Temple opened (v19)

In the Hebrew Old Testament, the last book is not Malachi as we have it, but 2 Chronicles, which finishes with the remnant of the Exile going up to rebuild the Temple:

> This is what Cyrus king of Persia says: 'The LORD, the God of heaven, has given me all the kingdoms of the earth, and He has appointed me to build Him a house in Jerusalem, which is in Judah. Whoever there is among you of all His people, may the LORD his God be with him; go up then!' (2 Chronicles 36:23)

In Revelation 21, we see there is no Temple in the New Jerusalem, because the Lord and the Lamb are the Temple, and dwell there with God's people. The Temple was not just a religious building, it was a house: God's home. Once God walked with Adam and Eve in the garden in the cool of the day, and He is still working to get back there and share life together with His people. It is God's greatest desire to dwell with His people again, but in order to get His house established He has to bring His Kingdom in, which as we have seen in Revelation 5, is through a Lamb slain upon the Throne. In the Tabernacle and the Temple, it was the Ark of the Covenant which was the Throne of God.

We saw in verse 1 how the Temple, the Altar and God's people are equivalent, and John measures them to see if they are big enough. At the end of Revelation 11, the Temple is opened, because it was now finished, complete with the Ark inside (see 1 Kings 8:6). Presumably, this is the point at which God's people reaches its 'full number'.

The Ark appears (v19)

Why does the Ark appear at this point? The tradition is that the Ark was buried during the Exile, but nobody knows where. Jeremiah 3:16 indicates that the people would no longer care about the Ark, because its purpose and service was over:

'It shall be in those days when you are multiplied and increased in the land,' declares the Lord, 'they will no longer say, "The ark of the covenant of the Lord." And it will not come to mind, nor will they remember it, nor will they miss it, nor will it be made again.'

The Ark spoke of God's presence in the midst of His people, and when it was absent it was a sign God was no longer with His people (see for example 1 Samuel 4:21–22). The Ark was the Throne of God on earth – the Mercy Seat. The Shekinah glory filled the Temple just as it had filled the Tabernacle (see for example Exodus 40:34, 2 Chronicles 7:1–3) – God, who is Spirit, appearing as a fiery cloud seated on His Throne. The Ark was a picture of Christ's incarnation: it was solid, you could look at it and touch it, but it also held the presence of God.

The Jerusalem Temple was different to any other temple in the world, whose gods were represented by idols. So much so, that when Pompey the leader of the Roman army came into Jerusalem in 69 BC, the High Priest pleaded with him not to go into the Most Holy Place, but he went in looked around and saw just a golden slab. There was no idol, so he called the Jews 'a-theists', because they seemed to have no god. Of course, the living and true God 'dwells in unapproachable light, whom no man has seen or can see' (1 Timothy 6:16).

The Ark represented God's promises to His covenant people, so after the great declaration of the Kingdom of God in verse 15, John looks up into heaven and sees that God is present with His people (who make up the Temple John measured), and He will keep His promises. The appearance of the Ark is fantastic news!

This confidence that God has not abandoned His people would be a very important message to John and his readers, who were suffering sustained persecution. This vision is saying: *See how My prophets and My saints are beaten up and trampled, and yet here they are in heavenly places, and I am there with them.* While our bodies may suffer persecution, in our spirits we have ascended into the heavenly places – this is the Christian life.

Just as we finish Revelation 11 and the 7th Trumpet with a sign of covenant, we will start the 7 Signs in chapter 12 with another covenant sign – a Woman in labour clothed with the sun and the moon and crowned with 12 Stars representing God's covenant people.

Parallels with the 7th Trumpet

There are echoes of the 7th Trumpet in the following chapters of Revelation, which map it onto events during the 7 Signs and 7 Bowls. In some cases the similarities are so strong it would seem the same thing is being described in two different places:

1. Loud voices

In Revelation 11:15:

> . . . there were **loud voices in heaven**, saying 'The kingdom of the world has become **the kingdom of our Lord and of His Christ**; and **He will reign** forever and ever.'

Then in Revelation 12:10:

> Then I heard **a loud voice in heaven**, saying, 'Now the salvation, and the power, and **the kingdom of our God** and the authority **of His Christ** have come . . .'

These voices from heaven are saying almost identical things – Christ's Kingdom is where He has authority, and the implication in both places is that He is come to reign forever. They are also the only places where the title 'Christ' ('anointed one') is used in the whole of Revelation, so are strongly linked. It may be surprising to find that a number of commentaries spend a lot of time and pages trying to demonstrate these passages are different, arguing Revelation 11 is strictly about the Second Coming, whereas Revelation 12 is *only* about the First Coming. It may not be helpful to be so definitive, and as we have looked at above, there are aspects of both First and Second Comings of Christ intermingled. So Revelation 11—12 may be describing Christ's coming in an overall sense.

We also see loud voices both before and after the 7 Bowls of Wrath are poured out (Revelation 16:1,17), as well as preceding the Marriage of the Lamb:

> I heard something like **a loud voice** of a great multitude **in heaven**, saying, 'Hallelujah! Salvation, glory, and power belong to our God' . . . Then I heard something like the voice of a great multitude and like the sound of many waters, and like the sound of mighty peals of thunder, saying, 'Hallelujah! For the Lord our God, the Almighty, **reigns**' (Revelation 19:1,6)

2. The Temple

The Temple is opened after both the 7th Trumpet sounds and after the 7th Sign (Revelation 15:5), and we see angels and hear loud voices coming out from it in Revelation 15 and 16. The Ark of His covenant in Revelation 11:19, is equivalent to the Tabernacle of testimony/witness. The Ark was testimony to God's promises to His covenant people – it contained the 10 Commandments, Aaron's staff and a jar of Manna, which together symbolized what God has done for His people.

3. Thunder, Lightning, Earthquake, Hailstorm

In both places we see lightning, rumblingss, thunder, earthquake and a great hailstorm (Revelation 11:19, cf 16:17–21, 19:6).

* ✵ *

So there is an intimate pattern of connections between Revelation 11 and what is coming up in chapters 12, 15 and 16. We should keep this movement in mind as it helps draw this section together as a whole.

Discussion Questions

What form do you think the 2 Witnesses might take?

How do you interpret the fire the 2 Witnesses breathe out?

Who are the 'sons of oil' in your life?
Are you a son/daughter of oil to others?

As with the Ark appearing in the Temple, what would be the sign that Jesus is with His Church today?

Summary of Revelation 1—11

Whilst we have just left the text at the end of Chapter 11 reading of further disasters: thunder, lightning, earthquake and hailstorms (Revelation 11:19), the first half of the Book of Revelation finishes on a high. After the darkness and disruption brought about by the 7 Seals being broken and the 7 Trumpets sounded, we have reached a climax: the 2 Witnesses going up to heaven after being resurrected with the breath of life from God, and the Temple opening to reveal the Ark of the Covenant (ie His promises to mankind).

This glorious scene is a natural place for us to divide the book. Even though we have seen a victory we know there is more to come — further birth pangs that increase in intensity (Mark 13:1–8). One purpose of John's Revelation is to forewarn believers and allow them in responding both to prepare and to forearm.

In this pause, then, we should consider one broad but pressing question followed by three elements to it:

—→ What should our response be individually and as the Church?

As I have argued from a gestational perspective: many of these events, aside from being highly symbolic – even hyperbolic – imagery, signify continuing and escalating turmoil in Creation that is, and always has been, current and not just reserved for the End of the Age. Therefore, in seeking how we integrate ourselves into this imagery and see it as relevant to the here and now:

—→ Should we be happy that Seals break and Trumpets blow, for that means God's destiny for us is back on track, or should we mourn and cry out to God to stay his hand because of all the necessary suffering they unleash?

—→ Should we be working to prevent catastrophe from striking, or should we welcome it, whilst opposing it?

—→ How should you or I aspire to be Overcomers in this unfolding epic to reflect the 2 Witnesses, the 24 Elders, the Martyrs and the host of believers?

God shares this tension with us. He does not want harm inflicted, yet knows that it's an inevitable consequence of the birth pangs necessary for our passage to the New Creation. Childbirth is a perfect illustration, for a woman wants her child born and healthy whilst not wanting the pain and pressure that this necessarily entails.

To move on in Chapters 11—22 to the second part of this Manifesto of Jesus that John writes, we will see the culmination in the New Jerusalem. The 'now and the not yet' is to live in the fullness of that and what we could experience. It is seen if you like as the zenith of human life in living this way with God and with mankind. It is the restoration of the Garden of Eden and more.

The Overcomers, the Martyrs, the Elders in this epoch are essential for the fulfillment of God's dream through loving sacrifice, witness and worship. It is fulfilling and exhilarating to wonder where you and I fit in to bring this about.

Volume II will continue to explore how this is coming about and we will see His activity more clearly as we move on through to Revelation's conclusion.

Reference material

List of Discussion Topics

Literal interpretation of Scripture	11
The reliability of prophecy	23
The Last Days	65
King–Priests	73
The First and the Last	79
Sheol and Hades	97
Overcoming	108
Rewards and Losses	118
Tree of Life	127
Who are True Israel?	130
The Book of Life	158
Once saved always saved?	161
The heavens	192
Crowns	214
The Second Coming	236
The Wrath of God	237
Crowns in Revelation	251
Physical vs spiritual death	258
The Angel of the Lord	359
The Mystery of God	374
The Gospel in Revelation	376

Select Bibliography

DE Aune (2014) *Revelation 1–5: Volume 52a – Word Biblical Commentary*

DE Aune (2014) *Revelation 6–8: Volume 52b – Word Biblical Commentary*

GK Beale (1999) *The Book of Revelation – The New International Greek Testament Commentary*

J Ellul (1977) *Apocalypse – The Book of Revelation*

S Gregg (1997) *Revelation: Four Views – A Parallel Commentary*

GH Lang (1948) *The Revelation of Jesus Christ*

MC Tenney (1962) *Interpreting Revelation*

Other books by the author

Gold, Silver & Precious Stones – The Doctrine of Rewards and Losses

The Kingdom of Jesus

Prayer – Living in the Breath of God

Suffering and the Love of God – The book of Job

Trinity – Song and Dance God

with Faith Forster

Women and the Kingdom

with Paul Marston

Christianity: The Evidence

God's Strategy in Human History – Vol 1: God's Path to Victory

God's Strategy in Human History – Vol 2: Reconsidering Key Biblical Ideas

Paul's Gospel in Romans and Galatians

About the author

Roger studied mathematics and theology at St John's College, Cambridge. After a period in the Royal Air Force, he worked as an itinerant evangelist before starting Ichthus Christian Fellowship with his wife Faith, in 1974. Roger was one of the founders of March for Jesus, was on the board of the AD2000 Movement and the Council of the Evangelical Missionary Alliance for many years. He has been involved with the Evangelical Alliance since the early 1970s as a member of the Council, and has served on a number of EA committees.

Among his many responsibilities he has been Chairman of the Council for the UK Evangelical Alliance and honorary Vice President of Tearfund, and is honoured to be on the Council of Reference for Aglow International (Britain), and together with Faith is a patron of Springs Dance Company.

Roger and Faith have a son and two daughters: Christen, Juliet and Deborah.